RECORD OF GRANCREST WAR

1

Original Story by **Ryo Mizuno**
Story & Art by **Makoto Yotsuba**
Character Design by **Miyuu**

Contents

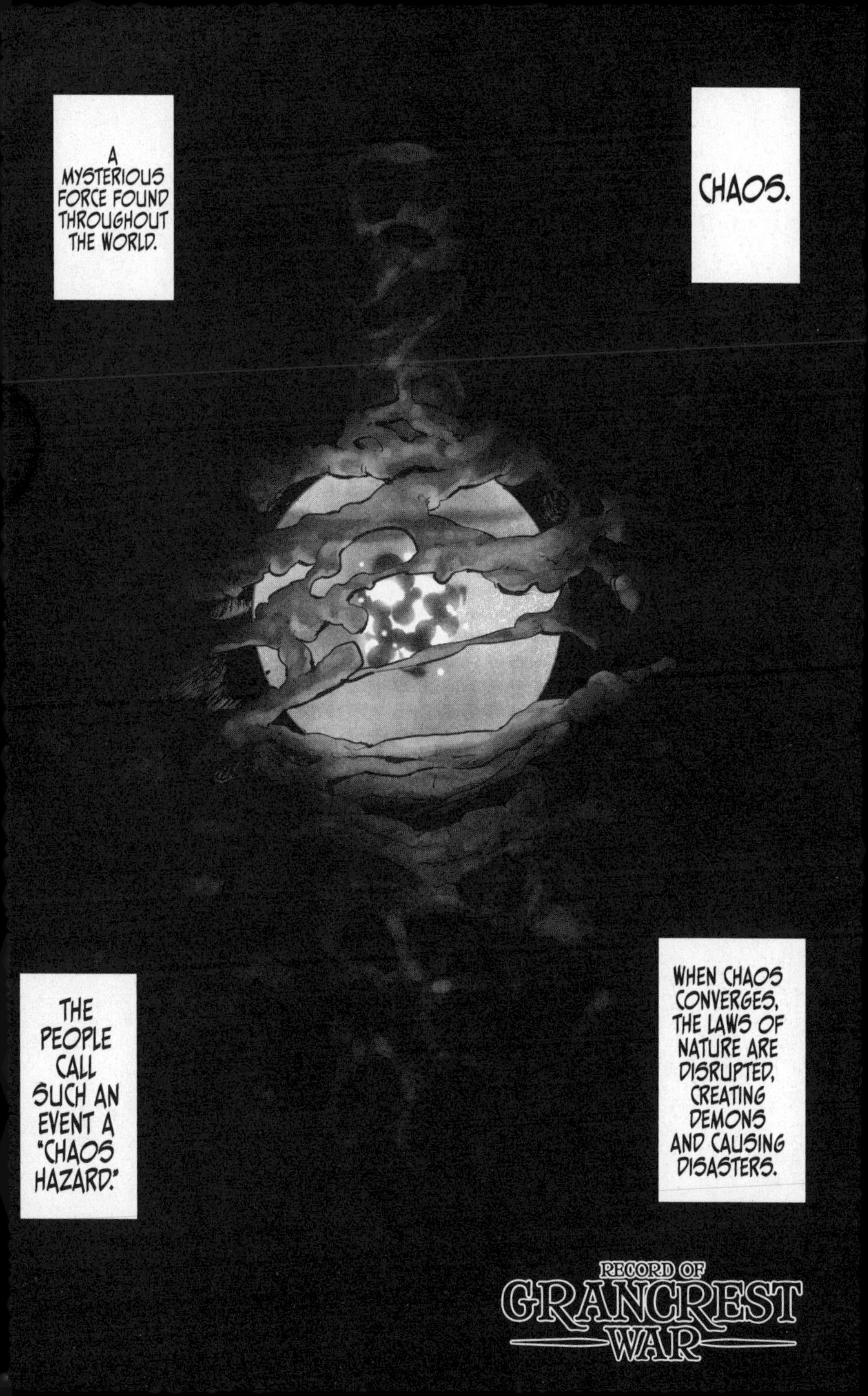
CHAOS.
A MYSTERIOUS FORCE FOUND THROUGHOUT THE WORLD.
WHEN CHAOS CONVERGES, THE LAWS OF NATURE ARE DISRUPTED, CREATING DEMONS AND CAUSING DISASTERS.
THE PEOPLE CALL SUCH AN EVENT A "CHAOS HAZARD."
RECORD OF GRANCREST WAR

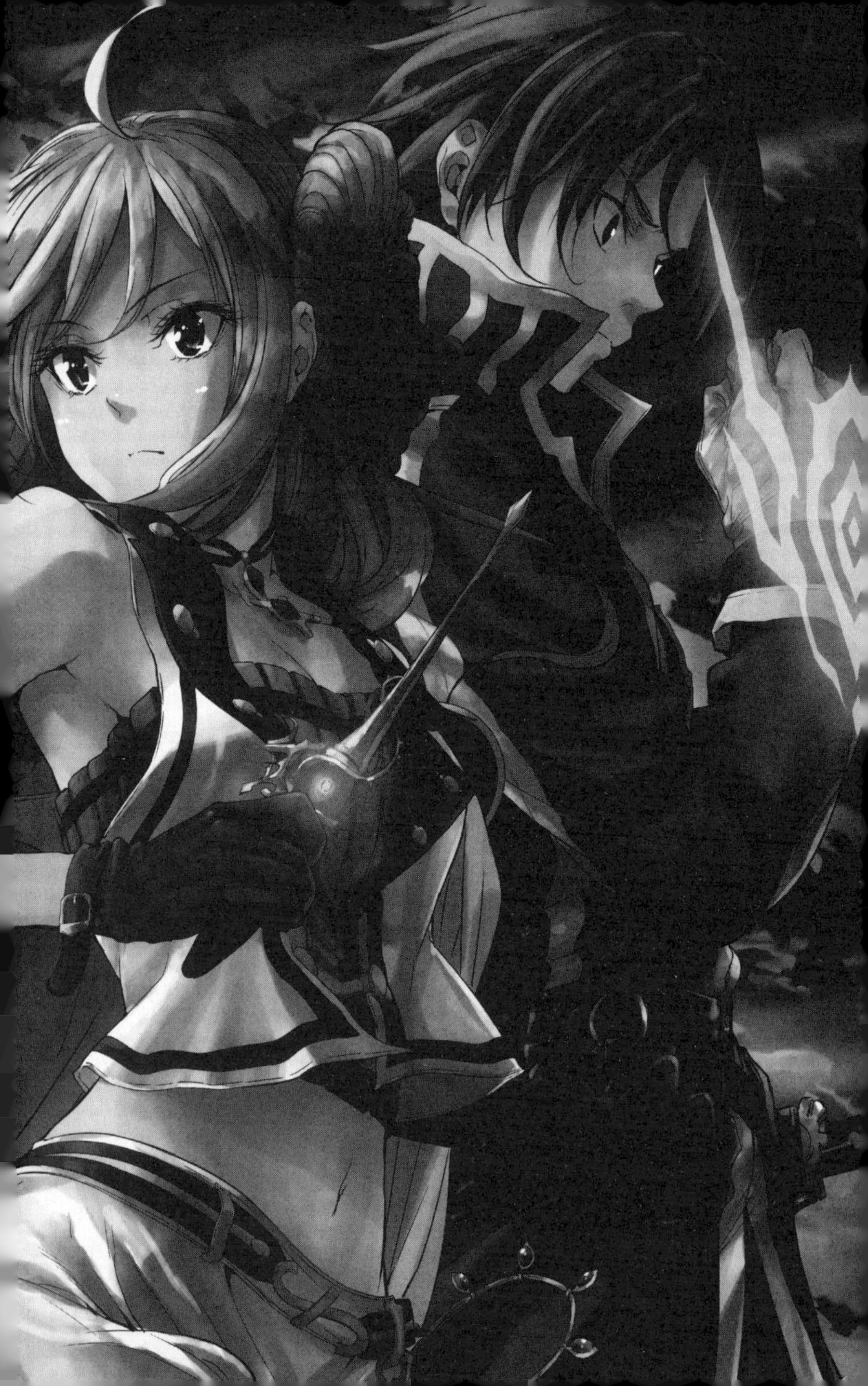

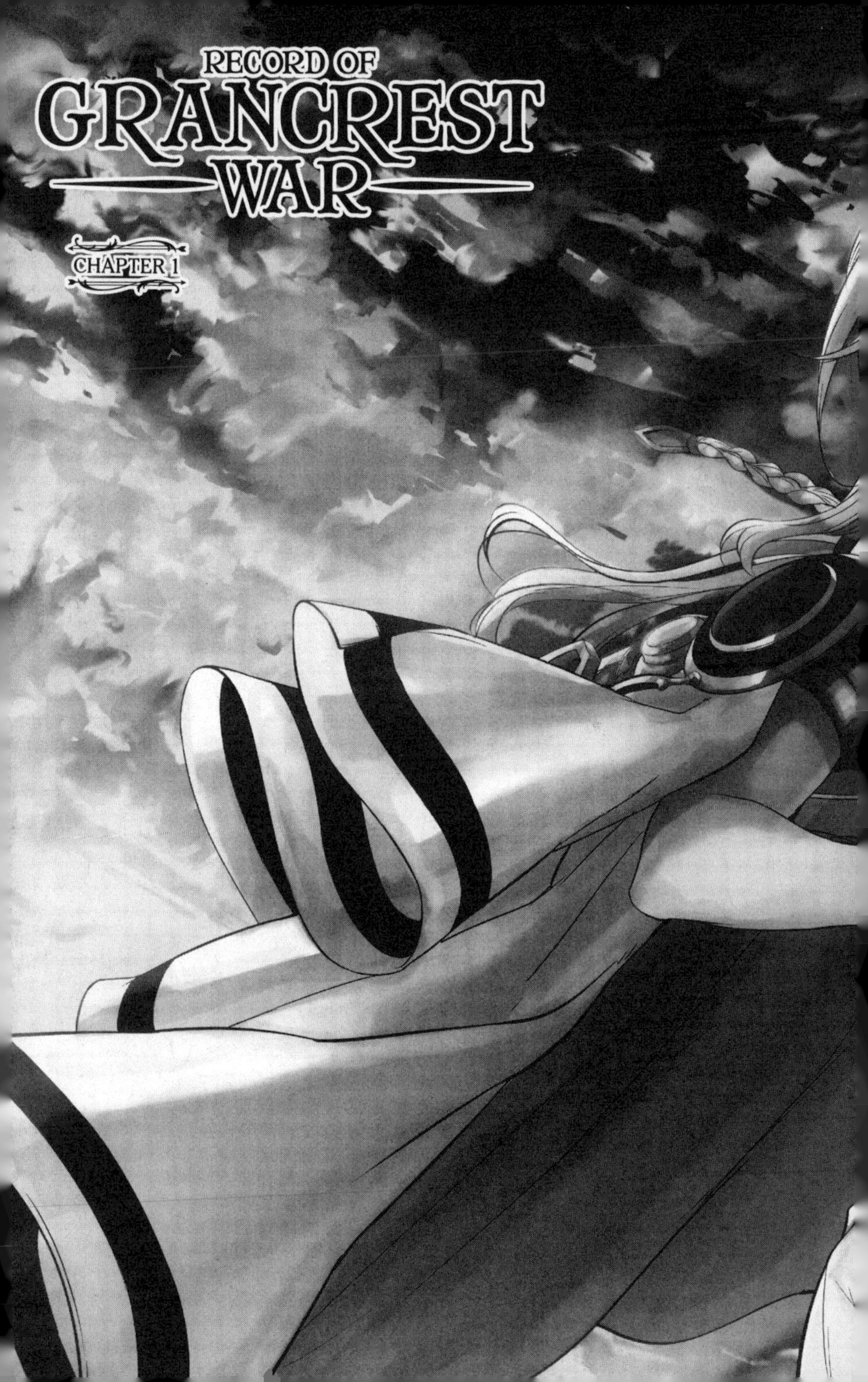
RECORD OF
GRANCREST
WAR
CHAPTER 1

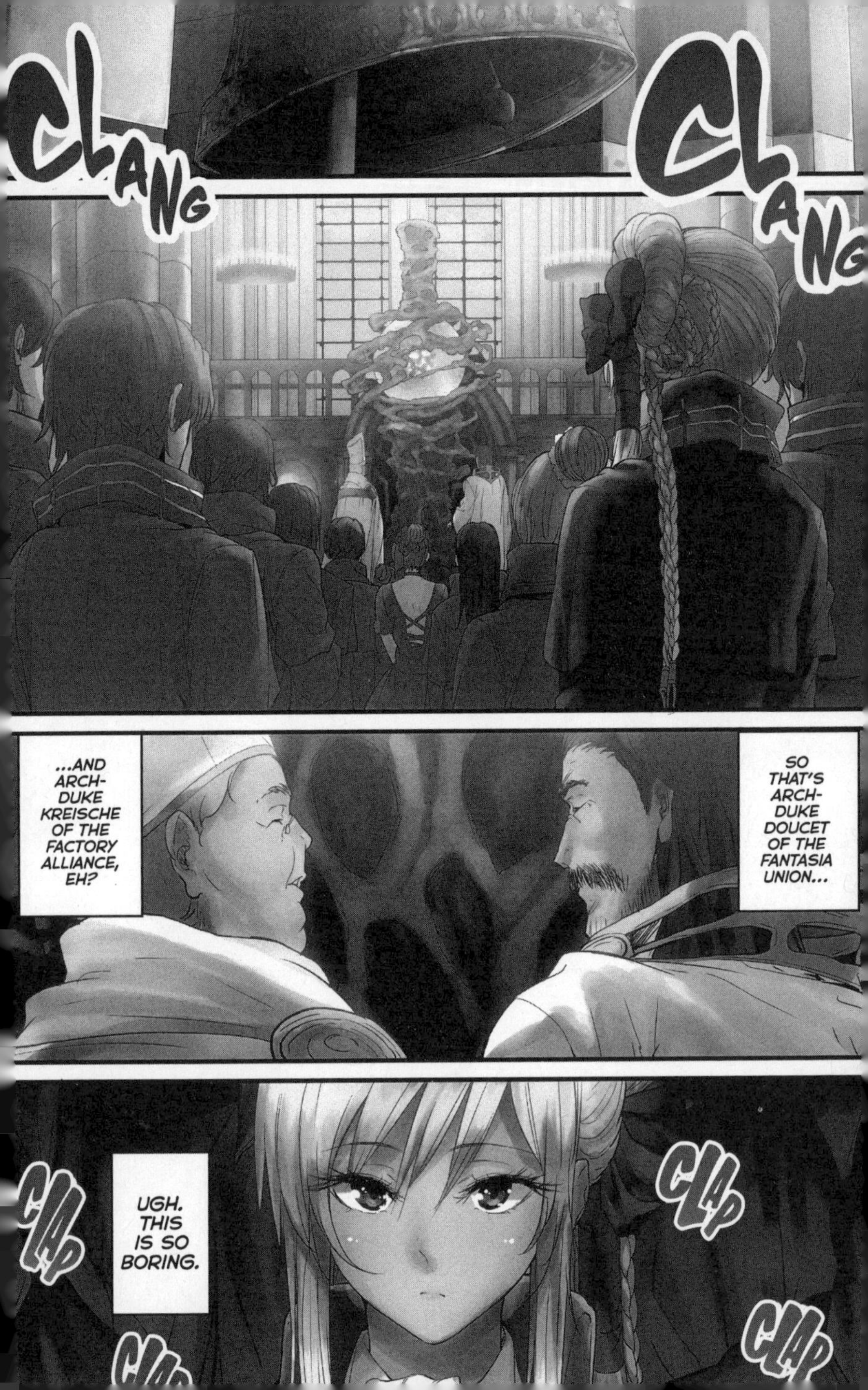
CLANG
CLANG
SO THAT'S ARCH-DUKE DOUCET OF THE FANTASIA UNION...
...AND ARCH-DUKE KREISCHE OF THE FACTORY ALLIANCE, EH?
CLAP
UGH. THIS IS SO BORING.
CLAP
CLAP

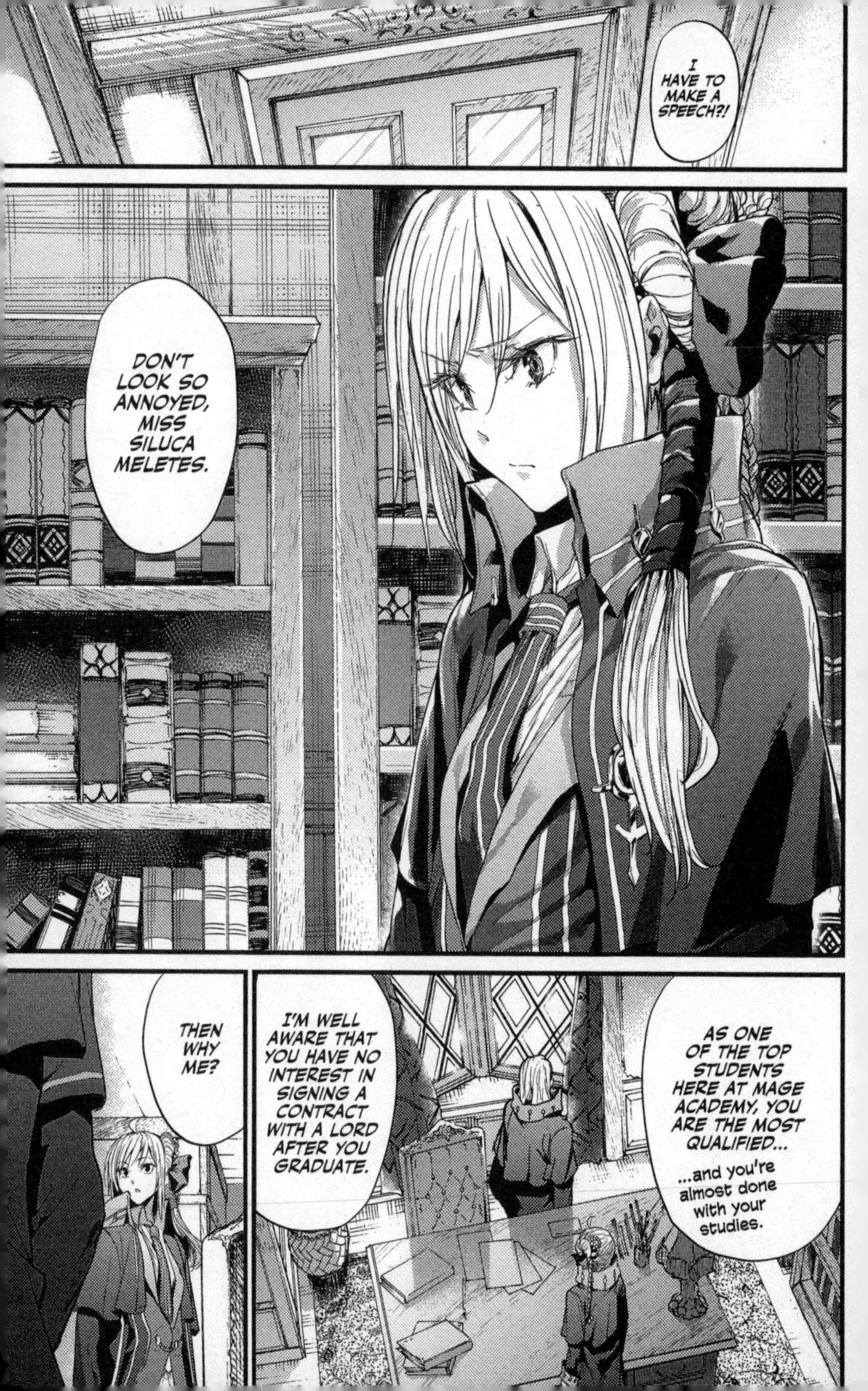
I HAVE TO MAKE A SPEECH?!
DON'T LOOK SO ANNOYED, MISS SILUCA MELETES.
AS ONE OF THE TOP STUDENTS HERE AT MAGE ACADEMY, YOU ARE THE MOST QUALIFIED...
...and you're almost done with your studies.
I'M WELL AWARE THAT YOU HAVE NO INTEREST IN SIGNING A CONTRACT WITH A LORD AFTER YOU GRADUATE.
THEN WHY ME?

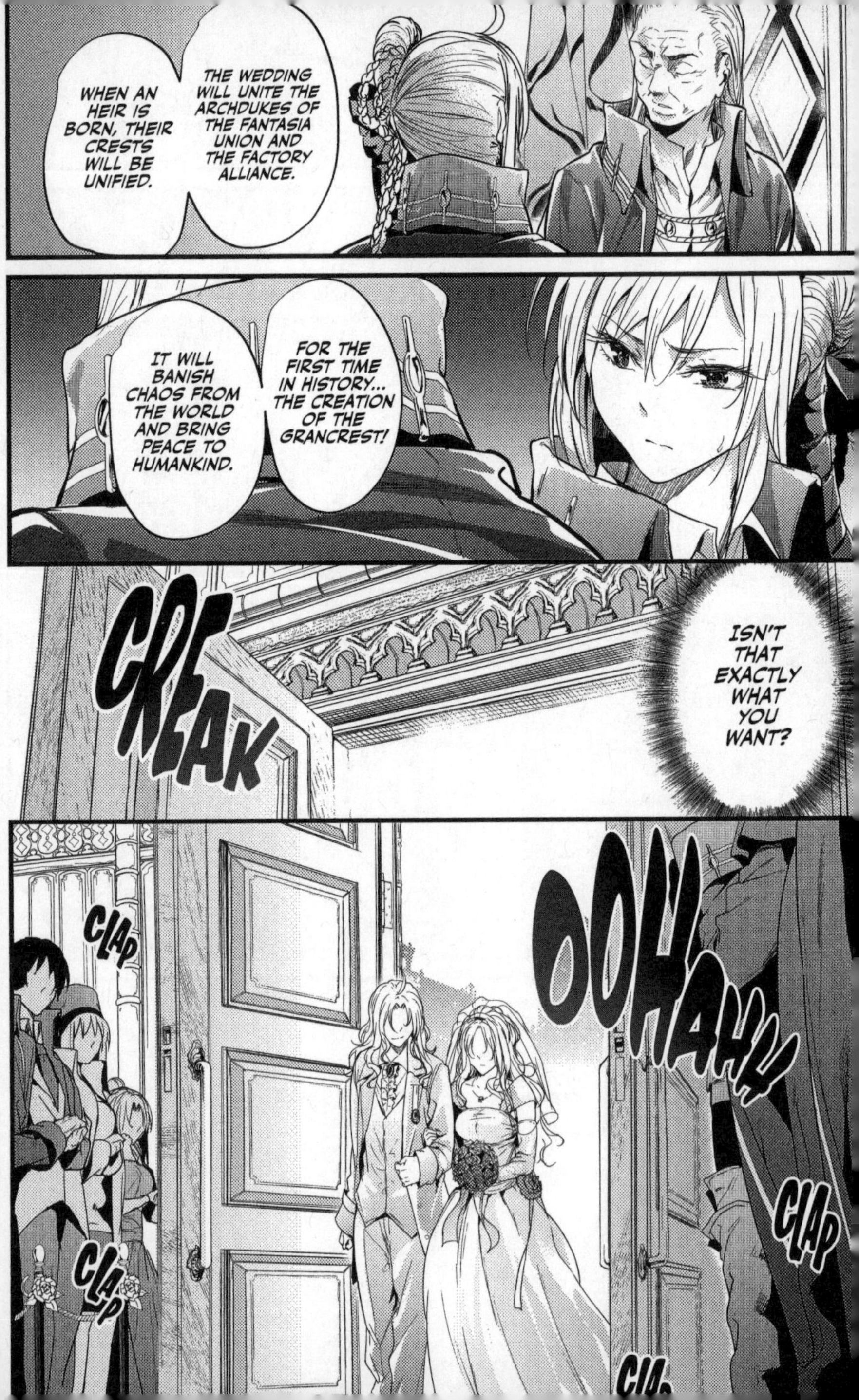
THE WEDDING WILL UNITE THE ARCHDUKES OF THE FANTASIA UNION AND THE FACTORY ALLIANCE.
WHEN AN HEIR IS BORN, THEIR CRESTS WILL BE UNIFIED.
FOR THE FIRST TIME IN HISTORY... THE CREATION OF THE GRANCREST!
IT WILL BANISH CHAOS FROM THE WORLD AND BRING PEACE TO HUMANKIND.
ISN'T THAT EXACTLY WHAT YOU WANT?
CREEAK
OOHAHH
CLAP
CLAP
CLAP
CLAP

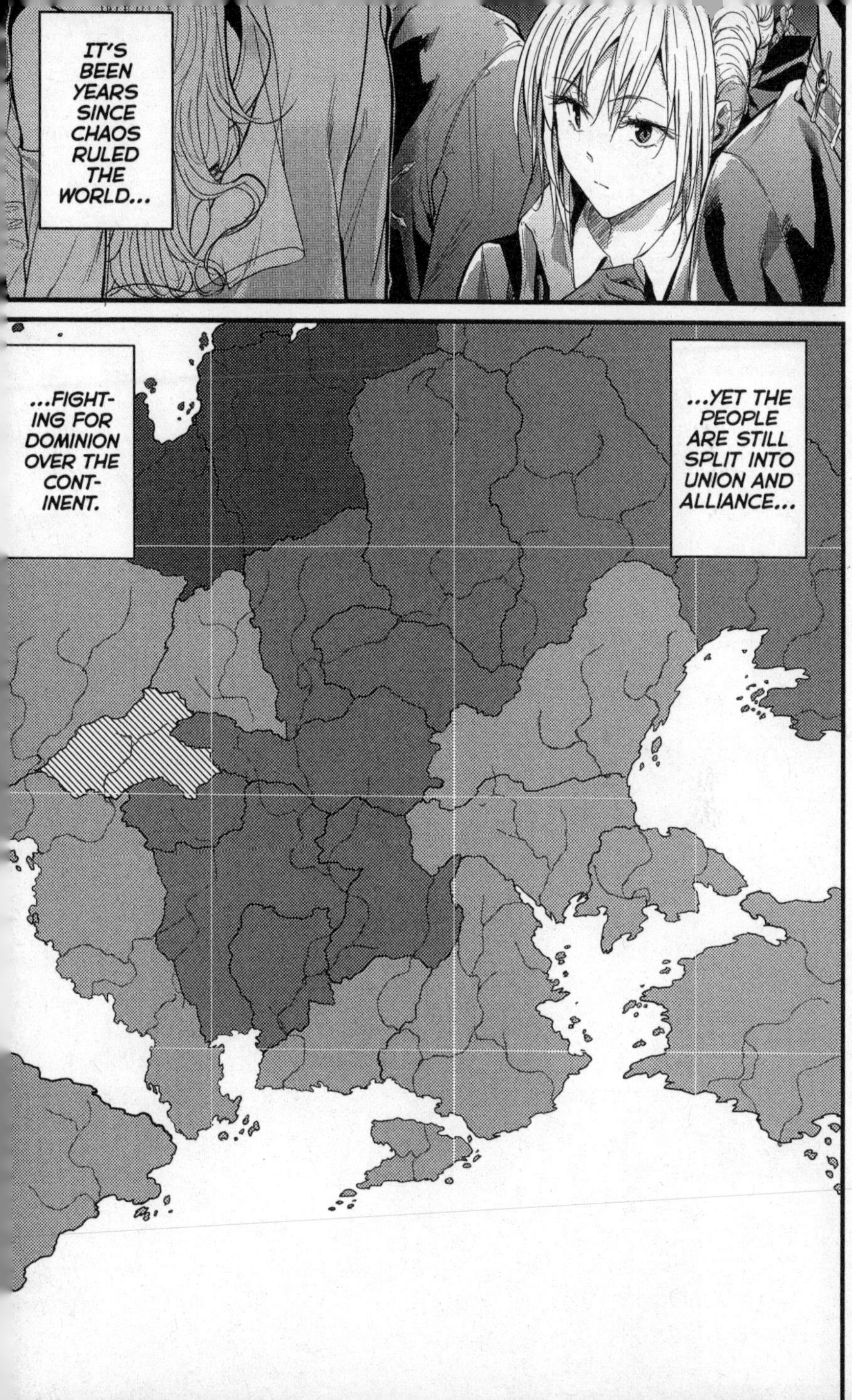
IT'S BEEN YEARS SINCE CHAOS RULED THE WORLD...
...YET THE PEOPLE ARE STILL SPLIT INTO UNION AND ALLIANCE...
...FIGHT-ING FOR DOMINION OVER THE CONT-INENT.

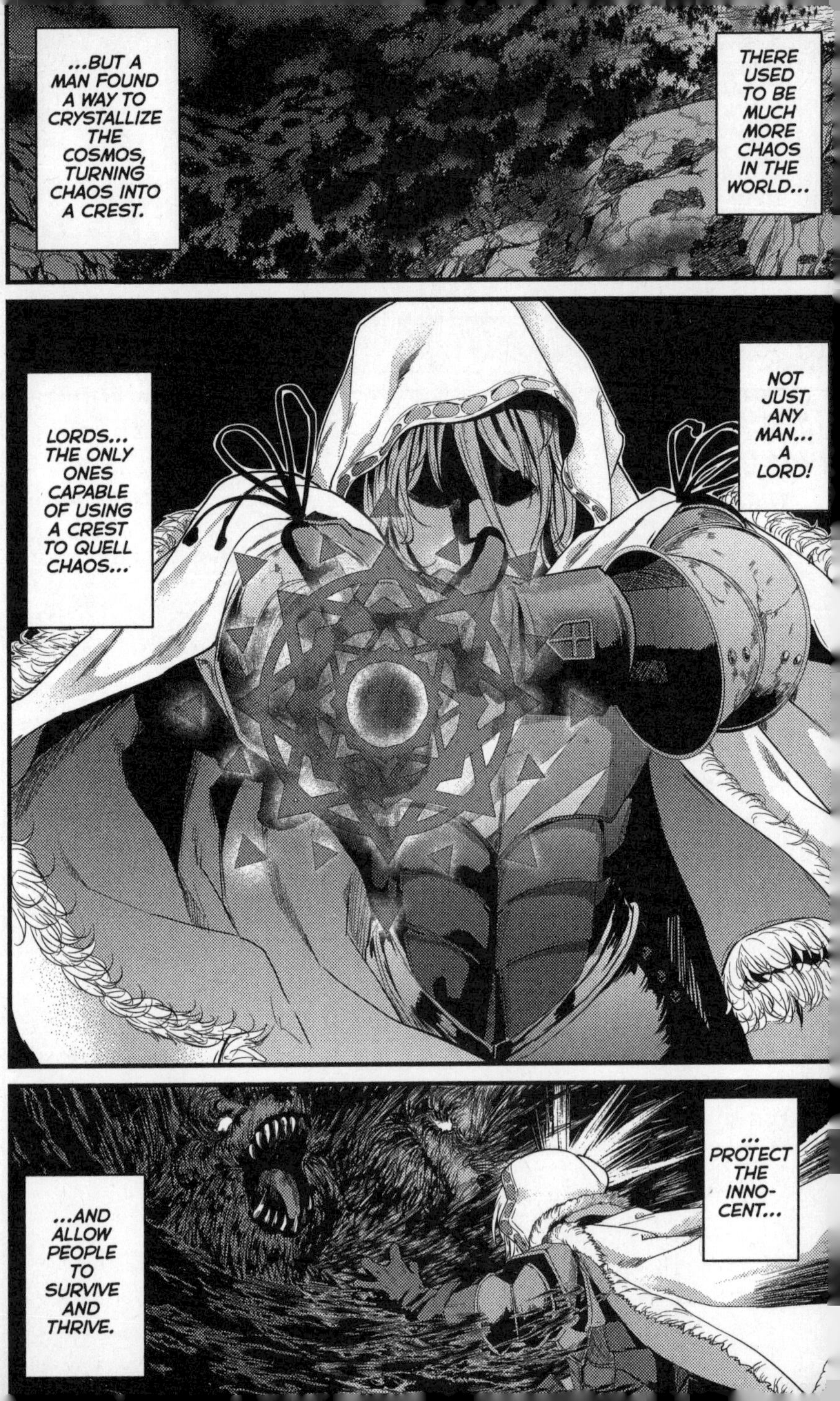
THERE USED TO BE MUCH MORE CHAOS IN THE WORLD...
...BUT A MAN FOUND A WAY TO CRYSTALLIZE THE COSMOS, TURNING CHAOS INTO A CREST.
NOT JUST ANY MAN... A LORD!
LORDS... THE ONLY ONES CAPABLE OF USING A CREST TO QUELL CHAOS...
...PROTECT THE INNO-CENT...
...AND ALLOW PEOPLE TO SURVIVE AND THRIVE.

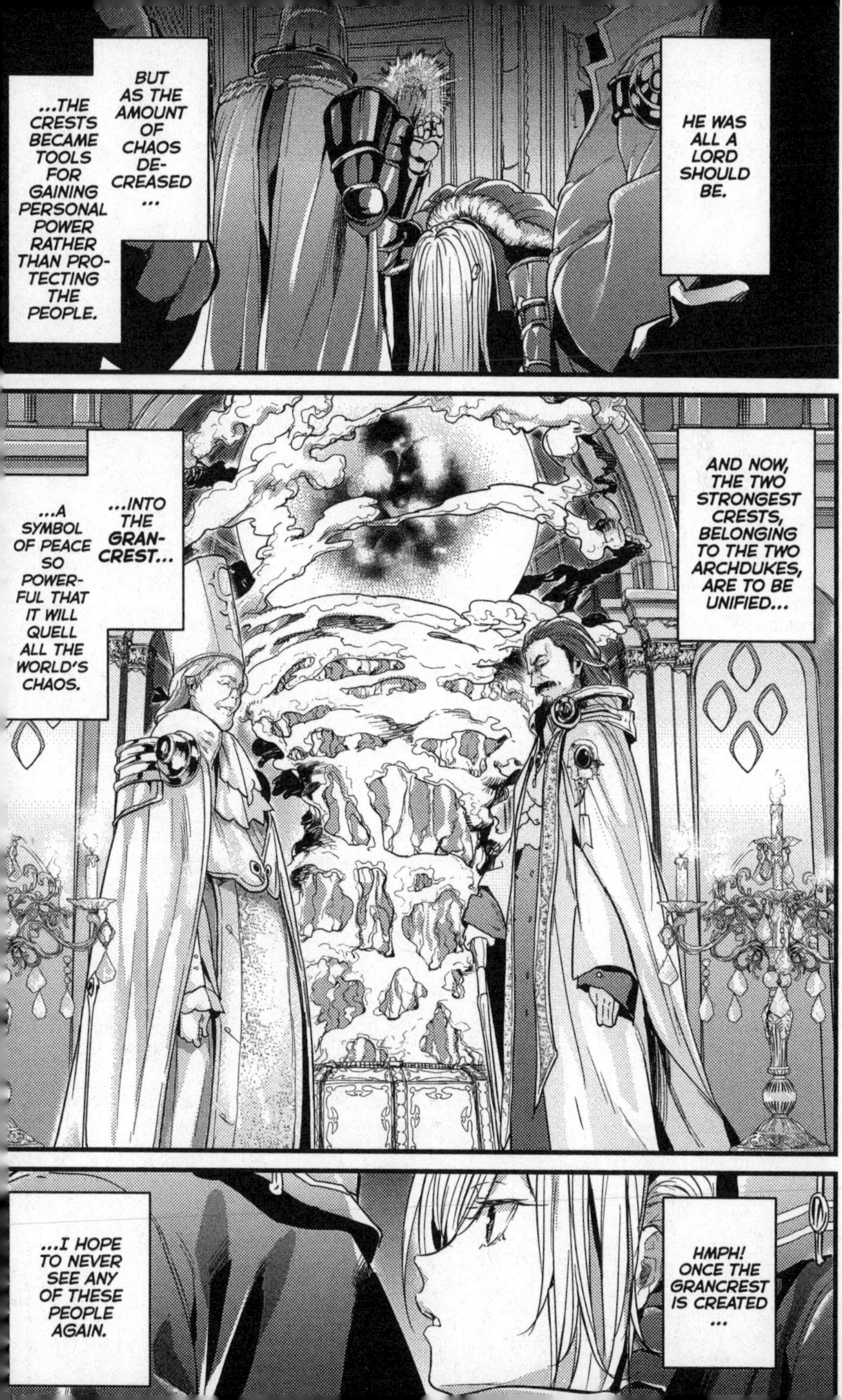
HE WAS ALL A LORD SHOULD BE.
BUT AS THE AMOUNT OF CHAOS DECREASED...
...THE CRESTS BECAME TOOLS FOR GAINING PERSONAL POWER RATHER THAN PROTECTING THE PEOPLE.
AND NOW, THE TWO STRONGEST CRESTS, BELONGING TO THE TWO ARCHDUKES, ARE TO BE UNIFIED...
...INTO THE GRANCREST...
...A SYMBOL OF PEACE SO POWERFUL THAT IT WILL QUELL ALL THE WORLD'S CHAOS.
HMPH! ONCE THE GRANCREST IS CREATED...
...I HOPE TO NEVER SEE ANY OF THESE PEOPLE AGAIN.

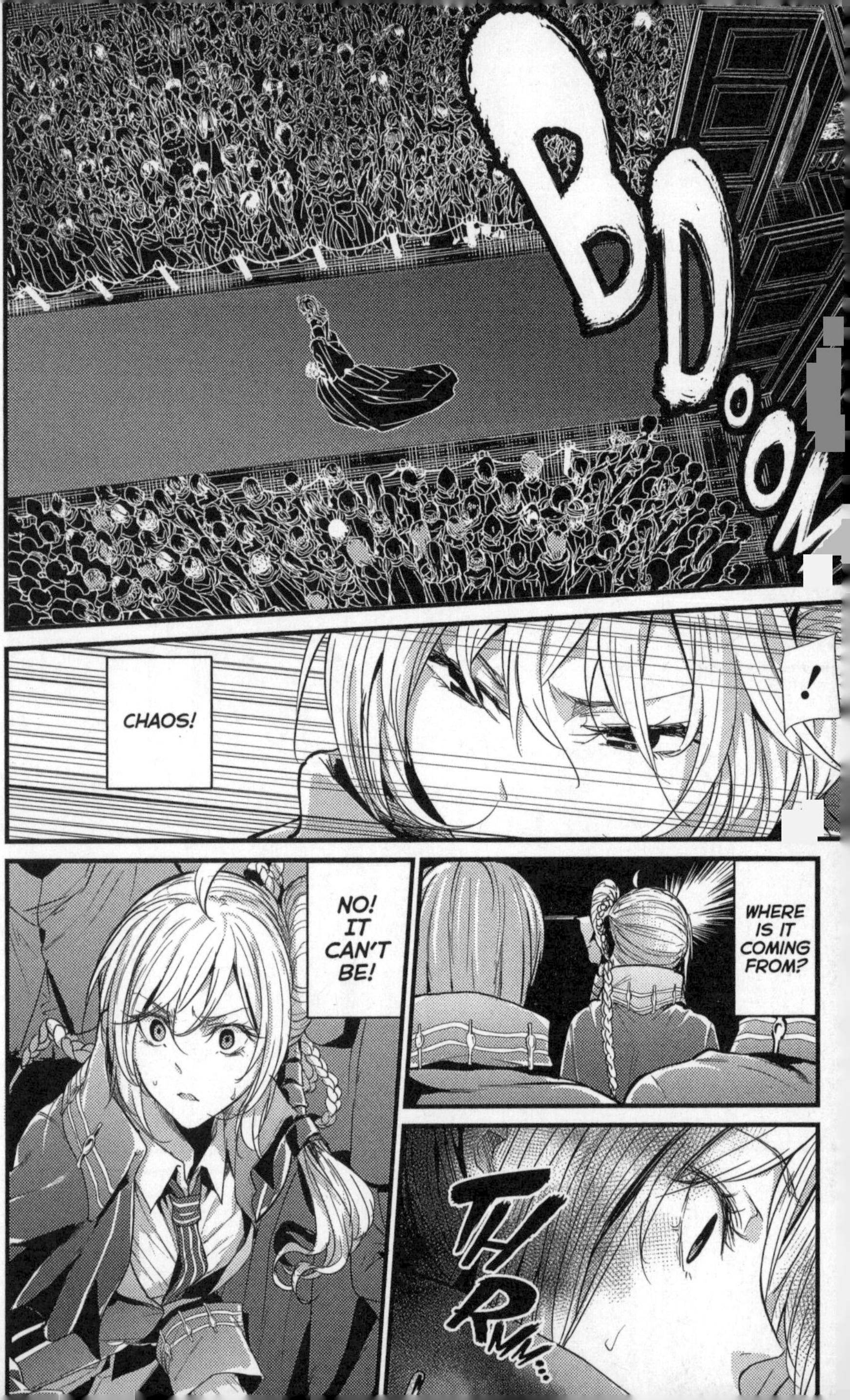
BDOOM
!
CHAOS!
WHERE IS IT COMING FROM?
NO! IT CAN'T BE!
THRMM...

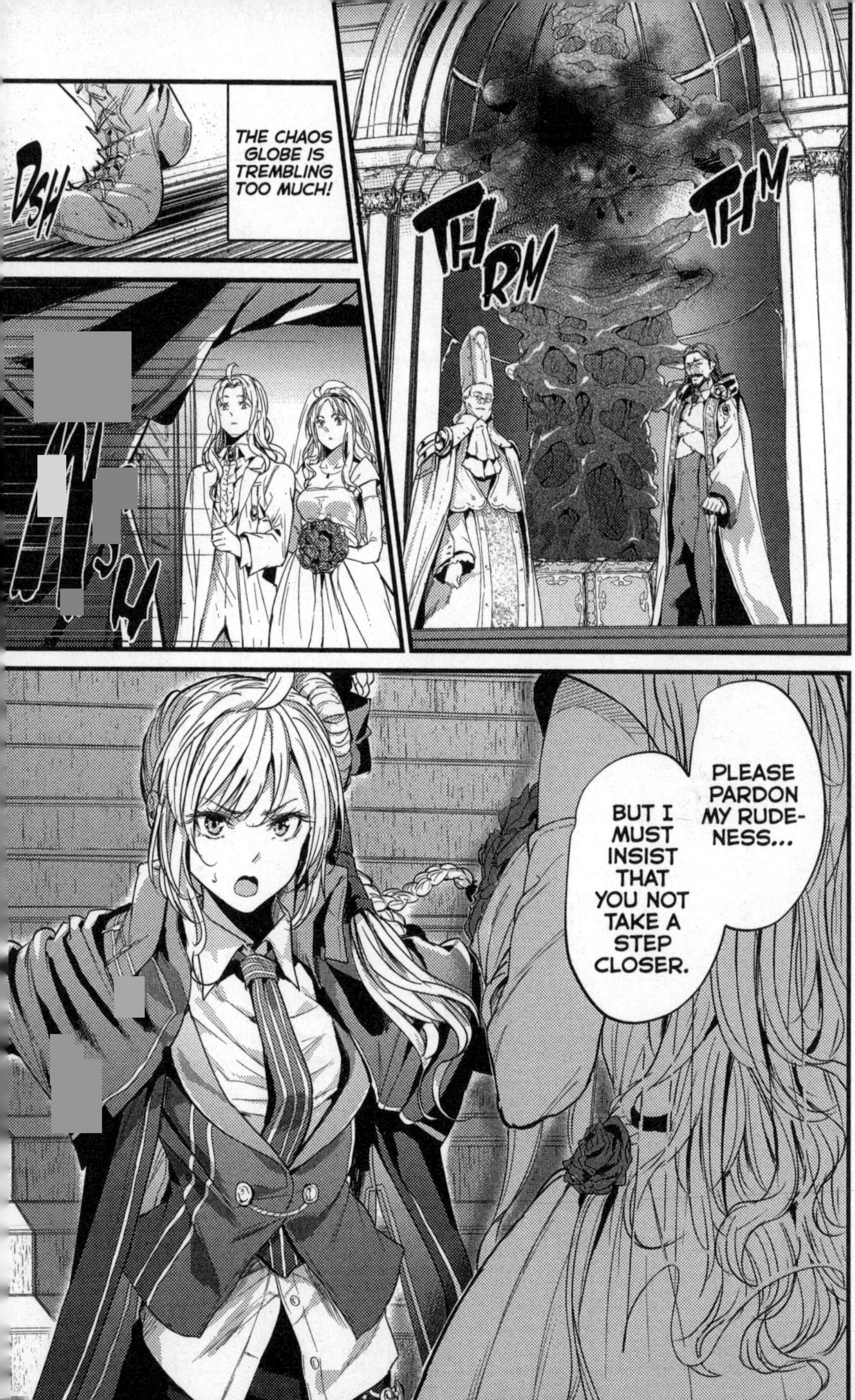
THRM
THM
DSH
THE CHAOS GLOBE IS TREMBLING TOO MUCH!
PLEASE PARDON MY RUDENESS...
BUT I MUST INSIST THAT YOU NOT TAKE A STEP CLOSER.

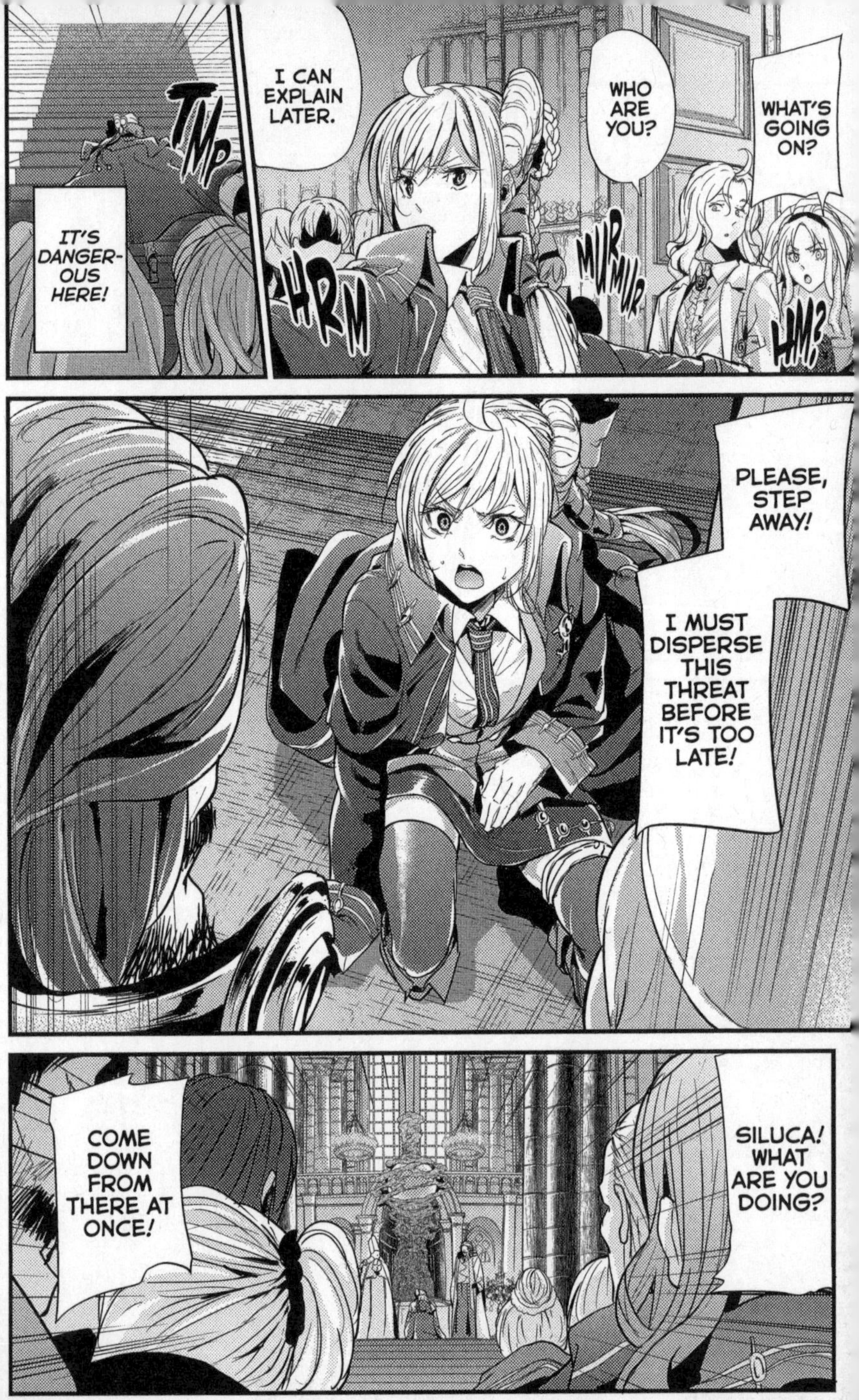
WHAT'S GOING ON?
WHO ARE YOU?
HM?
MURMUR
I CAN EXPLAIN LATER.
HRM
TMP
IT'S DANGER-OUS HERE!
PLEASE, STEP AWAY!
I MUST DISPERSE THIS THREAT BEFORE IT'S TOO LATE!
SILUCA! WHAT ARE YOU DOING?
COME DOWN FROM THERE AT ONCE!

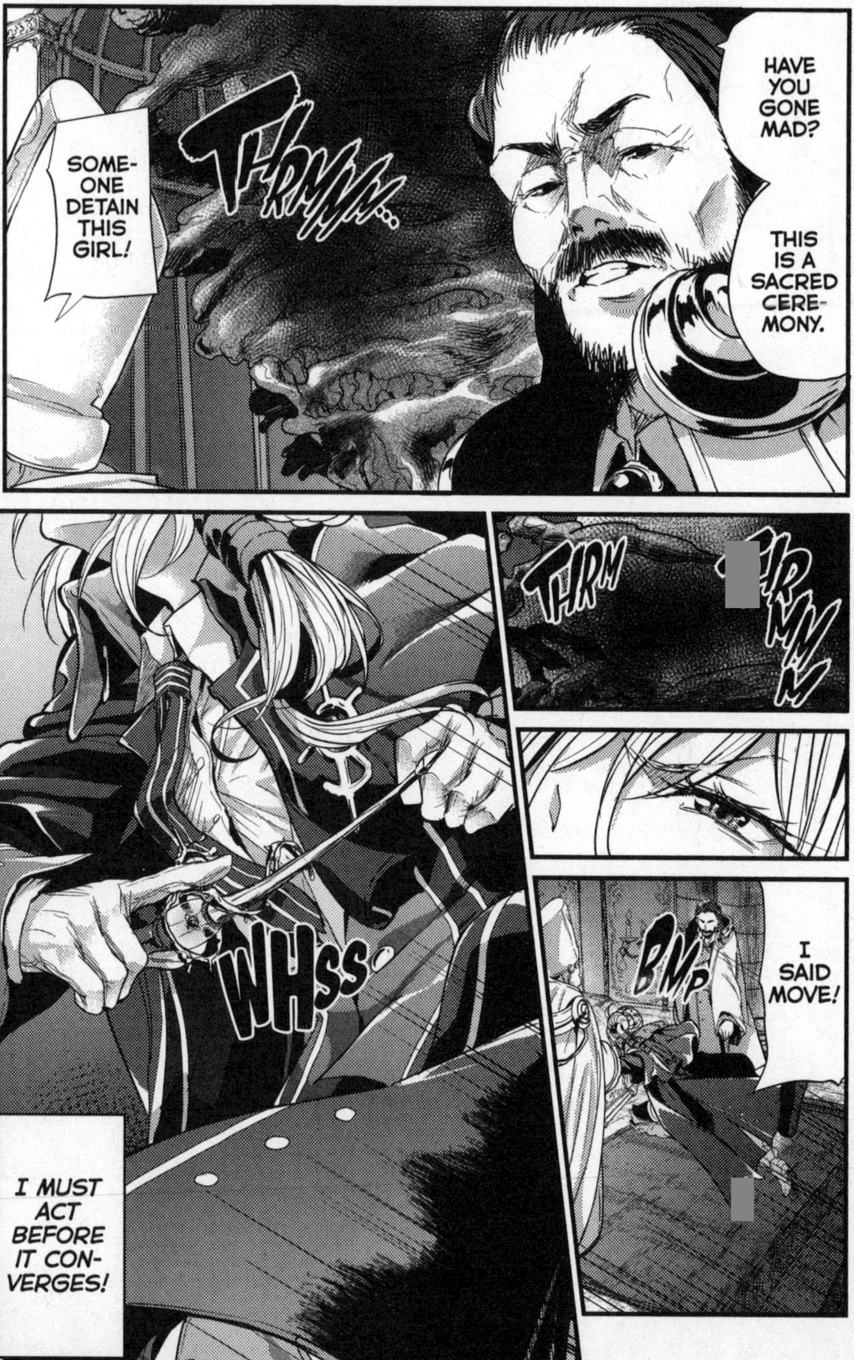
HAVE YOU GONE MAD?
THIS IS A SACRED CEREMONY.
THRMMM...
SOMEONE DETAIN THIS GIRL!
THRM
THRMMMM
BMP
I SAID MOVE!
WHSS
I MUST ACT BEFORE IT CONVERGES!

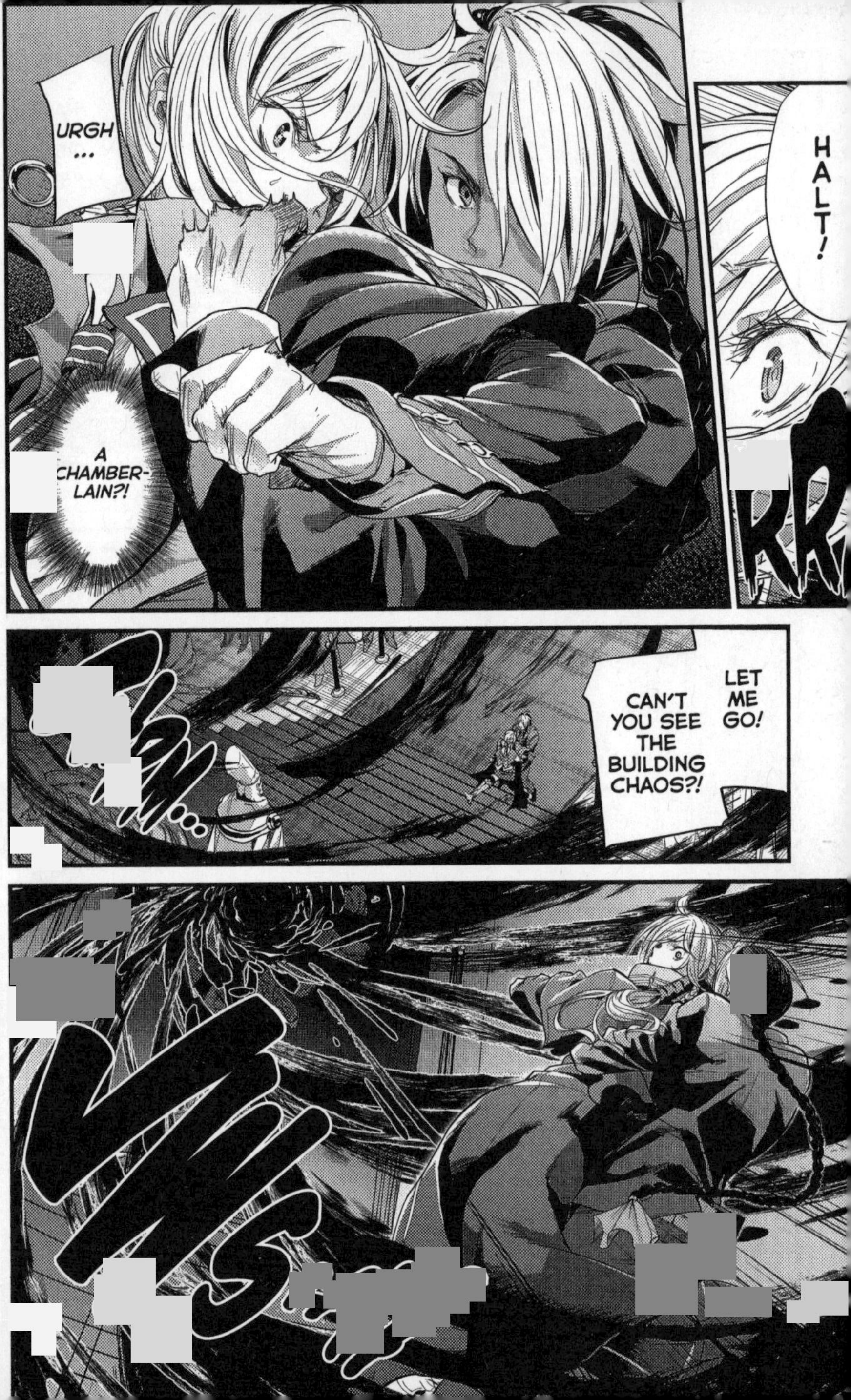
HALT!
URGH ...
A CHAMBER-LAIN?!
LET ME GO!
CAN'T YOU SEE THE BUILDING CHAOS?!

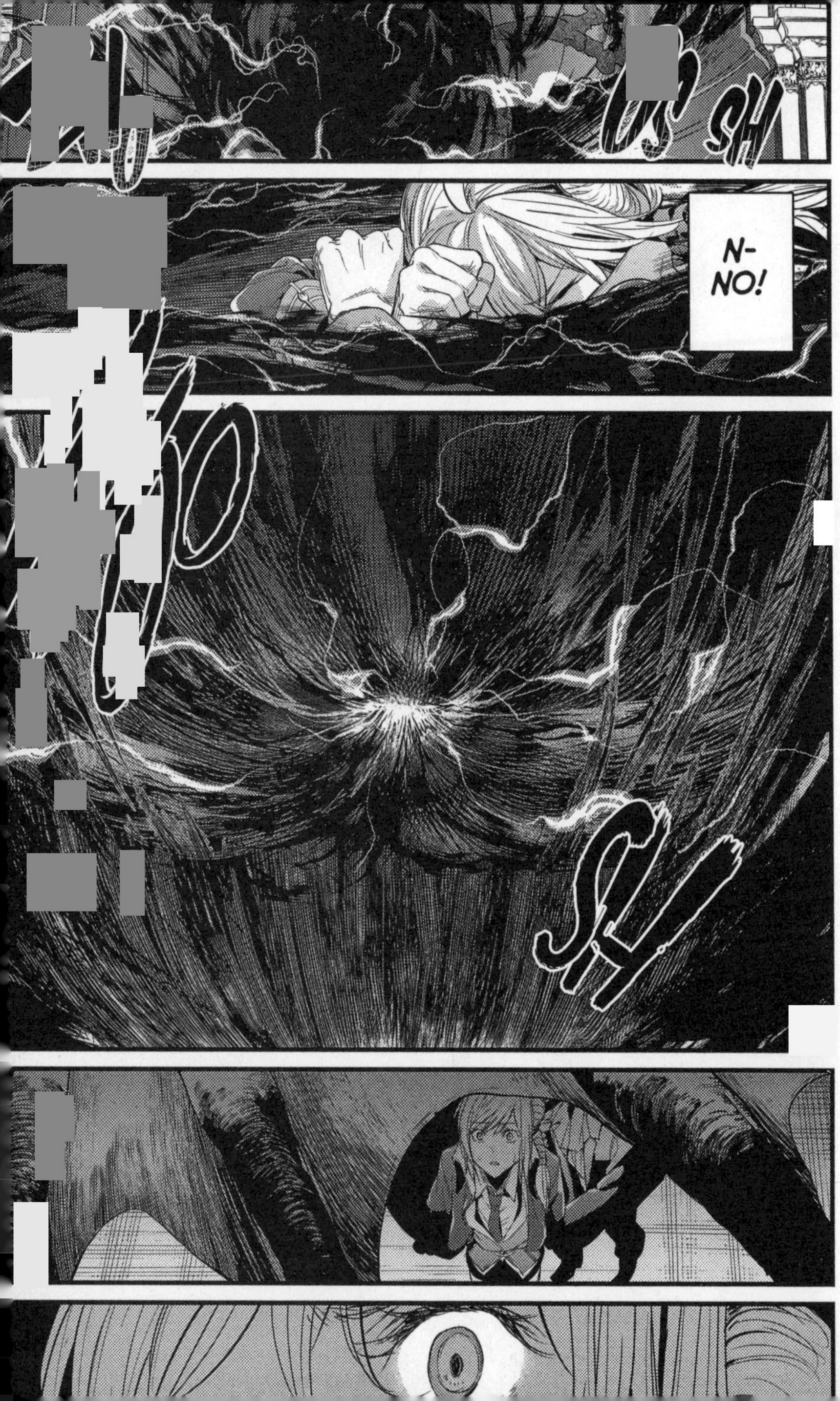
N-NO!

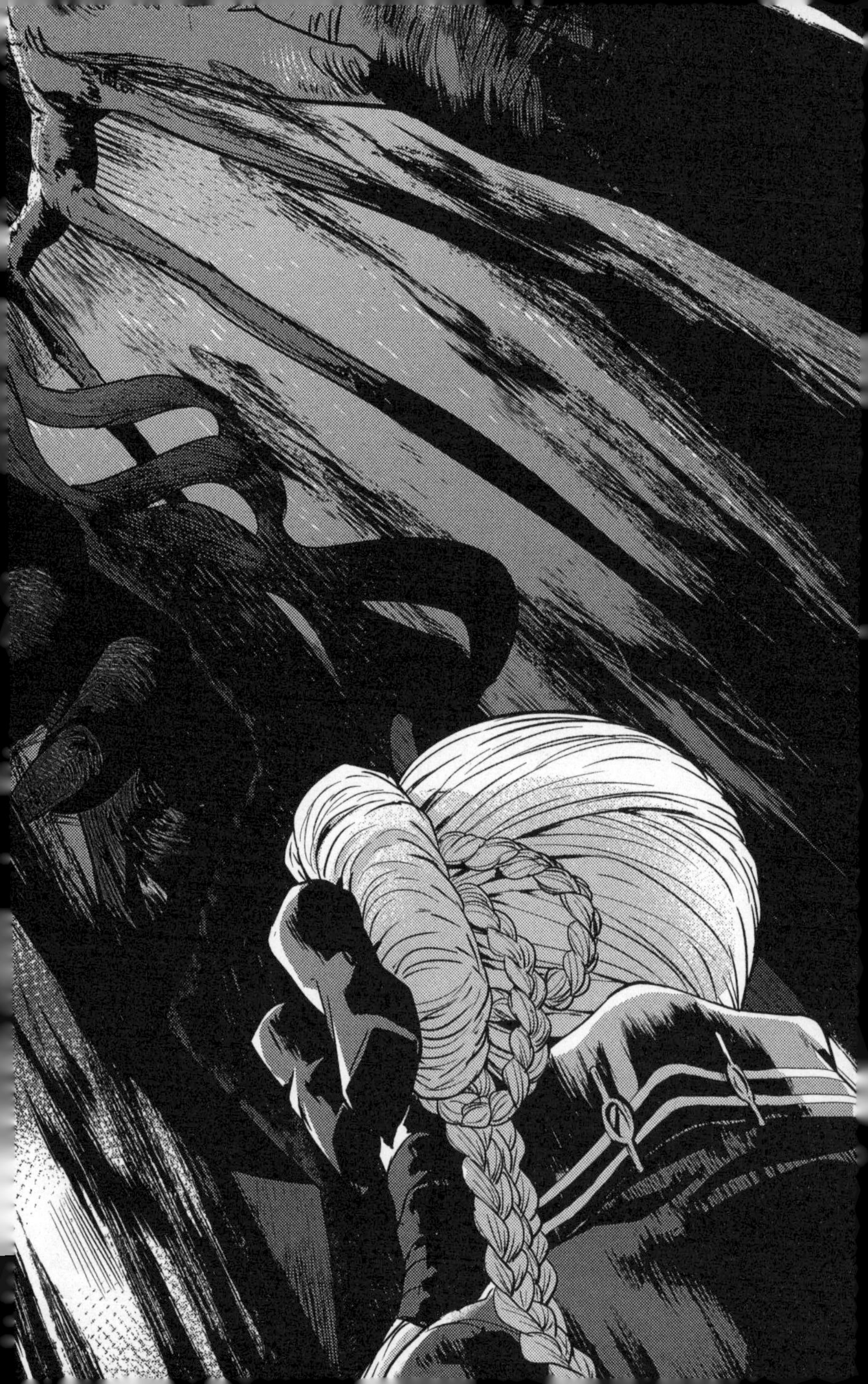

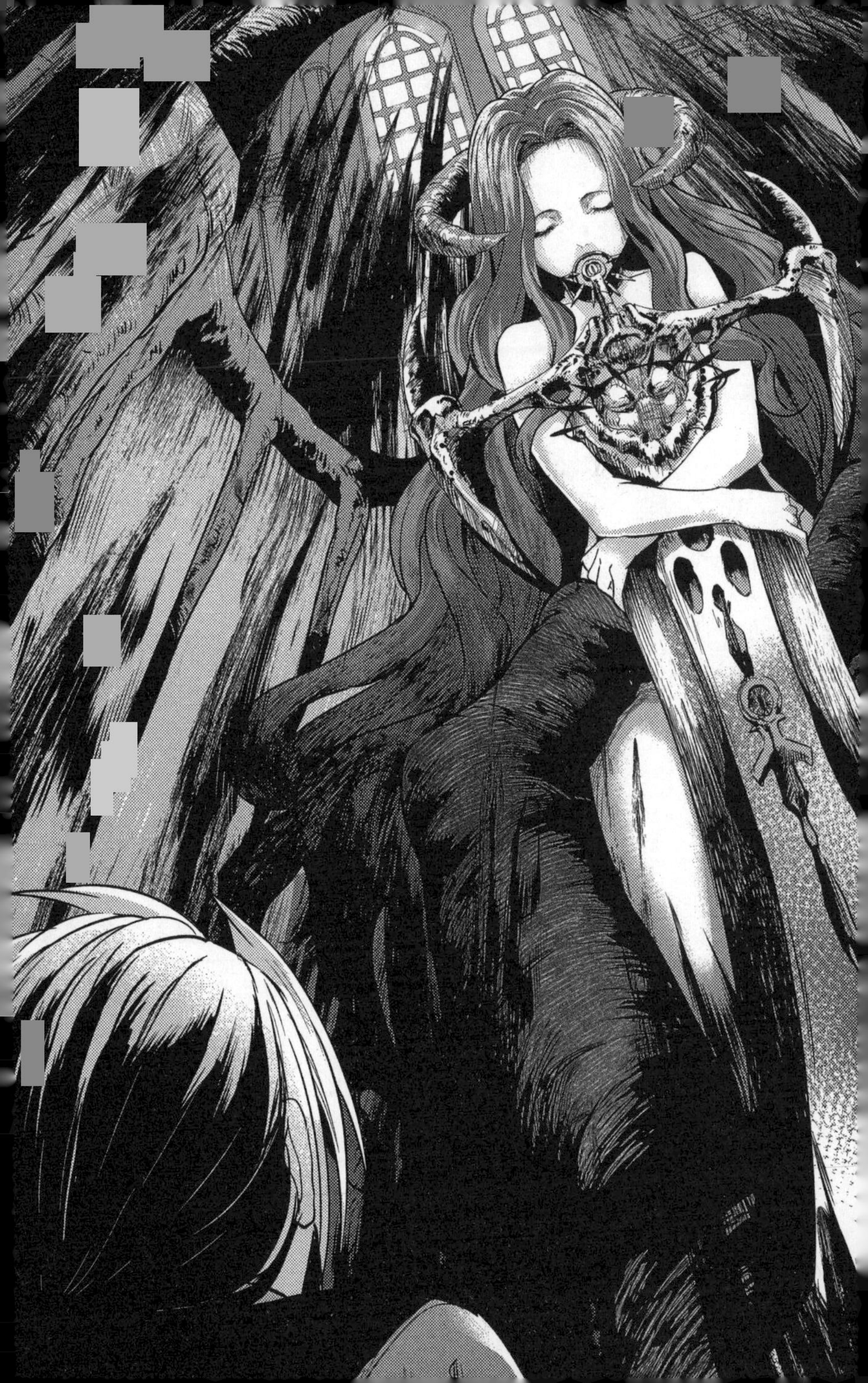

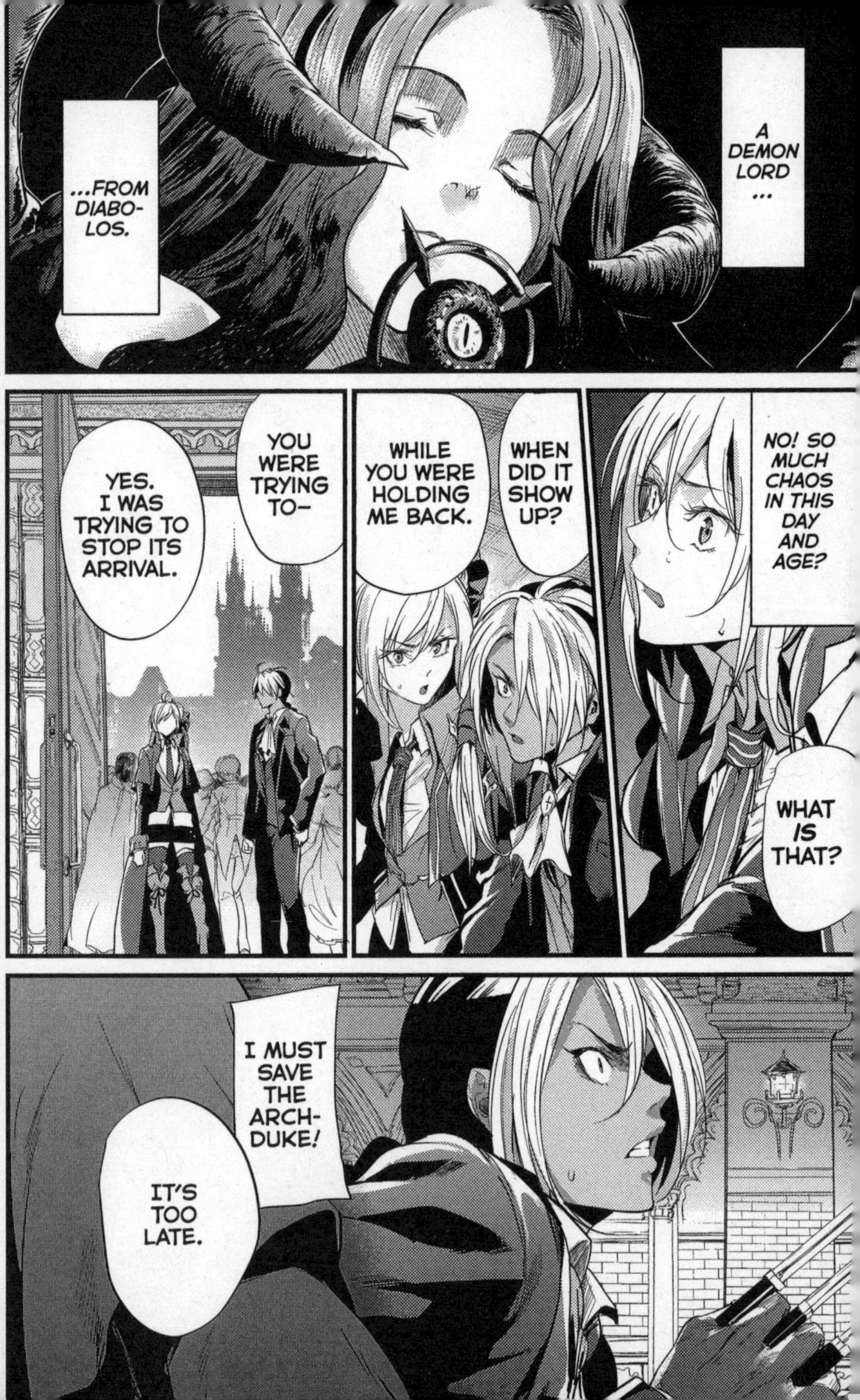
A DEMON LORD ...
...FROM DIABOLOS.
NO! SO MUCH CHAOS IN THIS DAY AND AGE?
WHAT *IS* THAT?
WHEN DID IT SHOW UP?
WHILE YOU WERE HOLDING ME BACK.
YOU WERE TRYING TO–
YES. I WAS TRYING TO STOP ITS ARRIVAL.
I MUST SAVE THE ARCH-DUKE!
IT'S TOO LATE.

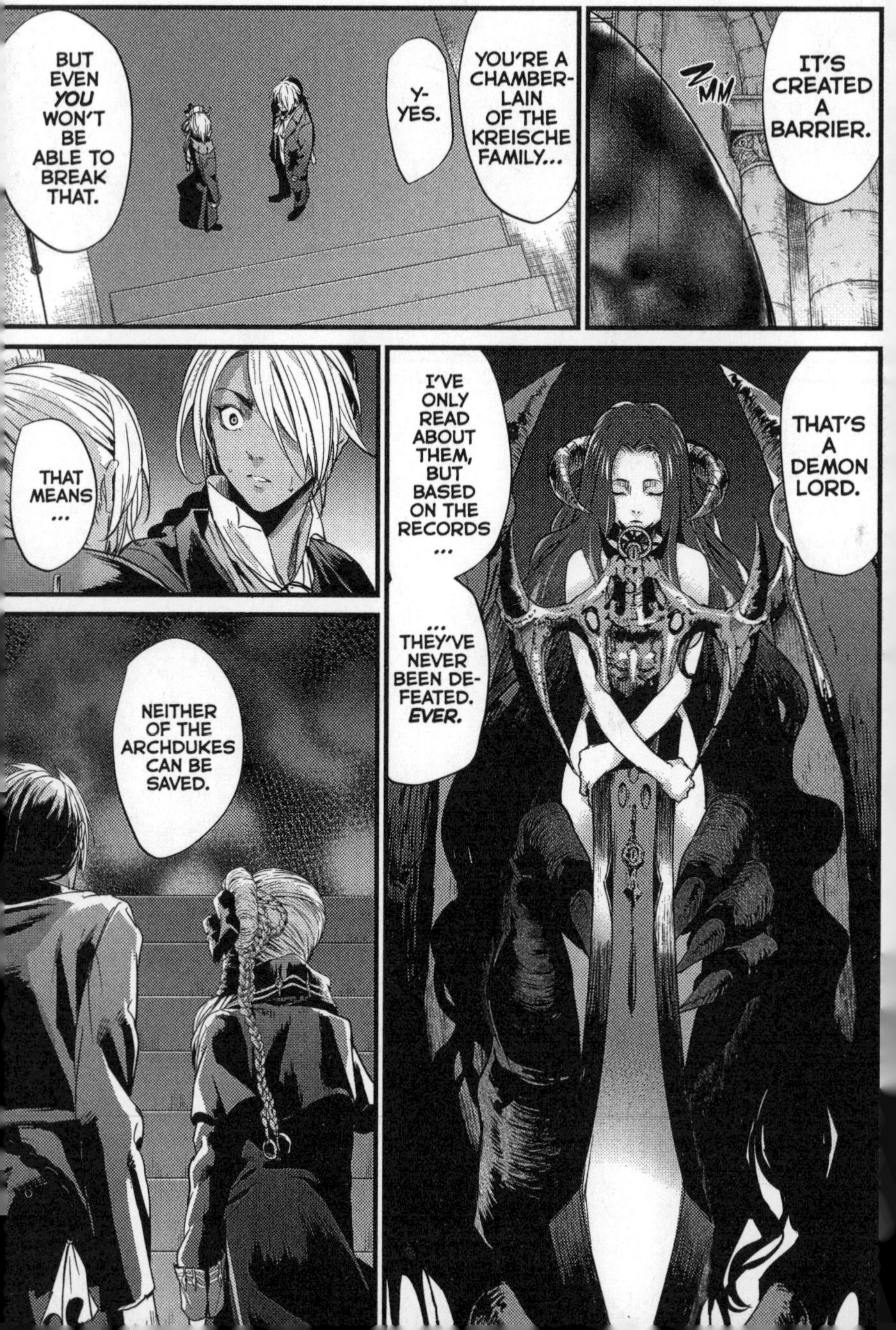
IT'S CREATED A BARRIER.
ZMM
YOU'RE A CHAMBERLAIN OF THE KREISCHE FAMILY...
Y-YES.
BUT EVEN *YOU* WON'T BE ABLE TO BREAK THAT.
THAT'S A DEMON LORD.
I'VE ONLY READ ABOUT THEM, BUT BASED ON THE RECORDS...
...THEY'VE NEVER BEEN DEFEATED. *EVER.*
THAT MEANS...
NEITHER OF THE ARCHDUKES CAN BE SAVED.

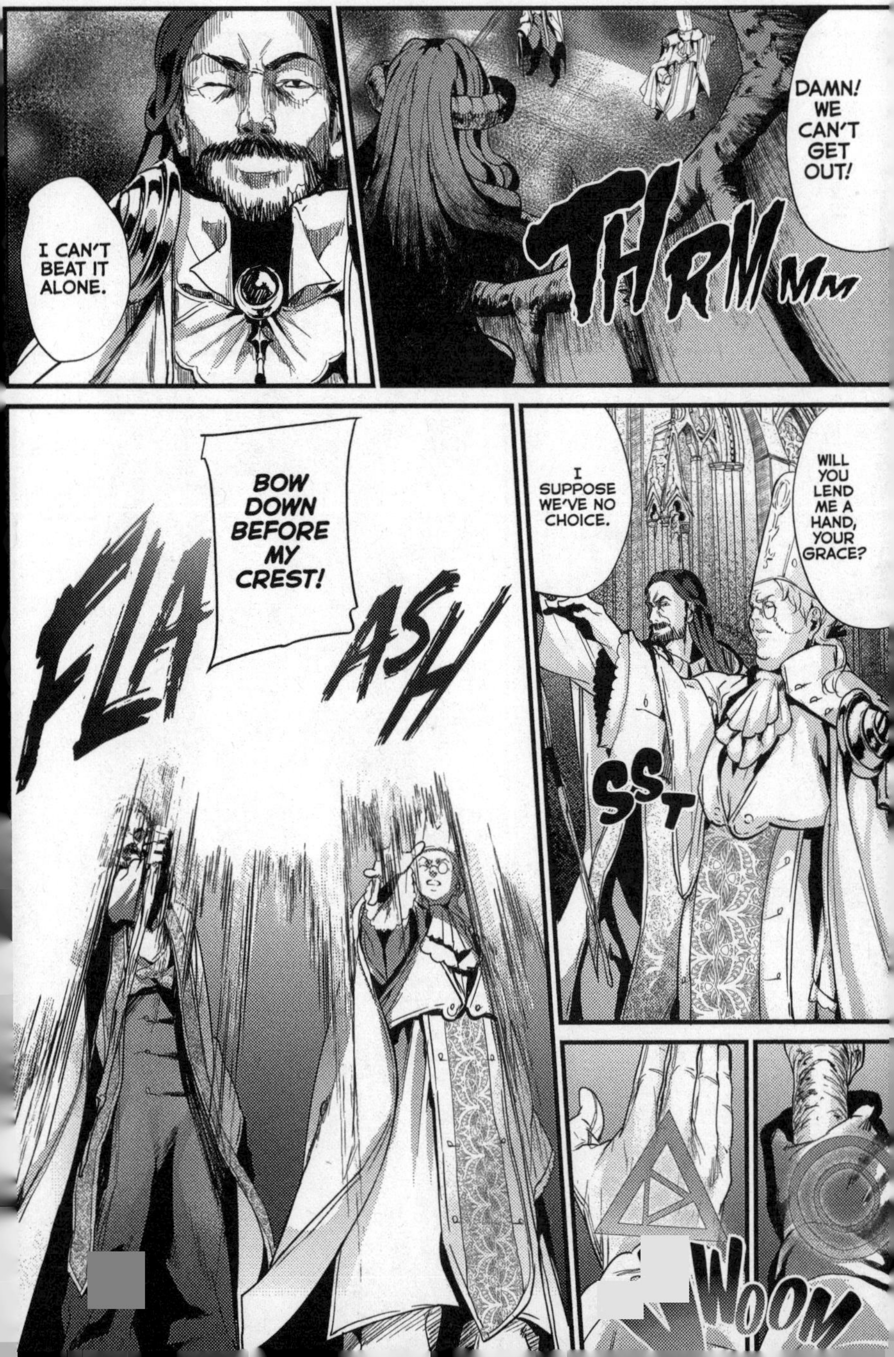
DAMN! WE CAN'T GET OUT!
THRMMM
I CAN'T BEAT IT ALONE.
WILL YOU LEND ME A HAND, YOUR GRACE?
I SUPPOSE WE'VE NO CHOICE.
SSST
WOOM
BOW DOWN BEFORE MY CREST!
FLAASH

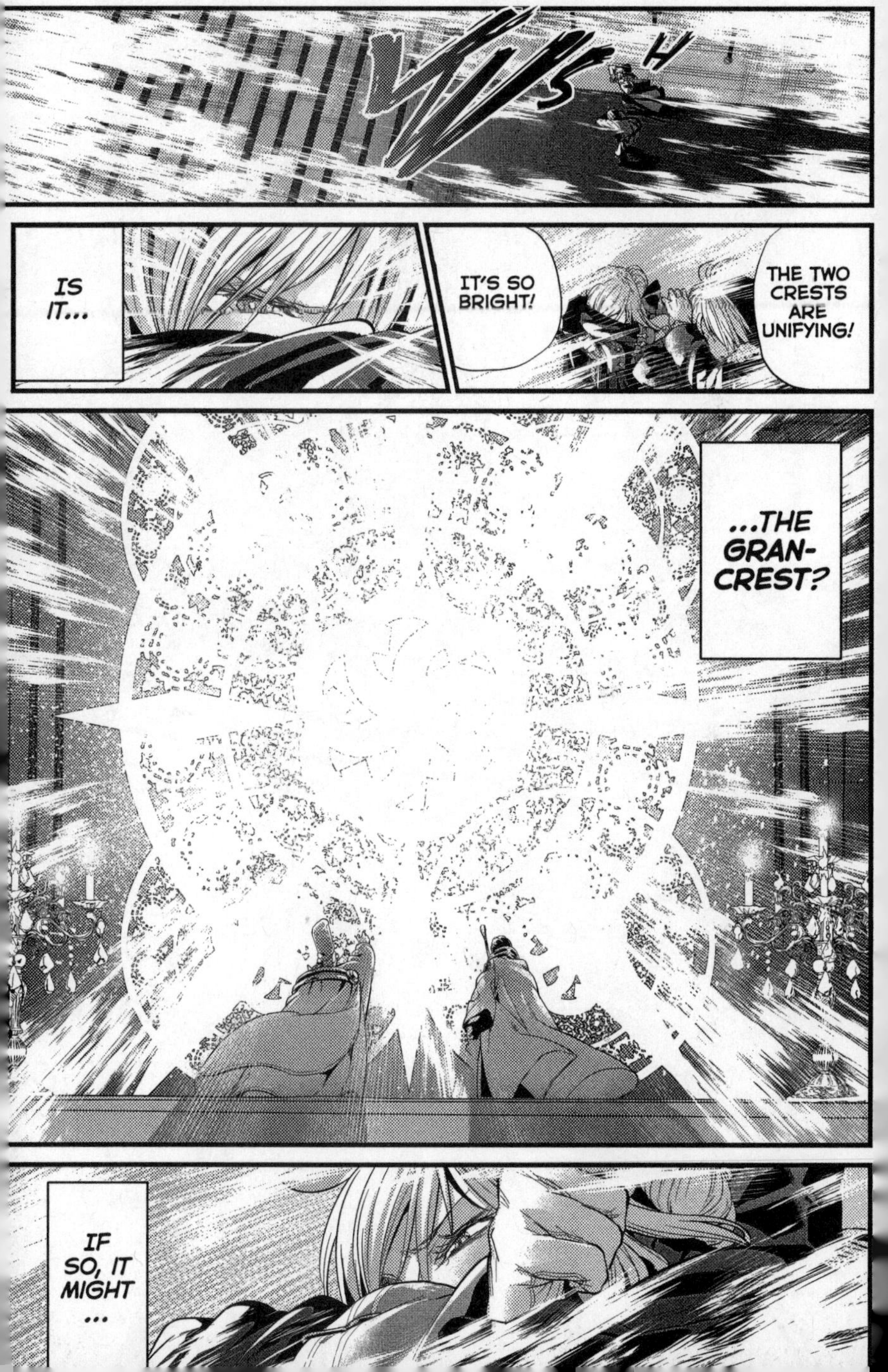
THE TWO CRESTS ARE UNIFYING!
IT'S SO BRIGHT!
IS IT...
...THE GRAN-CREST?
IF SO, IT MIGHT ...

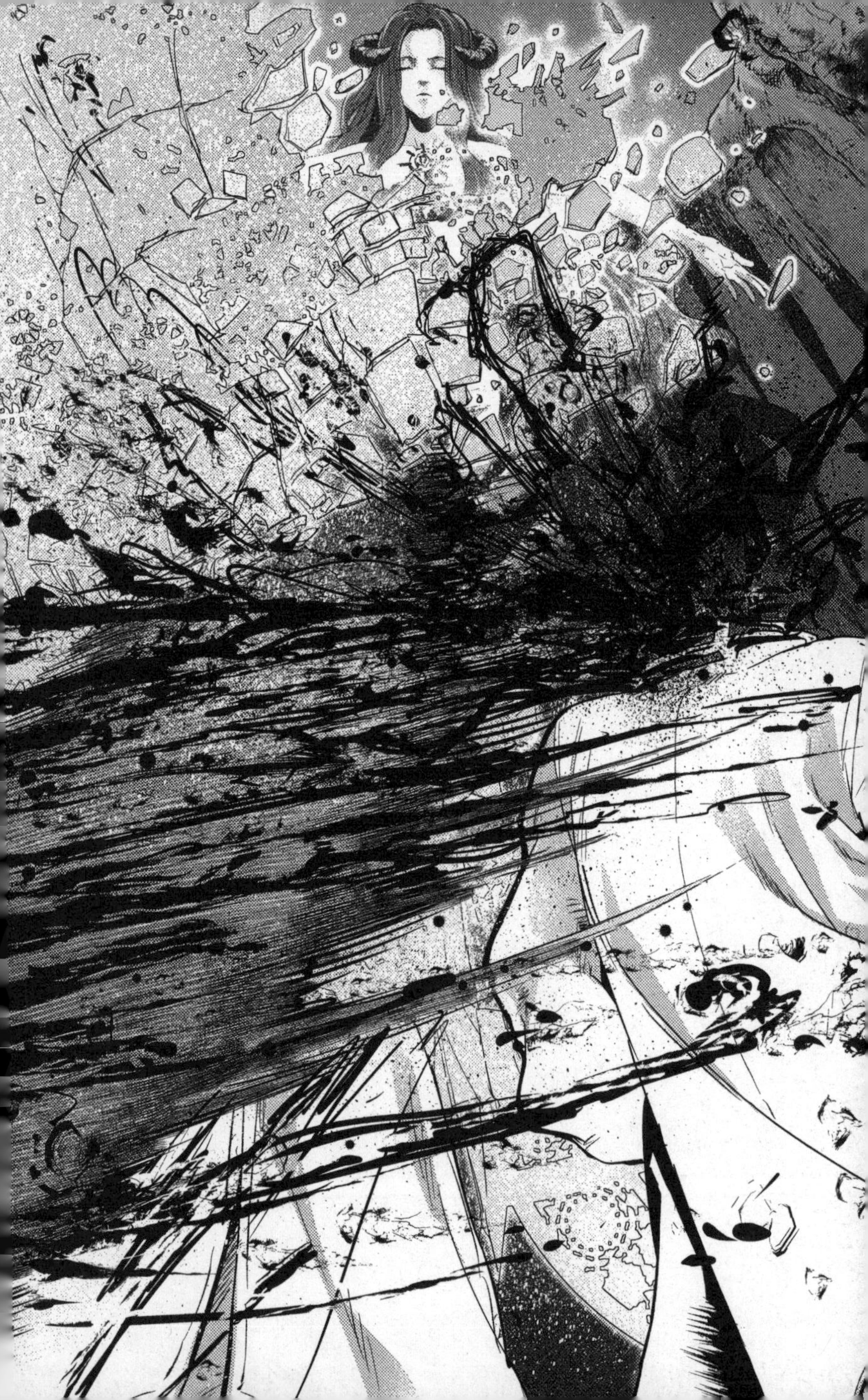

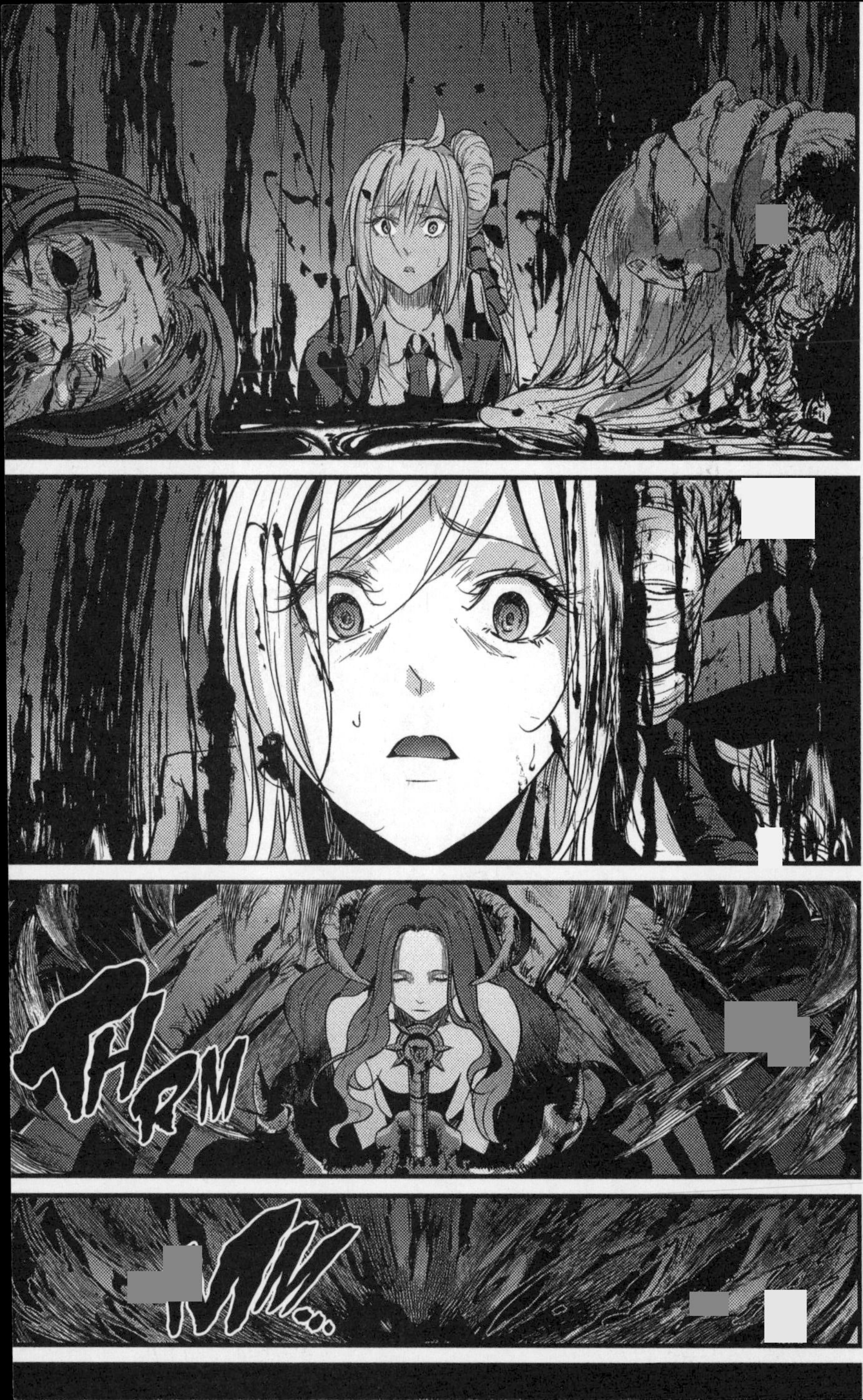
THRM
MM...

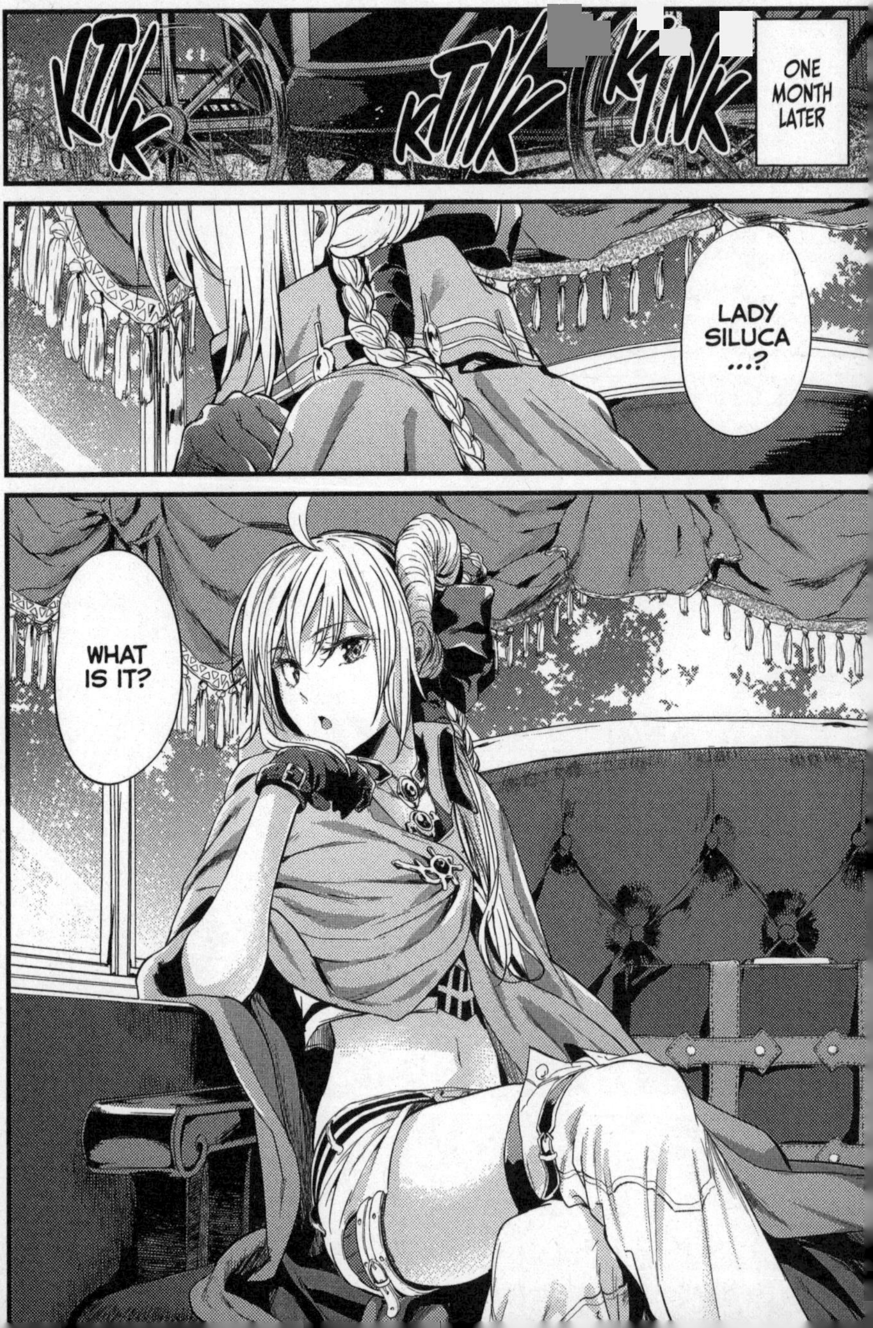
ONE MONTH LATER
KINK
KTINK
KTINK
LADY SILUCA ...?
WHAT IS IT?

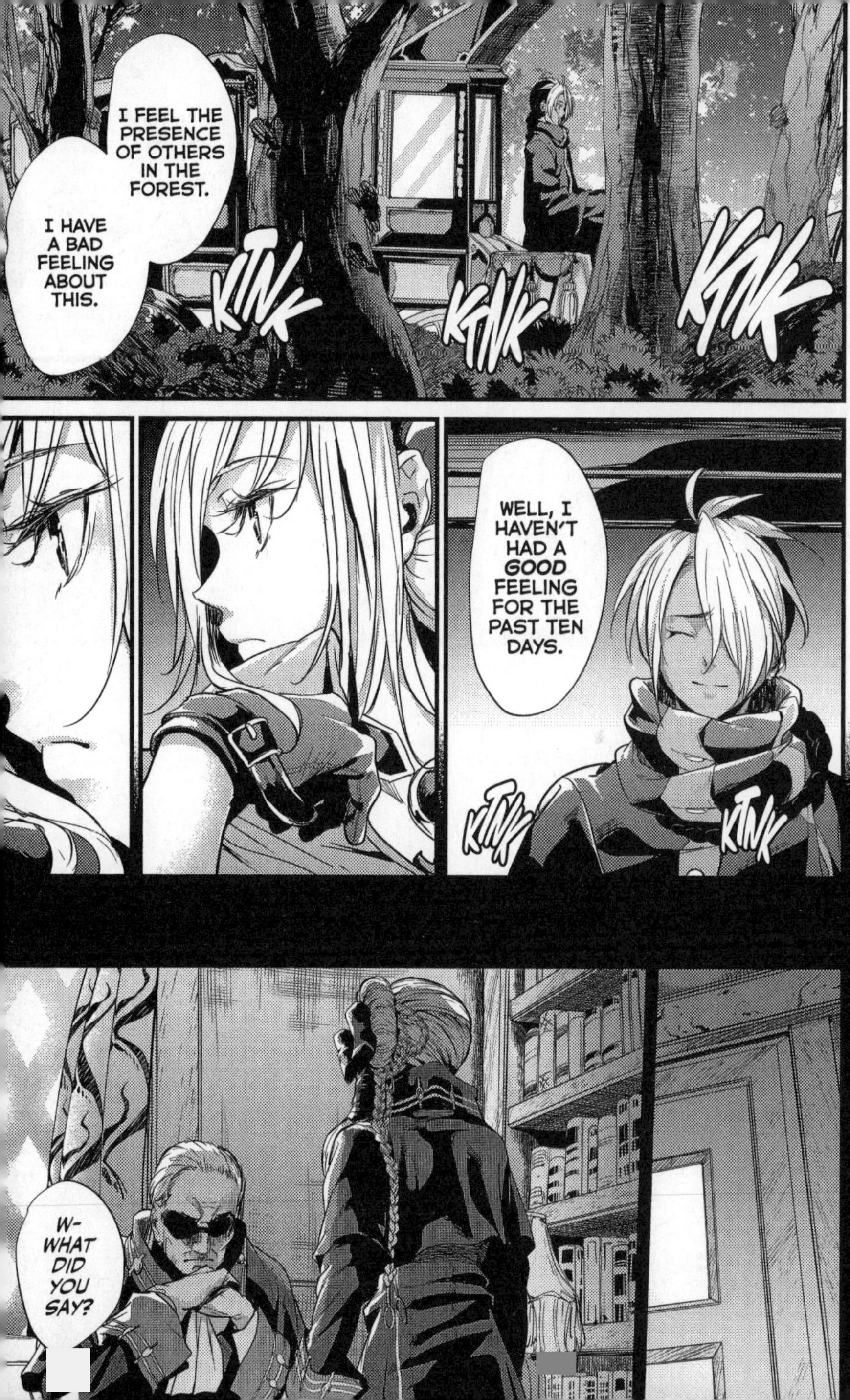
KTNK
KTNK
I FEEL THE PRESENCE OF OTHERS IN THE FOREST.
I HAVE A BAD FEELING ABOUT THIS.
KTNK
WELL, I HAVEN'T HAD A *GOOD* FEELING FOR THE PAST TEN DAYS.
KTNK
KTNK
W-WHAT DID YOU SAY?

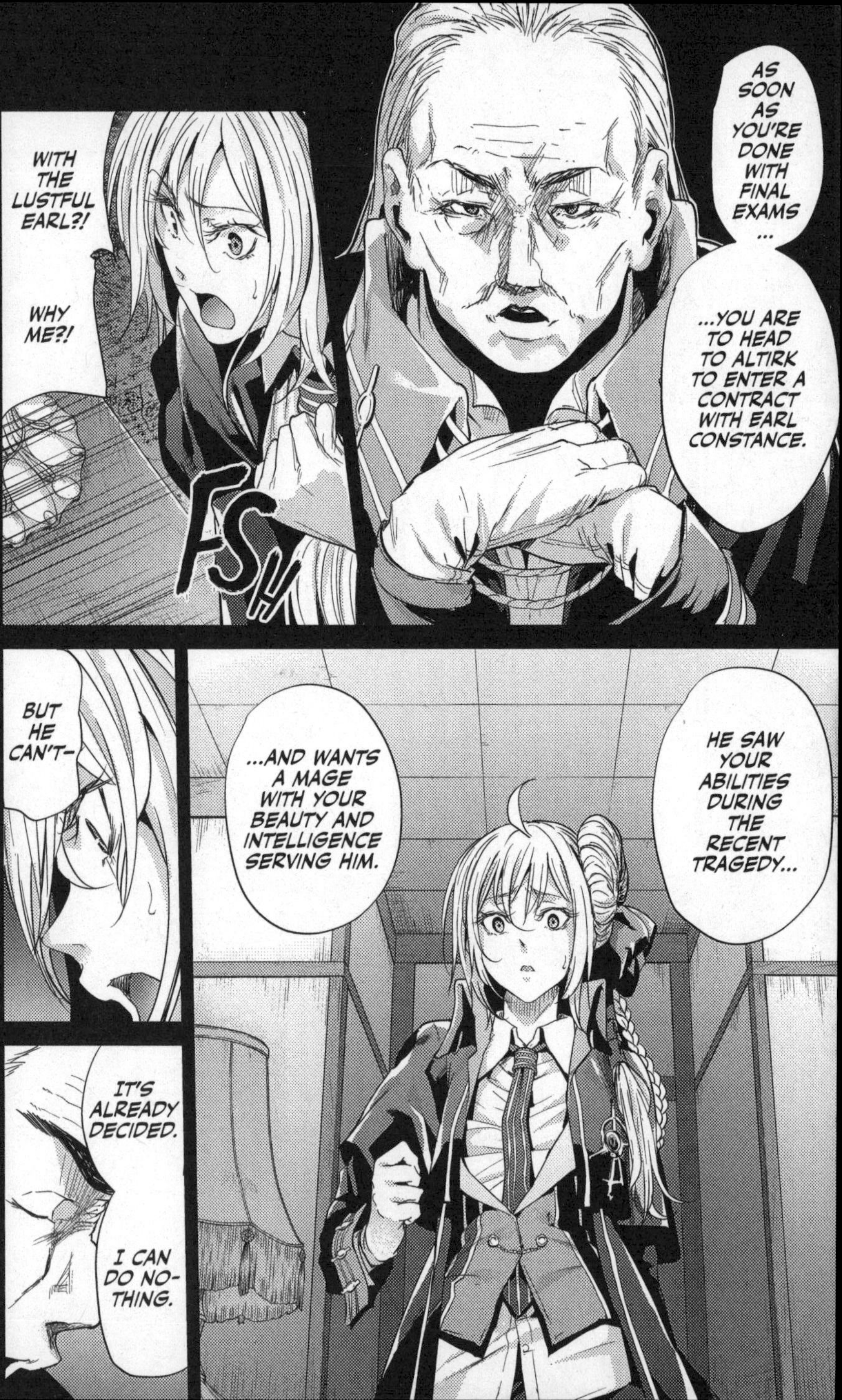
AS SOON AS YOU'RE DONE WITH FINAL EXAMS...
...YOU ARE TO HEAD TO ALTIRK TO ENTER A CONTRACT WITH EARL CONSTANCE.
WITH THE LUSTFUL EARL?!
WHY ME?!
FSH
HE SAW YOUR ABILITIES DURING THE RECENT TRAGEDY...
...AND WANTS A MAGE WITH YOUR BEAUTY AND INTELLIGENCE SERVING HIM.
BUT HE CAN'T-
IT'S ALREADY DECIDED.
I CAN DO NO-THING.

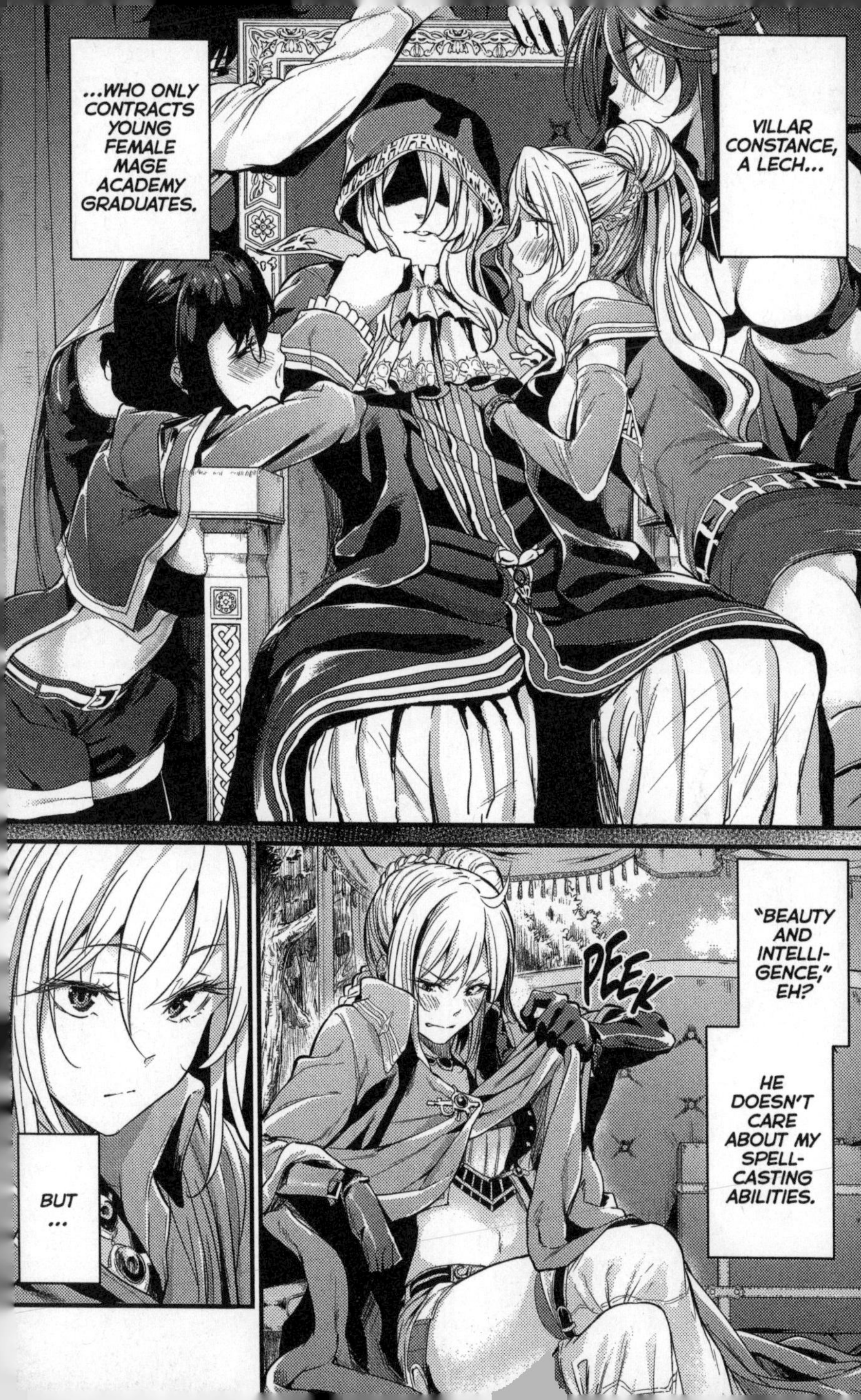
VILLAR CONSTANCE, A LECH...
...WHO ONLY CONTRACTS YOUNG FEMALE MAGE ACADEMY GRADUATES.
"BEAUTY AND INTELLI-GENCE," EH?
PEEK
HE DOESN'T CARE ABOUT MY SPELL-CASTING ABILITIES.
BUT ...

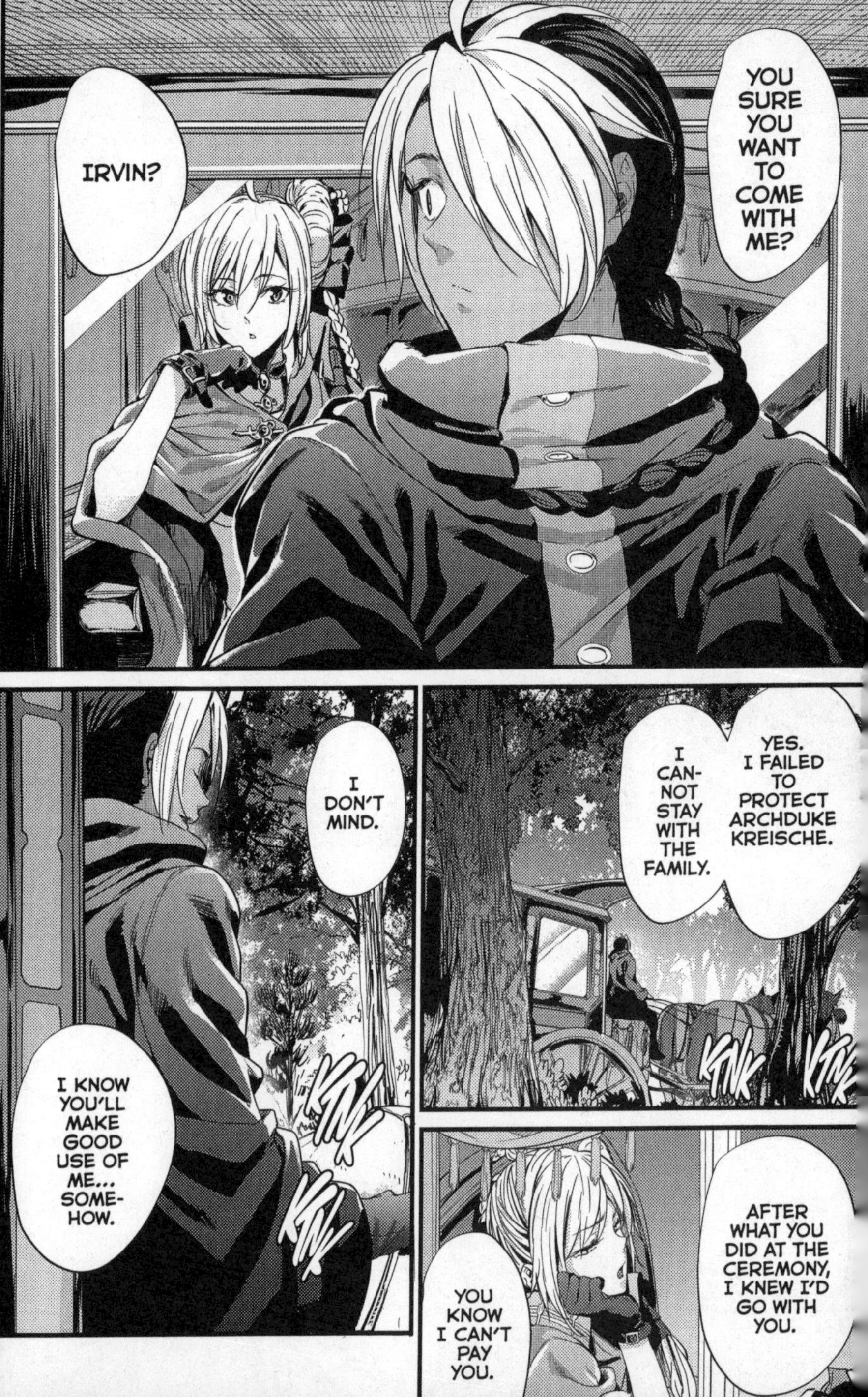
YOU SURE YOU WANT TO COME WITH ME?
IRVIN?
YES. I FAILED TO PROTECT ARCHDUKE KREISCHE.
I CAN-NOT STAY WITH THE FAMILY.
KINK
KINK
AFTER WHAT YOU DID AT THE CEREMONY, I KNEW I'D GO WITH YOU.
YOU KNOW I CAN'T PAY YOU.
I DON'T MIND.
I KNOW YOU'LL MAKE GOOD USE OF ME... SOME-HOW.
KINK
KINK

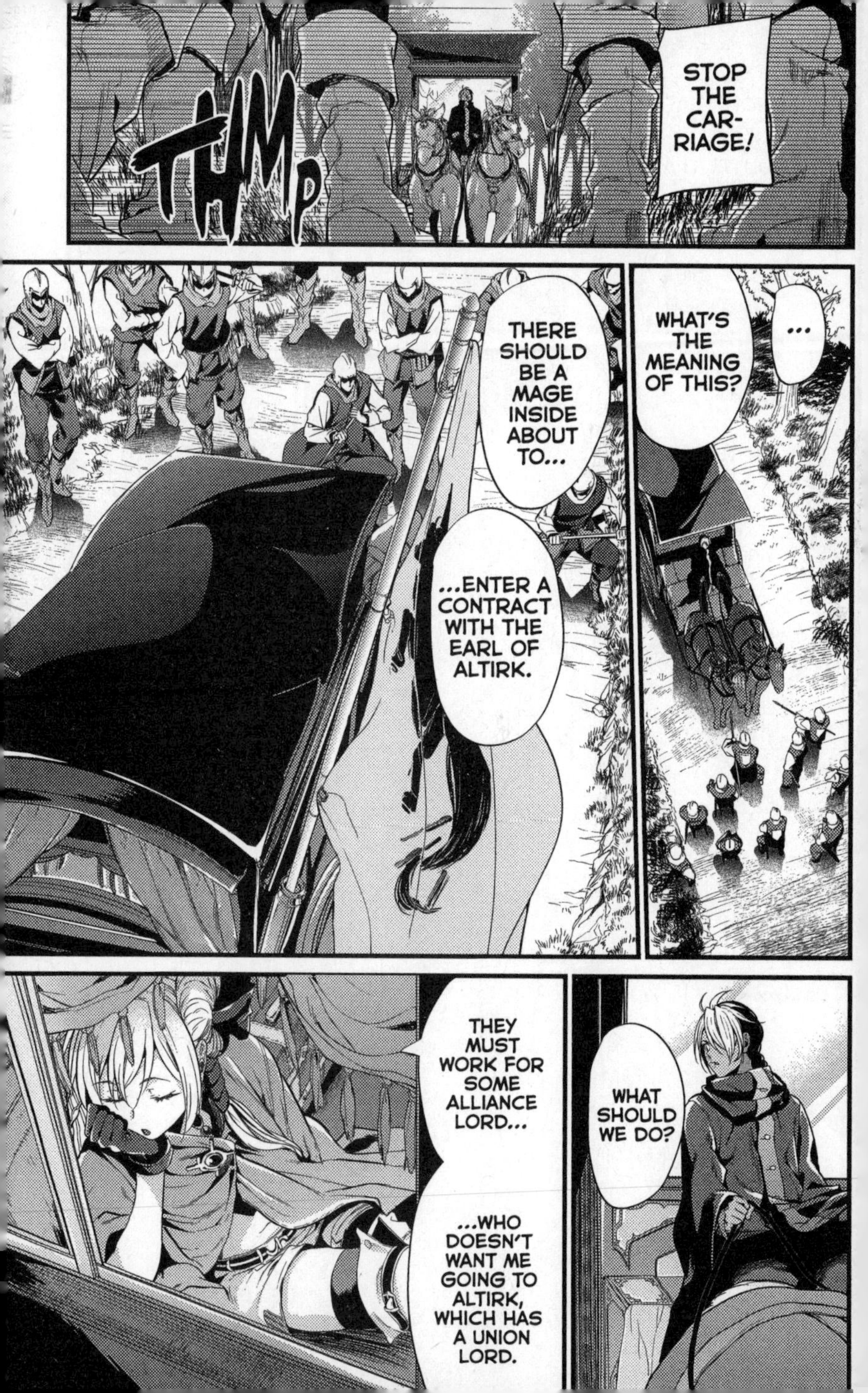
STOP THE CARRIAGE!
THMP
...
WHAT'S THE MEANING OF THIS?
THERE SHOULD BE A MAGE INSIDE ABOUT TO...
...ENTER A CONTRACT WITH THE EARL OF ALTIRK.
WHAT SHOULD WE DO?
THEY MUST WORK FOR SOME ALLIANCE LORD...
...WHO DOESN'T WANT ME GOING TO ALTIRK, WHICH HAS A UNION LORD.

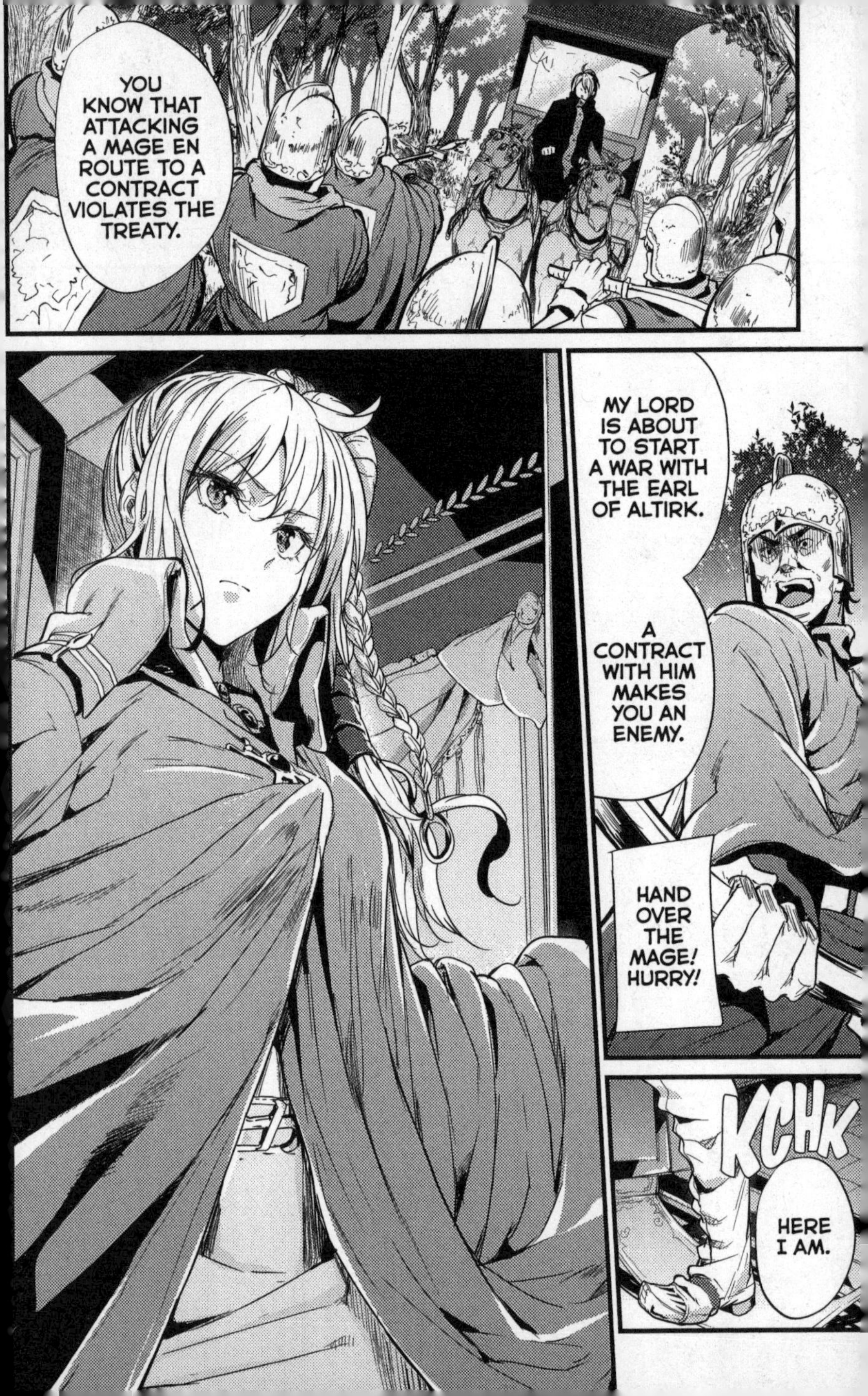
YOU KNOW THAT ATTACKING A MAGE EN ROUTE TO A CONTRACT VIOLATES THE TREATY.
MY LORD IS ABOUT TO START A WAR WITH THE EARL OF ALTIRK.
A CONTRACT WITH HIM MAKES YOU AN ENEMY.
HAND OVER THE MAGE! HURRY!
KCHK
HERE I AM.

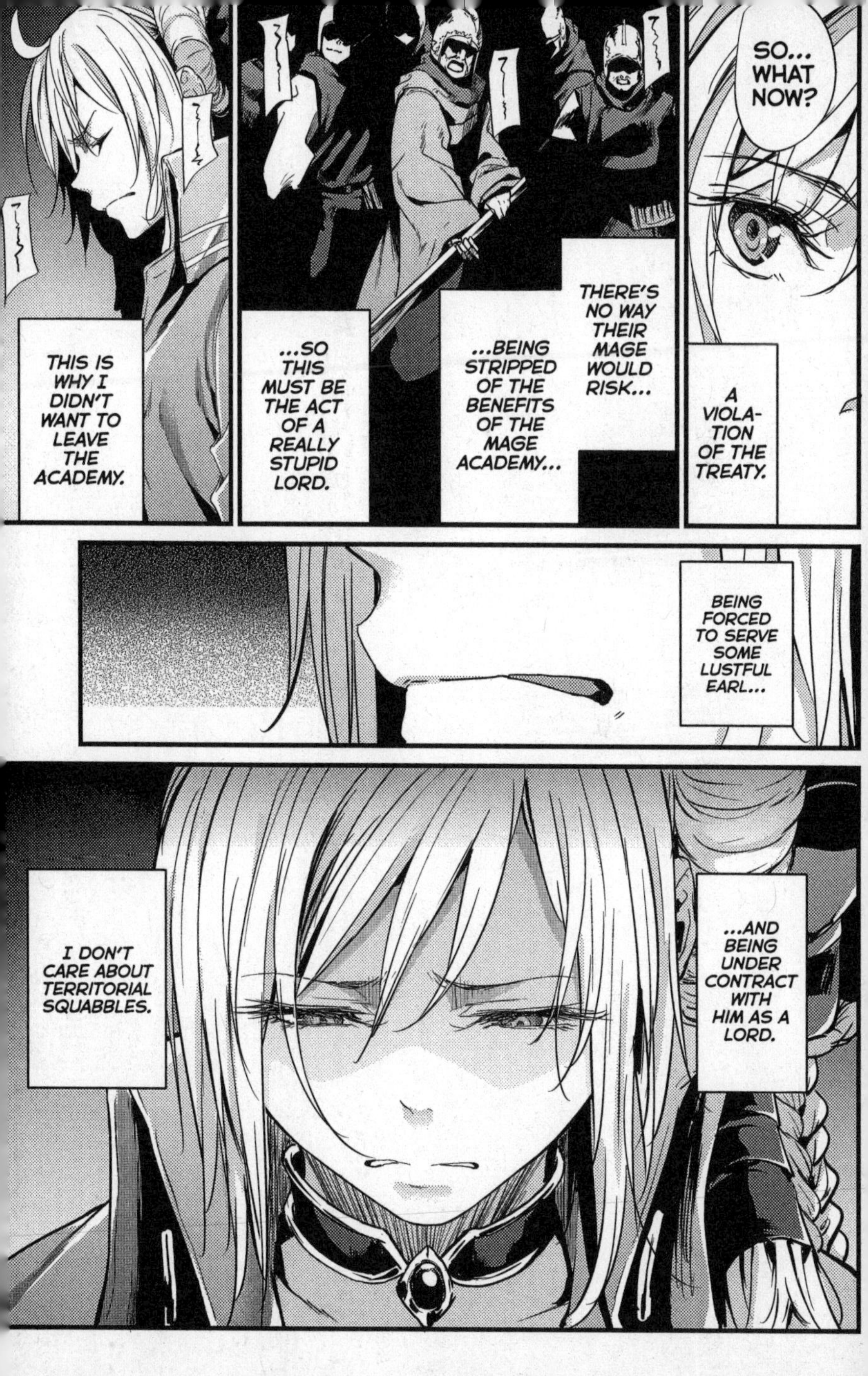
SO... WHAT NOW?
A VIOLATION OF THE TREATY.
THERE'S NO WAY THEIR MAGE WOULD RISK...
...BEING STRIPPED OF THE BENEFITS OF THE MAGE ACADEMY...
...SO THIS MUST BE THE ACT OF A REALLY STUPID LORD.
THIS IS WHY I DIDN'T WANT TO LEAVE THE ACADEMY.
BEING FORCED TO SERVE SOME LUSTFUL EARL...
...AND BEING UNDER CONTRACT WITH HIM AS A LORD.
I DON'T CARE ABOUT TERRITORIAL SQUABBLES.

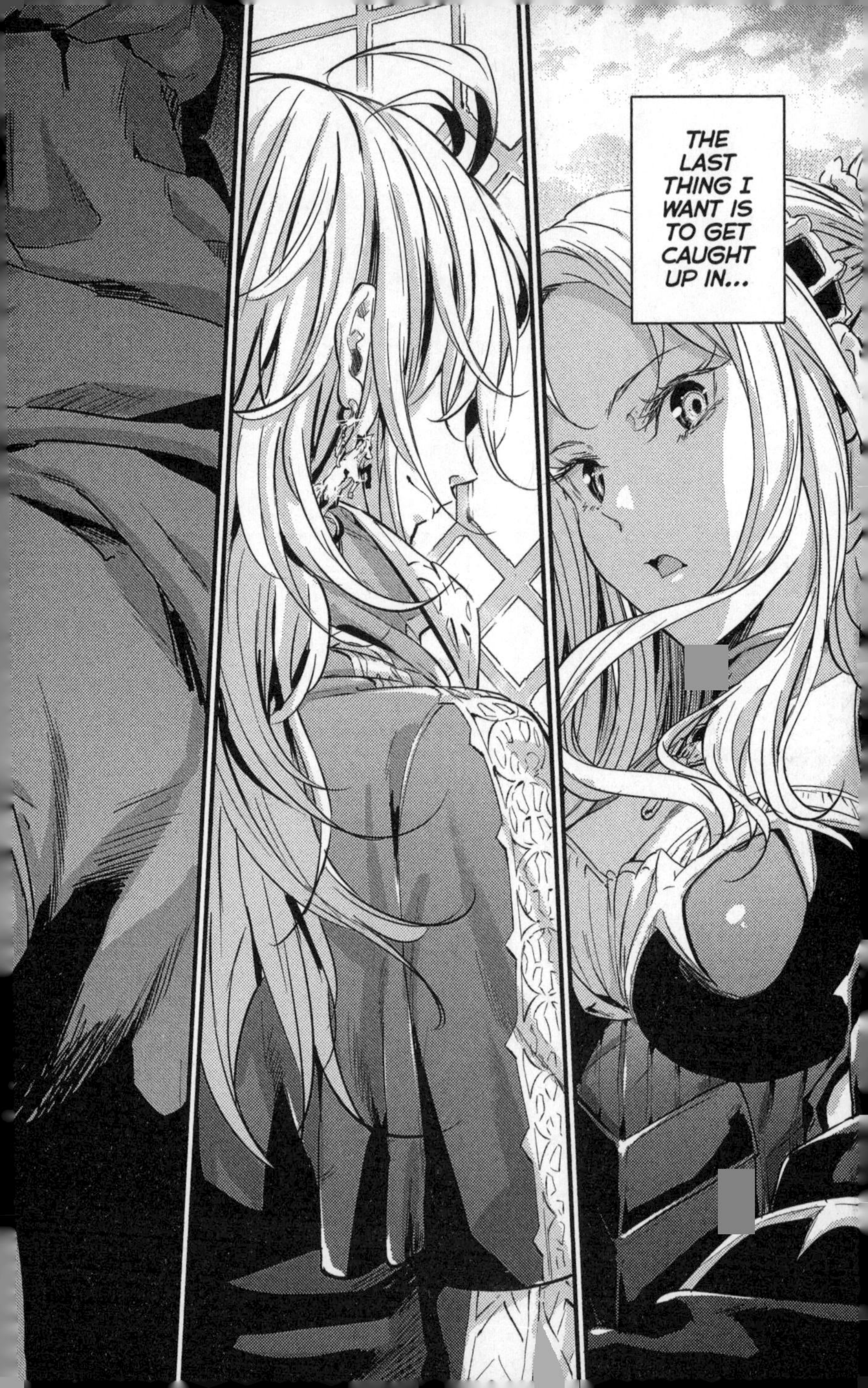
THE LAST THING I WANT IS TO GET CAUGHT UP IN...

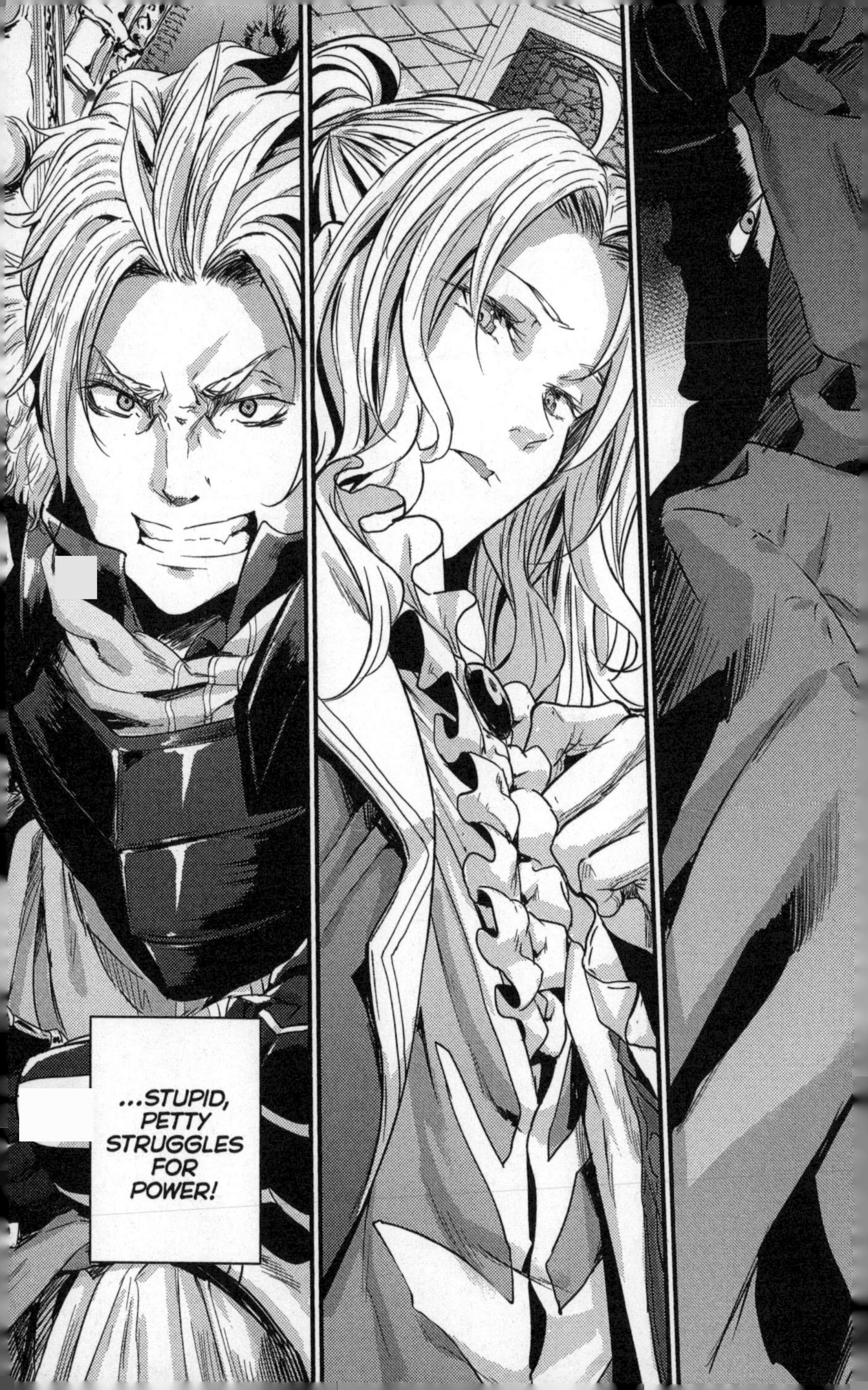
...STUPID, PETTY STRUGGLES FOR POWER!

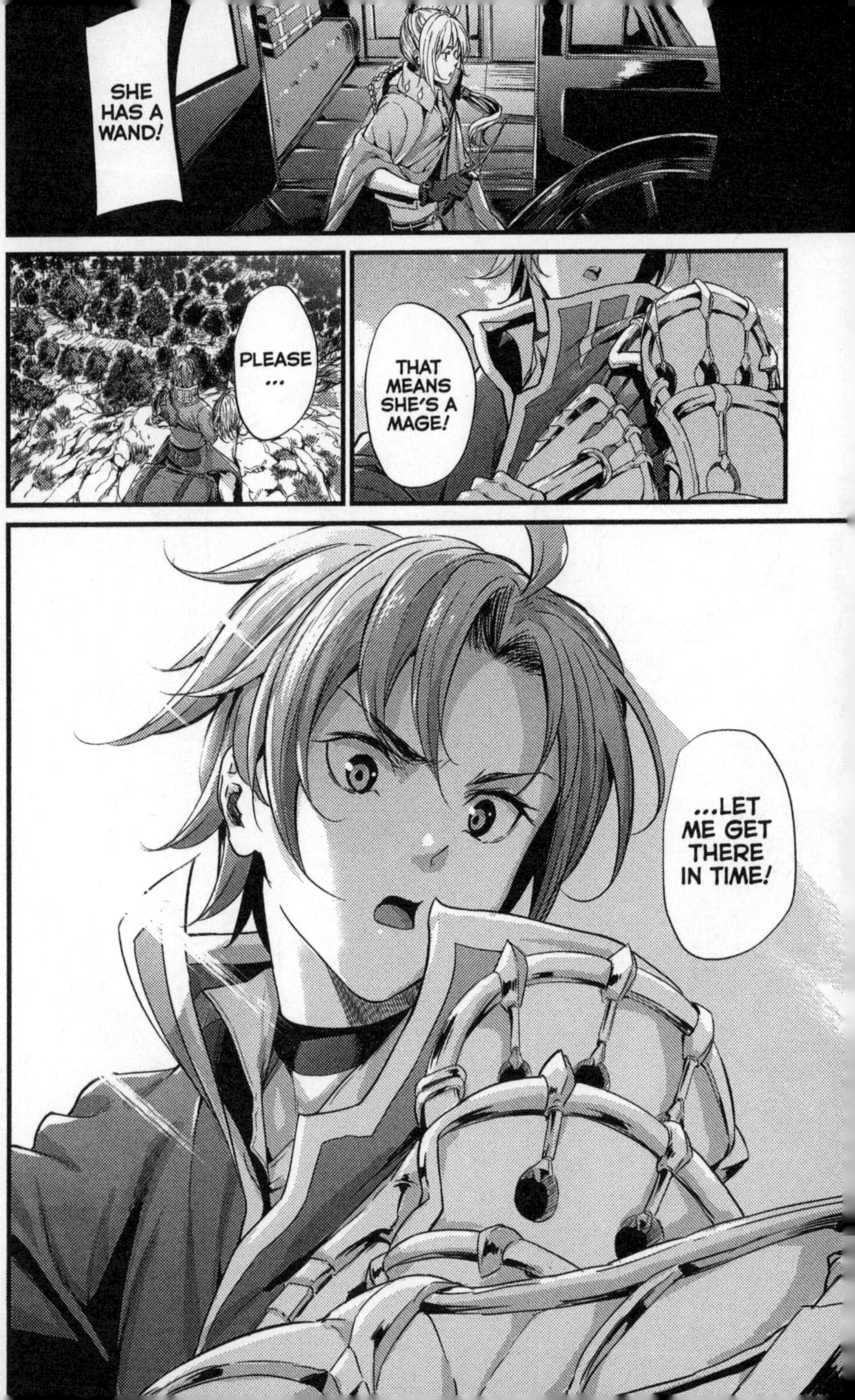
SHE HAS A WAND!
THAT MEANS SHE'S A MAGE!
PLEASE...
...LET ME GET THERE IN TIME!

RECORD OF
GRANCREST
WAR

RECORD OF
GRANCREST
WAR

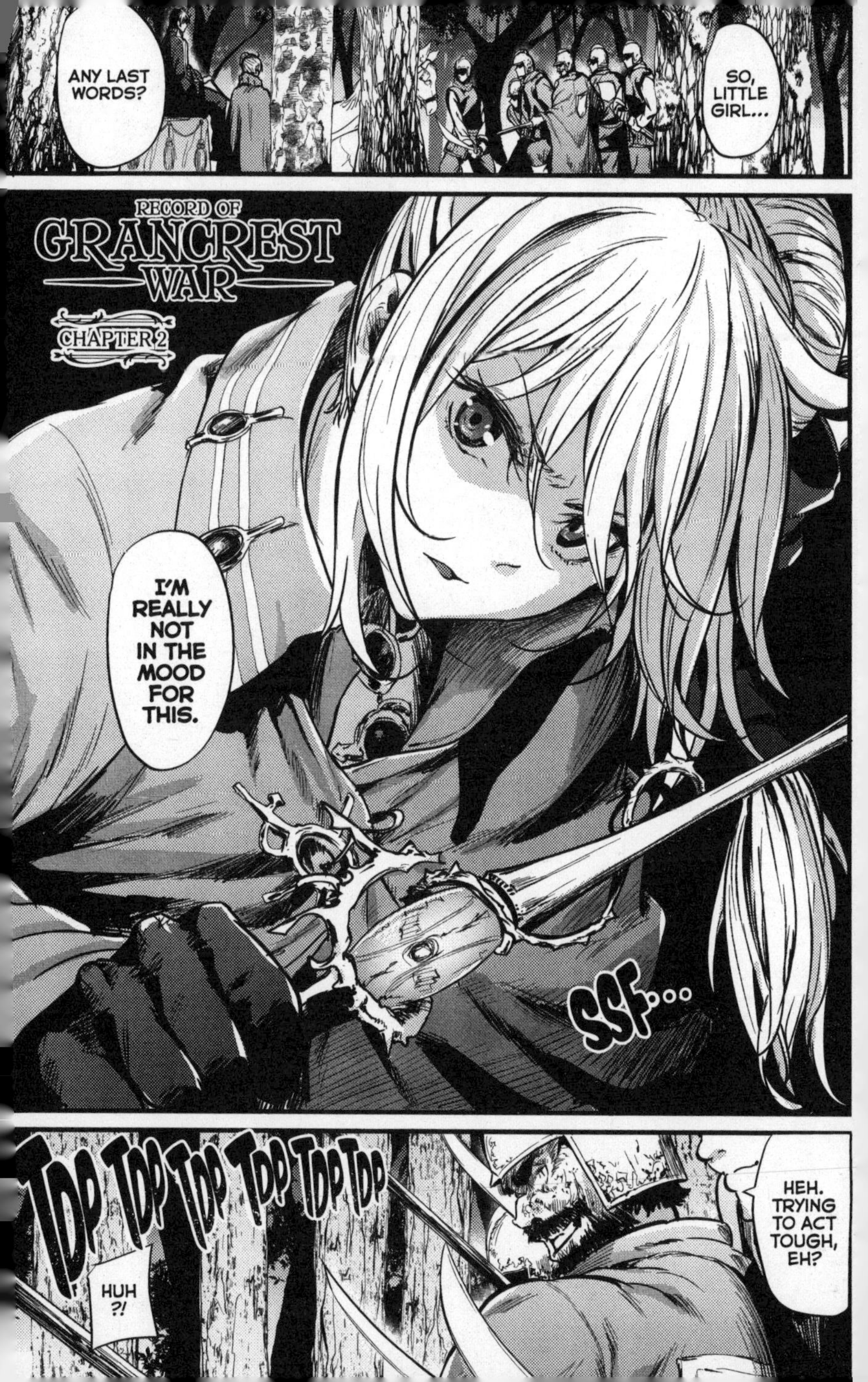
SO, LITTLE GIRL...
ANY LAST WORDS?
RECORD OF GRANCREST WAR
CHAPTER 2
I'M REALLY NOT IN THE MOOD FOR THIS.
SSF...
HEH. TRYING TO ACT TOUGH, EH?
TDP TDP TDP TDP TDP TDP
HUH ?!

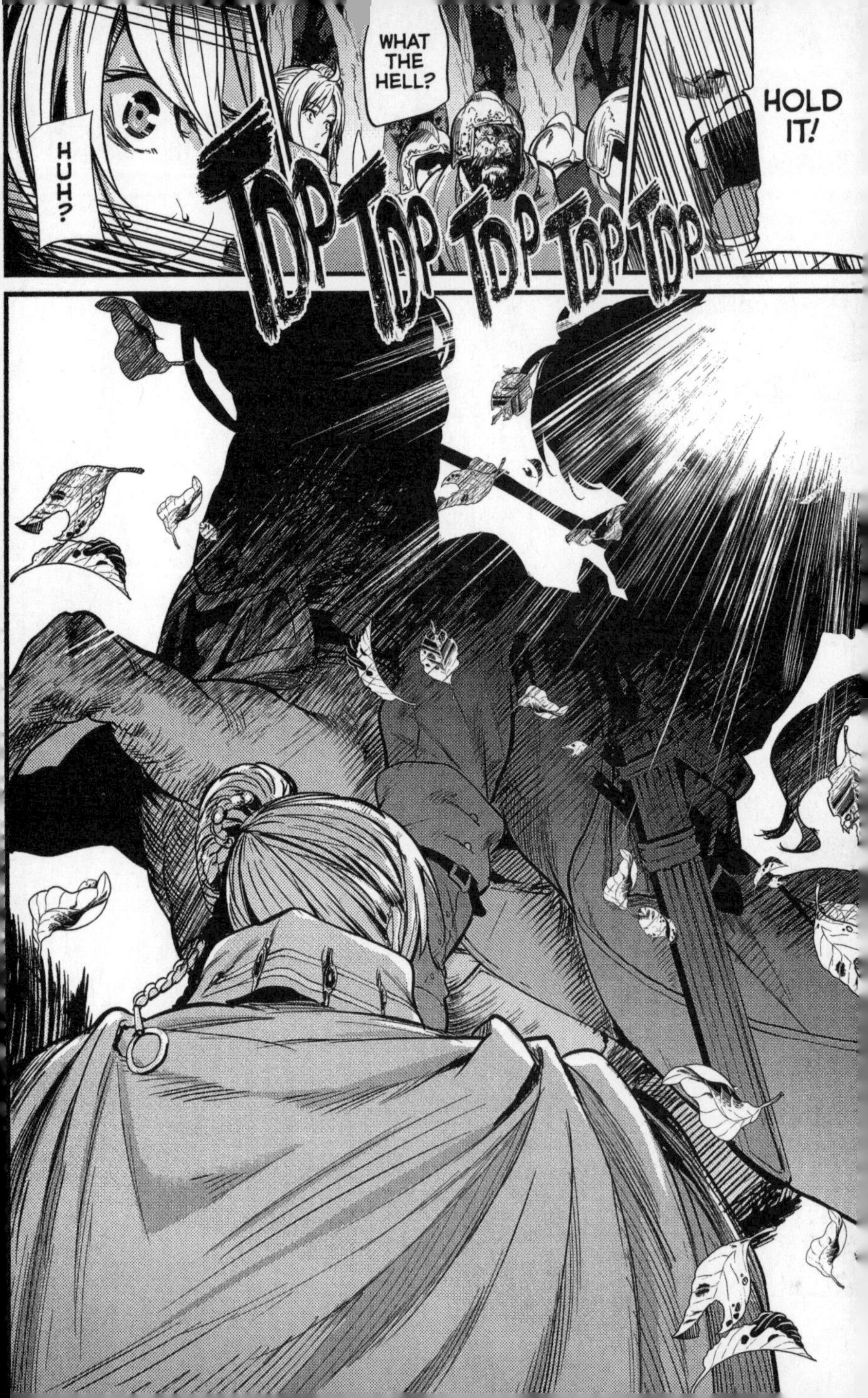
HOLD IT!
WHAT THE HELL?
HUH?
TDP TDP TDP TDP TDP

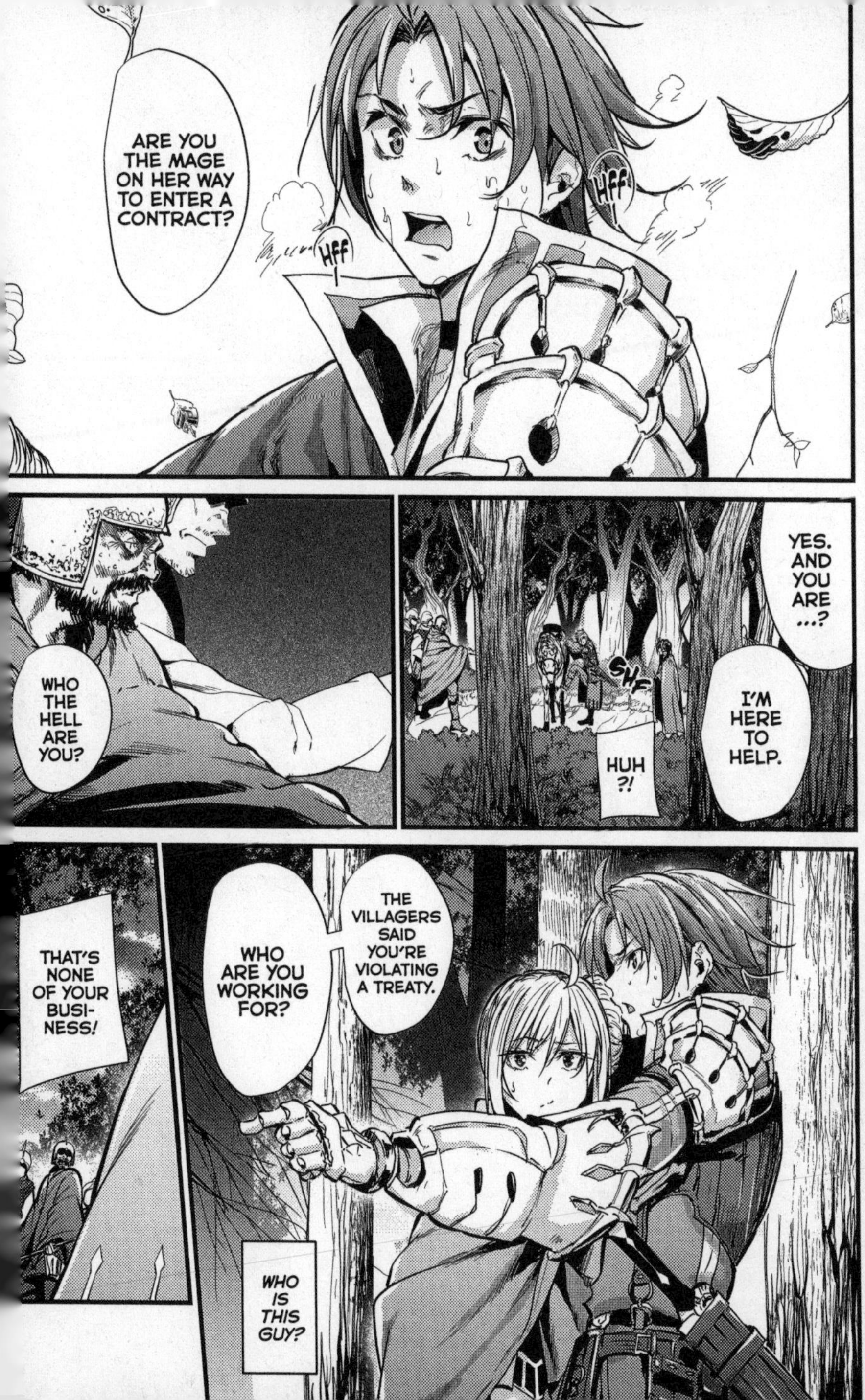

ARE YOU THE MAGE ON HER WAY TO ENTER A CONTRACT?
HFF
HFF
YES. AND YOU ARE ...?
SHF
I'M HERE TO HELP.
HUH ?!
WHO THE HELL ARE YOU?
THE VILLAGERS SAID YOU'RE VIOLATING A TREATY.
WHO ARE YOU WORKING FOR?
WHO IS THIS GUY?
THAT'S NONE OF YOUR BUSI-NESS!

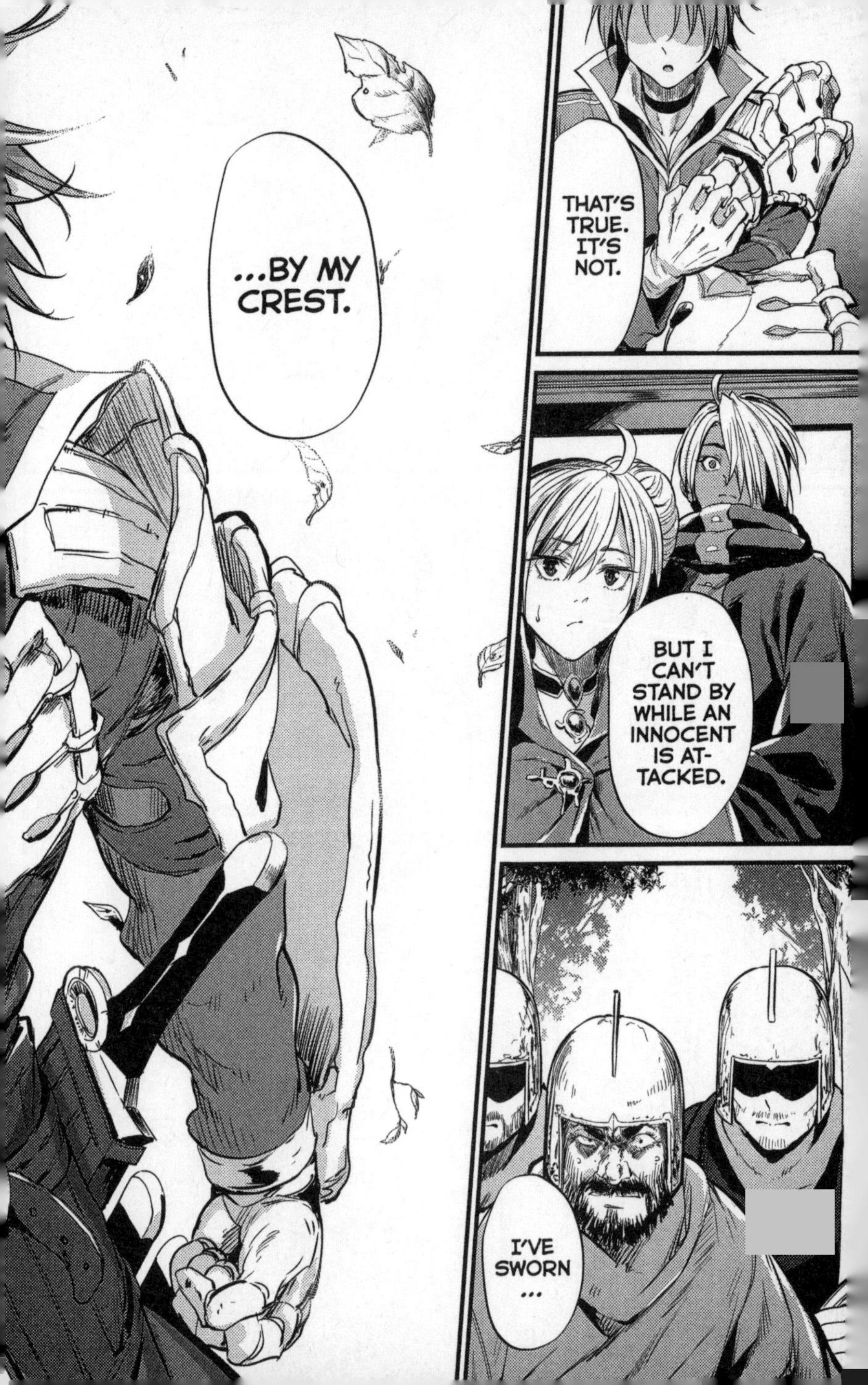
THAT'S TRUE. IT'S NOT.
BUT I CAN'T STAND BY WHILE AN INNOCENT IS AT-TACKED.
I'VE SWORN ...
...BY MY CREST.

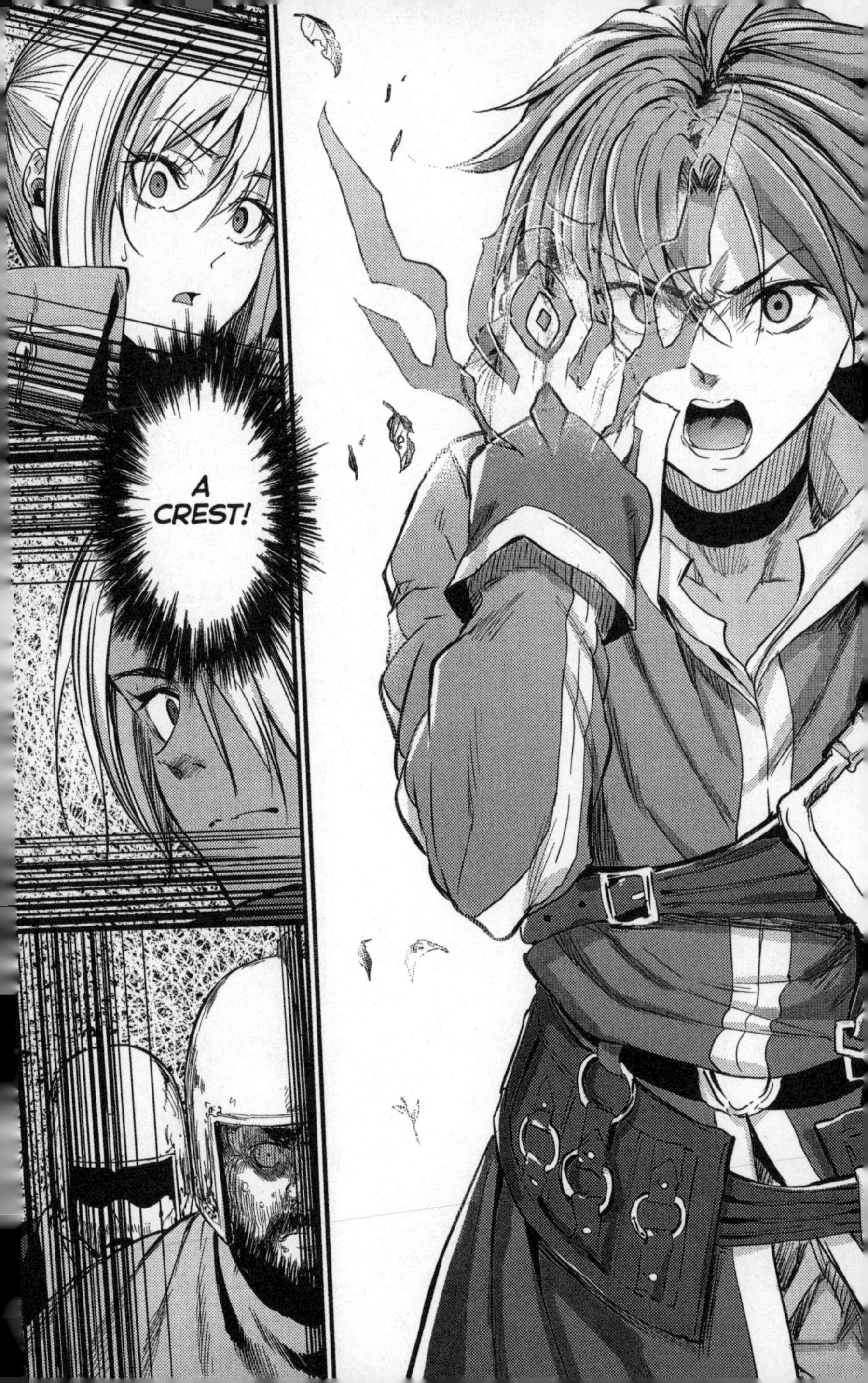
A CREST!

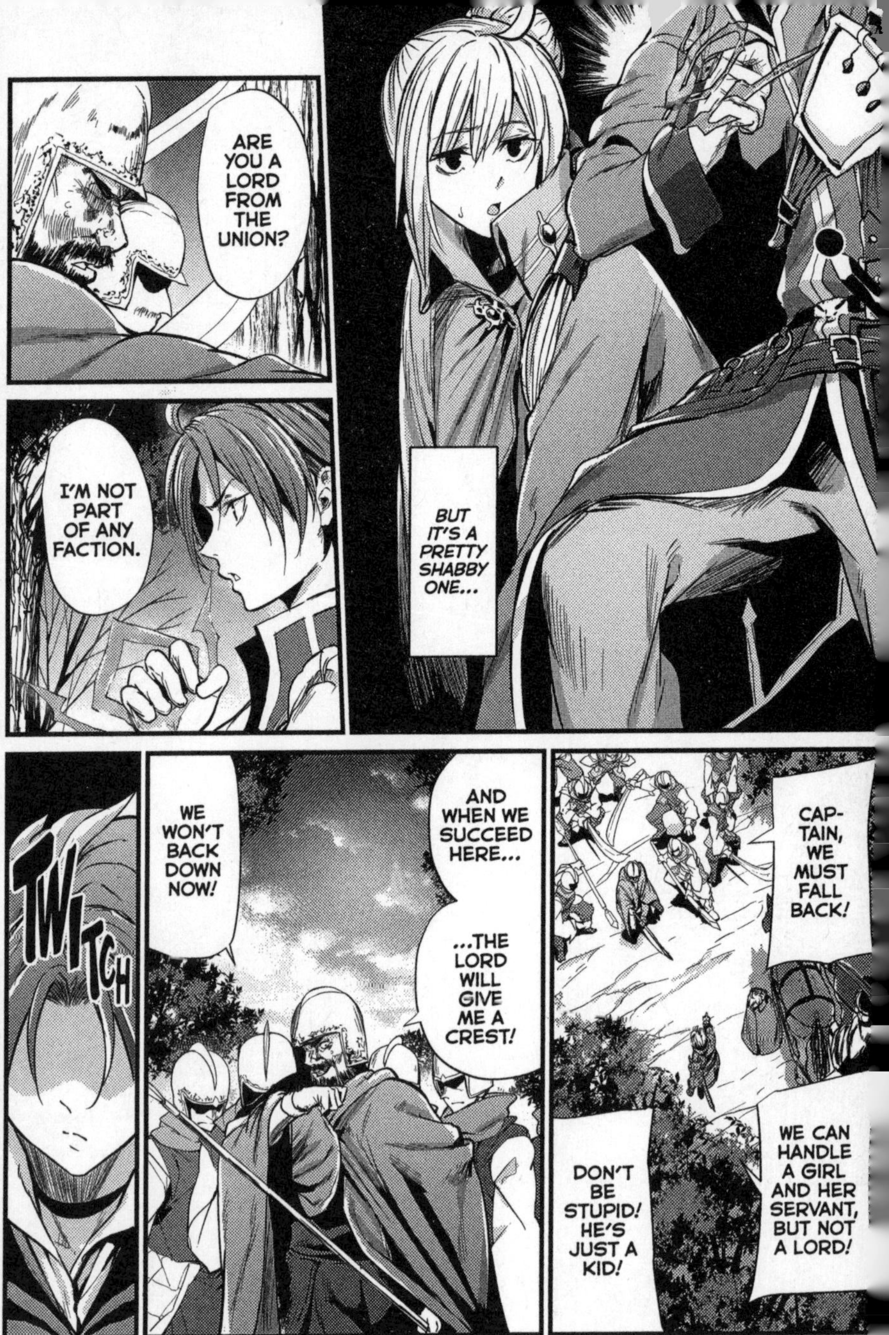
BUT IT'S A PRETTY SHABBY ONE...
ARE YOU A LORD FROM THE UNION?
I'M NOT PART OF ANY FACTION.
CAP-TAIN, WE MUST FALL BACK!
WE CAN HANDLE A GIRL AND HER SERVANT, BUT NOT A LORD!
DON'T BE STUPID! HE'S JUST A KID!
AND WHEN WE SUCCEED HERE...
...THE LORD WILL GIVE ME A CREST!
WE WON'T BACK DOWN NOW!
TWITCH

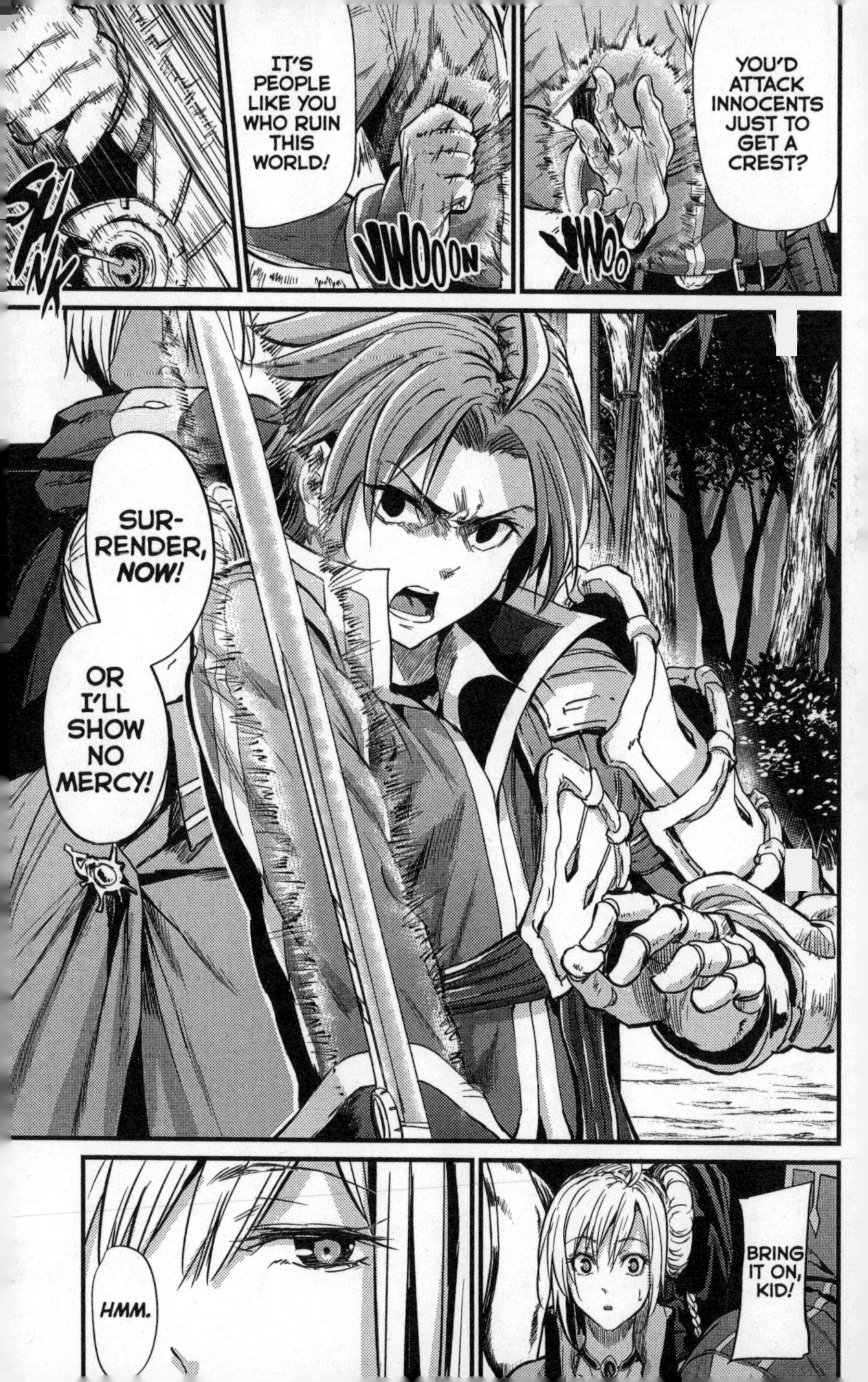
YOU'D ATTACK INNOCENTS JUST TO GET A CREST?
VWOO
IT'S PEOPLE LIKE YOU WHO RUIN THIS WORLD!
VWOOON
SHNK
SUR-RENDER, NOW!
OR I'LL SHOW NO MERCY!
BRING IT ON, KID!
HMM.

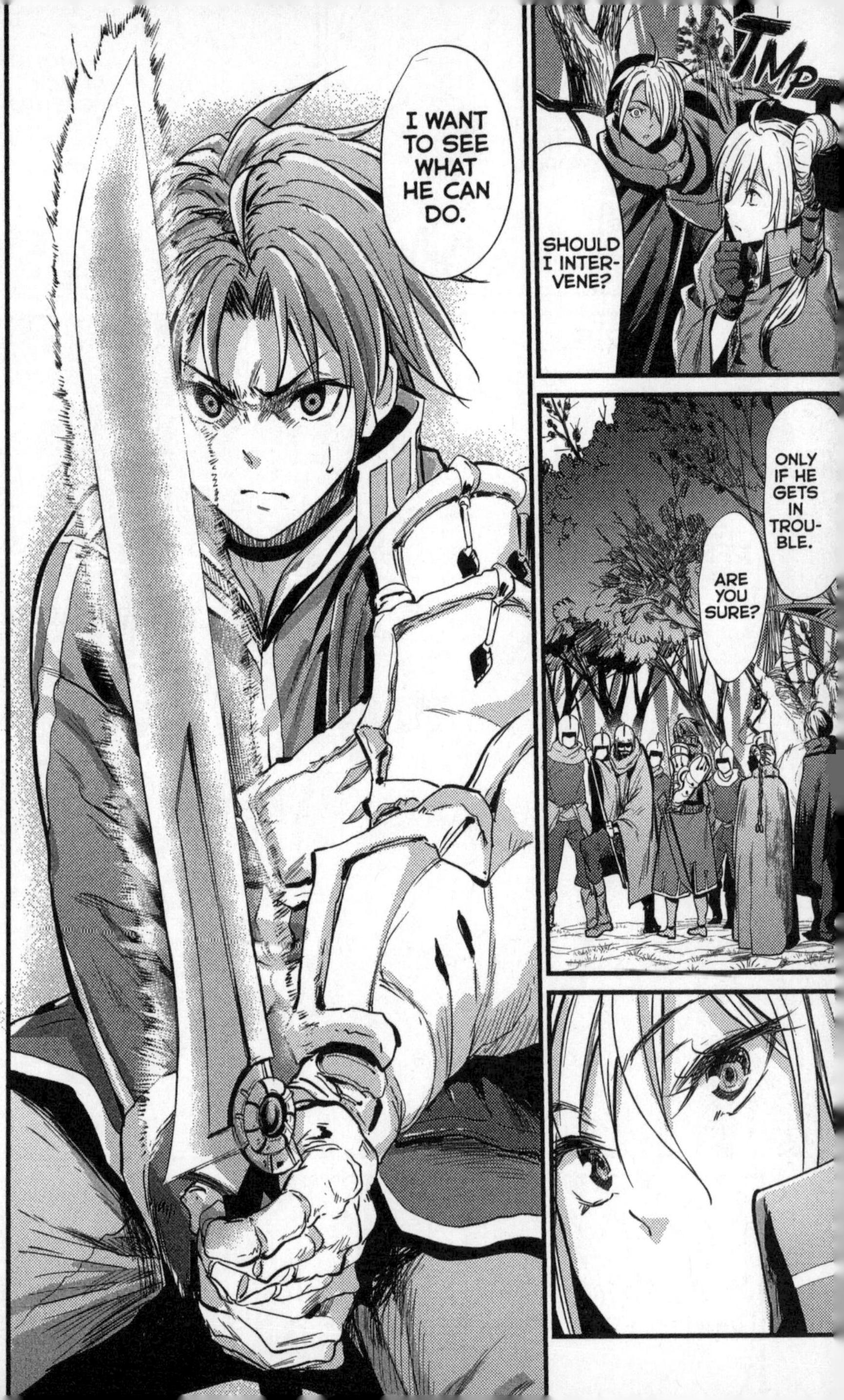
TMP
SHOULD I INTERVENE?
ONLY IF HE GETS IN TROUBLE.
ARE YOU SURE?
I WANT TO SEE WHAT HE CAN DO.

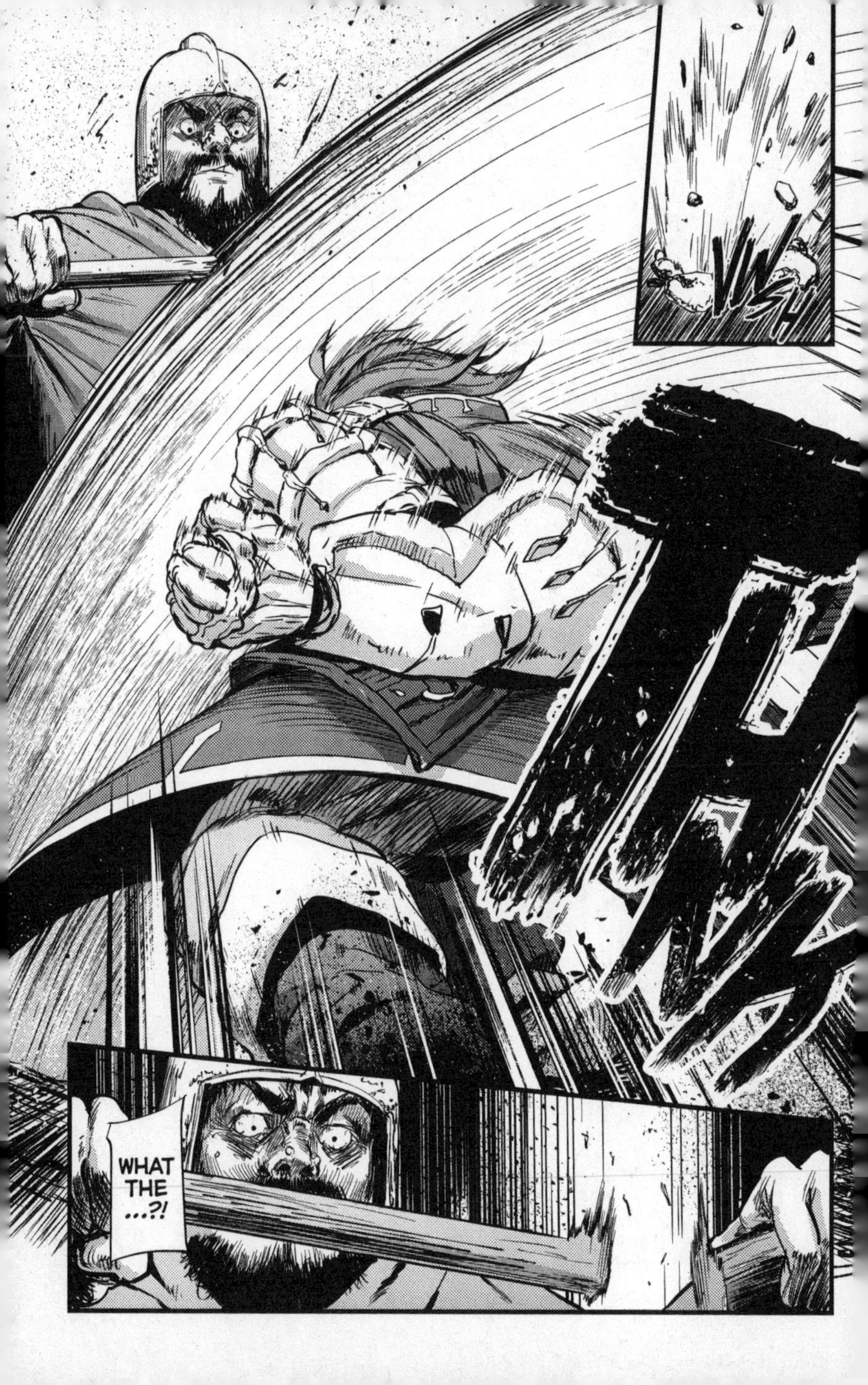
VWSH
WHAT THE ...?!

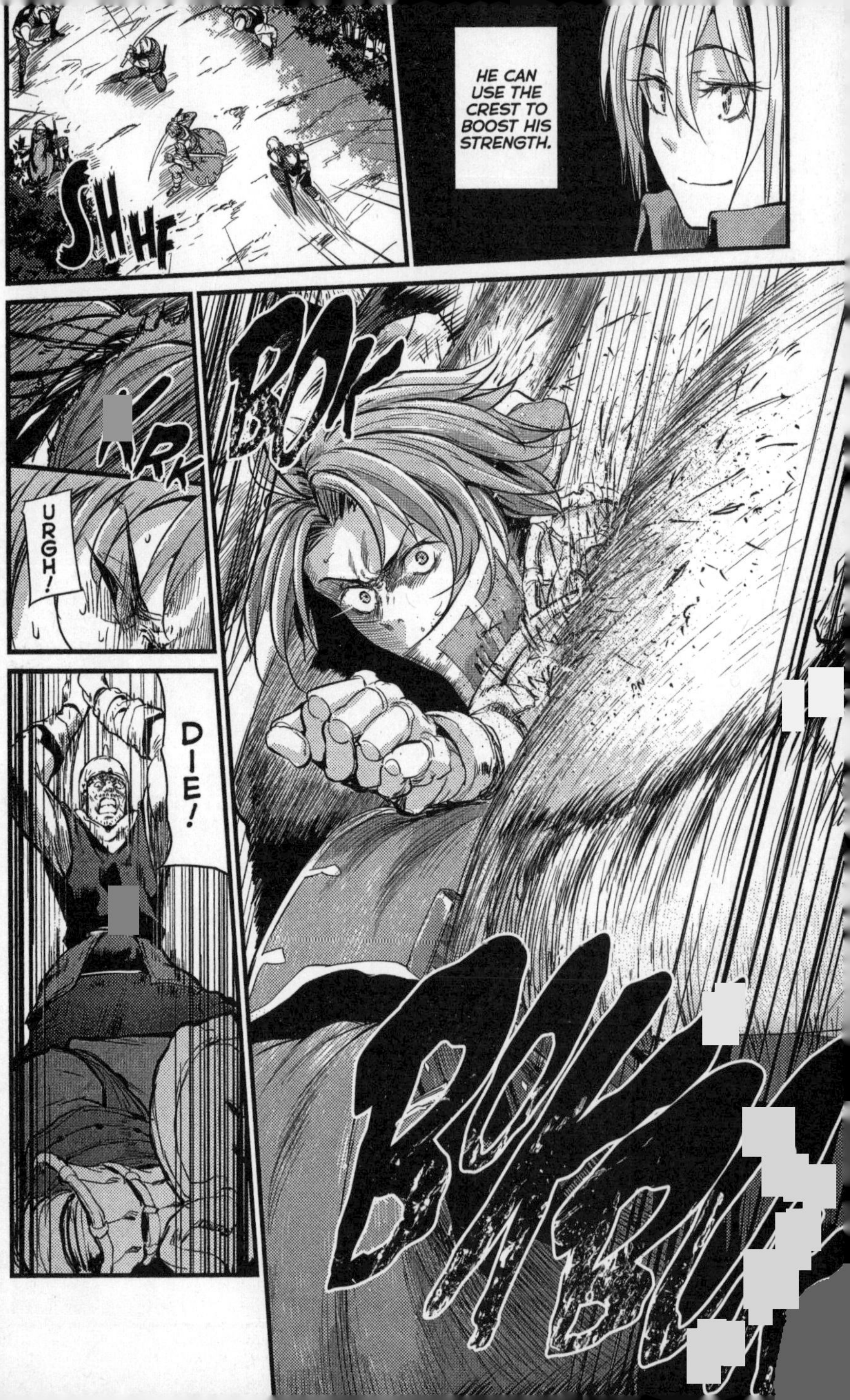
HE CAN USE THE CREST TO BOOST HIS STRENGTH.
SHHF
BOK
URGH!
DIE!

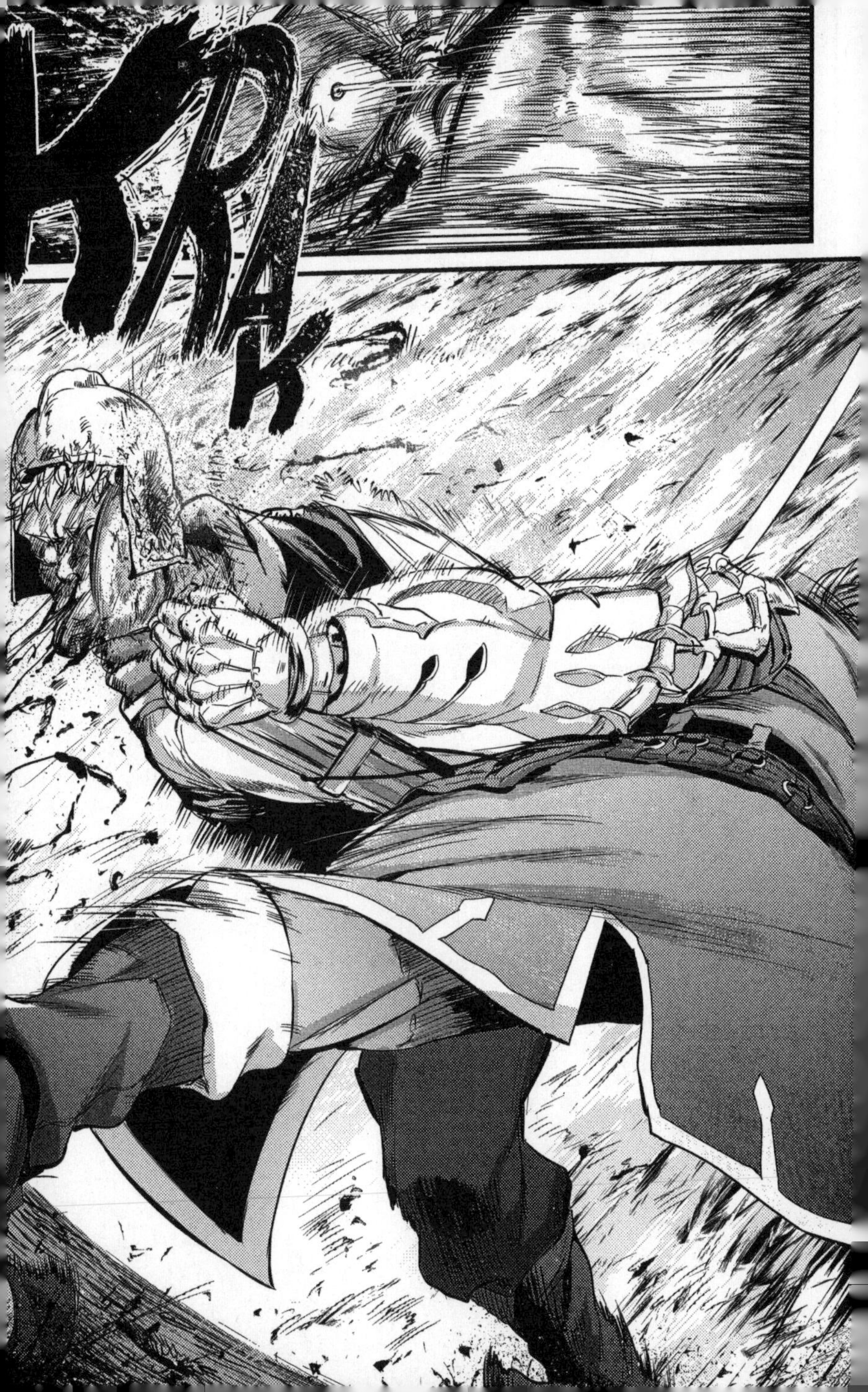
KRAK

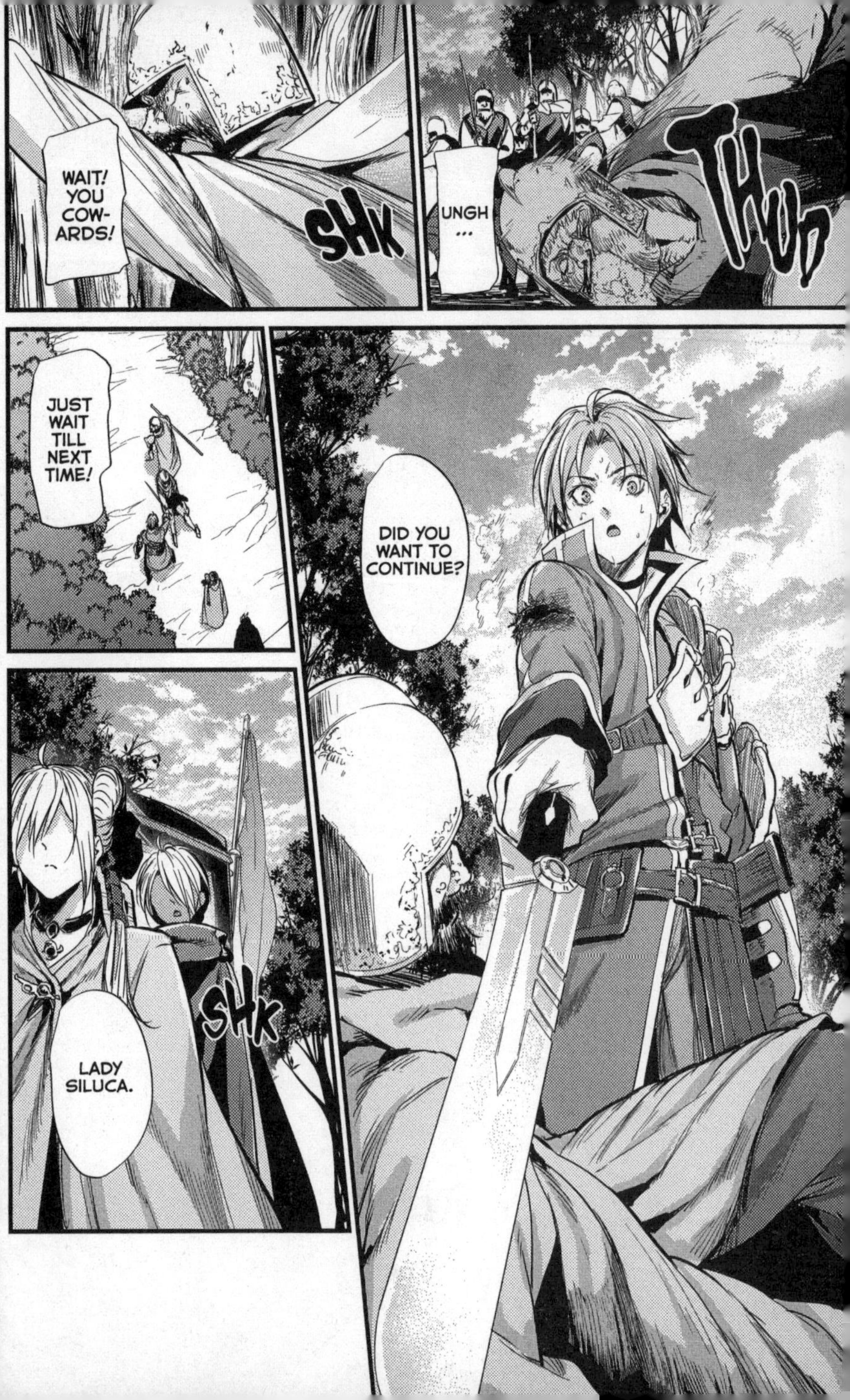
UNGH ...
THUD
WAIT! YOU COW-ARDS!
SHK
DID YOU WANT TO CONTINUE?
JUST WAIT TILL NEXT TIME!
SHK
LADY SILUCA.

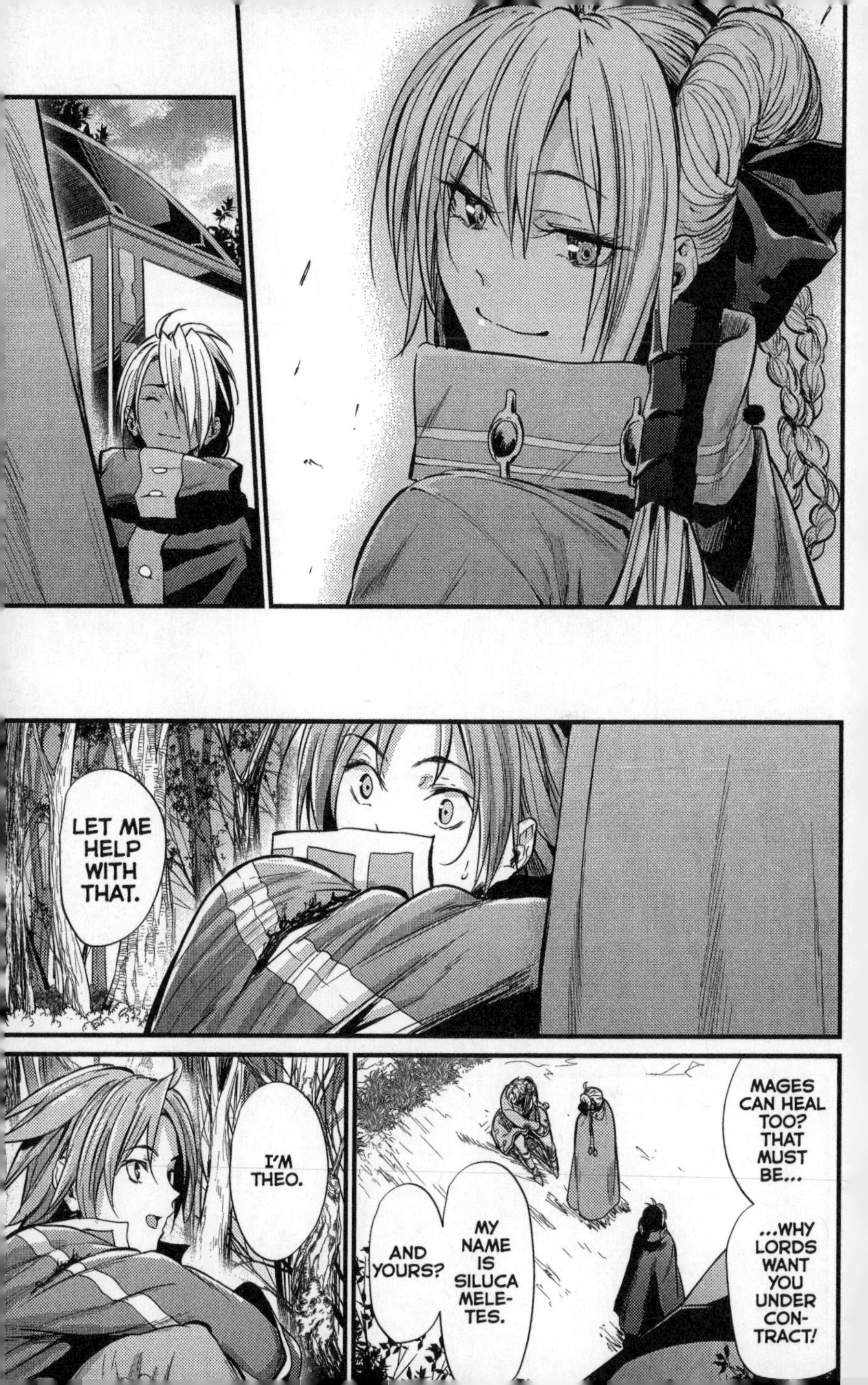
LET ME HELP WITH THAT.
MAGES CAN HEAL TOO? THAT MUST BE...
...WHY LORDS WANT YOU UNDER CONTRACT!
MY NAME IS SILUCA MELETES.
AND YOURS?
I'M THEO.

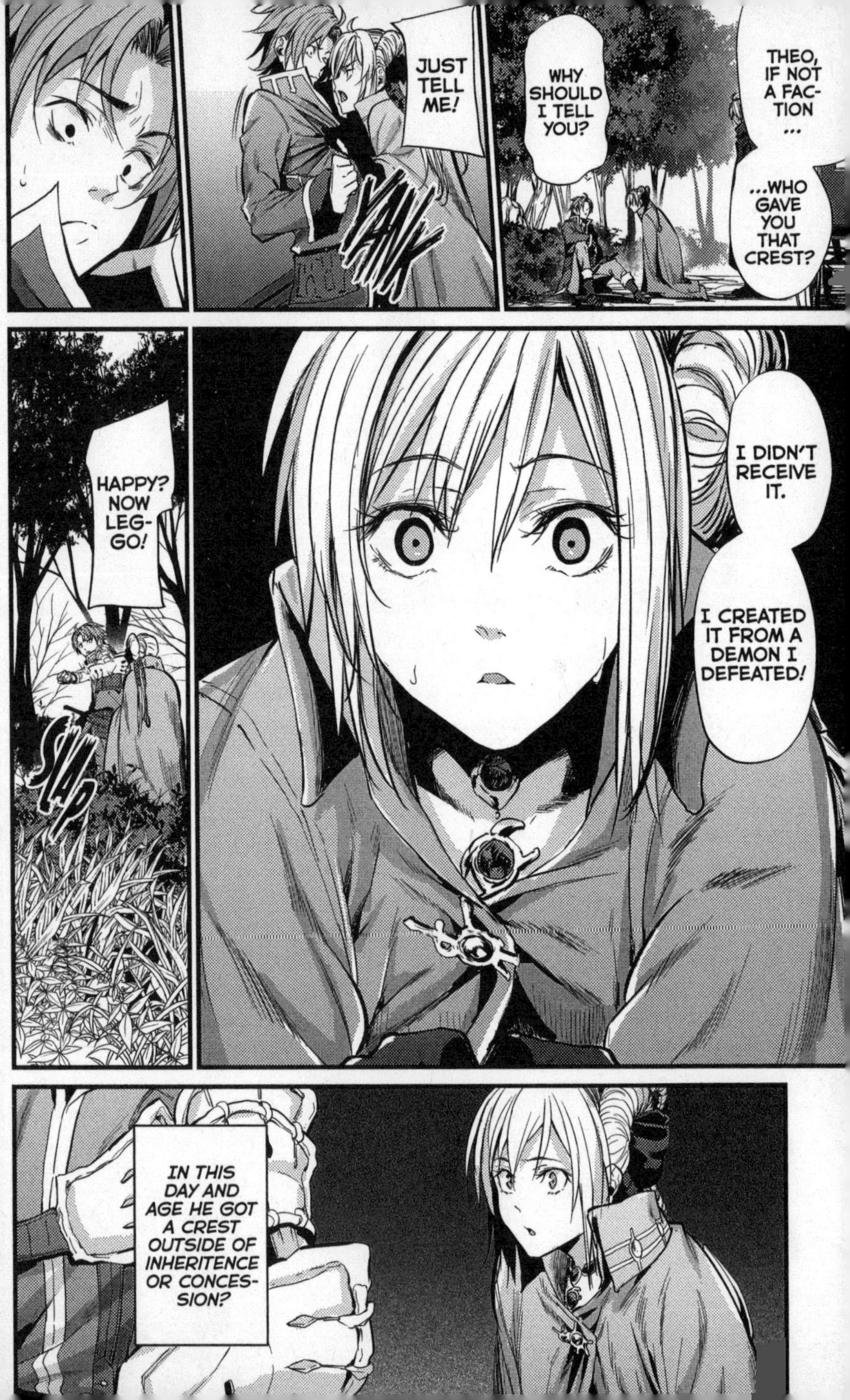
THEO, IF NOT A FAC-TION...
...WHO GAVE YOU THAT CREST?
WHY SHOULD I TELL YOU?
JUST TELL ME!
YANK
I DIDN'T RECEIVE IT.
I CREATED IT FROM A DEMON I DEFEATED!
HAPPY? NOW LEG-GO!
SLAP
IN THIS DAY AND AGE HE GOT A CREST OUTSIDE OF INHERITENCE OR CONCES-SION?

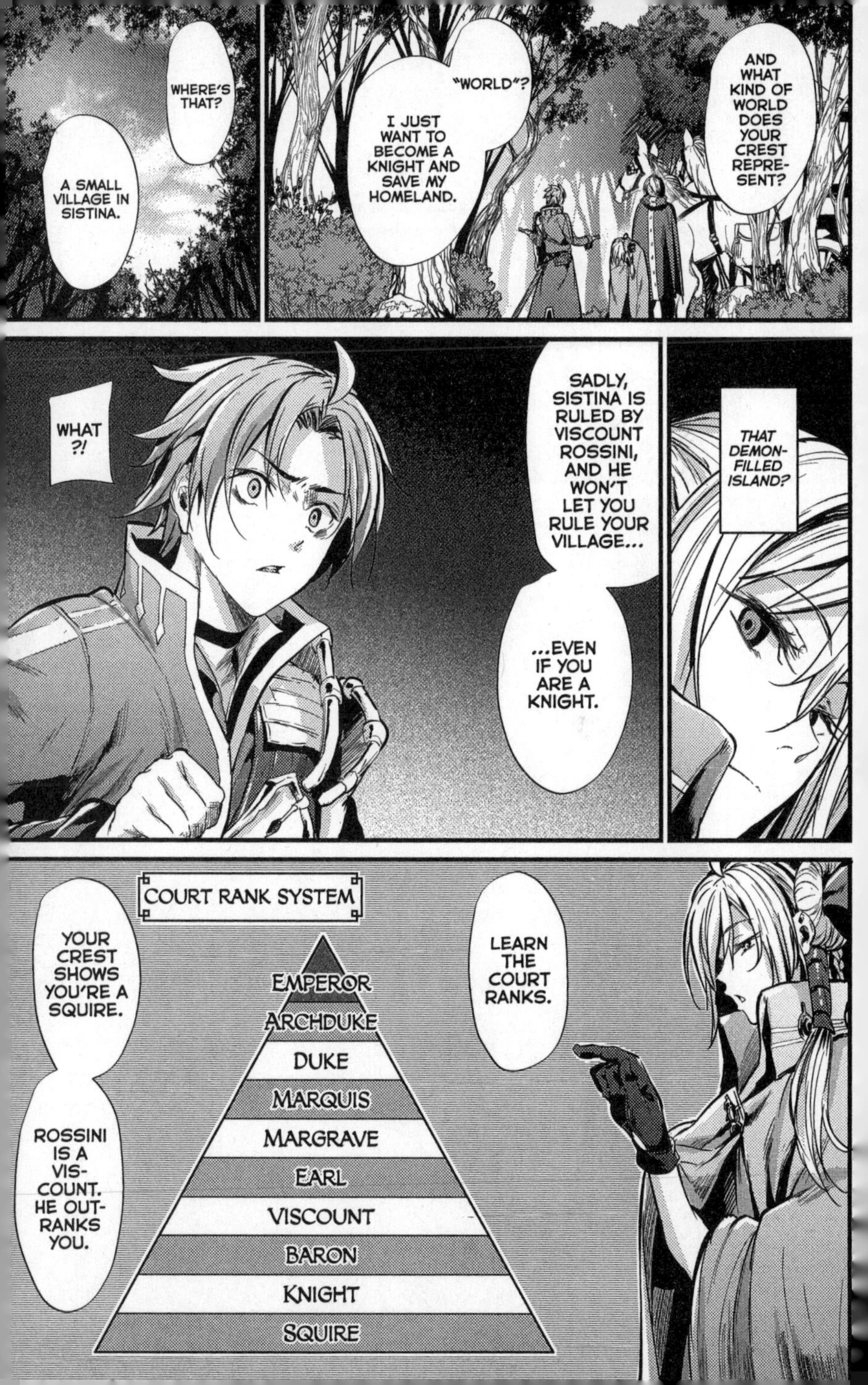
AND WHAT KIND OF WORLD DOES YOUR CREST REPRESENT?
"WORLD"?
I JUST WANT TO BECOME A KNIGHT AND SAVE MY HOMELAND.
WHERE'S THAT?
A SMALL VILLAGE IN SISTINA.
THAT DEMON-FILLED ISLAND?
SADLY, SISTINA IS RULED BY VISCOUNT ROSSINI, AND HE WON'T LET YOU RULE YOUR VILLAGE...
...EVEN IF YOU ARE A KNIGHT.
WHAT?!
LEARN THE COURT RANKS.
COURT RANK SYSTEM
EMPEROR
ARCHDUKE
DUKE
MARQUIS
MARGRAVE
EARL
VISCOUNT
BARON
KNIGHT
SQUIRE
YOUR CREST SHOWS YOU'RE A SQUIRE.
ROSSINI IS A VISCOUNT. HE OUTRANKS YOU.

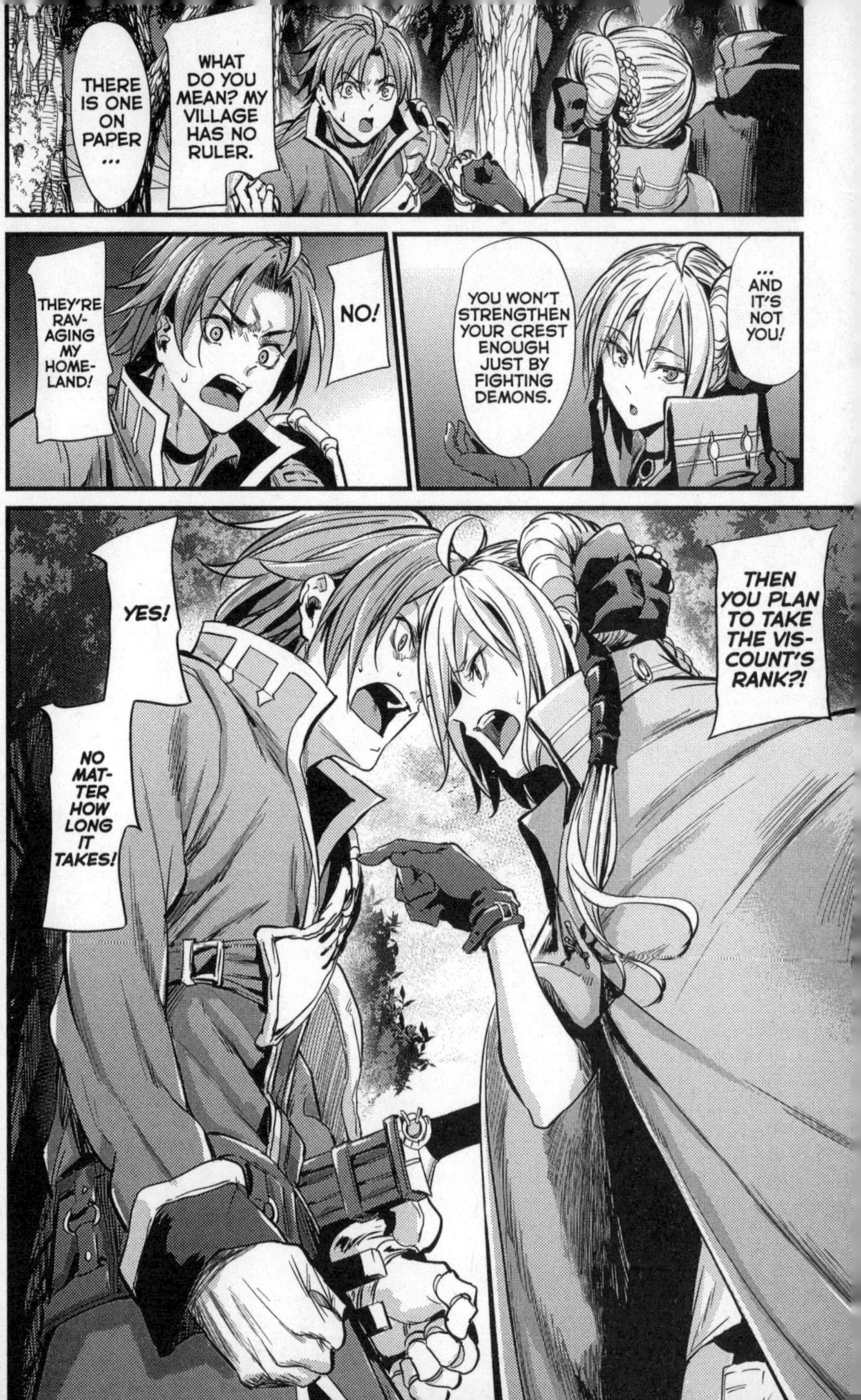

WHAT DO YOU MEAN? MY VILLAGE HAS NO RULER.
THERE IS ONE ON PAPER ...
... AND IT'S NOT YOU!
YOU WON'T STRENGTHEN YOUR CREST ENOUGH JUST BY FIGHTING DEMONS.
NO!
THEY'RE RAVAGING MY HOMELAND!
THEN YOU PLAN TO TAKE THE VISCOUNT'S RANK?!
YES!
NO MATTER HOW LONG IT TAKES!

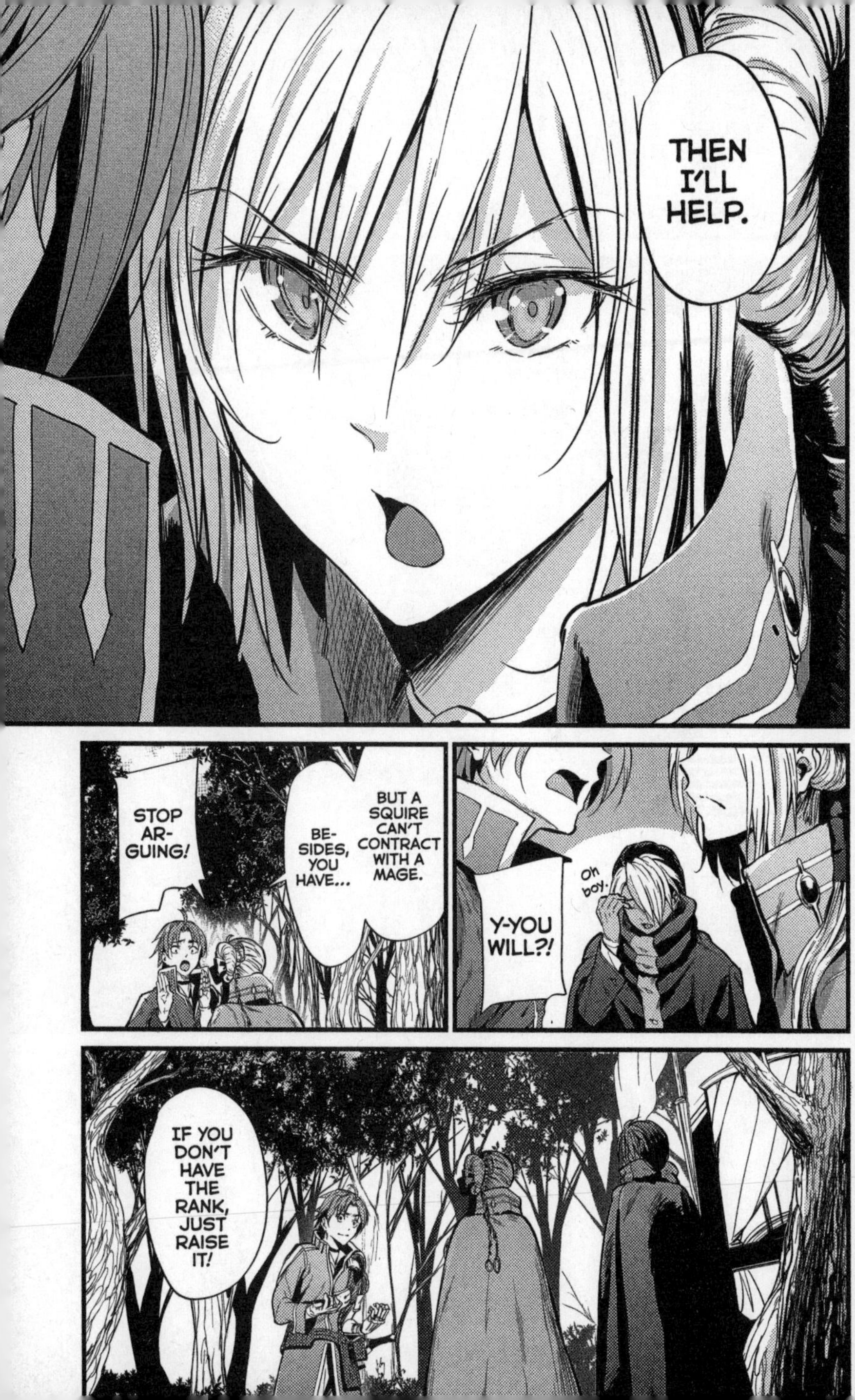
THEN I'LL HELP.
Oh boy.
Y-YOU WILL?!
BUT A SQUIRE CAN'T CONTRACT WITH A MAGE.
BE-SIDES, YOU HAVE...
STOP AR-GUING!
IF YOU DON'T HAVE THE RANK, JUST RAISE IT!

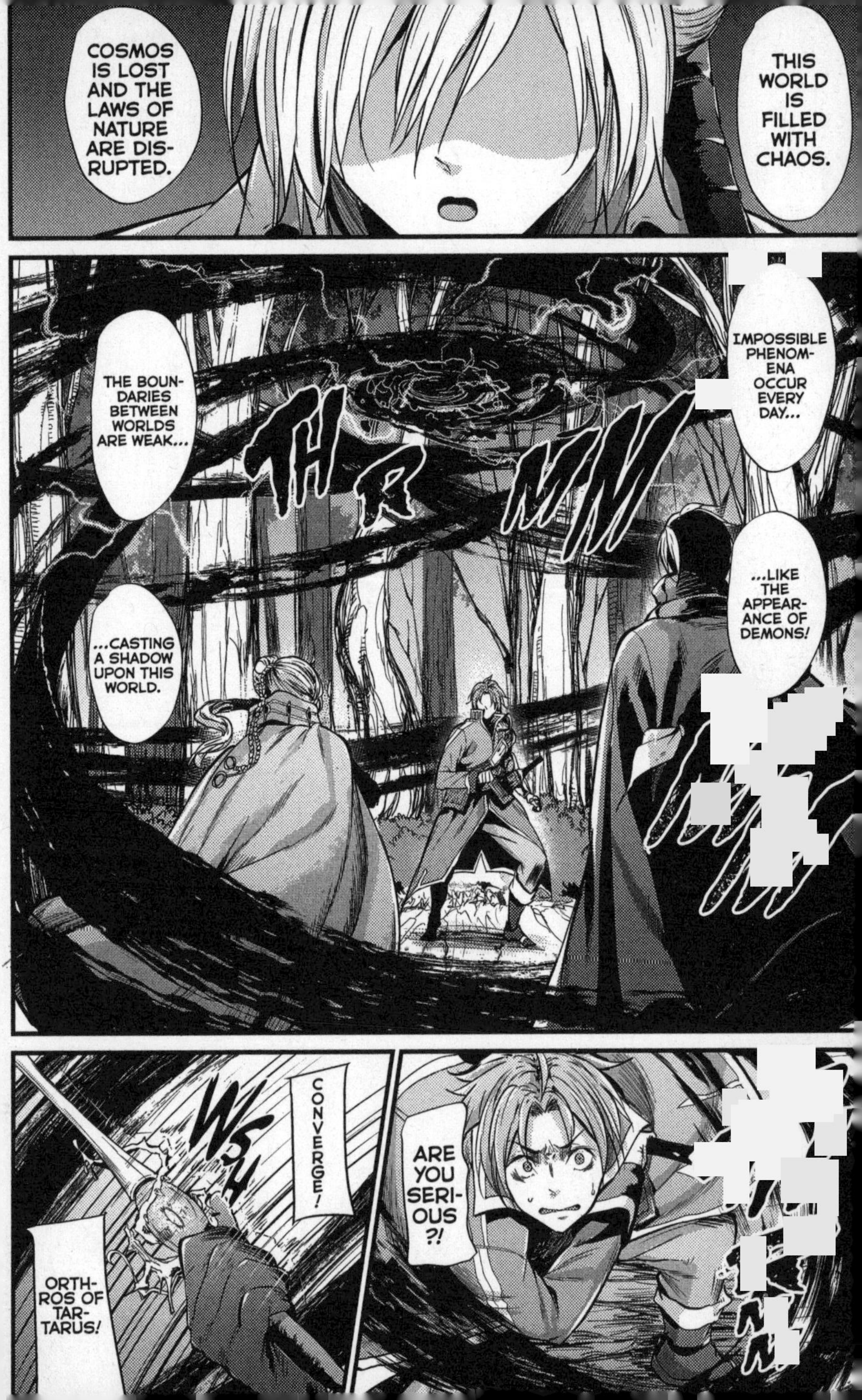
THIS WORLD IS FILLED WITH CHAOS.
COSMOS IS LOST AND THE LAWS OF NATURE ARE DISRUPTED.
IMPOSSIBLE PHENOMENA OCCUR EVERY DAY...
...LIKE THE APPEARANCE OF DEMONS!
THE BOUNDARIES BETWEEN WORLDS ARE WEAK...
...CASTING A SHADOW UPON THIS WORLD.
ARE YOU SERIOUS?!
CONVERGE!
WSH
ORTHROS OF TARTARUS!

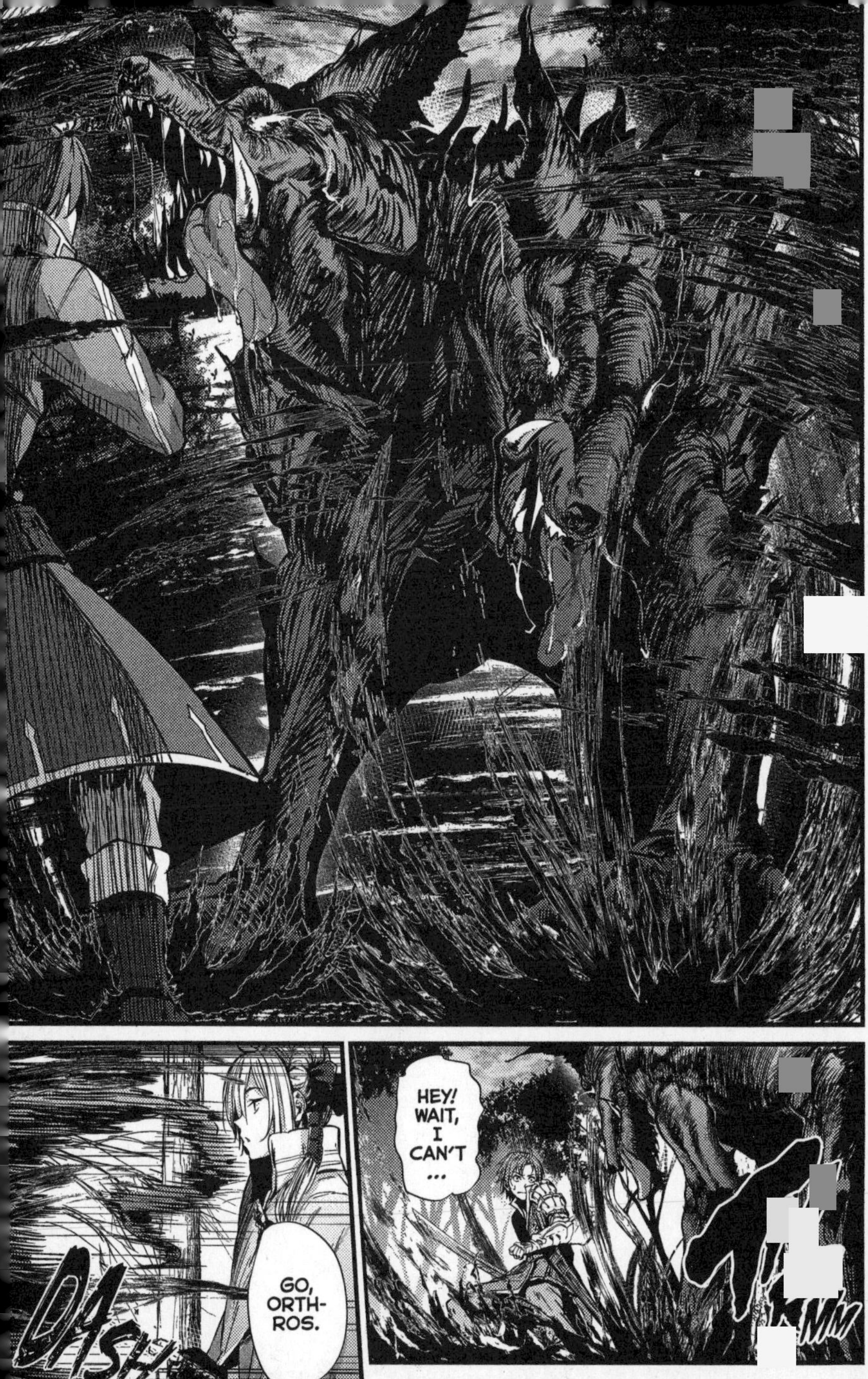
HEY! WAIT, I CAN'T ...
GO, ORTH-ROS.
DASH

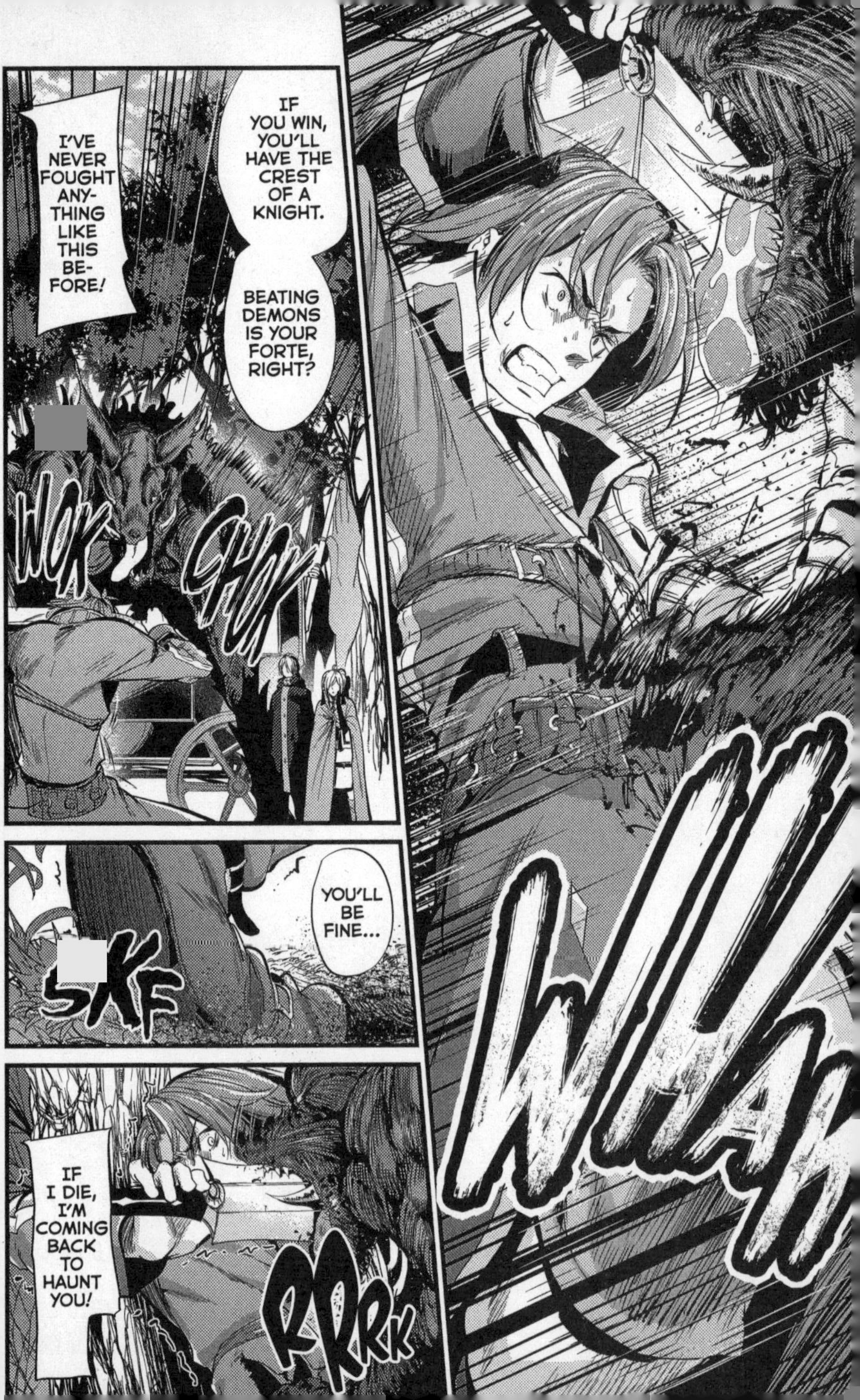
WHA
IF YOU WIN, YOU'LL HAVE THE CREST OF A KNIGHT.
BEATING DEMONS IS YOUR FORTE, RIGHT?
I'VE NEVER FOUGHT ANY-THING LIKE THIS BE-FORE!
CHUK
WOK
YOU'LL BE FINE...
SKF
IF I DIE, I'M COMING BACK TO HAUNT YOU!
RRRK

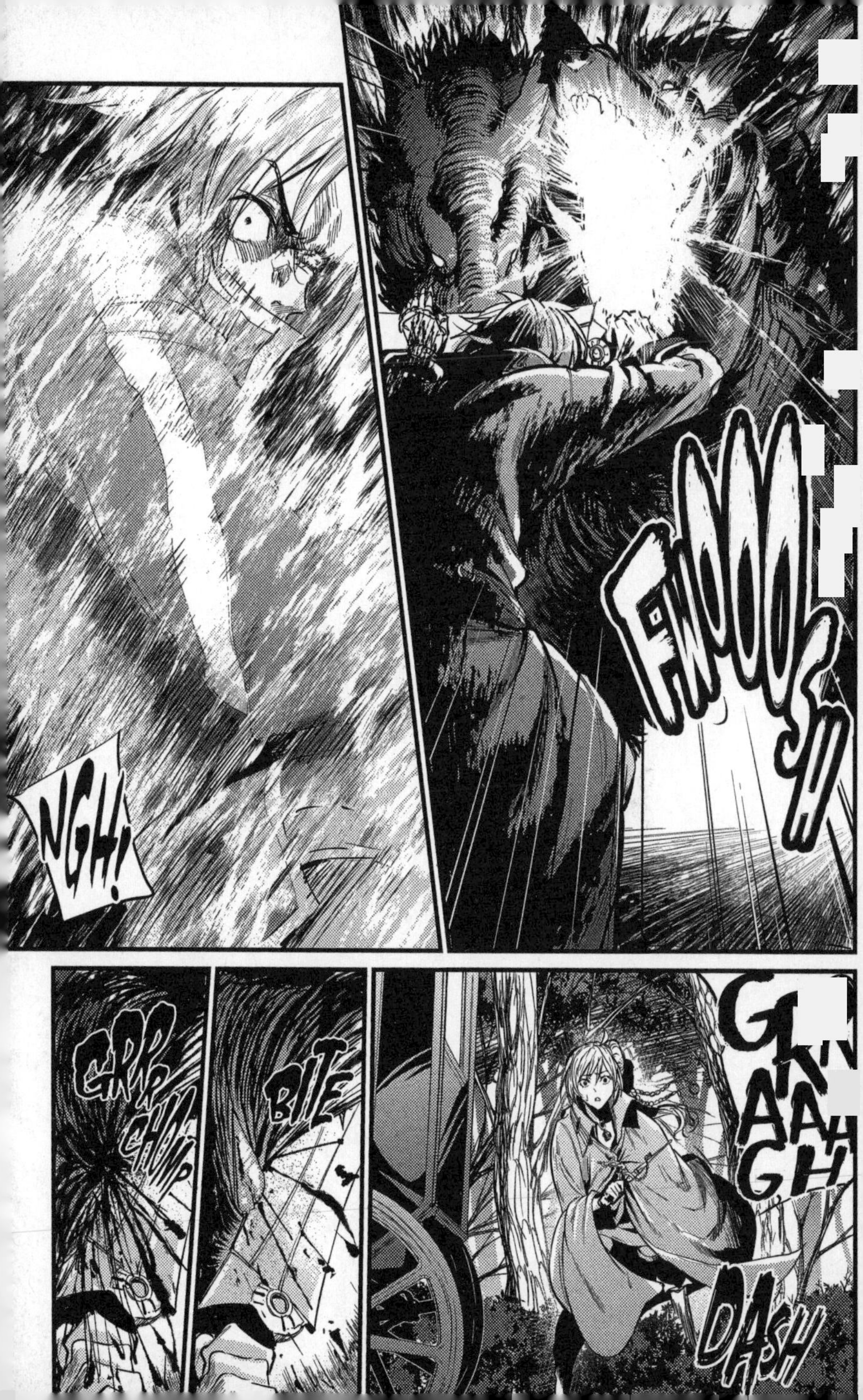
FWOOOSH
NGH!
GRAAAGH
DASH
BITE
GRRR
CHOMP

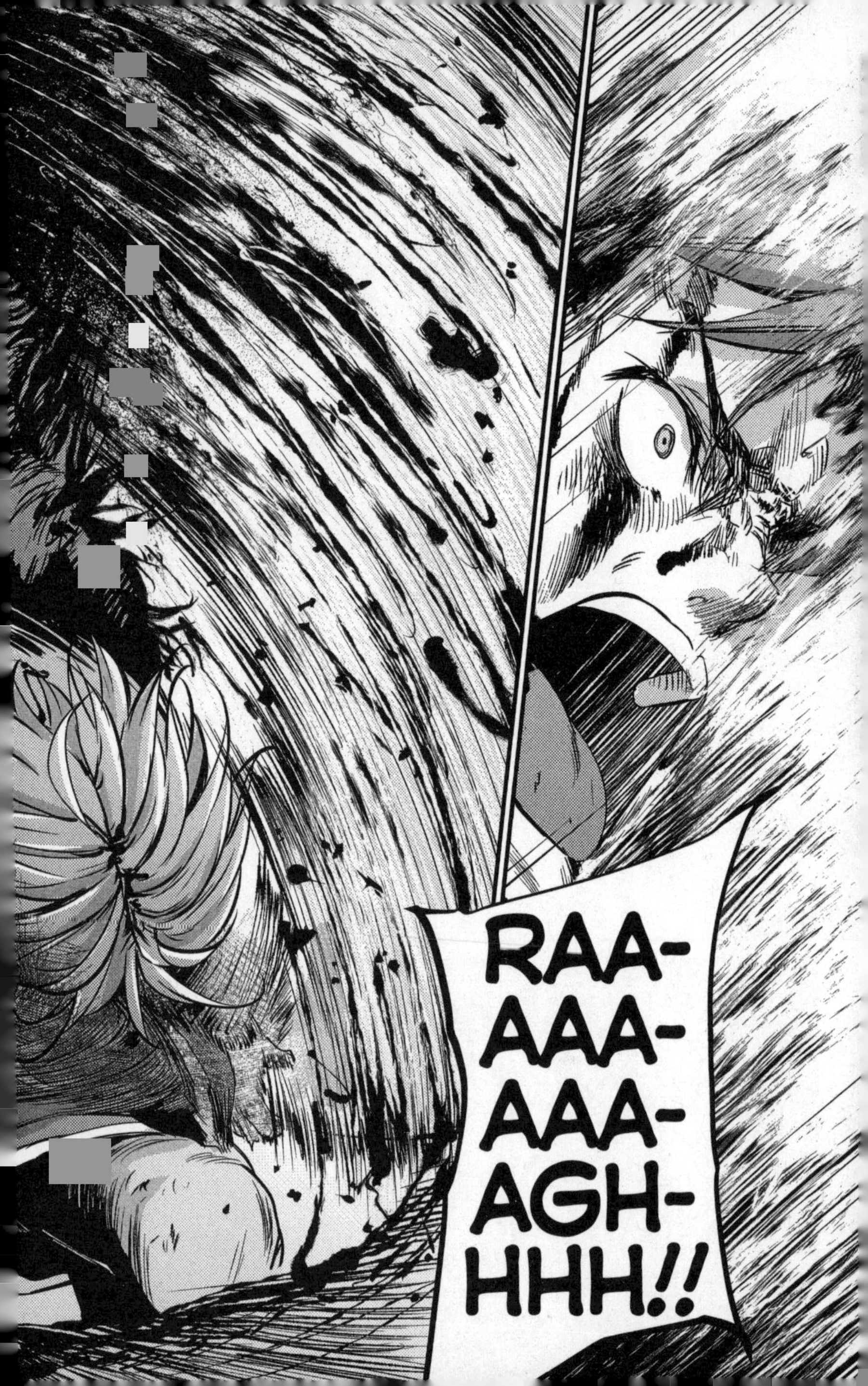
RAA-AAA-AAA-AGH-HHH!!

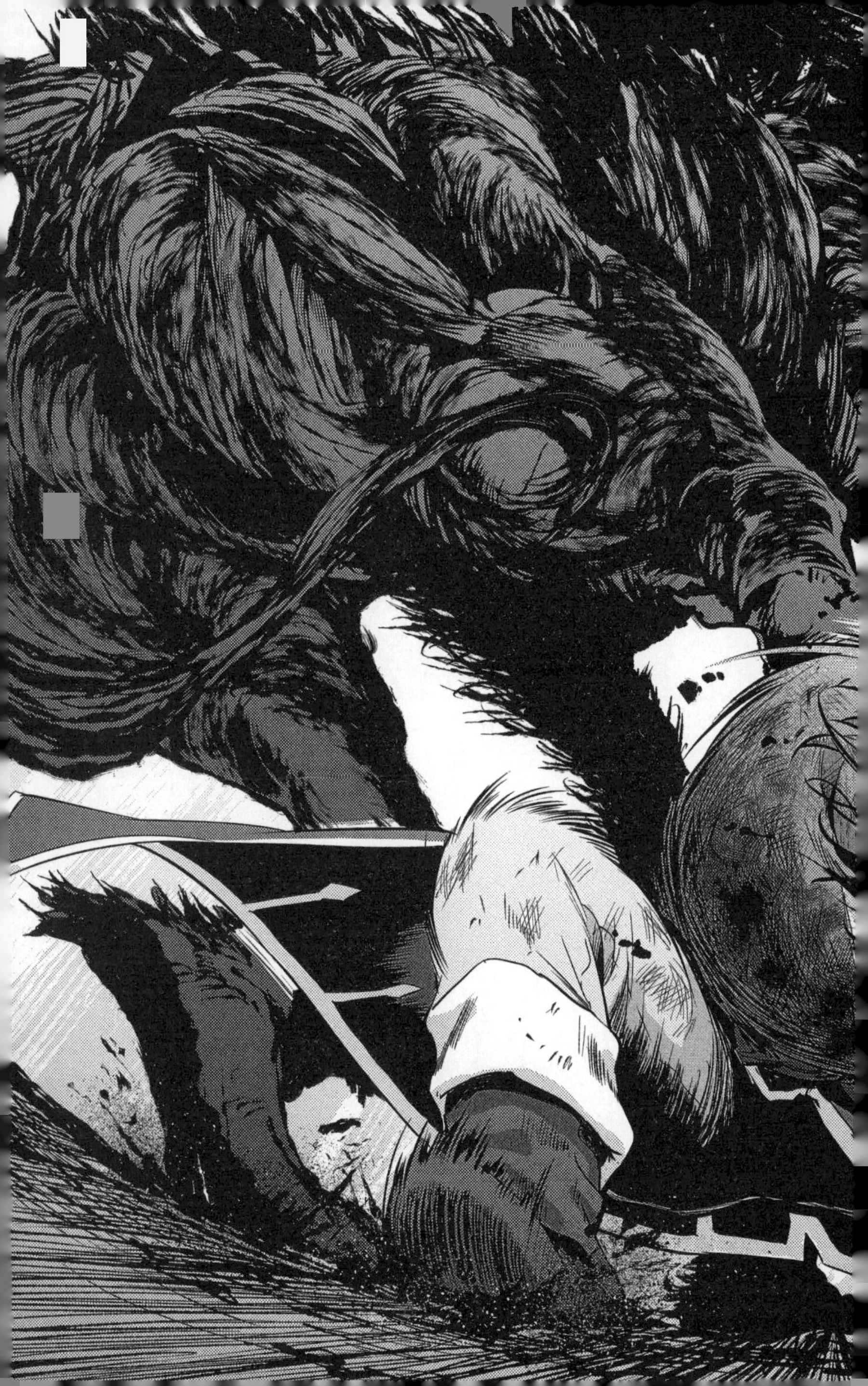

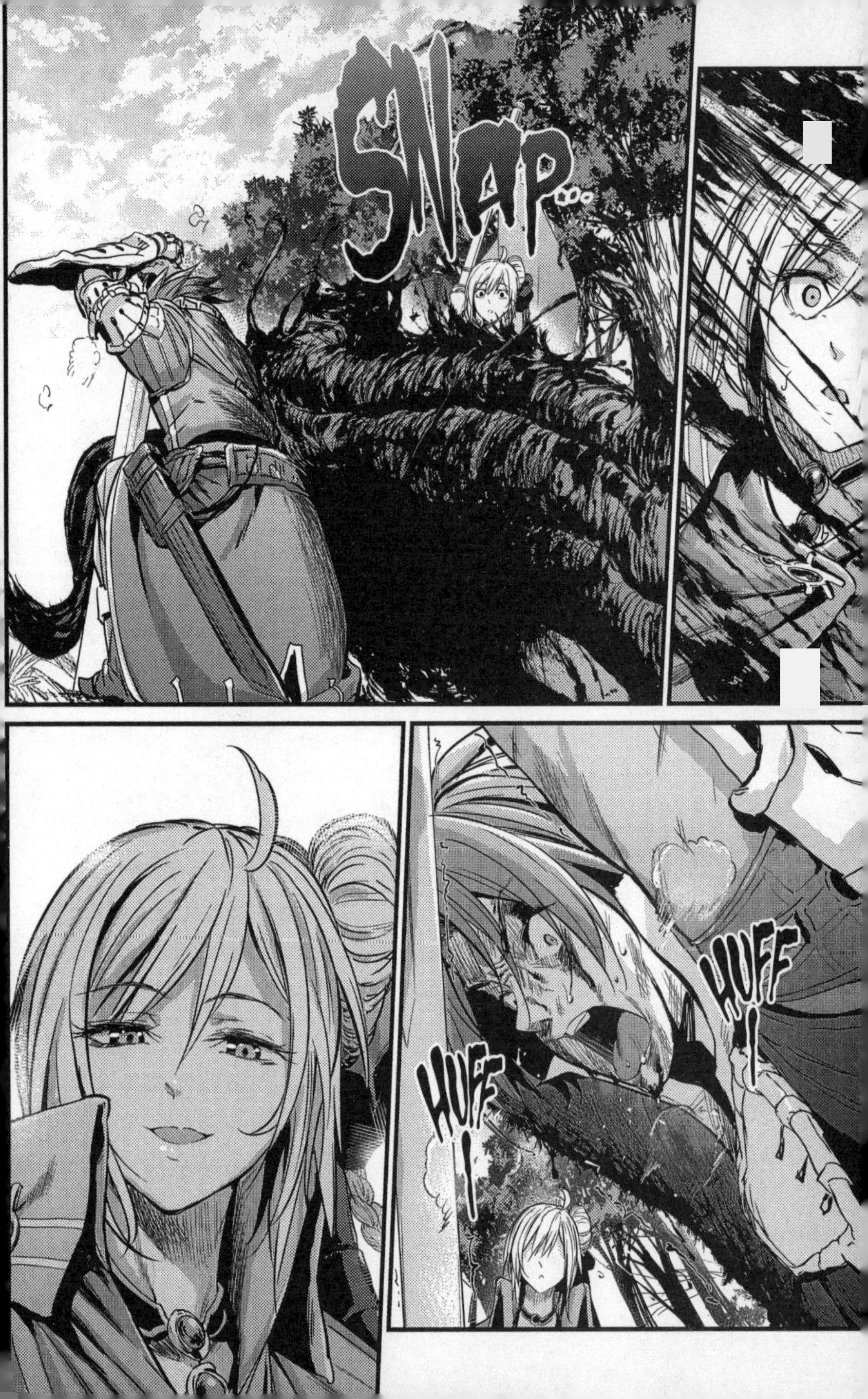

SNAP...
HUFF
HUFF

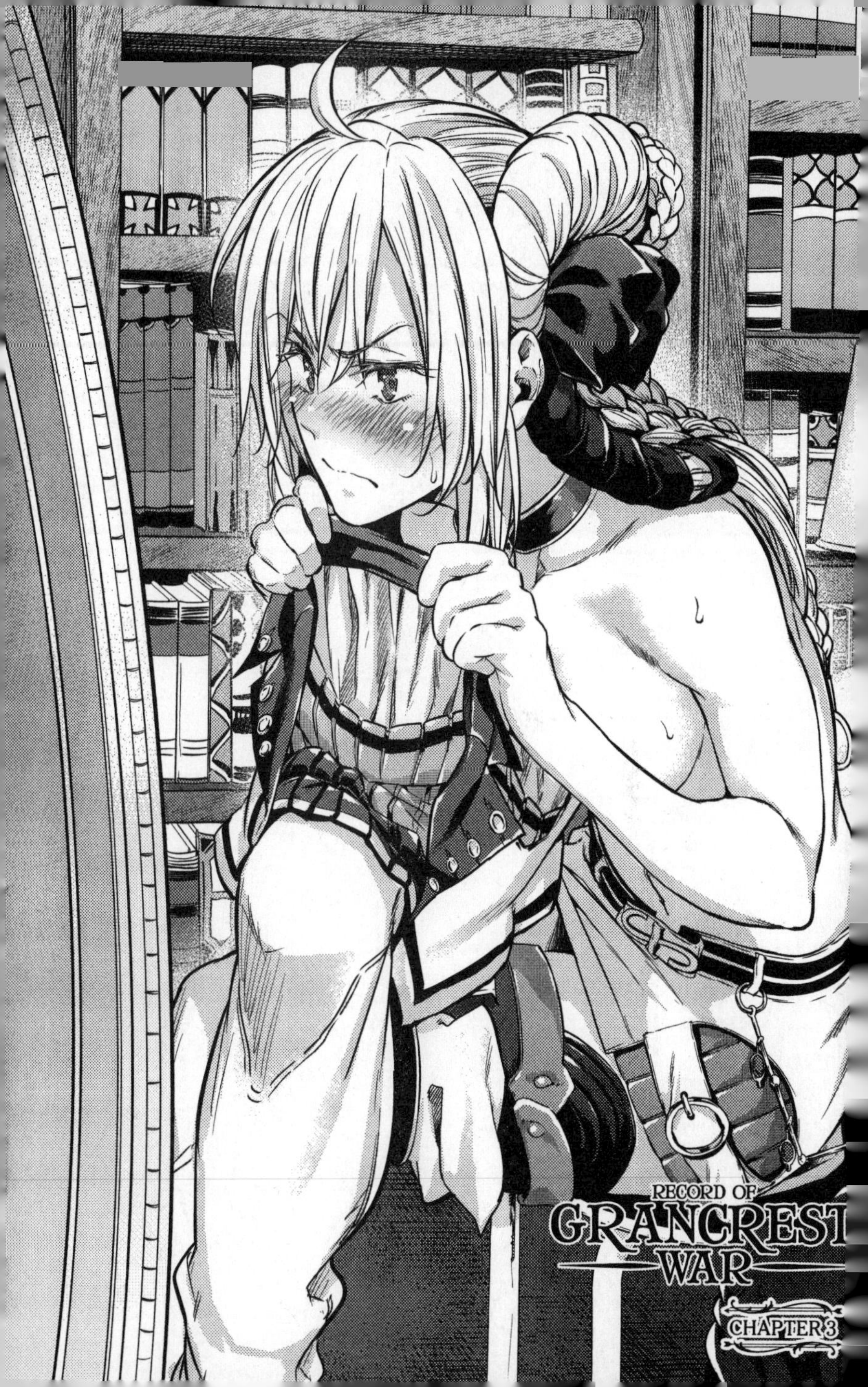
RECORD OF
GRANCREST
WAR
CHAPTER 3

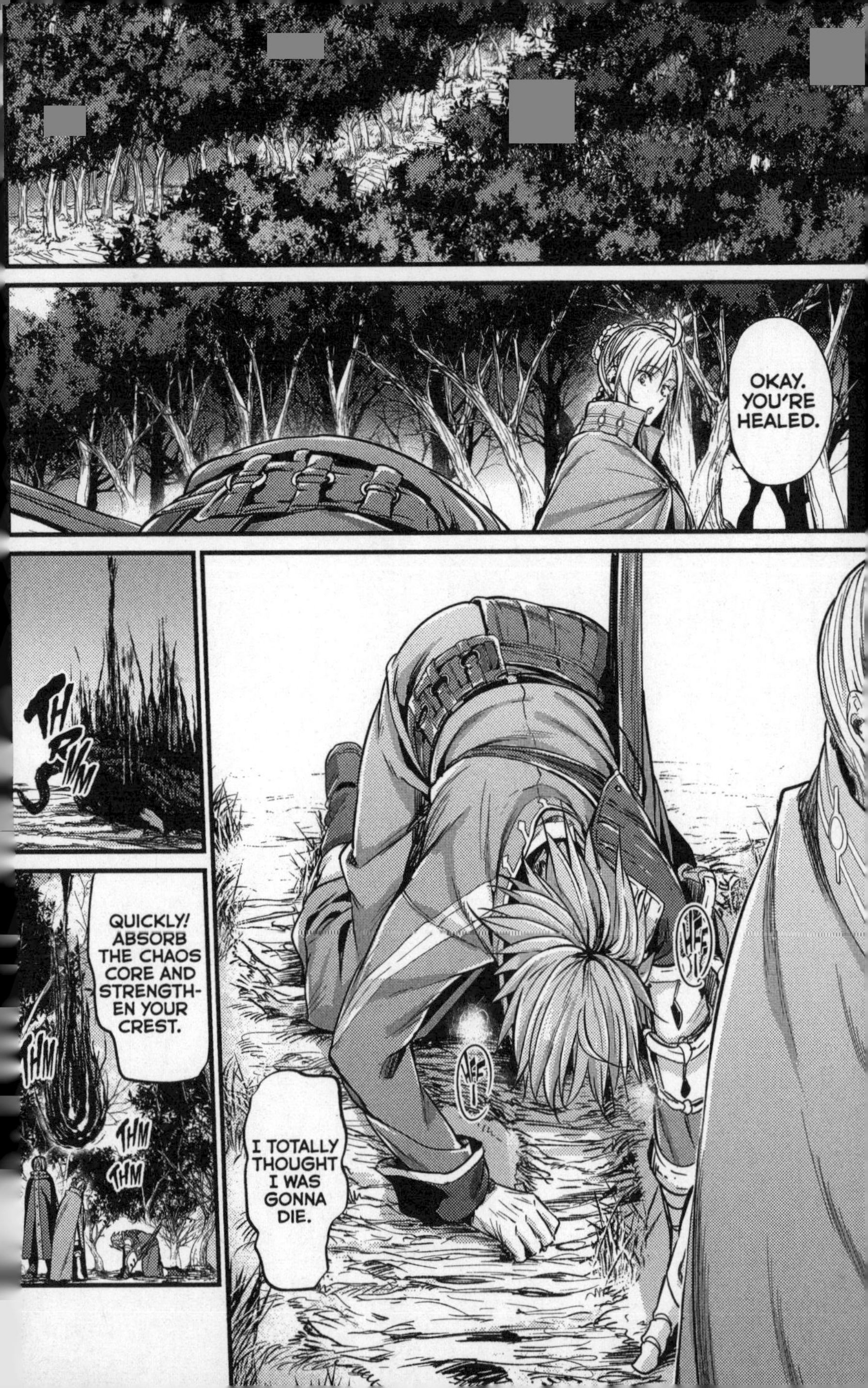
OKAY. YOU'RE HEALED.
HFF
HFF
I TOTALLY THOUGHT I WAS GONNA DIE.
THRMM
QUICKLY! ABSORB THE CHAOS CORE AND STRENGTH-EN YOUR CREST.
THM
THM
THM

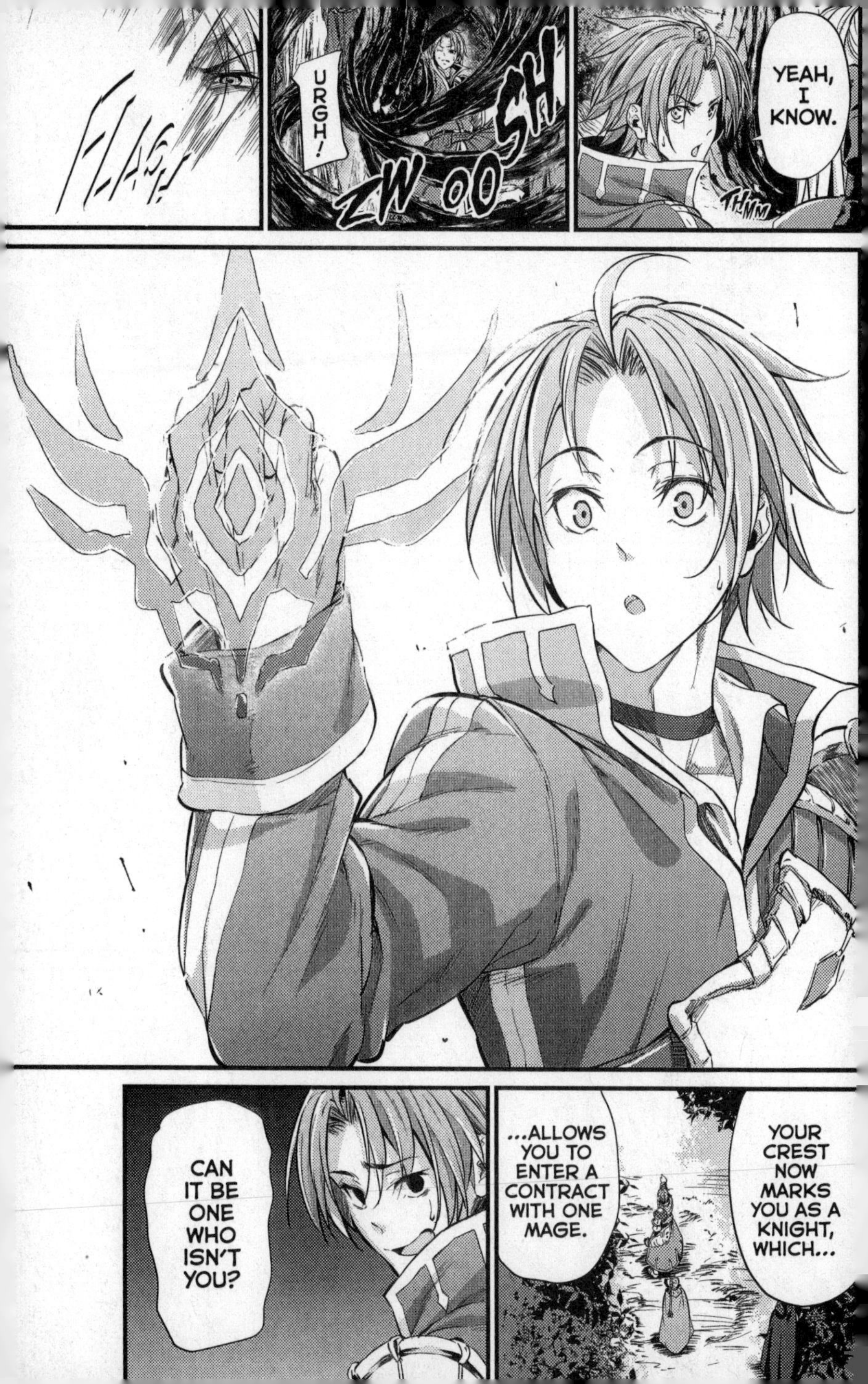
YEAH, I KNOW.
THMM
URGH!
ZWOOSH
FLASH
YOUR CREST NOW MARKS YOU AS A KNIGHT, WHICH...
...ALLOWS YOU TO ENTER A CONTRACT WITH ONE MAGE.
CAN IT BE ONE WHO ISN'T YOU?

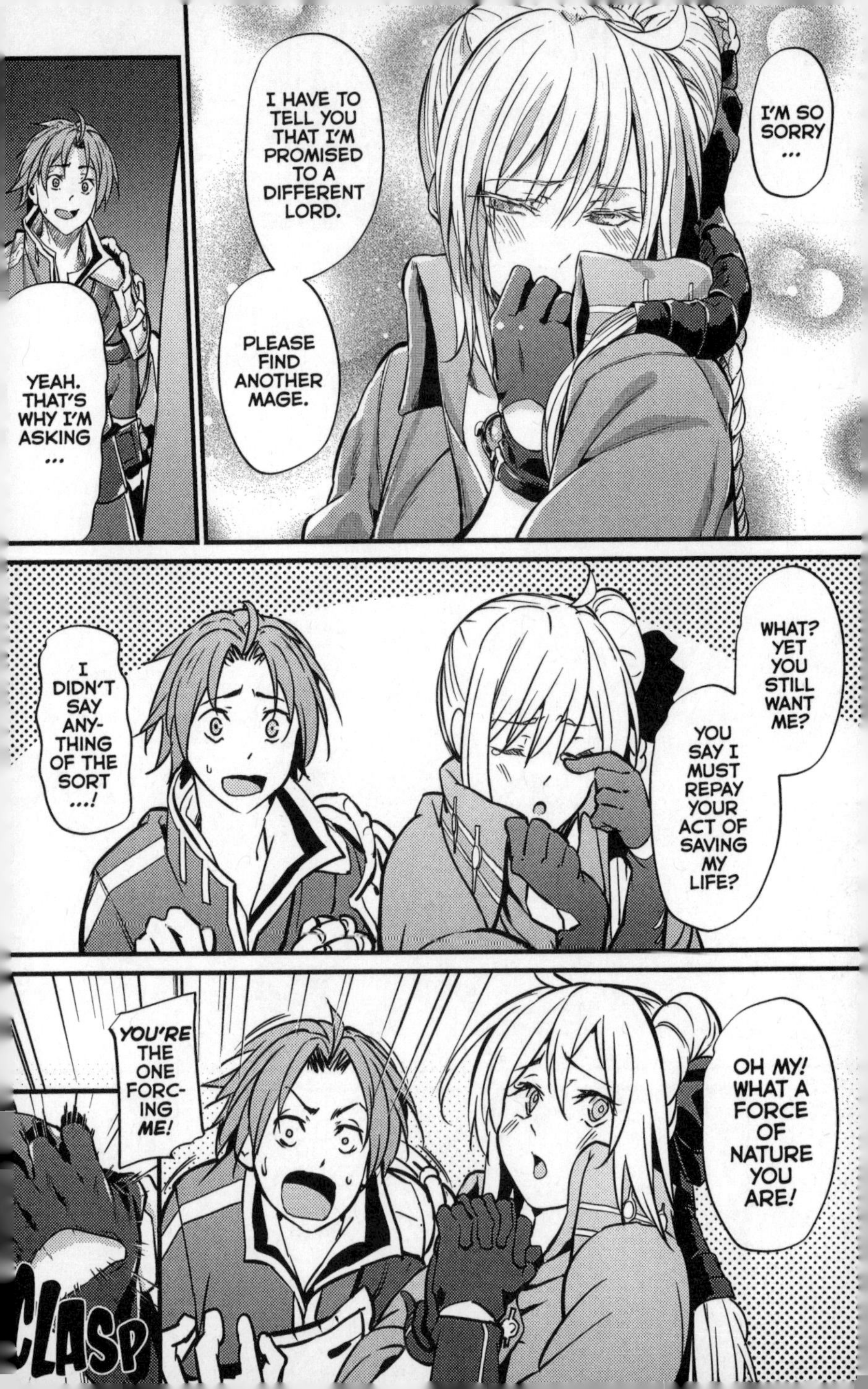
I'M SO SORRY ...
I HAVE TO TELL YOU THAT I'M PROMISED TO A DIFFERENT LORD.
PLEASE FIND ANOTHER MAGE.
YEAH. THAT'S WHY I'M ASKING ...
WHAT? YET YOU STILL WANT ME?
YOU SAY I MUST REPAY YOUR ACT OF SAVING MY LIFE?
I DIDN'T SAY ANYTHING OF THE SORT ...!
OH *MY*! WHAT A FORCE OF NATURE YOU ARE!
YOU'RE THE ONE FORCING *ME*!
CLASP

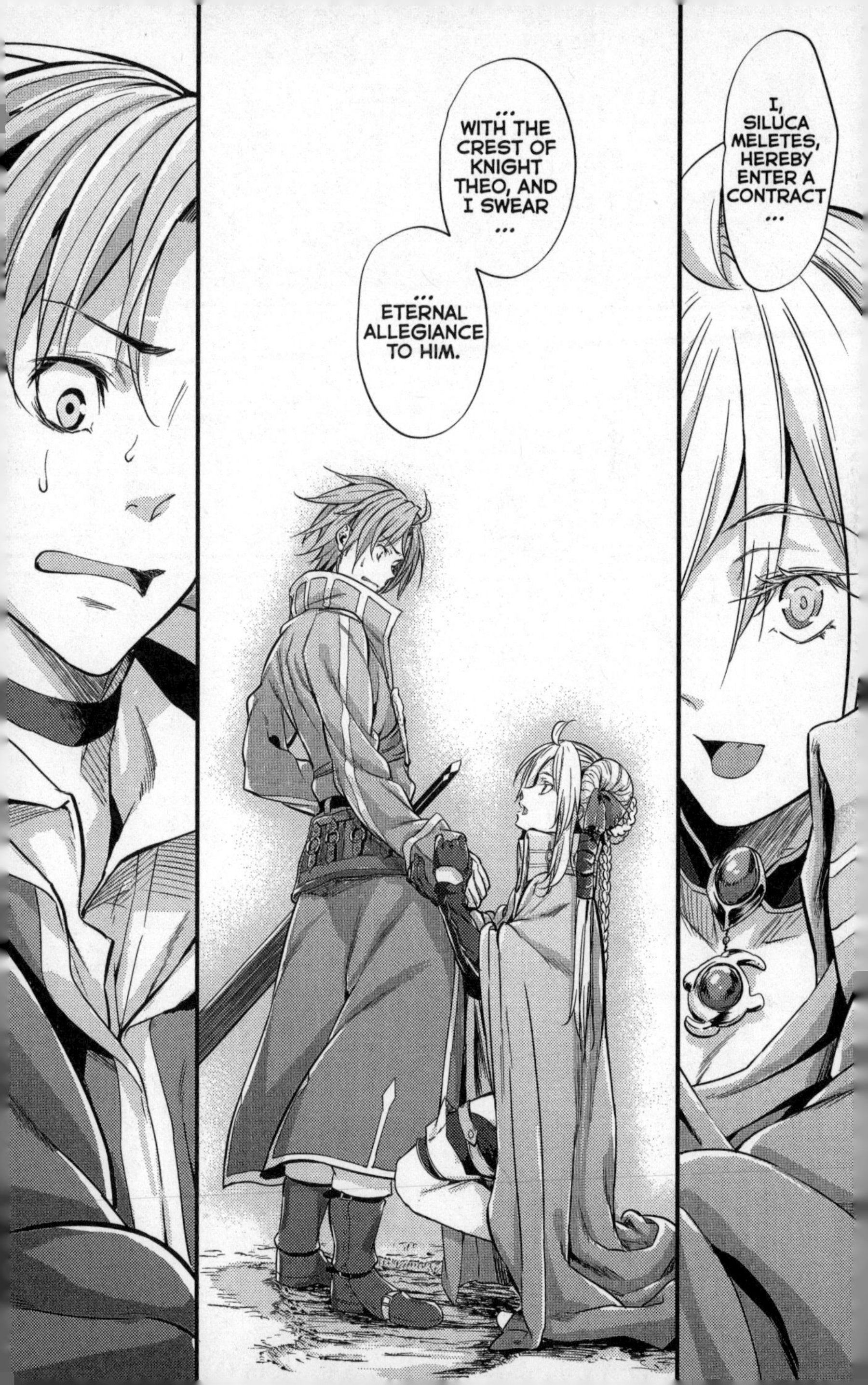
I, SILUCA MELETES, HEREBY ENTER A CONTRACT ...
... WITH THE CREST OF KNIGHT THEO, AND I SWEAR ...
... ETERNAL ALLEGIANCE TO HIM.

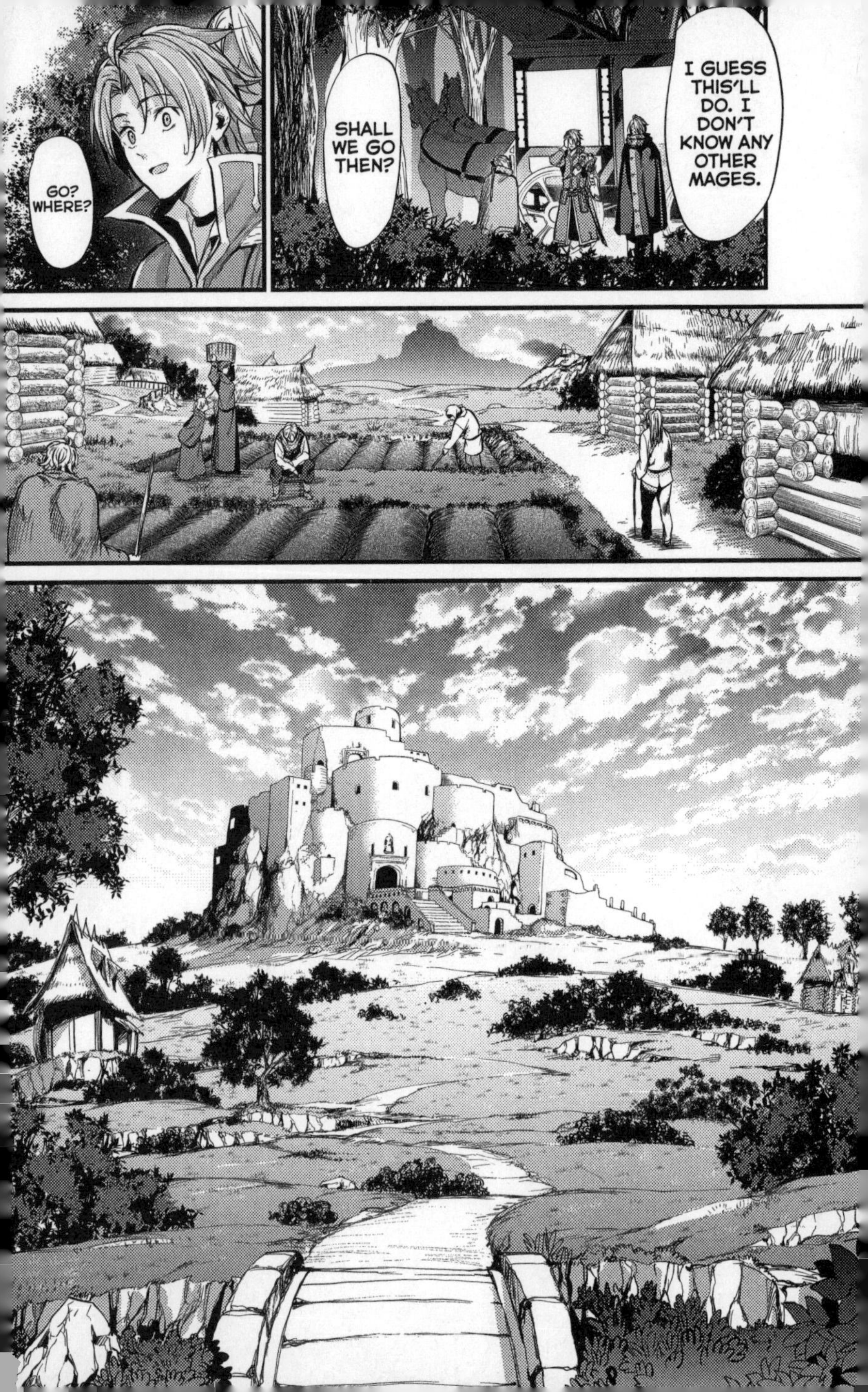
I GUESS THIS'LL DO. I DON'T KNOW ANY OTHER MAGES.
SHALL WE GO THEN?
GO? WHERE?

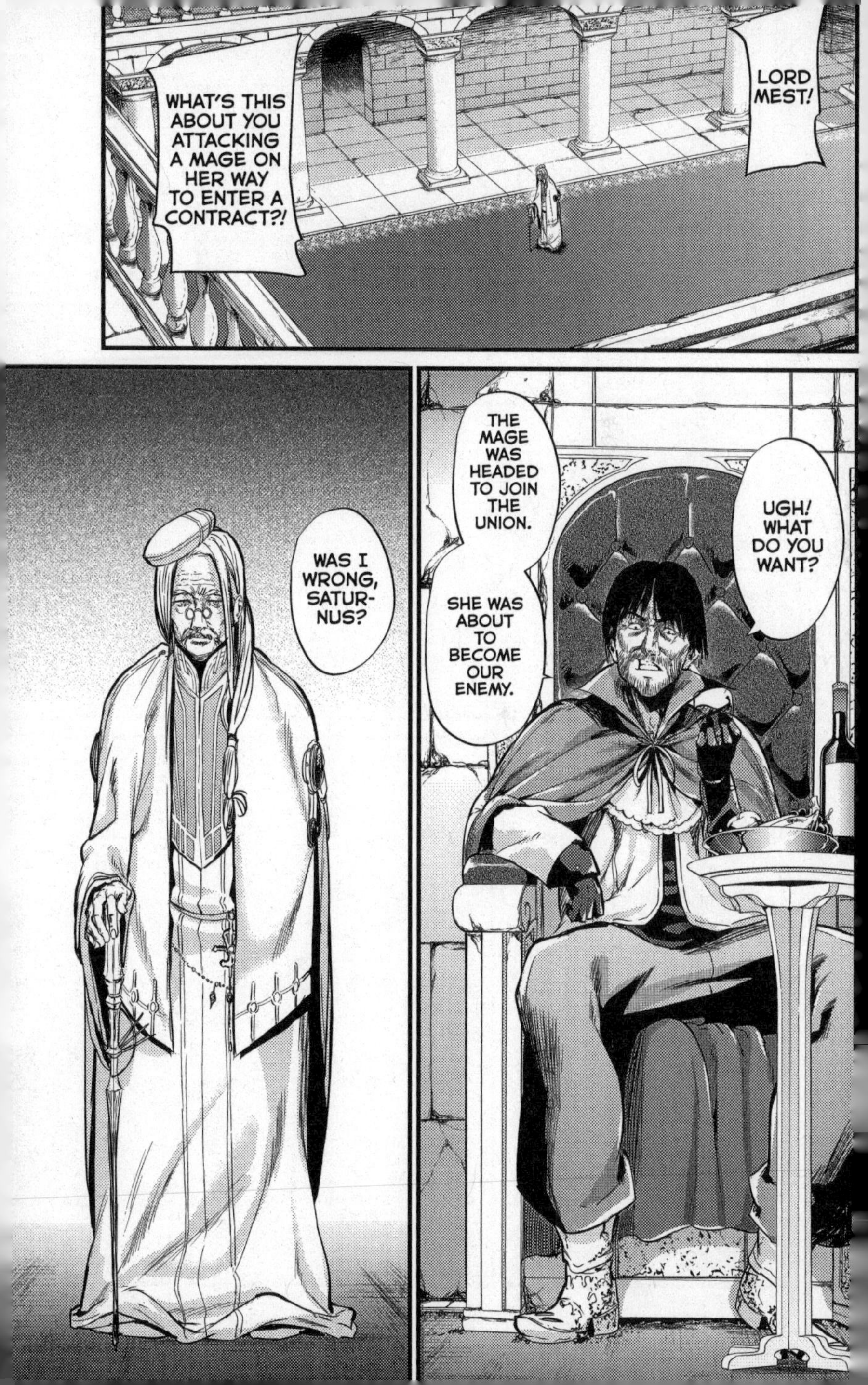
LORD MEST!
WHAT'S THIS ABOUT YOU ATTACKING A MAGE ON HER WAY TO ENTER A CONTRACT?!
UGH! WHAT DO YOU WANT?
THE MAGE WAS HEADED TO JOIN THE UNION.
SHE WAS ABOUT TO BECOME OUR ENEMY.
WAS I WRONG, SATURNUS?

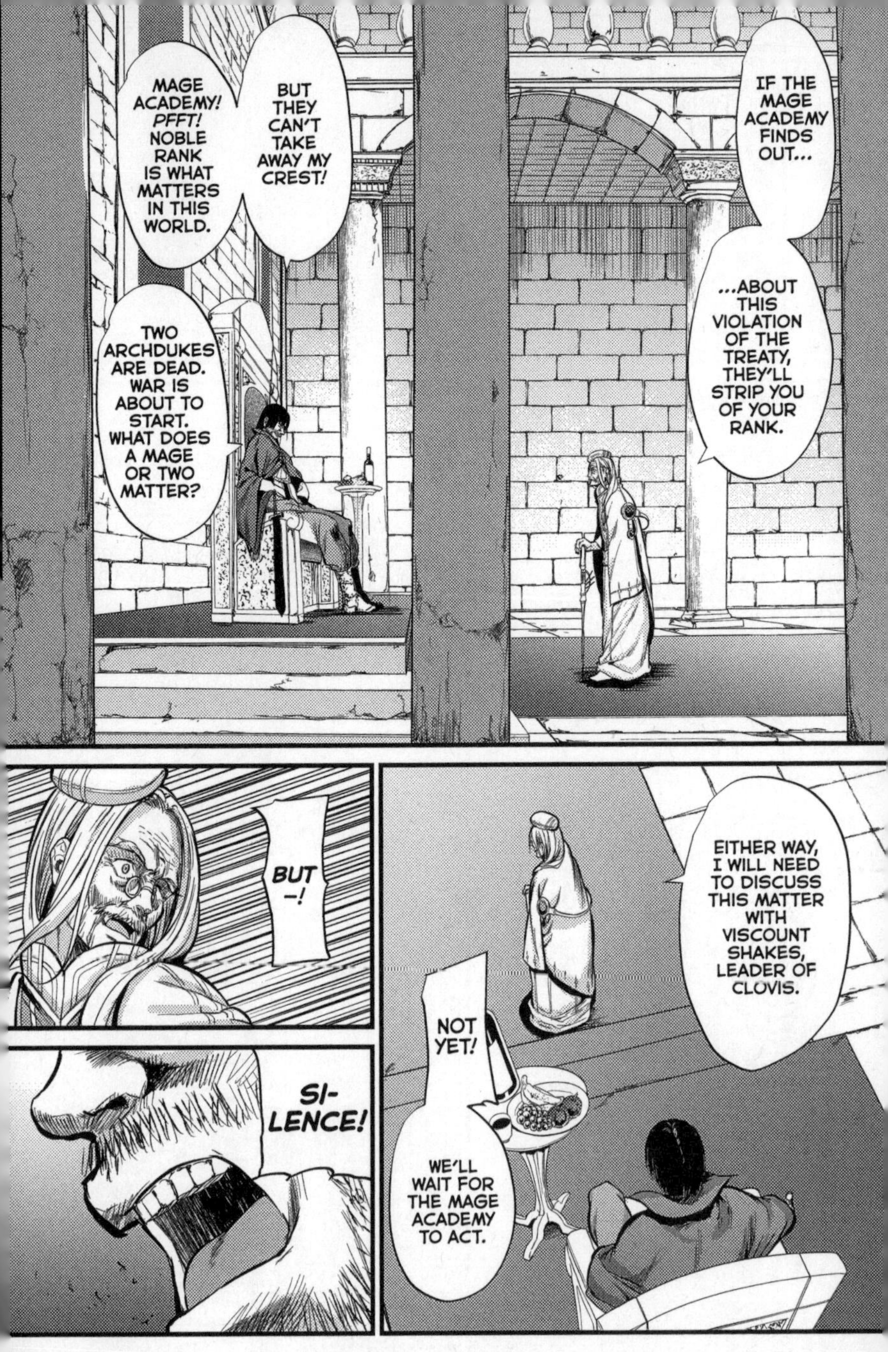
IF THE MAGE ACADEMY FINDS OUT...
...ABOUT THIS VIOLATION OF THE TREATY, THEY'LL STRIP YOU OF YOUR RANK.
BUT THEY CAN'T TAKE AWAY MY CREST!
MAGE ACADEMY! PFFT! NOBLE RANK IS WHAT MATTERS IN THIS WORLD.
TWO ARCHDUKES ARE DEAD. WAR IS ABOUT TO START. WHAT DOES A MAGE OR TWO MATTER?
EITHER WAY, I WILL NEED TO DISCUSS THIS MATTER WITH VISCOUNT SHAKES, LEADER OF CLOVIS.
NOT YET!
WE'LL WAIT FOR THE MAGE ACADEMY TO ACT.
BUT —!
SI-LENCE!

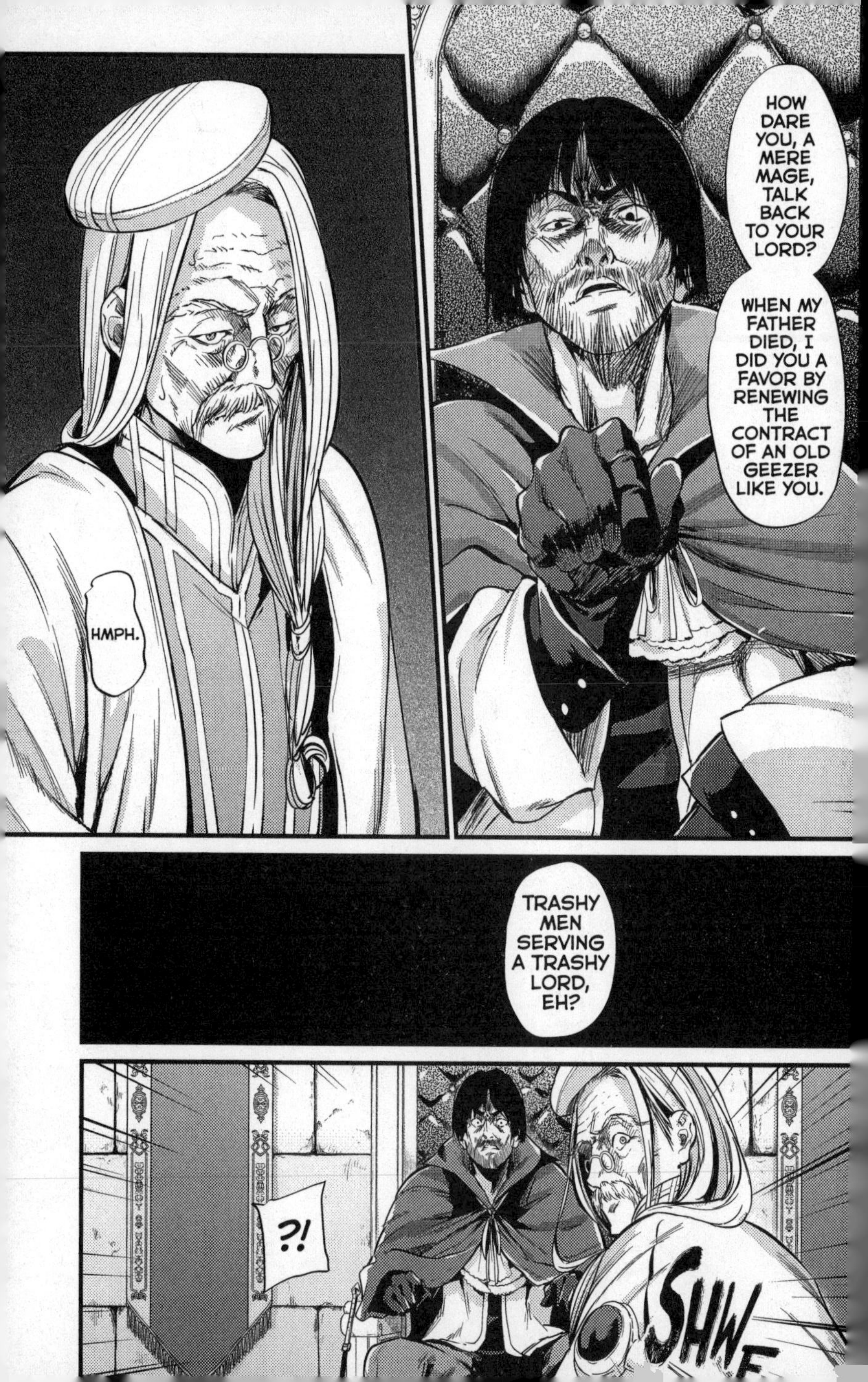
HOW DARE YOU, A MERE MAGE, TALK BACK TO YOUR LORD?
WHEN MY FATHER DIED, I DID YOU A FAVOR BY RENEWING THE CONTRACT OF AN OLD GEEZER LIKE YOU.
HMPH.
TRASHY MEN SERVING A TRASHY LORD, EH?
?!
SHW

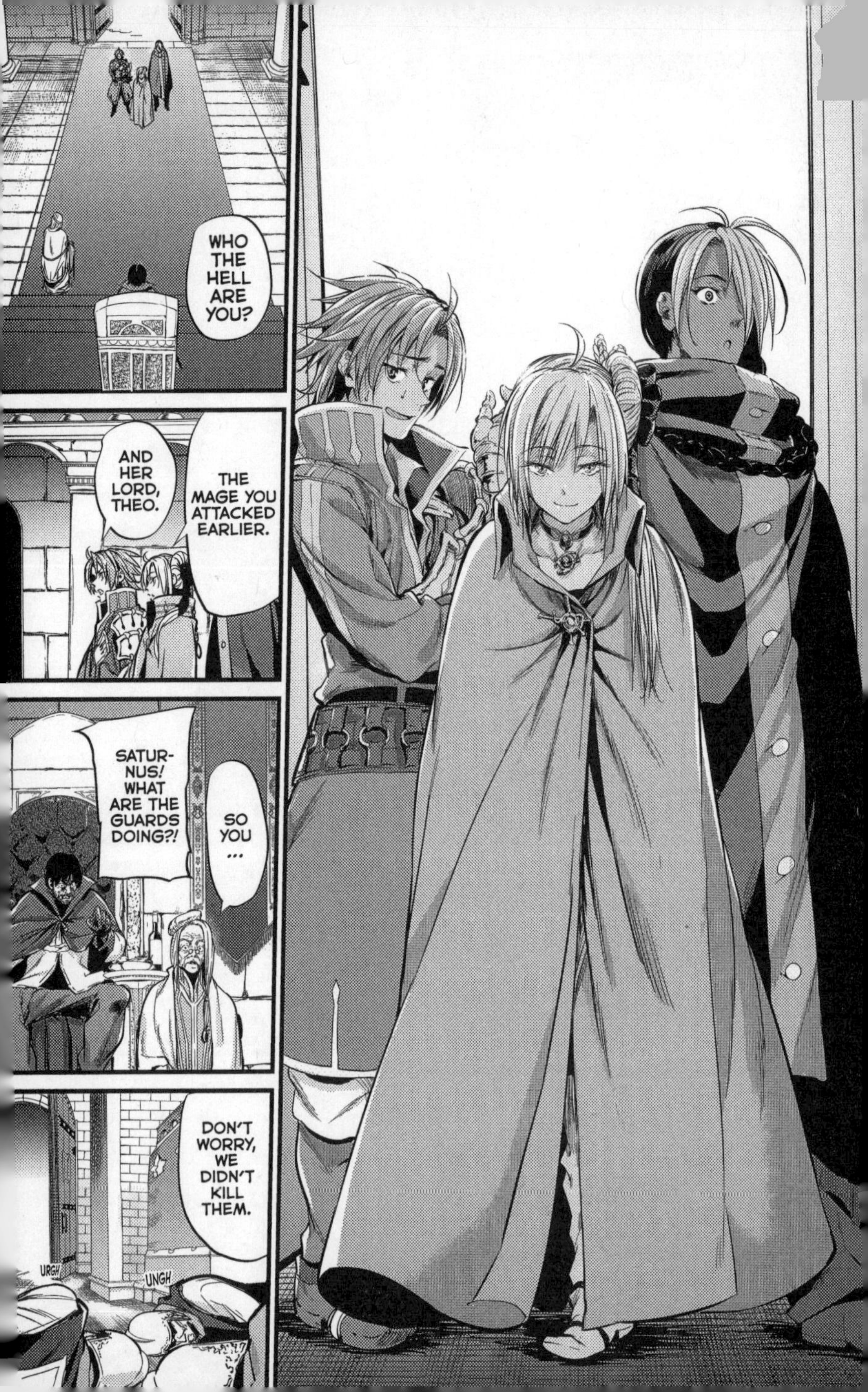
WHO THE HELL ARE YOU?
THE MAGE YOU ATTACKED EARLIER.
AND HER LORD, THEO.
SO YOU ...
SATURNUS! WHAT ARE THE GUARDS DOING?!
DON'T WORRY, WE DIDN'T KILL THEM.
URGH
UNGH

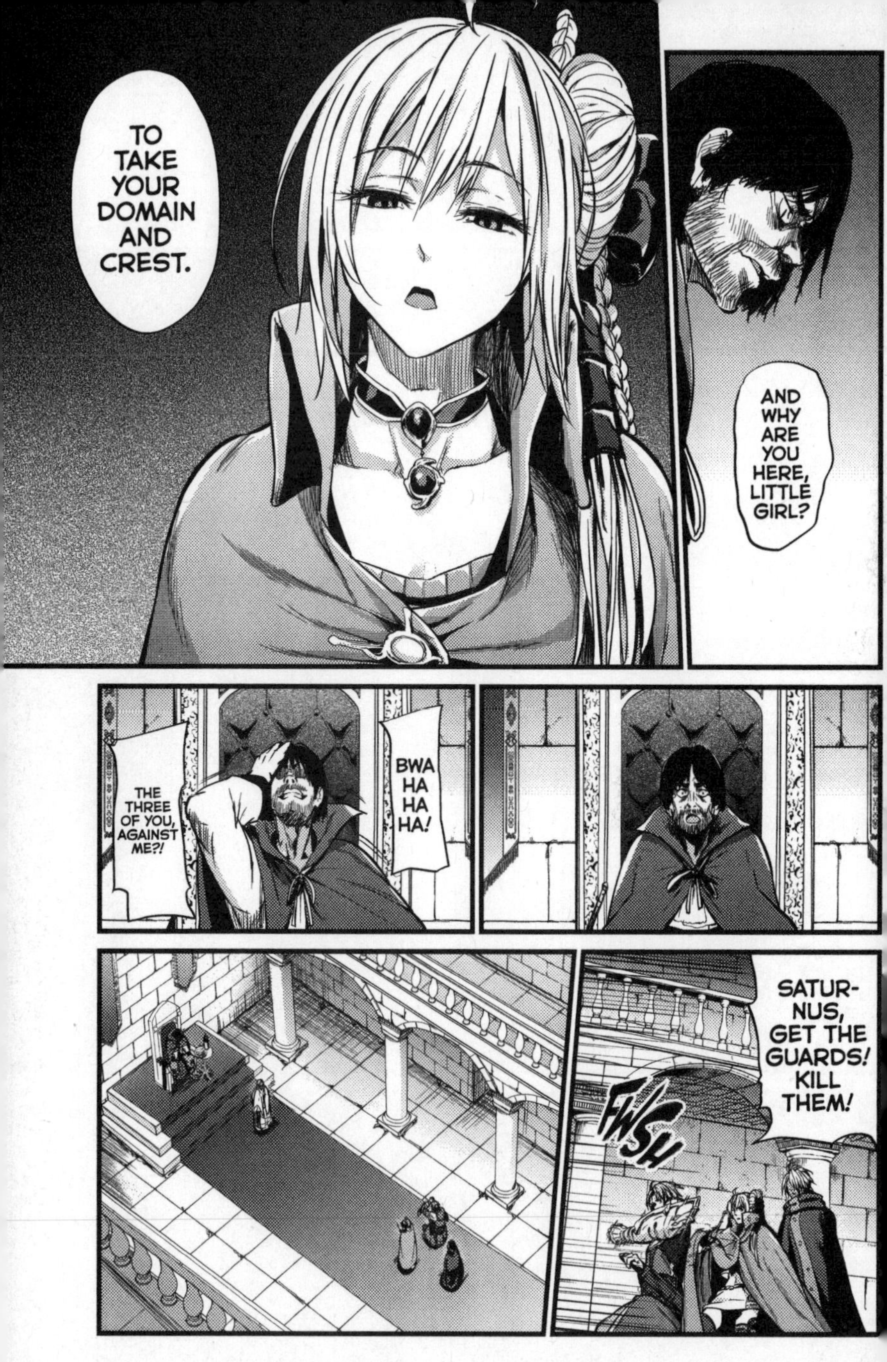
AND WHY ARE YOU HERE, LITTLE GIRL?
TO TAKE YOUR DOMAIN AND CREST.
BWA HA HA HA!
THE THREE OF YOU, AGAINST ME?!
SATURNUS, GET THE GUARDS! KILL THEM!
FWSH

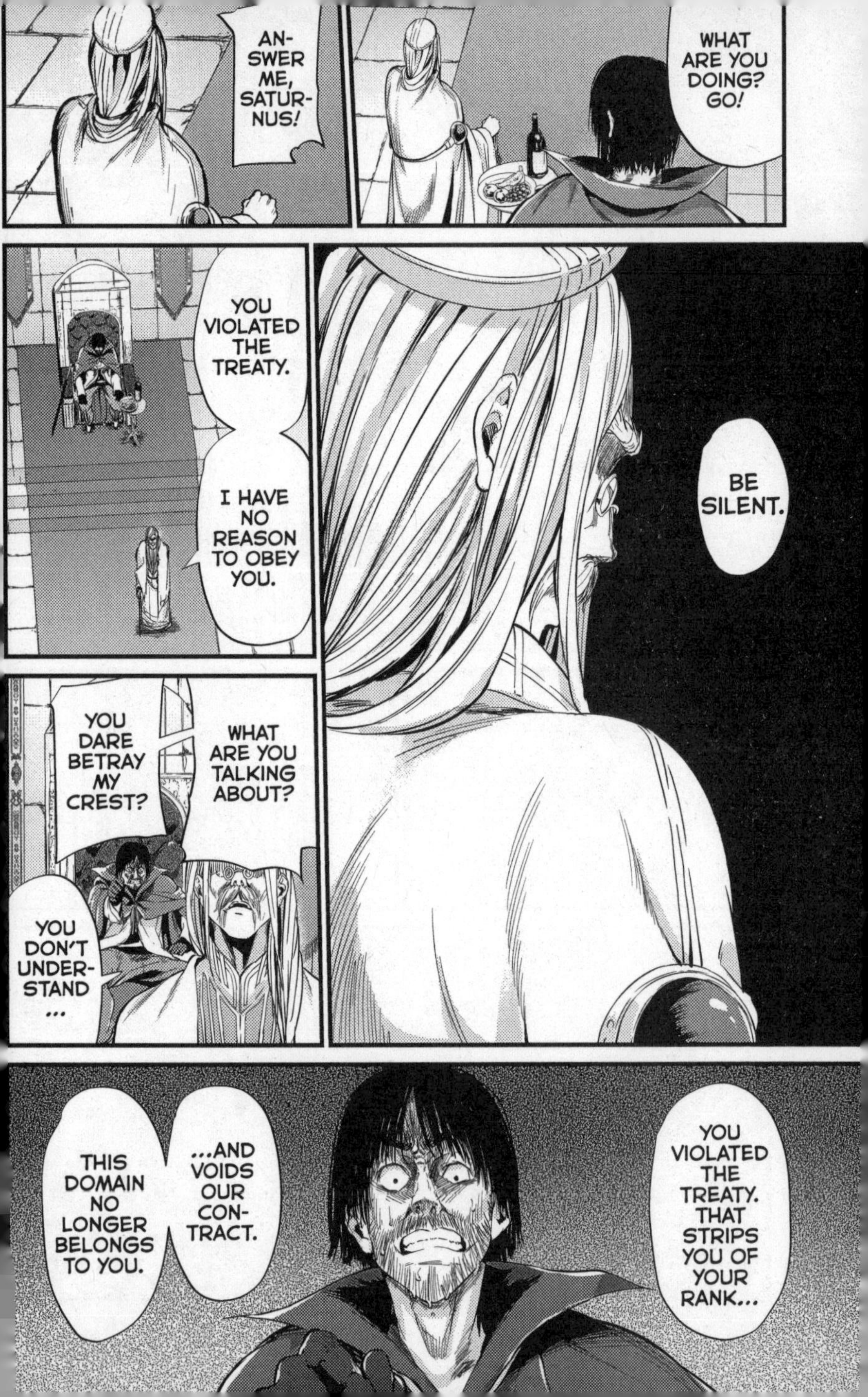
WHAT ARE YOU DOING? GO!
ANSWER ME, SATURNUS!
BE SILENT.
YOU VIOLATED THE TREATY.
I HAVE NO REASON TO OBEY YOU.
WHAT ARE YOU TALKING ABOUT?
YOU DARE BETRAY MY CREST?
YOU DON'T UNDERSTAND...
YOU VIOLATED THE TREATY. THAT STRIPS YOU OF YOUR RANK...
...AND VOIDS OUR CONTRACT.
THIS DOMAIN NO LONGER BELONGS TO YOU.

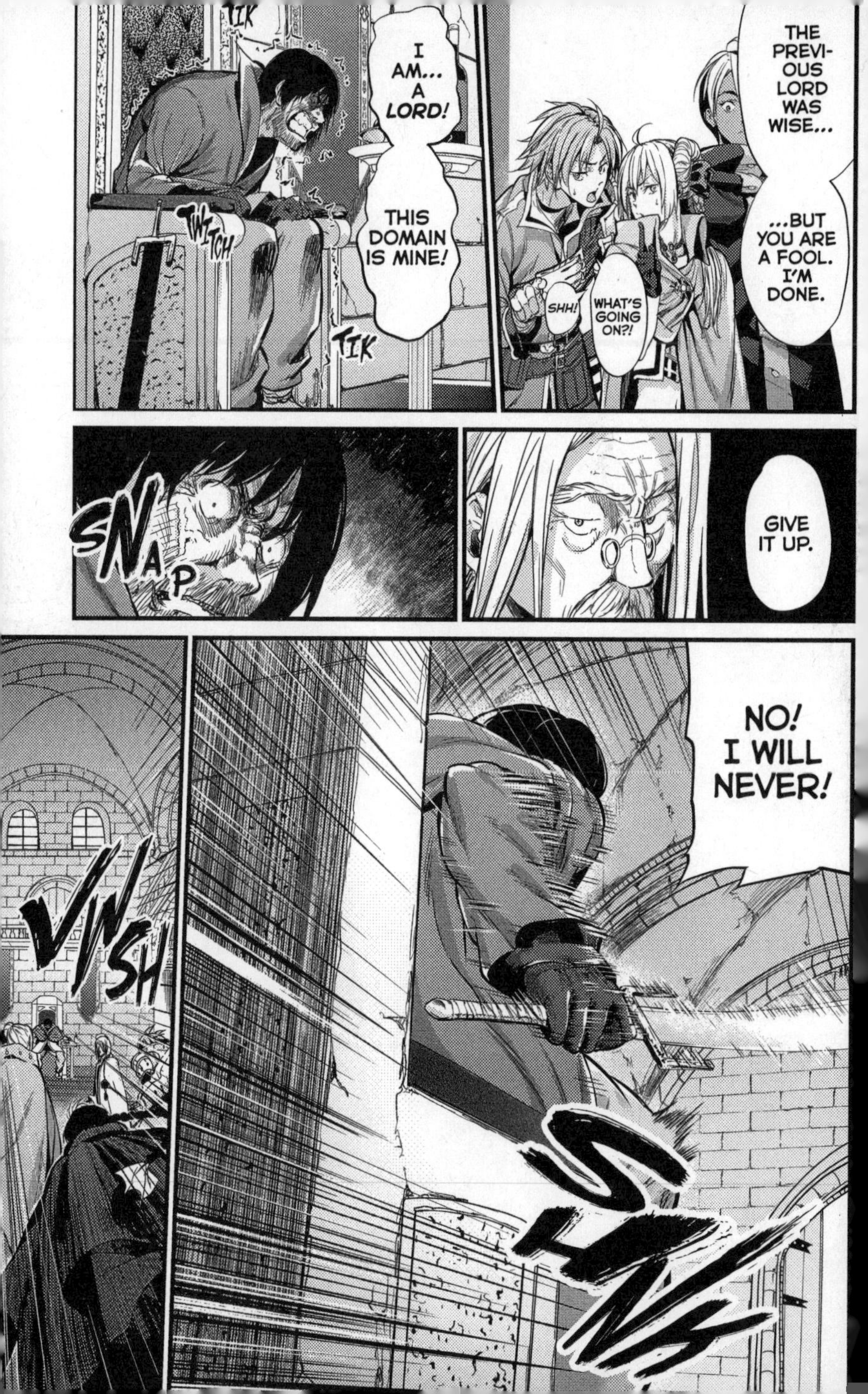
THE PREVIOUS LORD WAS WISE...
...BUT YOU ARE A FOOL. I'M DONE.
WHAT'S GOING ON?!
SHH!
TIK
I AM... A LORD!
THIS DOMAIN IS MINE!
TWITCH
TIK
GIVE IT UP.
SNAP
NO! I WILL NEVER!
SHNK
VWSH

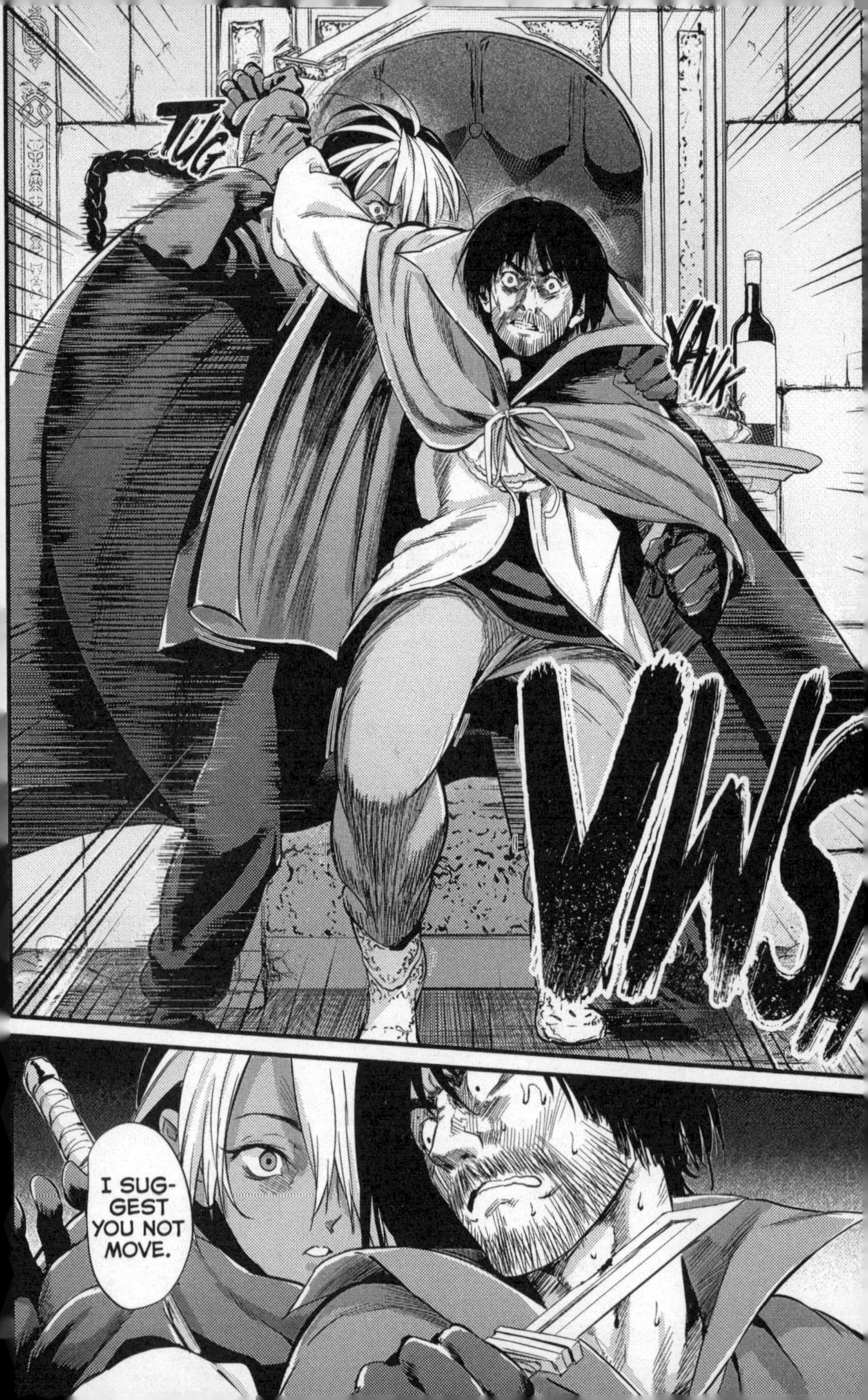
TUG
YANK
VWSH
I SUG-GEST YOU NOT MOVE.

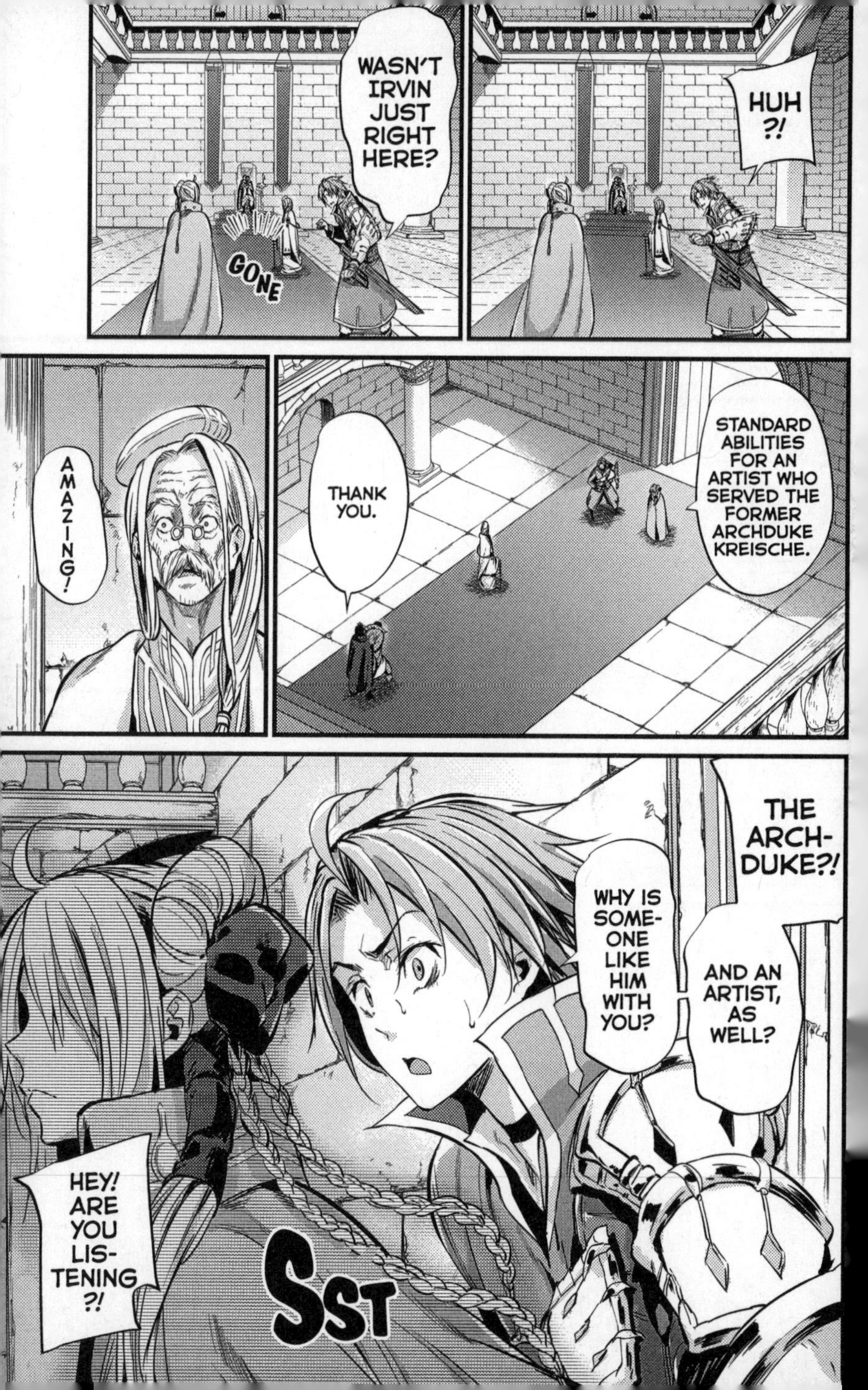
HUH ?!
WASN'T IRVIN JUST RIGHT HERE?
GONE
STANDARD ABILITIES FOR AN ARTIST WHO SERVED THE FORMER ARCHDUKE KREISCHE.
THANK YOU.
AMAZING!
THE ARCH-DUKE?!
AND AN ARTIST, AS WELL?
WHY IS SOME-ONE LIKE HIM WITH YOU?
HEY! ARE YOU LIS-TENING ?!
SST

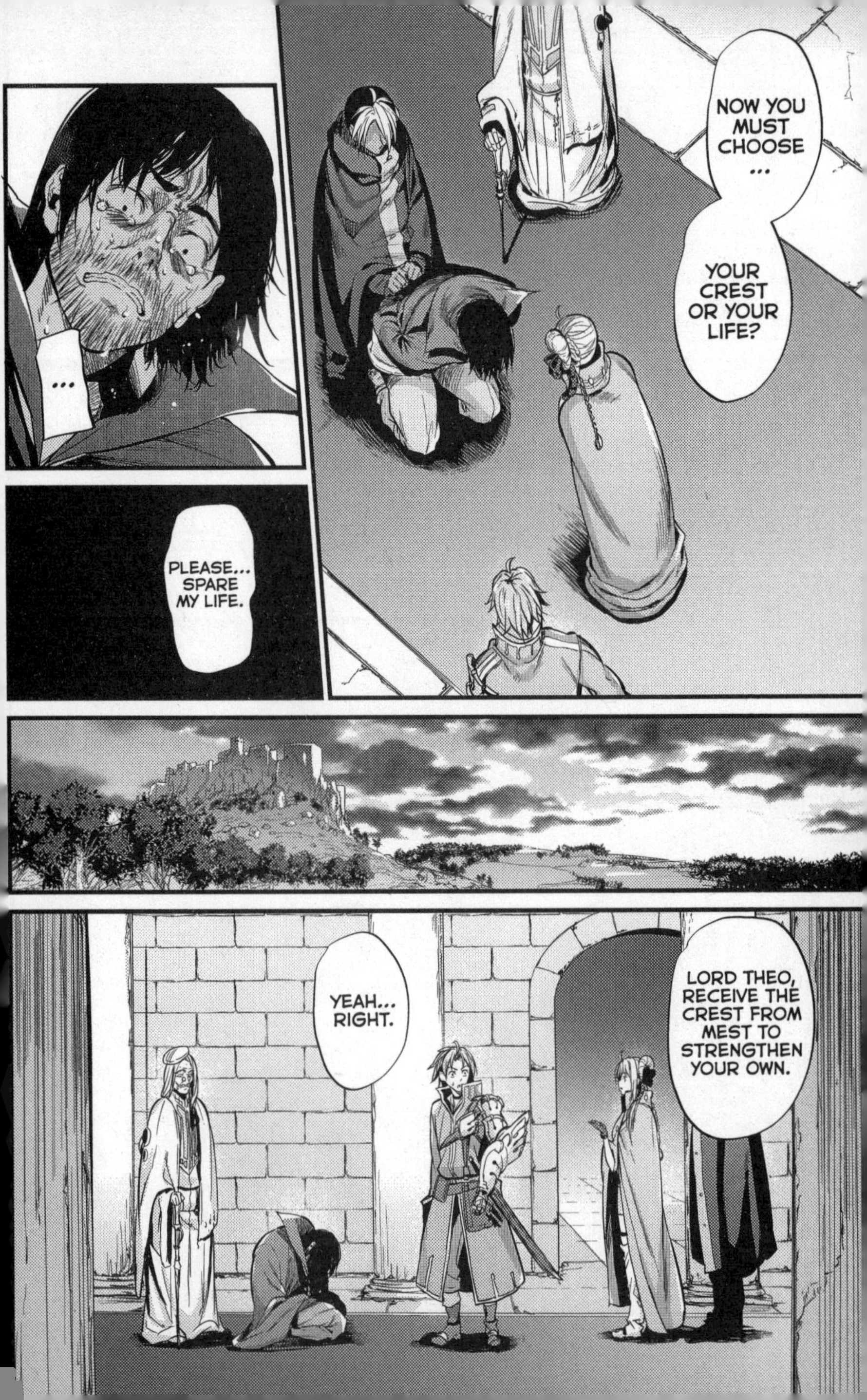
NOW YOU MUST CHOOSE ...
YOUR CREST OR YOUR LIFE?
...
PLEASE... SPARE MY LIFE.
LORD THEO, RECEIVE THE CREST FROM MEST TO STRENGTHEN YOUR OWN.
YEAH... RIGHT.

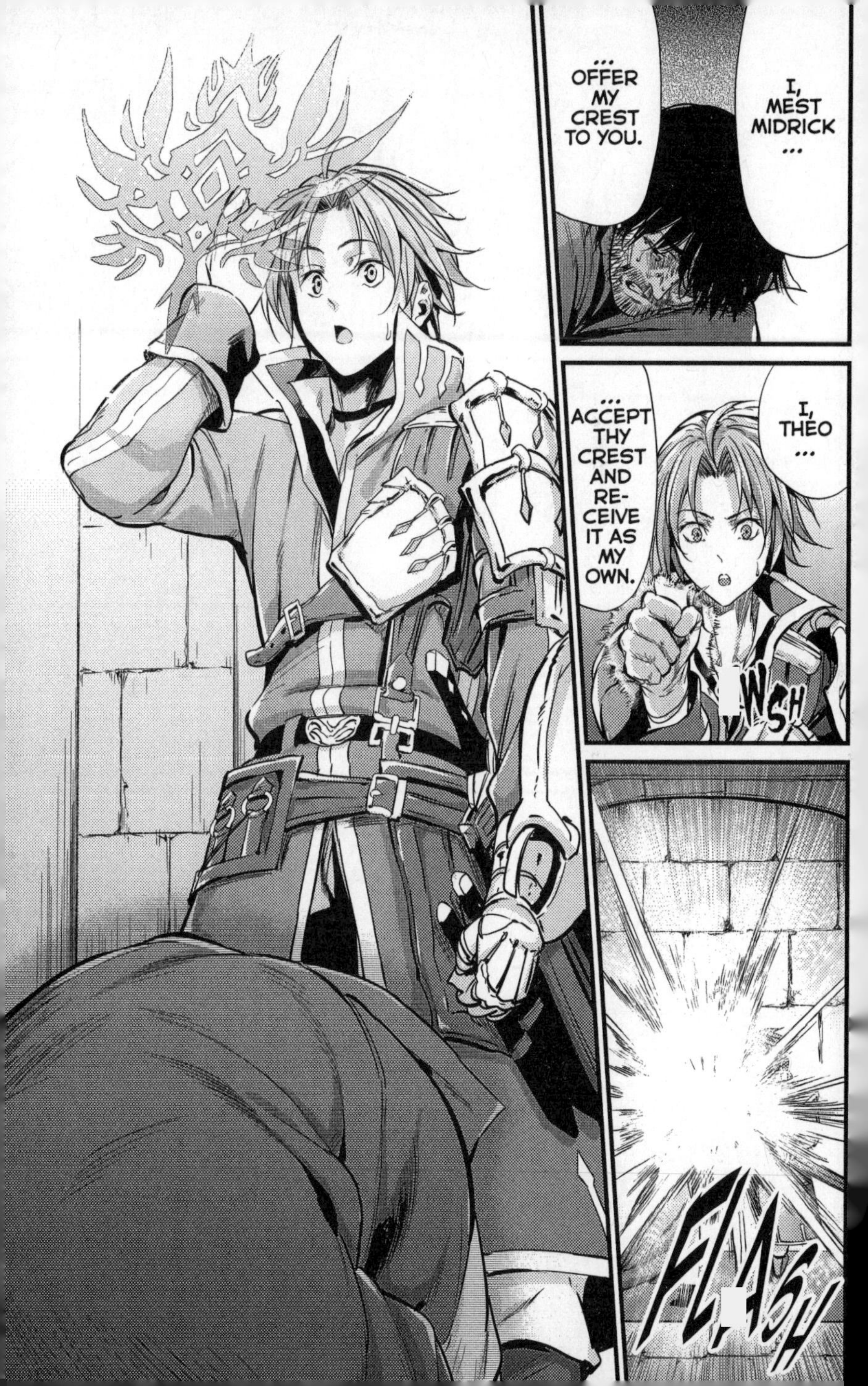
I, MEST MIDRICK ...
... OFFER MY CREST TO YOU.
I, THEO ...
... ACCEPT THY CREST AND RE-CEIVE IT AS MY OWN.
WSH
FLASH

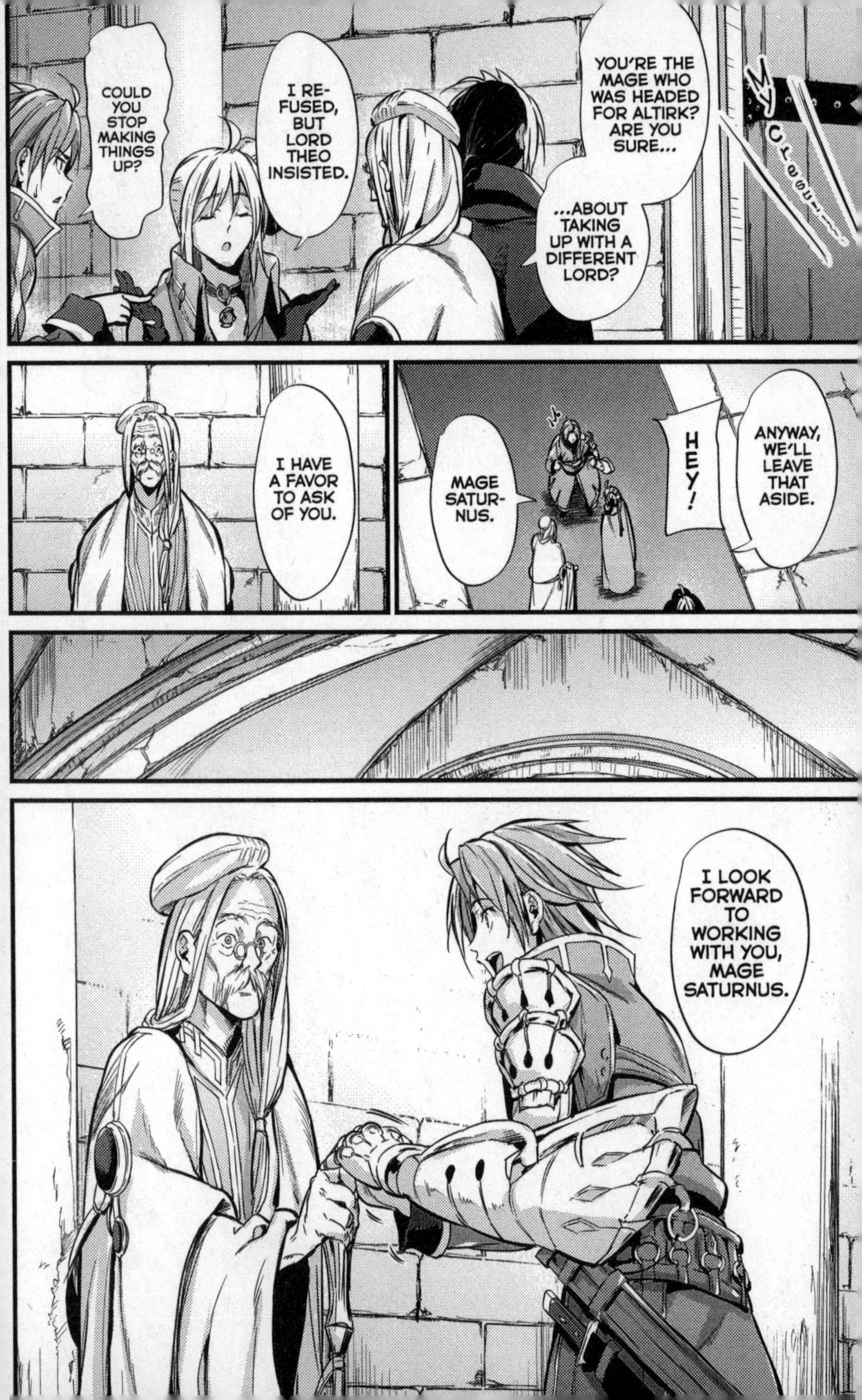
My Cresu!~
YOU'RE THE MAGE WHO WAS HEADED FOR ALTIRK? ARE YOU SURE...
...ABOUT TAKING UP WITH A DIFFERENT LORD?
I REFUSED, BUT LORD THEO INSISTED.
COULD YOU STOP MAKING THINGS UP?
ANYWAY, WE'LL LEAVE THAT ASIDE.
HEY!
MAGE SATURNUS.
I HAVE A FAVOR TO ASK OF YOU.
I LOOK FORWARD TO WORKING WITH YOU, MAGE SATURNUS.

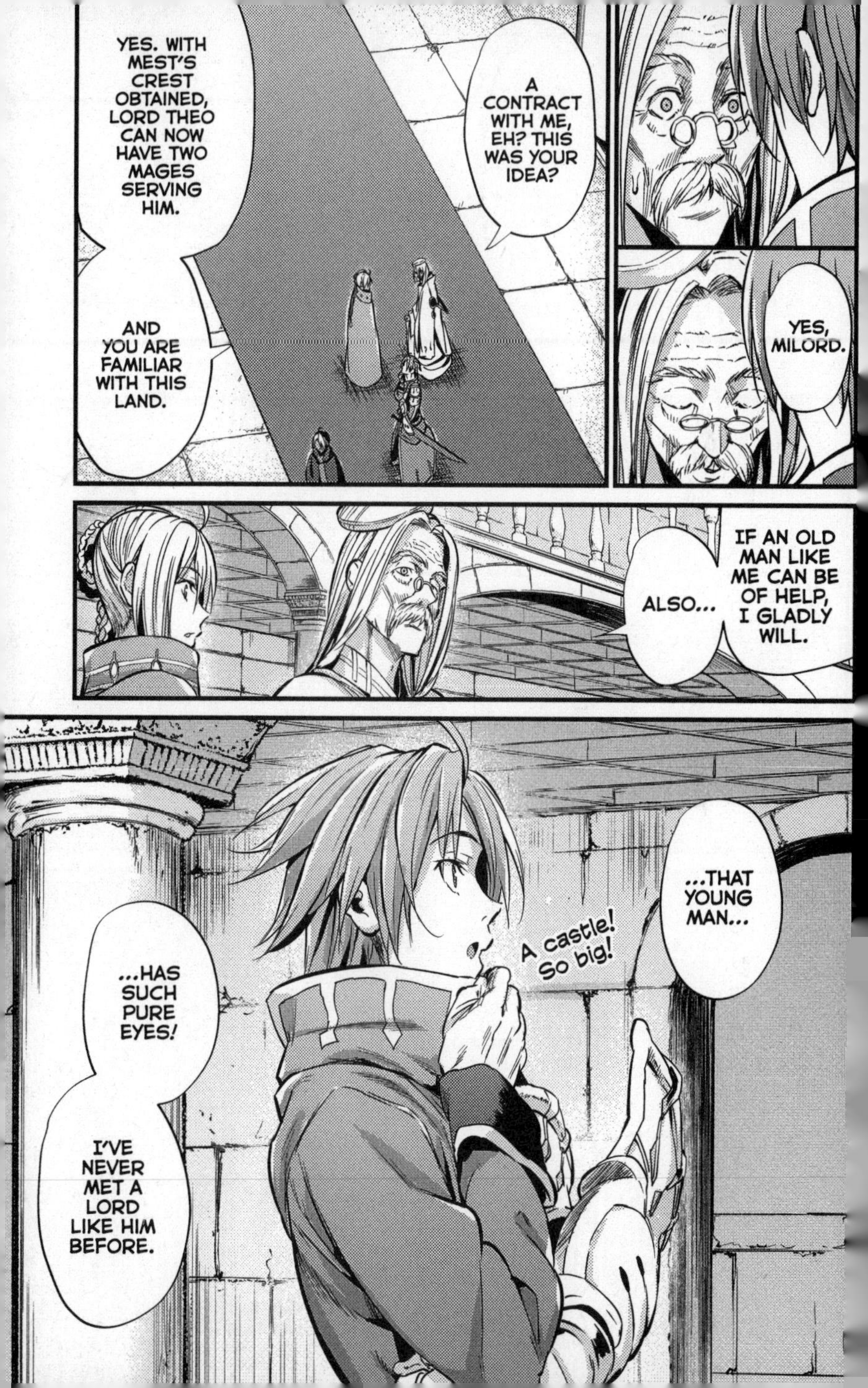
A CONTRACT WITH ME, EH? THIS WAS YOUR IDEA?
YES. WITH MEST'S CREST OBTAINED, LORD THEO CAN NOW HAVE TWO MAGES SERVING HIM.
AND YOU ARE FAMILIAR WITH THIS LAND.
YES, MILORD.
IF AN OLD MAN LIKE ME CAN BE OF HELP, I GLADLY WILL.
ALSO...
...THAT YOUNG MAN...
A castle! So big!
...HAS SUCH PURE EYES!
I'VE NEVER MET A LORD LIKE HIM BEFORE.

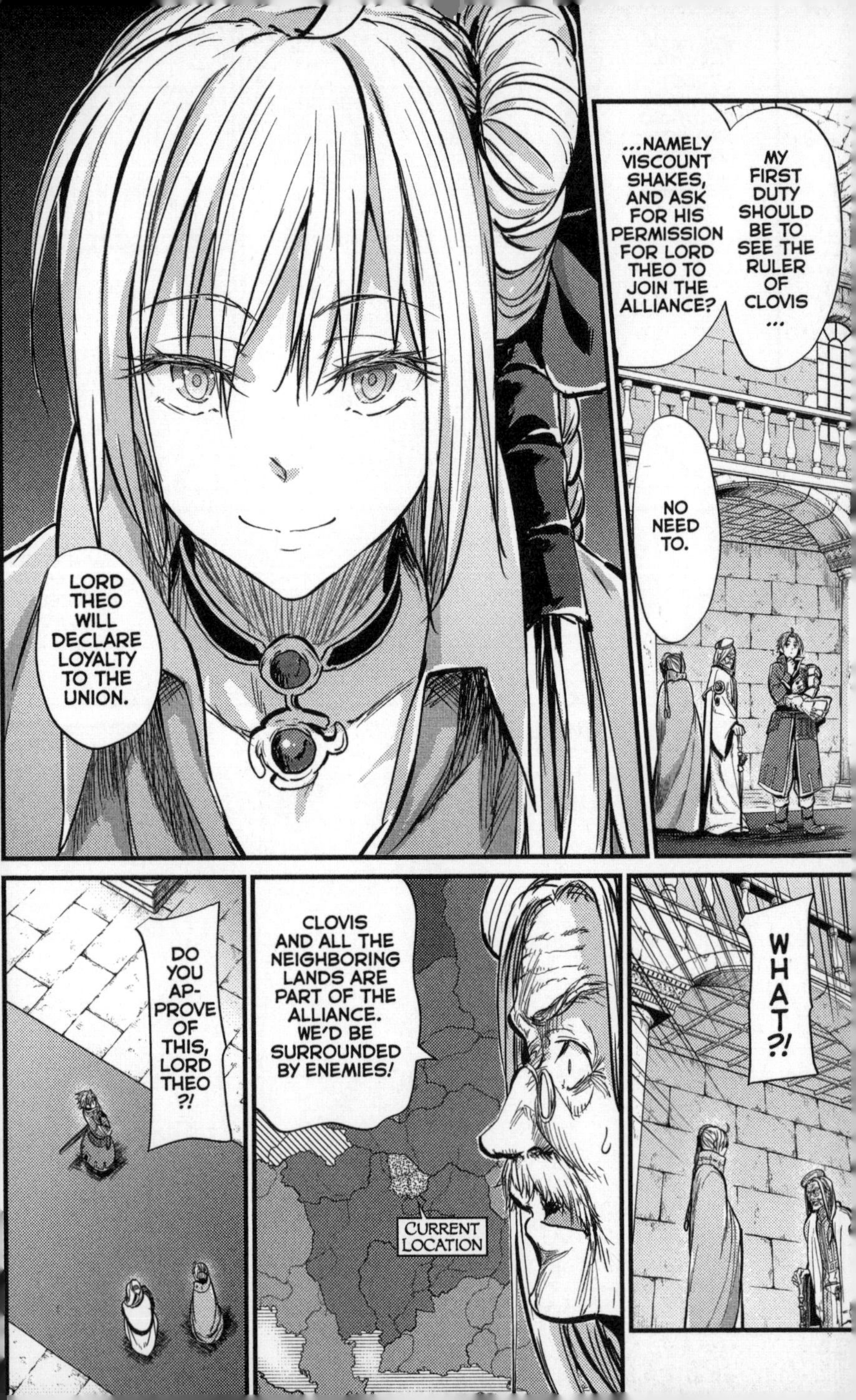
MY FIRST DUTY SHOULD BE TO SEE THE RULER OF CLOVIS ...
...NAMELY VISCOUNT SHAKES, AND ASK FOR HIS PERMISSION FOR LORD THEO TO JOIN THE ALLIANCE?
NO NEED TO.
LORD THEO WILL DECLARE LOYALTY TO THE UNION.
WHAT?!
CLOVIS AND ALL THE NEIGHBORING LANDS ARE PART OF THE ALLIANCE. WE'D BE SURROUNDED BY ENEMIES!
CURRENT LOCATION
DO YOU AP-PROVE OF THIS, LORD THEO?!

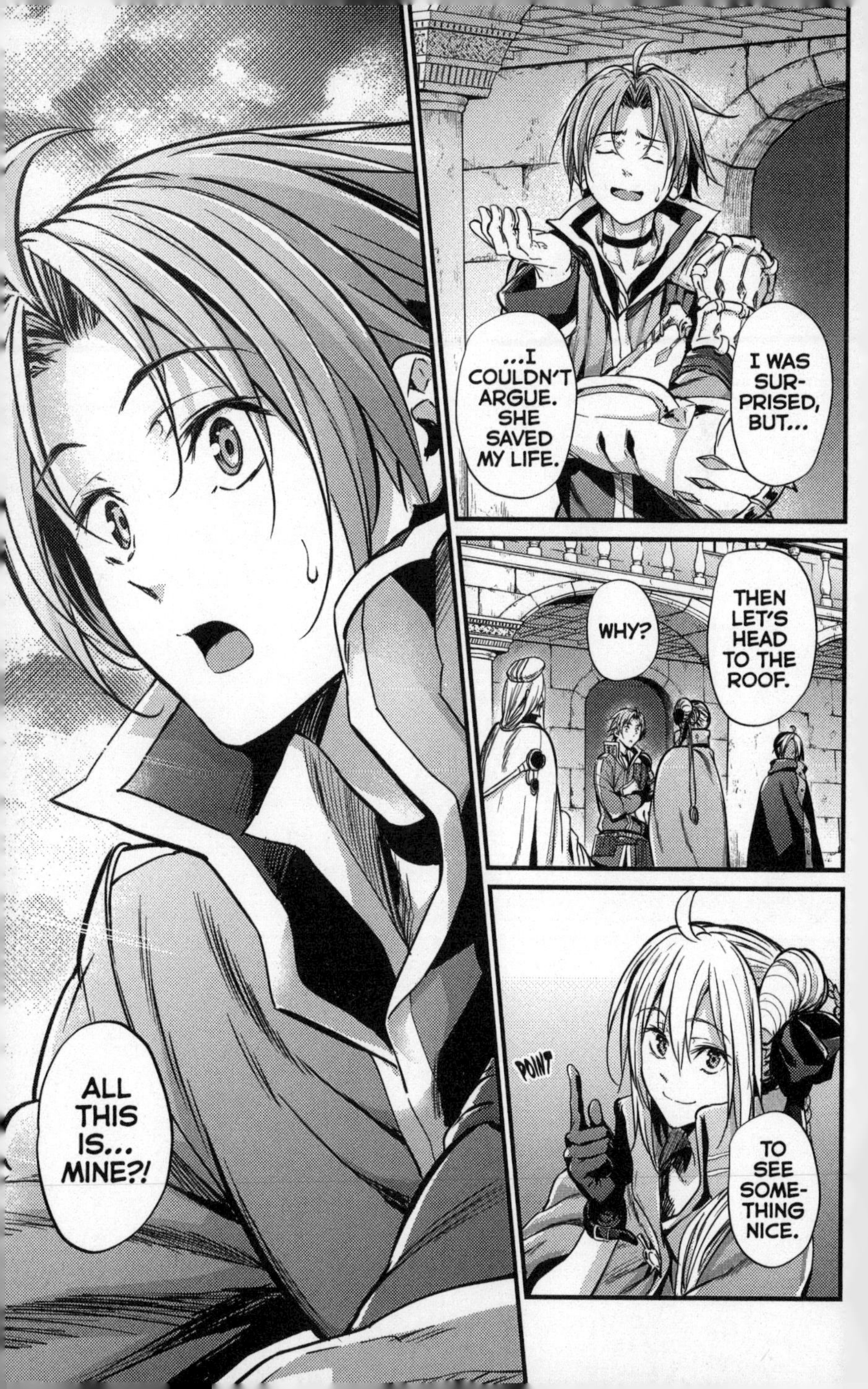
I WAS SURPRISED, BUT...
...I COULDN'T ARGUE. SHE SAVED MY LIFE.
THEN LET'S HEAD TO THE ROOF.
WHY?
POINT
TO SEE SOMETHING NICE.
ALL THIS IS... MINE?!

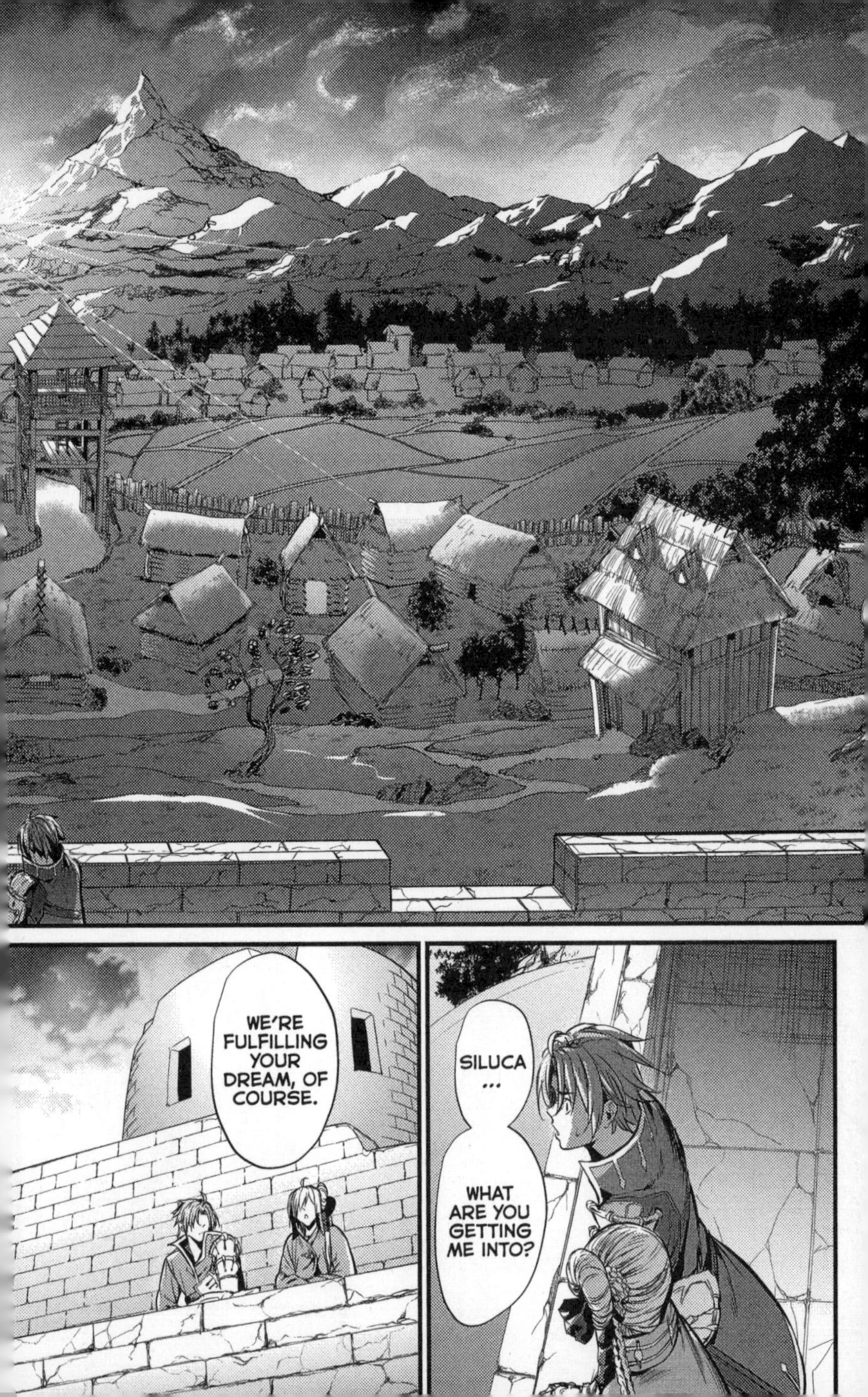
SILUCA...
WHAT ARE YOU GETTING ME INTO?
WE'RE FULFILLING YOUR DREAM, OF COURSE.

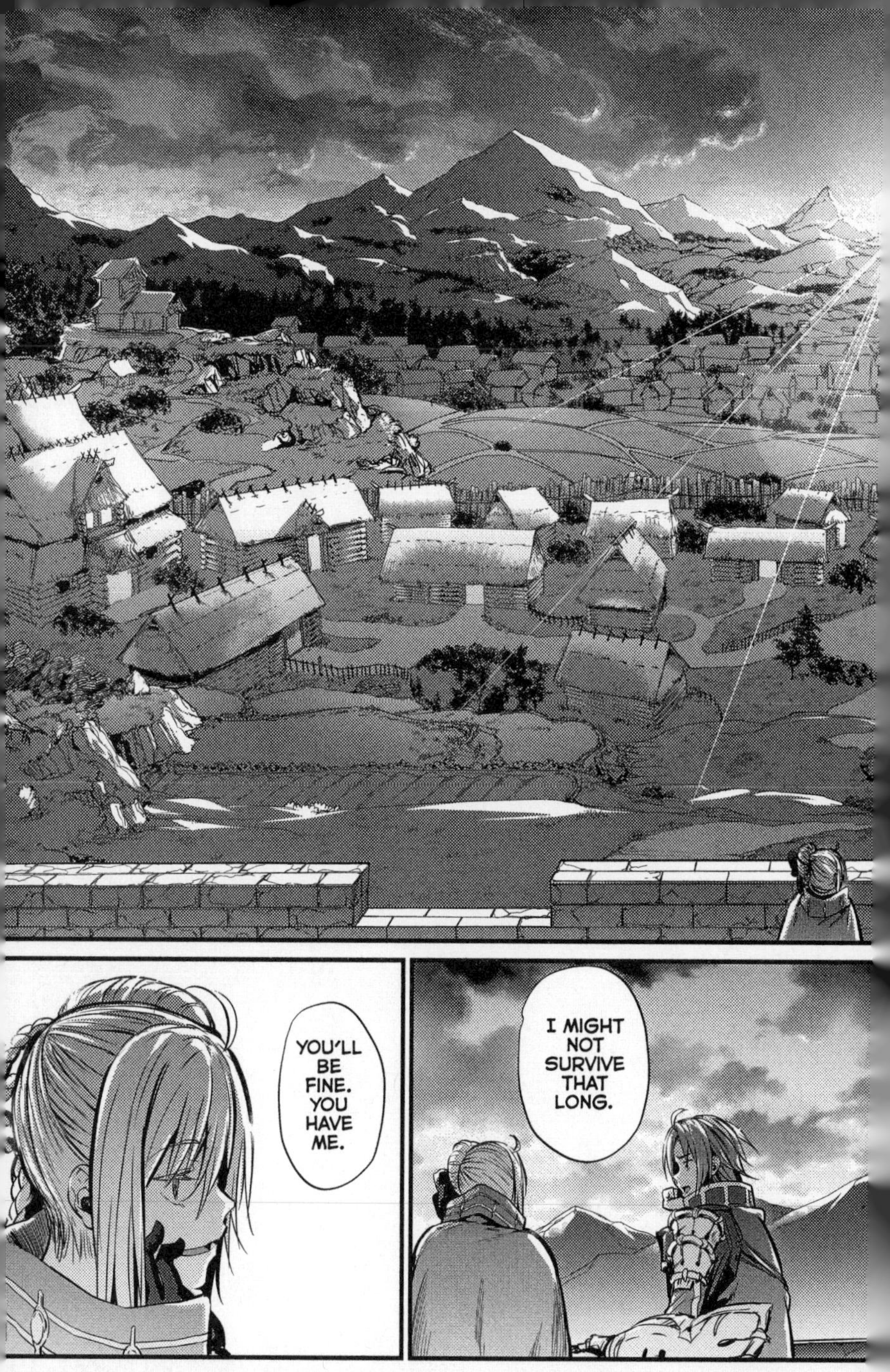
I MIGHT NOT SURVIVE THAT LONG.
YOU'LL BE FINE. YOU HAVE ME.

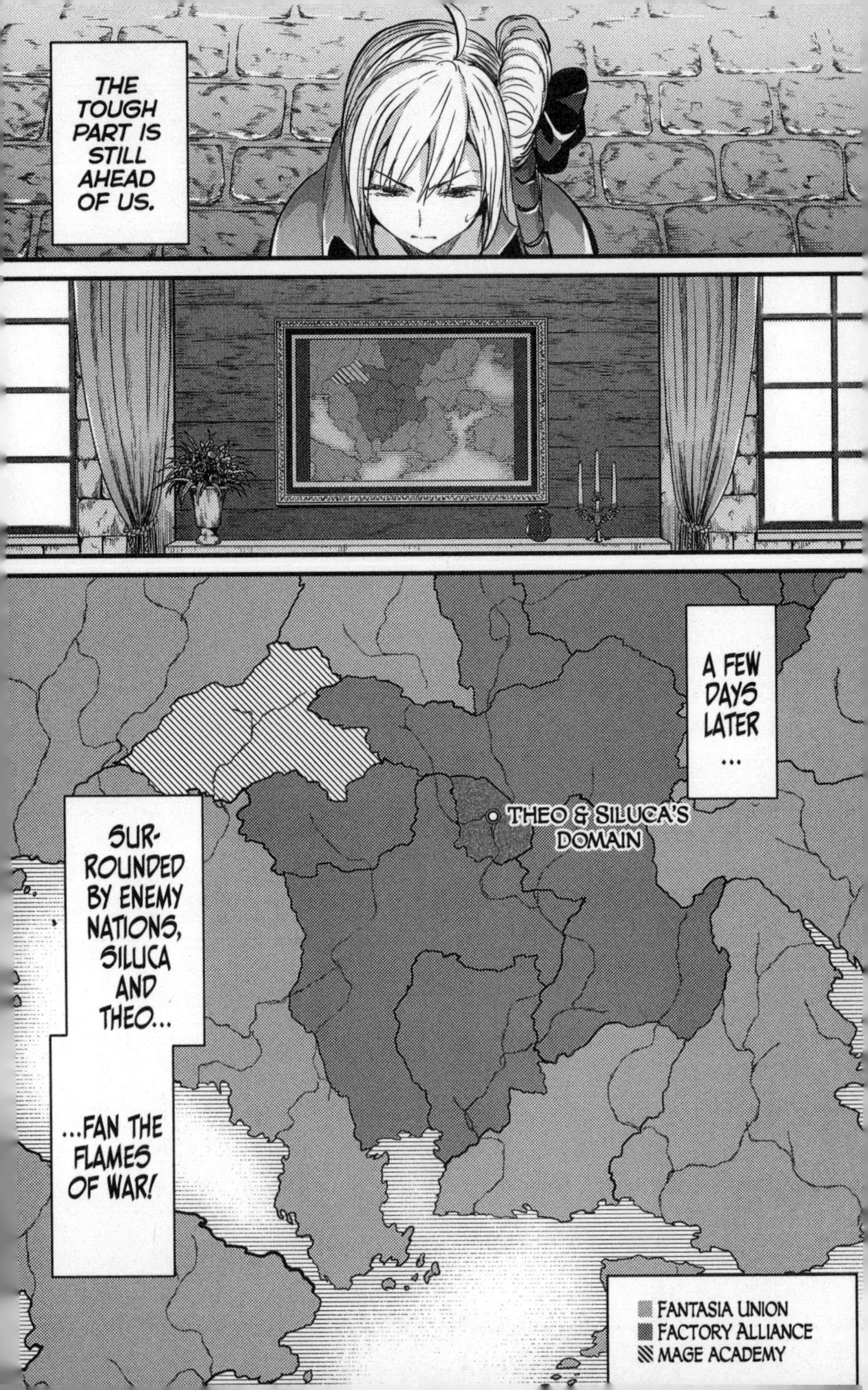
THE TOUGH PART IS STILL AHEAD OF US.
A FEW DAYS LATER...
SUR-ROUNDED BY ENEMY NATIONS, SILUCA AND THEO...
...FAN THE FLAMES OF WAR!
THEO & SILUCA'S DOMAIN
FANTASIA UNION
FACTORY ALLIANCE
MAGE ACADEMY

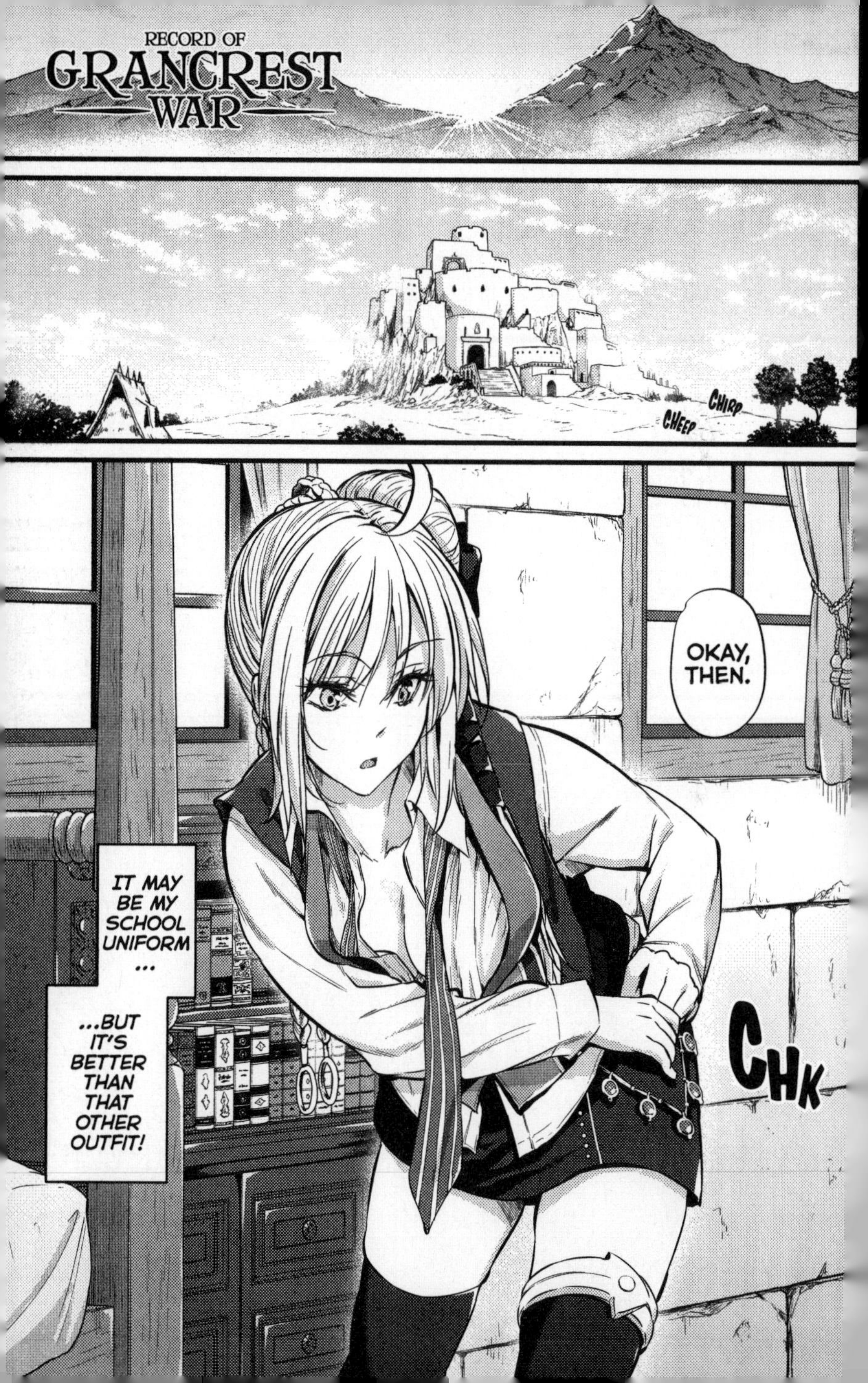

RECORD OF GRANCREST WAR
CHIRP
CHEEP
OKAY, THEN.
IT MAY BE MY SCHOOL UNIFORM...
...BUT IT'S BETTER THAN THAT OTHER OUTFIT!
CHK

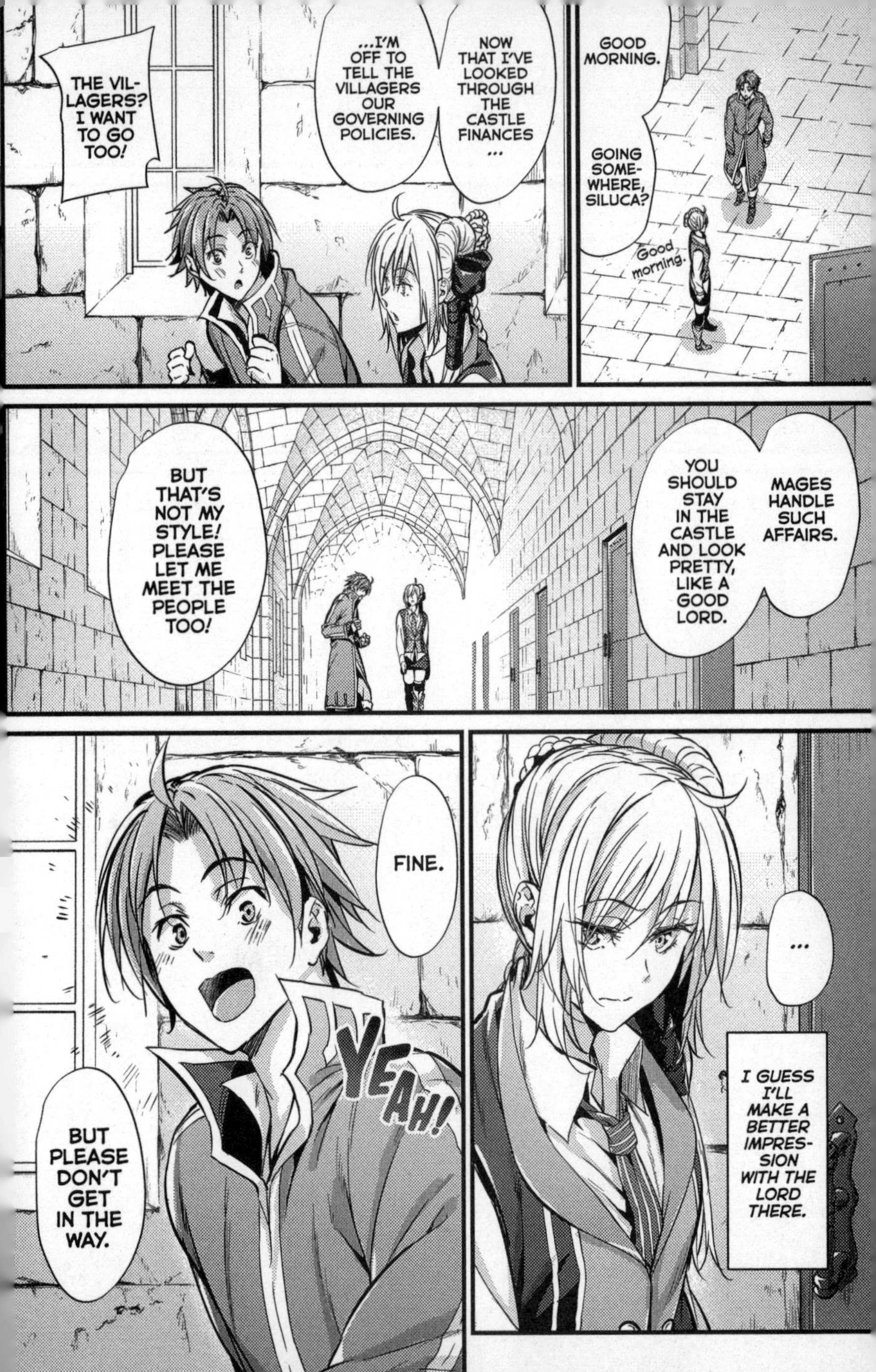
GOOD MORNING.
GOING SOMEWHERE, SILUCA?
Good morning.
NOW THAT I'VE LOOKED THROUGH THE CASTLE FINANCES...
...I'M OFF TO TELL THE VILLAGERS OUR GOVERNING POLICIES.
THE VILLAGERS? I WANT TO GO TOO!
MAGES HANDLE SUCH AFFAIRS.
YOU SHOULD STAY IN THE CASTLE AND LOOK PRETTY, LIKE A GOOD LORD.
BUT THAT'S NOT MY STYLE! PLEASE LET ME MEET THE PEOPLE TOO!
...
I GUESS I'LL MAKE A BETTER IMPRESSION WITH THE LORD THERE.
FINE.
YEAH!
BUT PLEASE DON'T GET IN THE WAY.

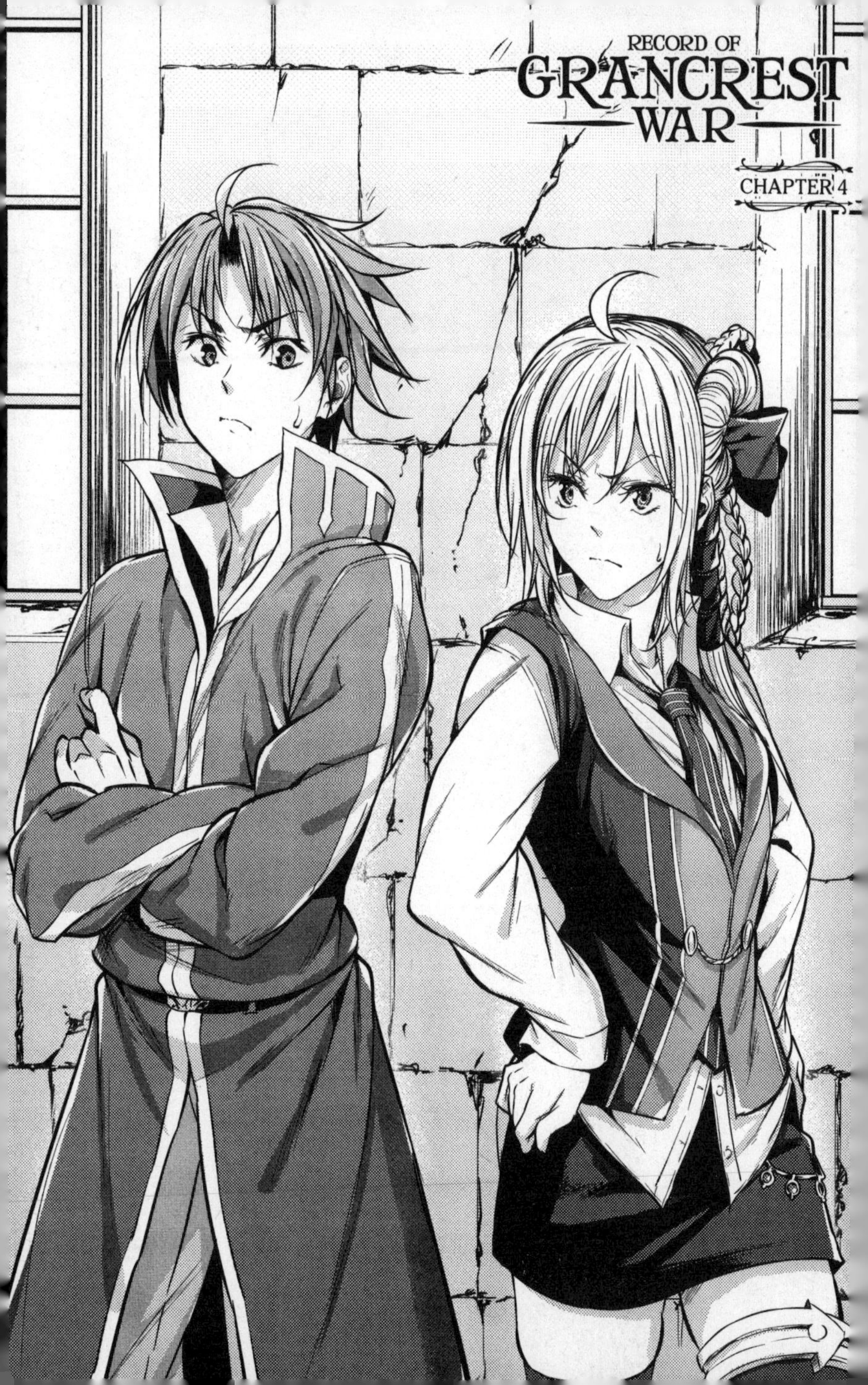
RECORD OF
GRANCREST
WAR
CHAPTER 4

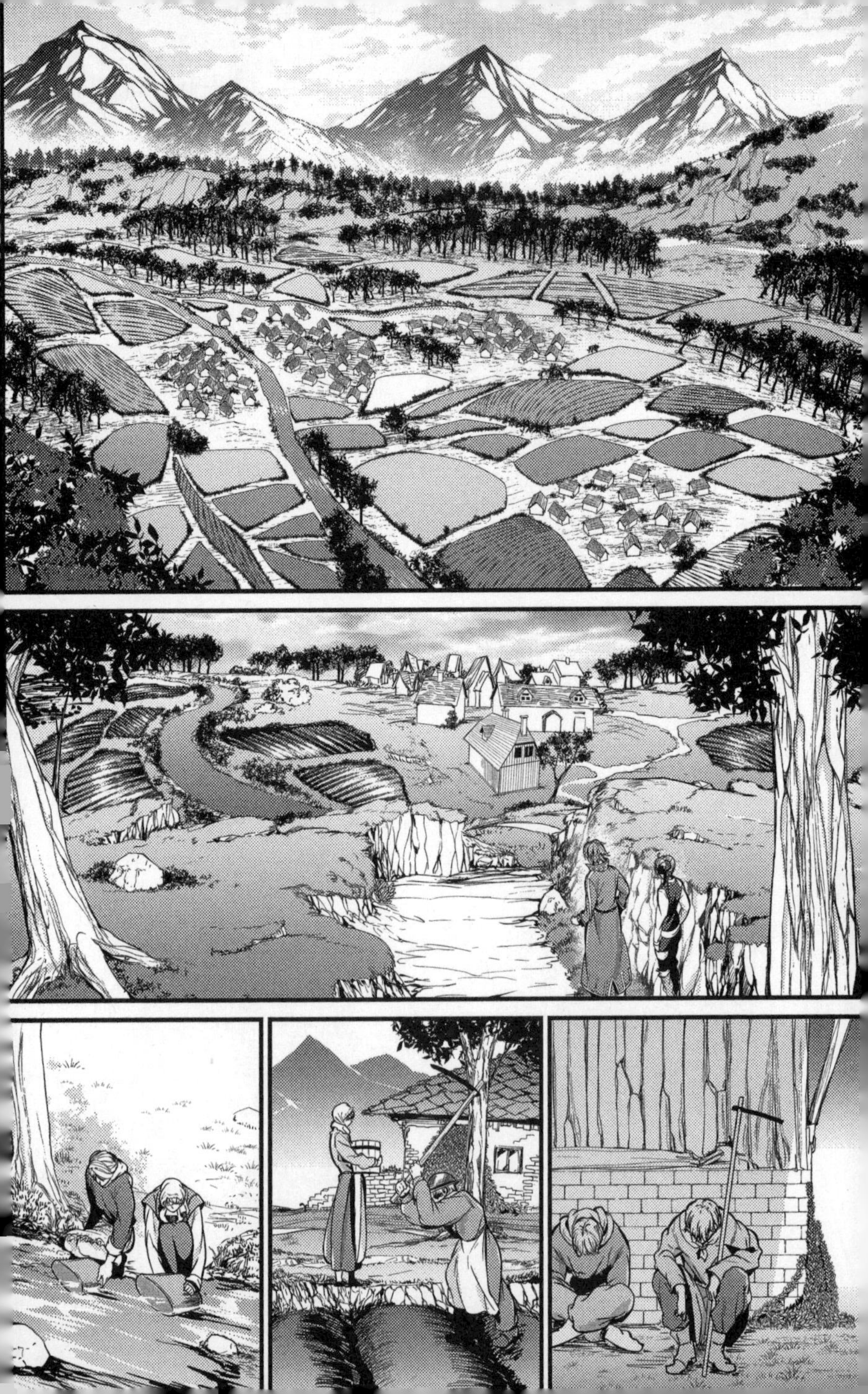

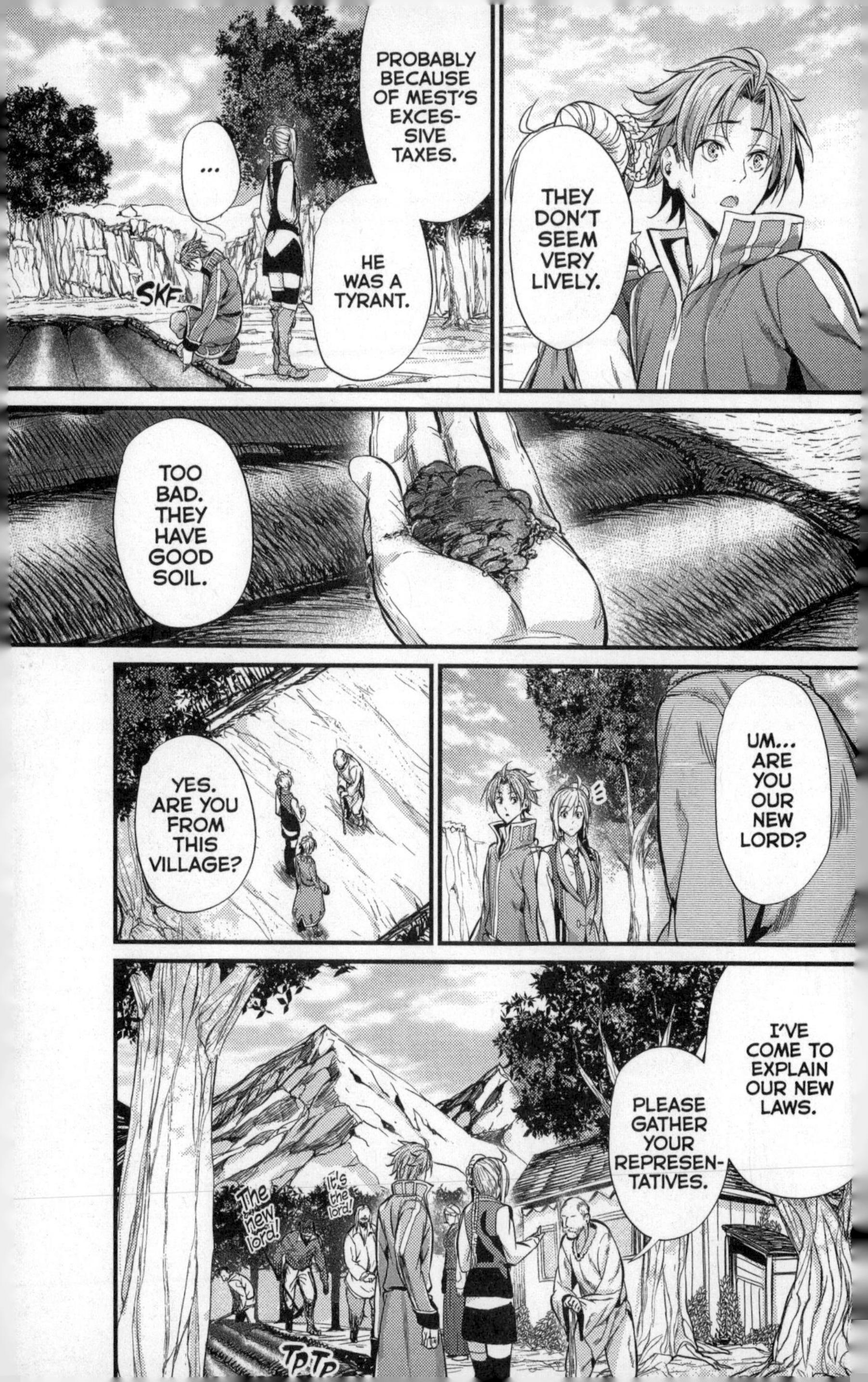
THEY DON'T SEEM VERY LIVELY.
PROBABLY BECAUSE OF MEST'S EXCES-SIVE TAXES.
HE WAS A TYRANT.
...
SKF
TOO BAD. THEY HAVE GOOD SOIL.
UM... ARE YOU OUR NEW LORD?
YES. ARE YOU FROM THIS VILLAGE?
I'VE COME TO EXPLAIN OUR NEW LAWS.
PLEASE GATHER YOUR REPRESEN-TATIVES.
It's the lord!
The new lord!
TP TP

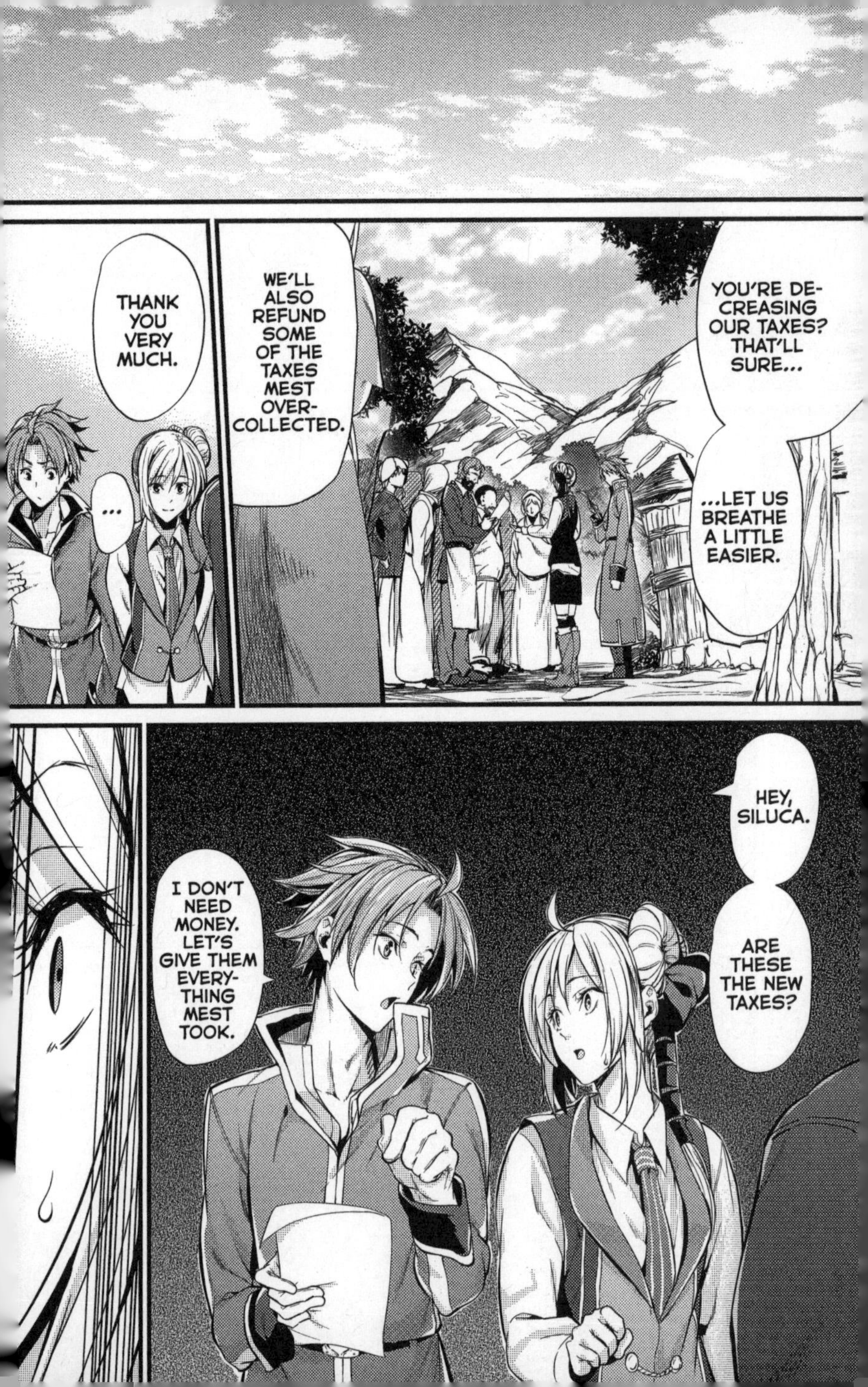
YOU'RE DE-CREASING OUR TAXES? THAT'LL SURE...
...LET US BREATHE A LITTLE EASIER.
WE'LL ALSO REFUND SOME OF THE TAXES MEST OVER-COLLECTED.
THANK YOU VERY MUCH.
...
HEY, SILUCA.
ARE THESE THE NEW TAXES?
I DON'T NEED MONEY. LET'S GIVE THEM EVERY-THING MEST TOOK.

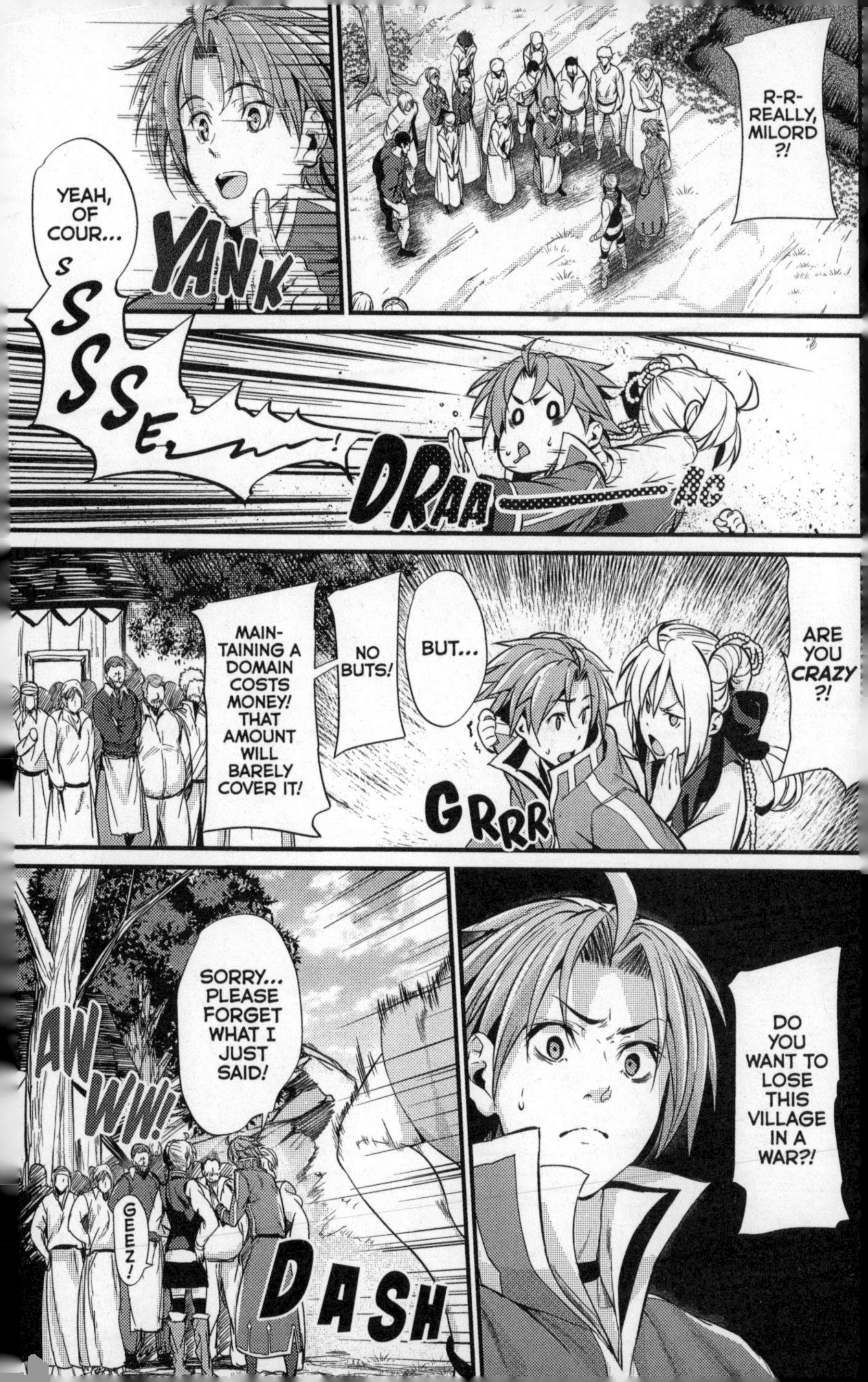
R-R-REALLY, MILORD?!
YEAH, OF COUR...
YANK
sSSSE—!
DRAA—AG
ARE YOU CRAZY?!
GRRR
BUT...
NO BUTS!
MAIN-TAINING A DOMAIN COSTS MONEY! THAT AMOUNT WILL BARELY COVER IT!
DO YOU WANT TO LOSE THIS VILLAGE IN A WAR?!
SORRY... PLEASE FORGET WHAT I JUST SAID!
AWWW!
GEEZ!
DASH

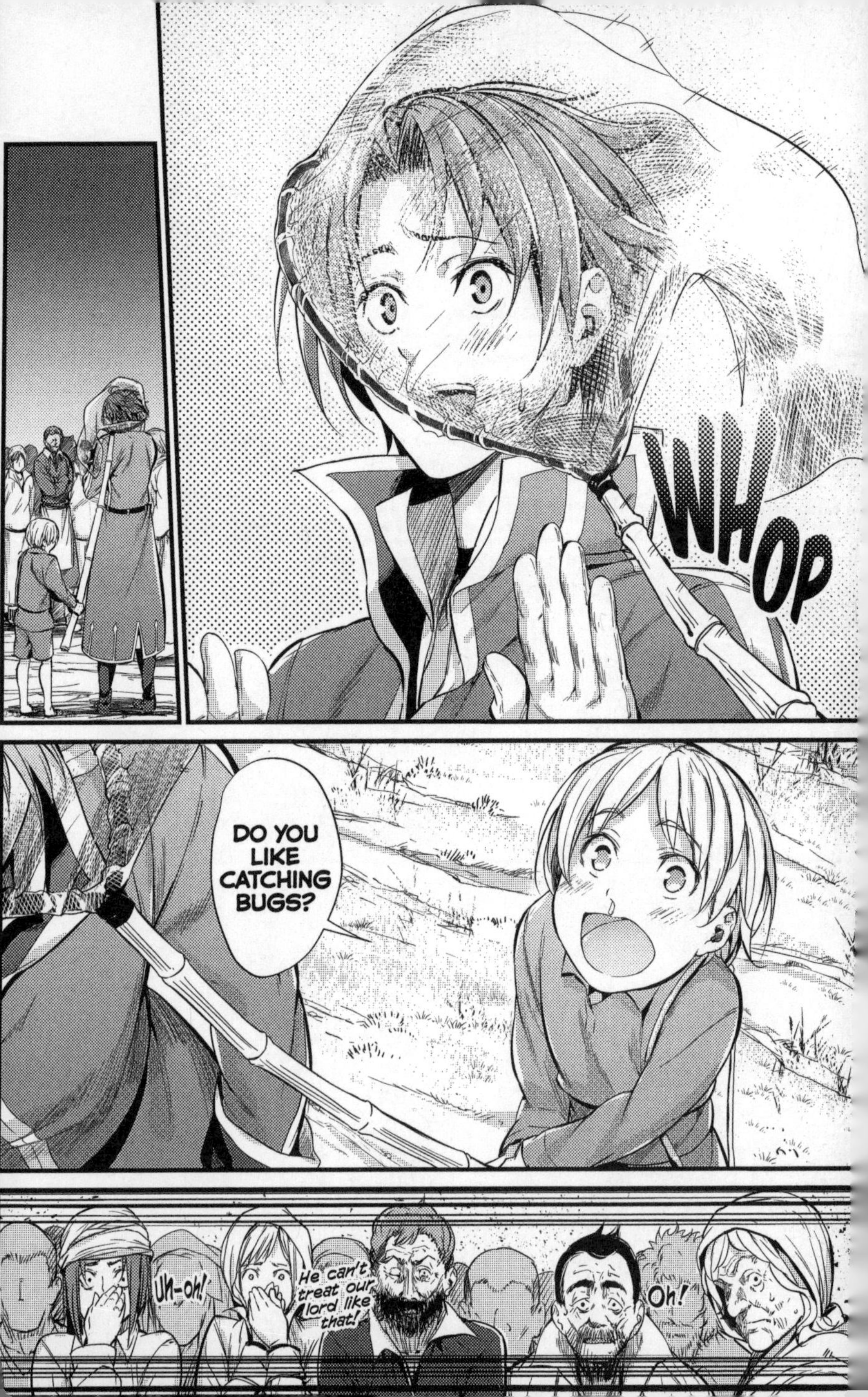
WHOP
DO YOU LIKE CATCHING BUGS?
Oh!
He can't treat our lord like that!
Uh-oh!

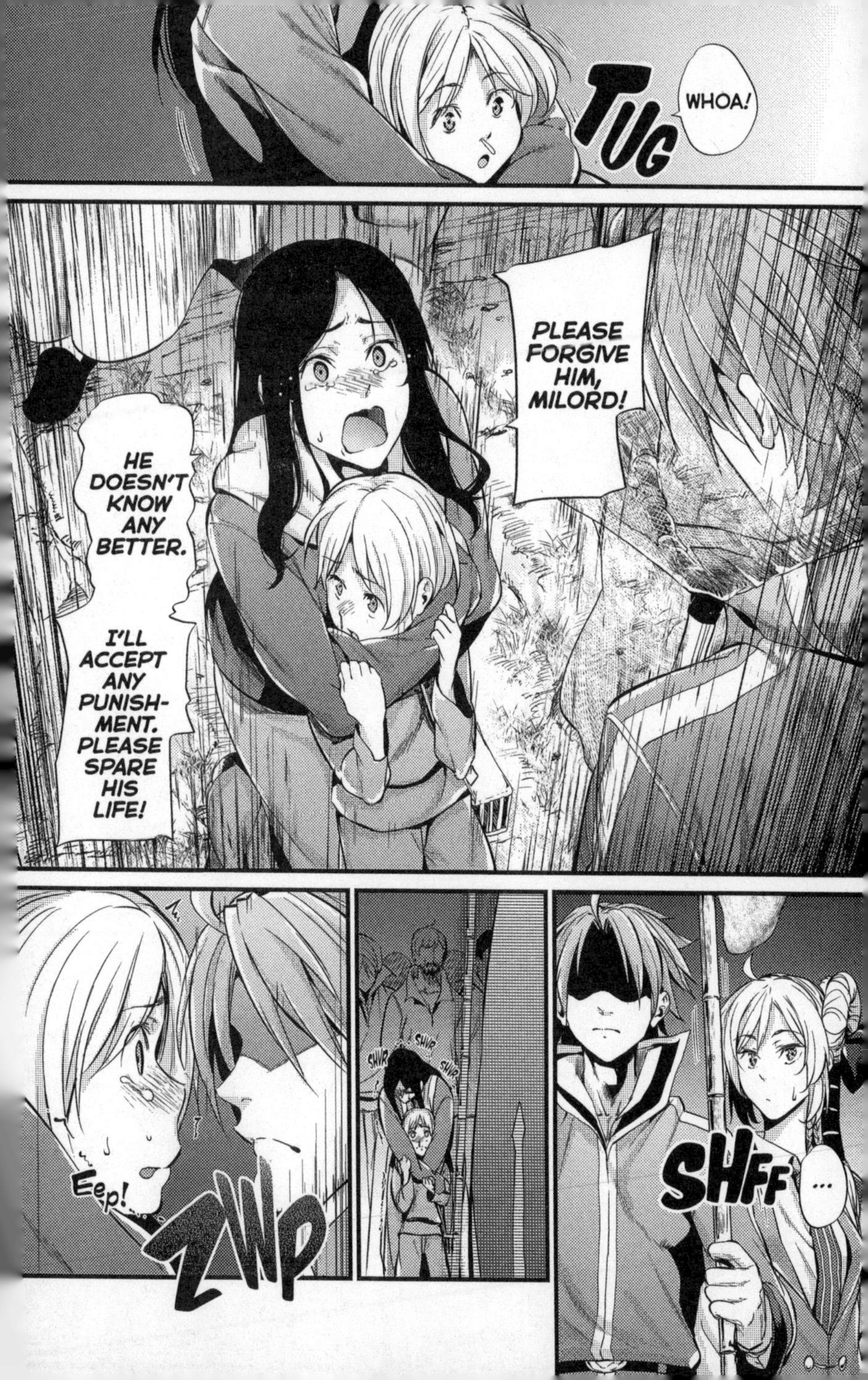
TUG
WHOA!
PLEASE FORGIVE HIM, MILORD!
HE DOESN'T KNOW ANY BETTER.
I'LL ACCEPT ANY PUNISHMENT. PLEASE SPARE HIS LIFE!
SHFF
...
SHVR
SHVR
SHVR
Eep!
ZWP

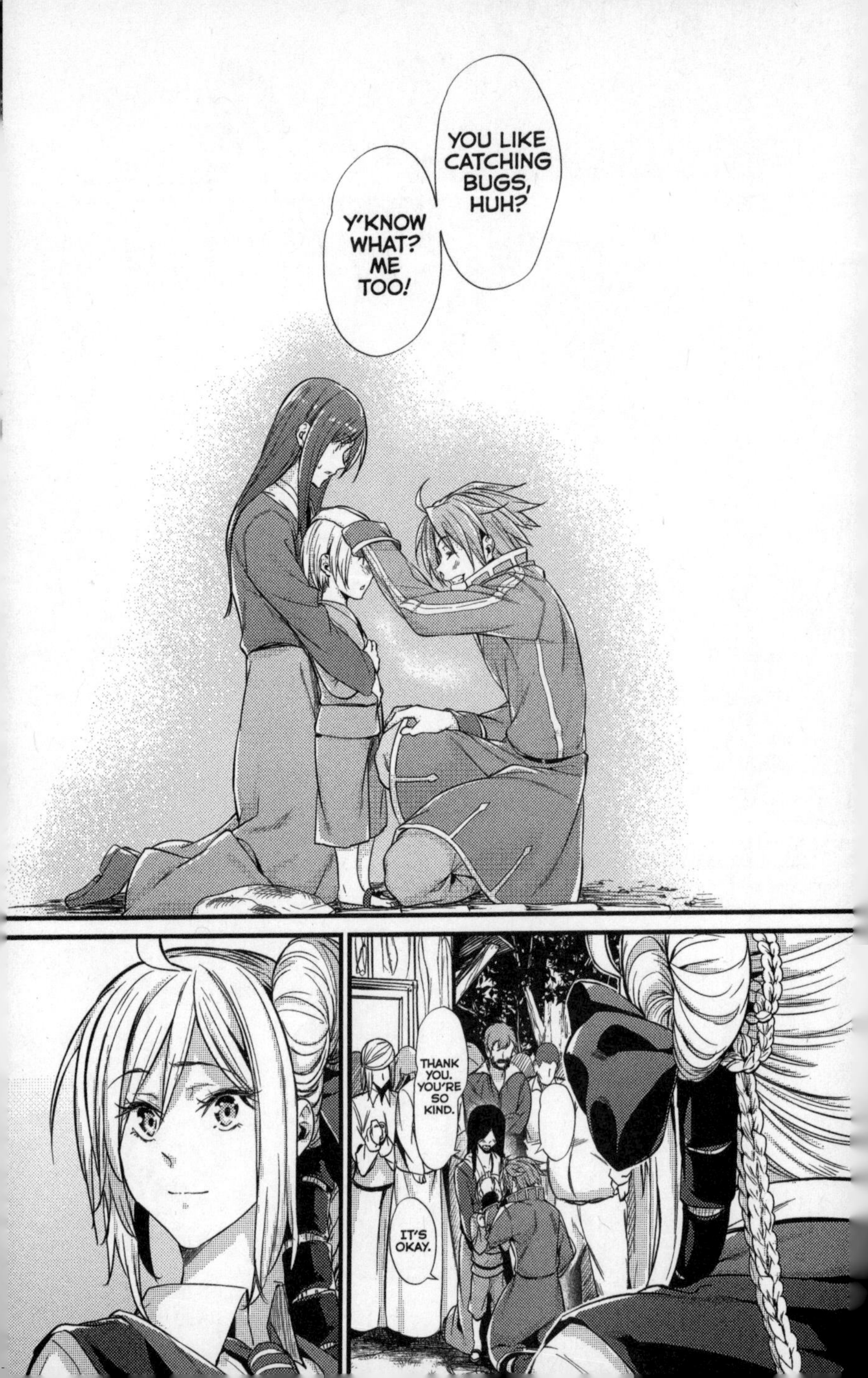
YOU LIKE CATCHING BUGS, HUH?
Y'KNOW WHAT? ME TOO!
THANK YOU. YOU'RE SO KIND.
IT'S OKAY.

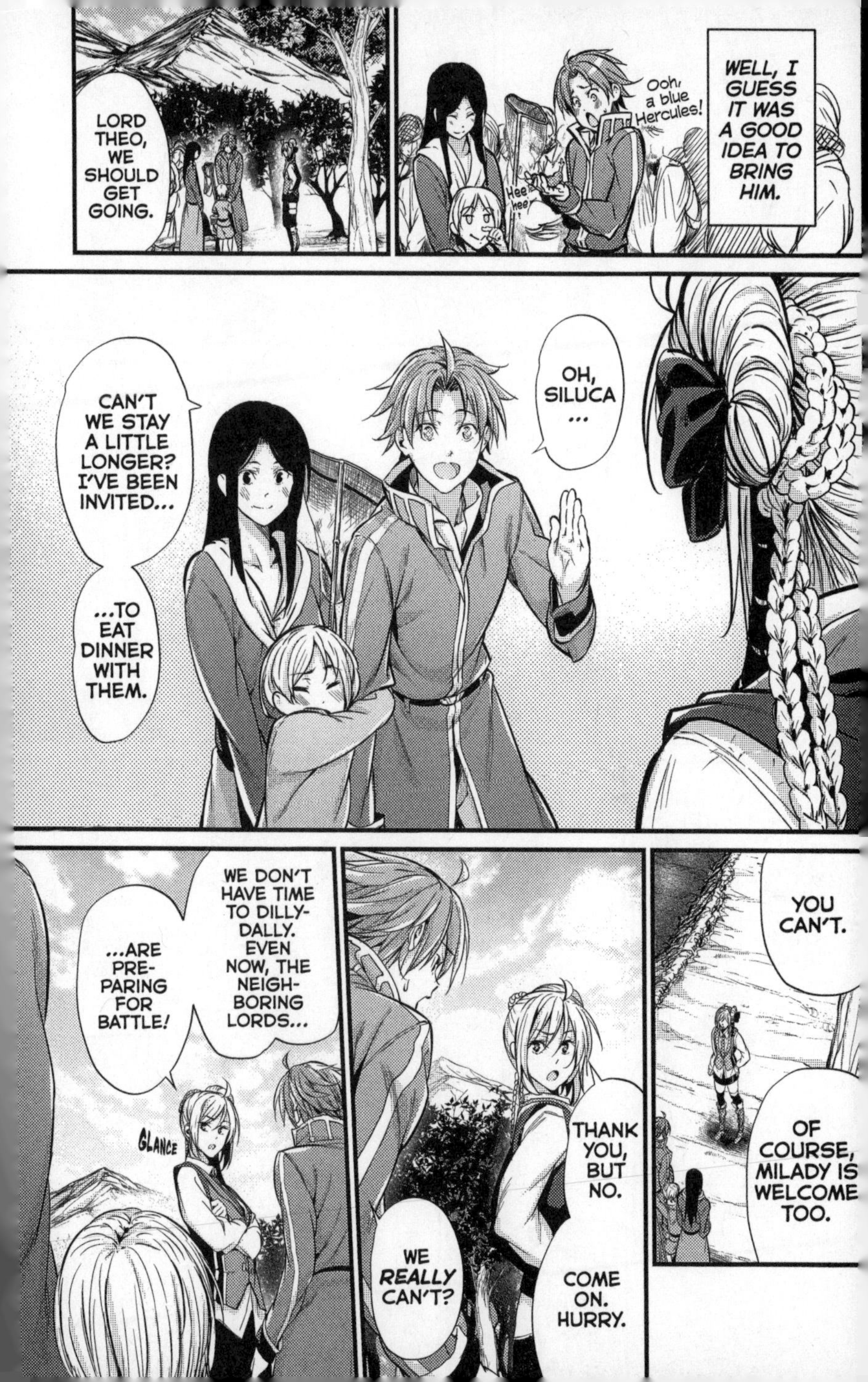
WELL, I GUESS IT WAS A GOOD IDEA TO BRING HIM.
Ooh, a blue Hercules!
Hee hee!
LORD THEO, WE SHOULD GET GOING.
OH, SILUCA...
CAN'T WE STAY A LITTLE LONGER? I'VE BEEN INVITED...
...TO EAT DINNER WITH THEM.
YOU CAN'T.
OF COURSE, MILADY IS WELCOME TOO.
THANK YOU, BUT NO.
WE REALLY CAN'T?
COME ON. HURRY.
WE DON'T HAVE TIME TO DILLY-DALLY. EVEN NOW, THE NEIGHBORING LORDS...
...ARE PREPARING FOR BATTLE!
GLANCE

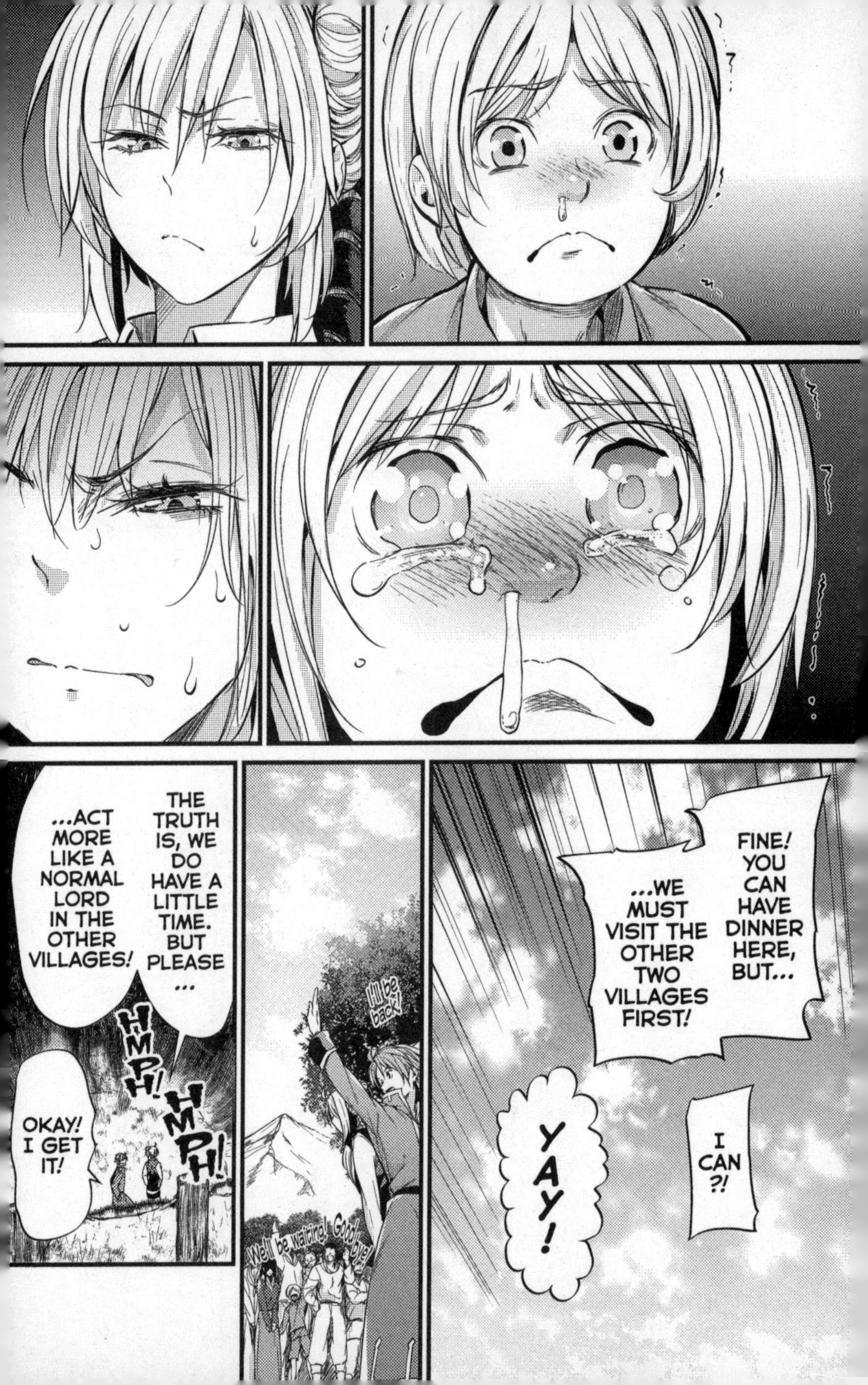
FINE! YOU CAN HAVE DINNER HERE, BUT...
...WE MUST VISIT THE OTHER TWO VILLAGES FIRST!
I CAN ?!
YAY!
I'll be back!
We'll be waiting! Good-bye!
THE TRUTH IS, WE DO HAVE A LITTLE TIME. BUT PLEASE...
...ACT MORE LIKE A NORMAL LORD IN THE OTHER VILLAGES!
HMPH! HMPH!
OKAY! I GET IT!

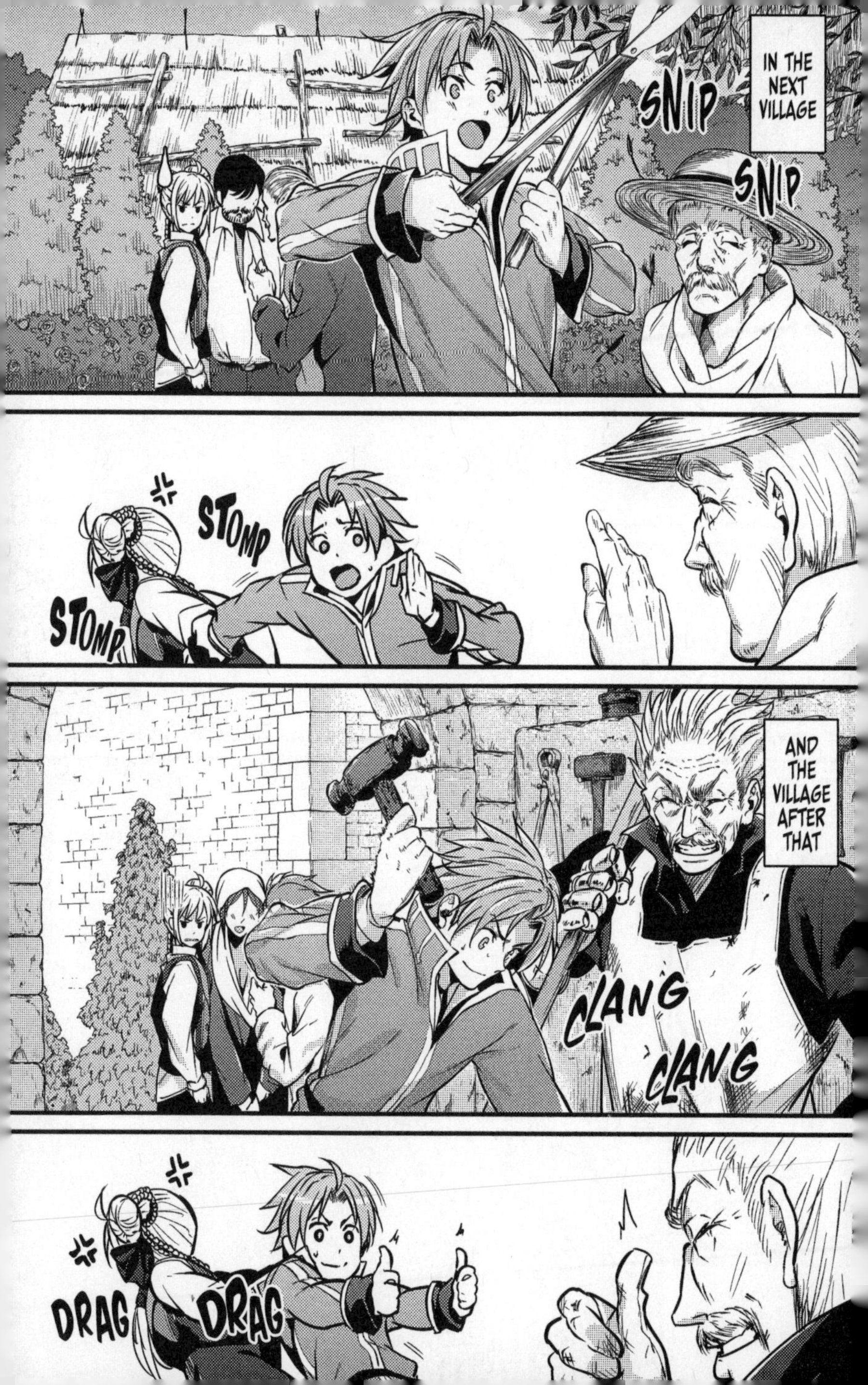
IN THE NEXT VILLAGE
SNIP
SNIP
STOMP
STOMP
AND THE VILLAGE AFTER THAT
CLANG
CLANG
DRAG
DRAG

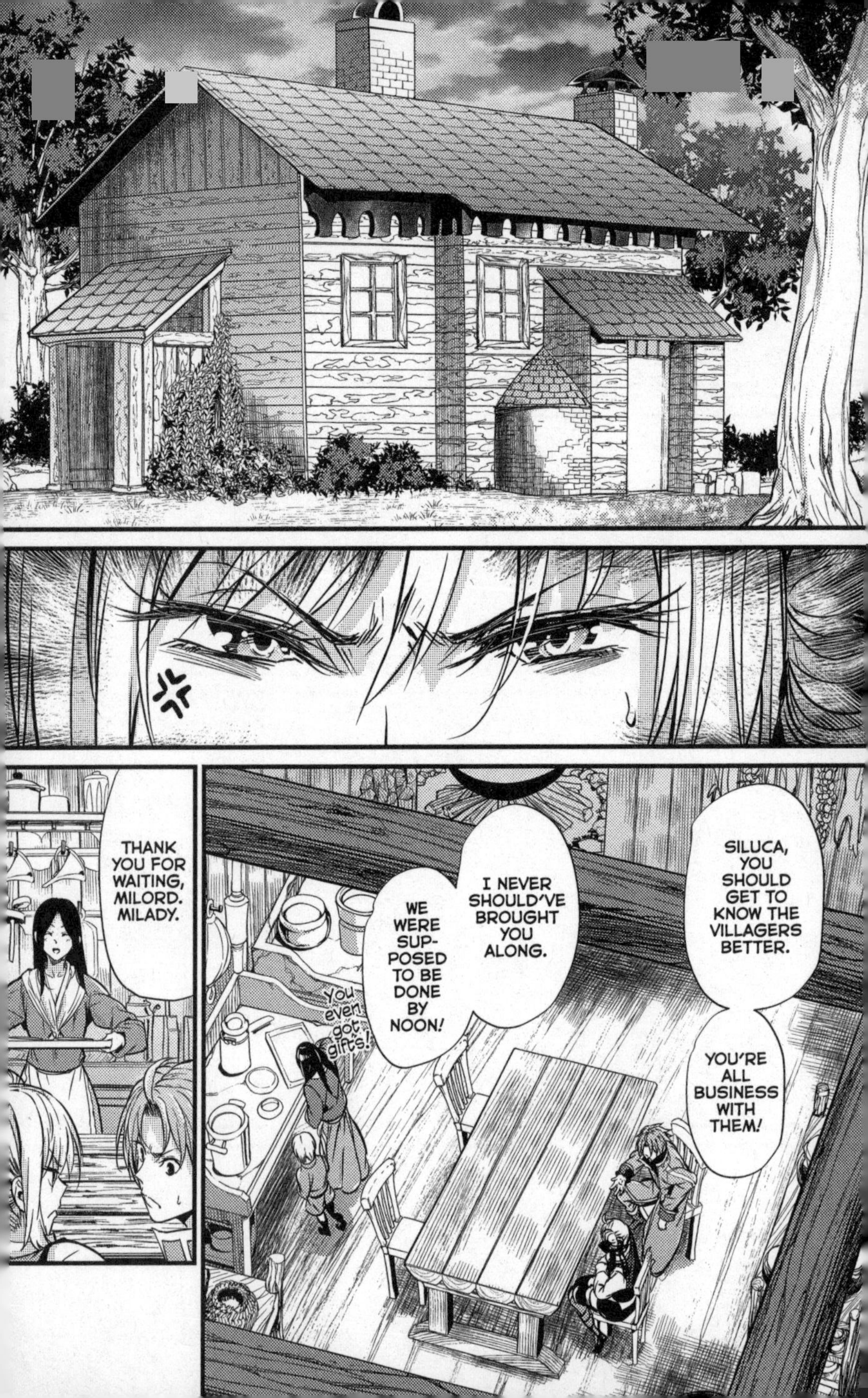
SILUCA, YOU SHOULD GET TO KNOW THE VILLAGERS BETTER.
YOU'RE ALL BUSINESS WITH THEM!
I NEVER SHOULD'VE BROUGHT YOU ALONG.
WE WERE SUP-POSED TO BE DONE BY NOON!
You even got gifts!
THANK YOU FOR WAITING, MILORD. MILADY.

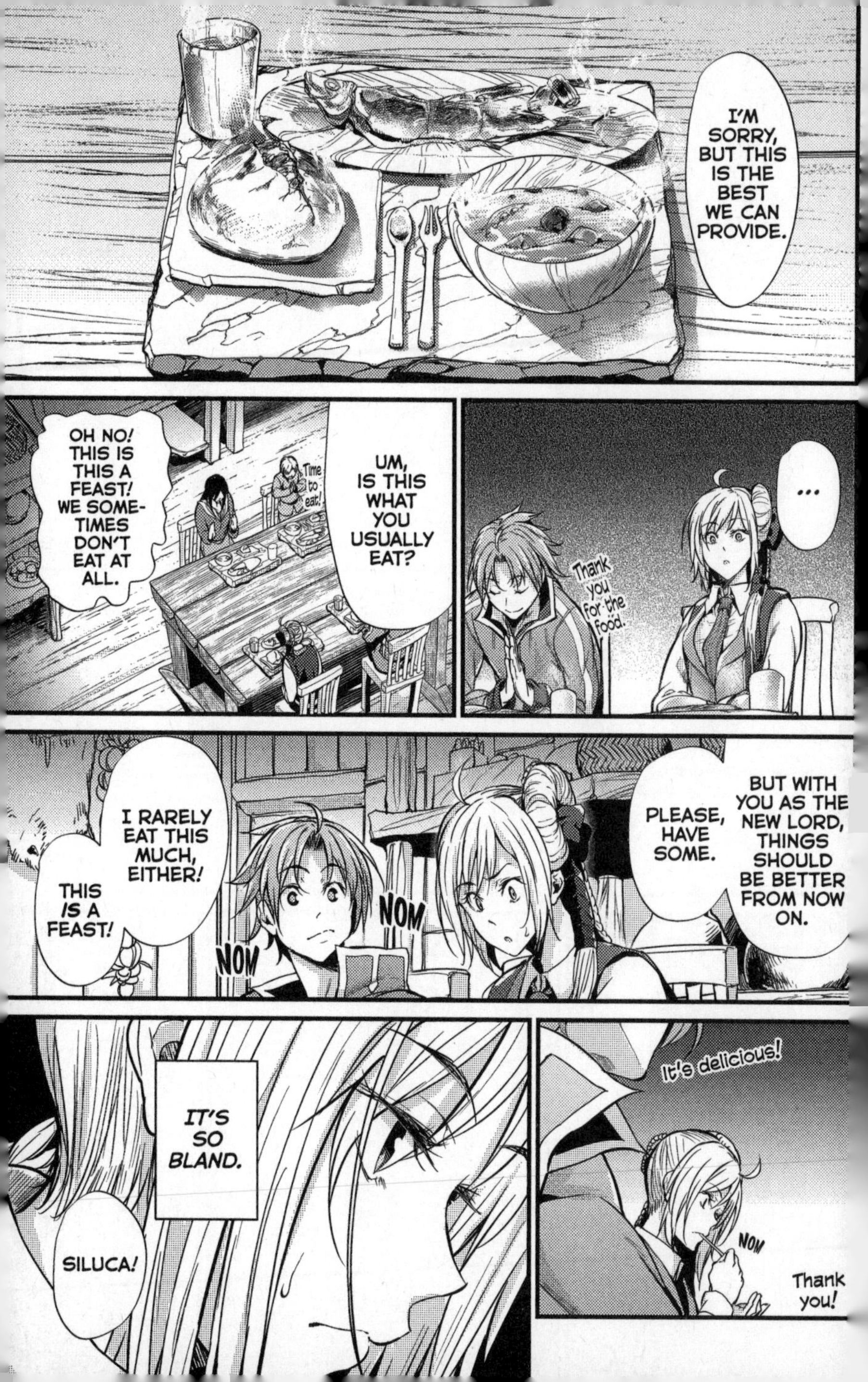
I'M SORRY, BUT THIS IS THE BEST WE CAN PROVIDE.
...
Thank you for the food.
UM, IS THIS WHAT YOU USUALLY EAT?
Time to eat!
OH NO! THIS IS THIS A FEAST! WE SOME-TIMES DON'T EAT AT ALL.
BUT WITH YOU AS THE NEW LORD, THINGS SHOULD BE BETTER FROM NOW ON.
PLEASE, HAVE SOME.
NOM
NOM
I RARELY EAT THIS MUCH, EITHER!
THIS *IS* A FEAST!
It's delicious!
NOM
Thank you!
IT'S SO BLAND.
SILUCA!

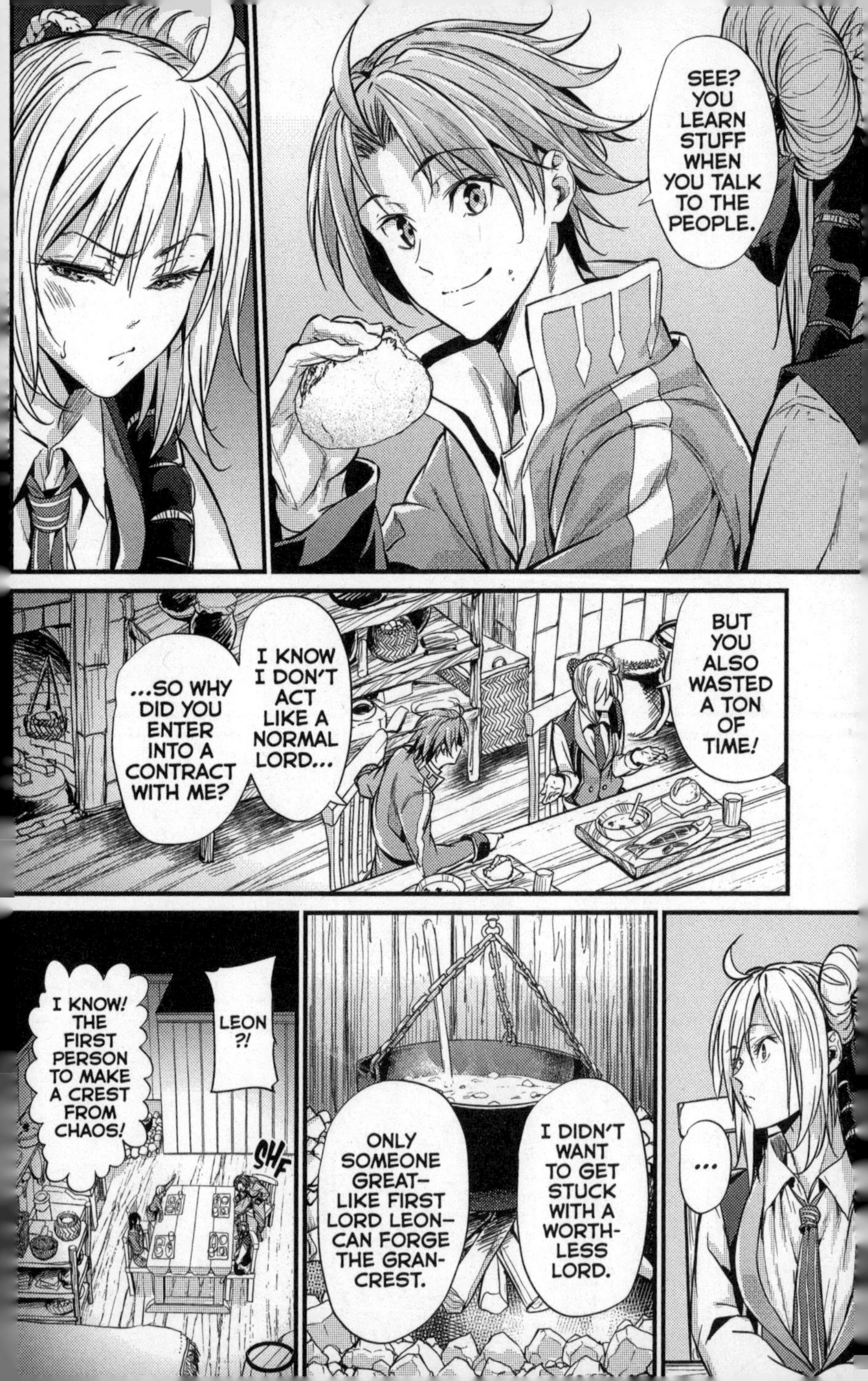
SEE? YOU LEARN STUFF WHEN YOU TALK TO THE PEOPLE.
BUT YOU ALSO WASTED A TON OF TIME!
I KNOW I DON'T ACT LIKE A NORMAL LORD...
...SO WHY DID YOU ENTER INTO A CONTRACT WITH ME?
...
I DIDN'T WANT TO GET STUCK WITH A WORTHLESS LORD.
ONLY SOMEONE GREAT—LIKE FIRST LORD LEON—CAN FORGE THE GRANCREST.
LEON?!
I KNOW! THE FIRST PERSON TO MAKE A CREST FROM CHAOS!
SHF

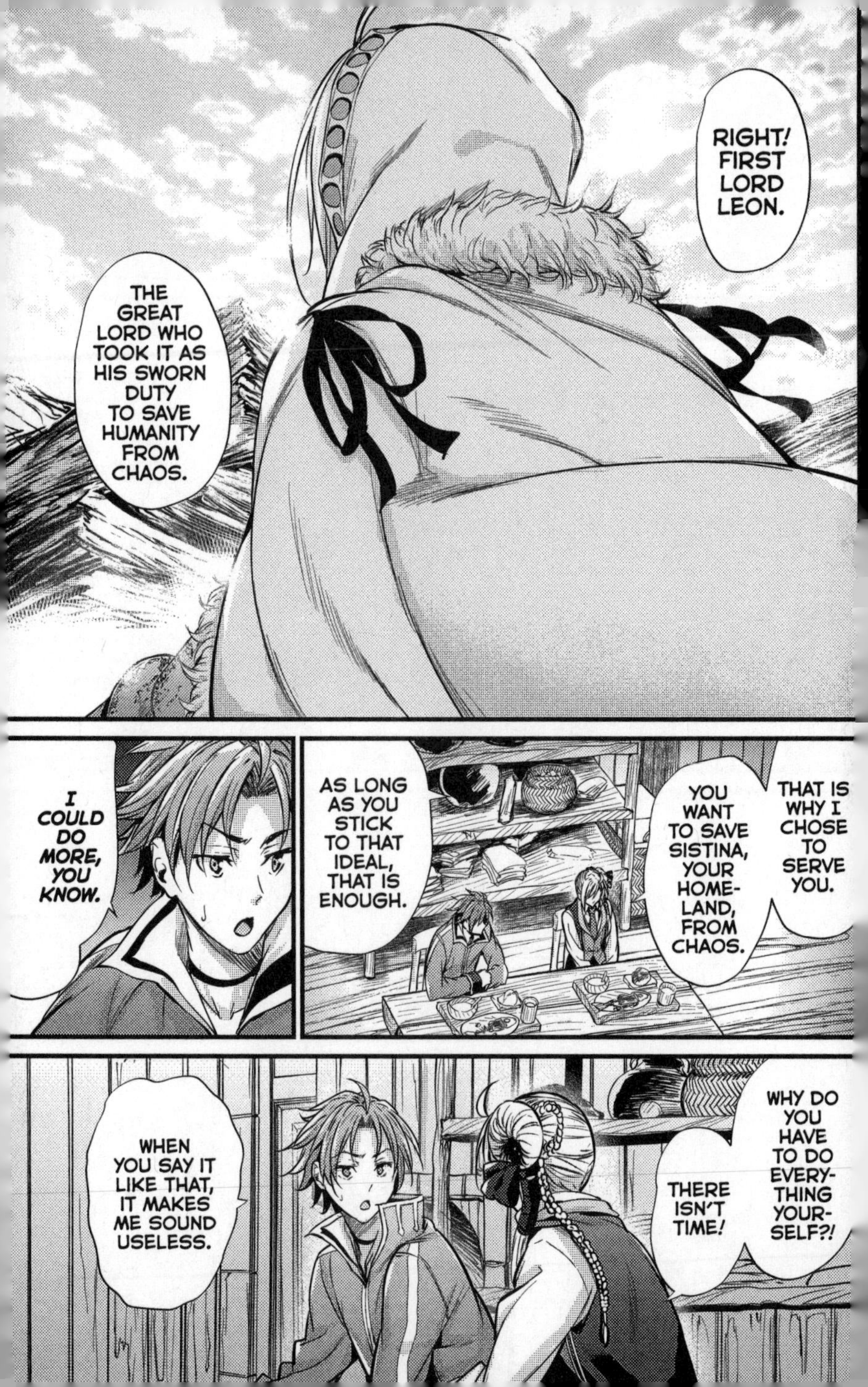

RIGHT! FIRST LORD LEON.
THE GREAT LORD WHO TOOK IT AS HIS SWORN DUTY TO SAVE HUMANITY FROM CHAOS.
THAT IS WHY I CHOSE TO SERVE YOU.
YOU WANT TO SAVE SISTINA, YOUR HOME-LAND, FROM CHAOS.
AS LONG AS YOU STICK TO THAT IDEAL, THAT IS ENOUGH.
I COULD DO MORE, YOU KNOW.
WHY DO YOU HAVE TO DO EVERY-THING YOUR-SELF?!
THERE ISN'T TIME!
WHEN YOU SAY IT LIKE THAT, IT MAKES ME SOUND USELESS.

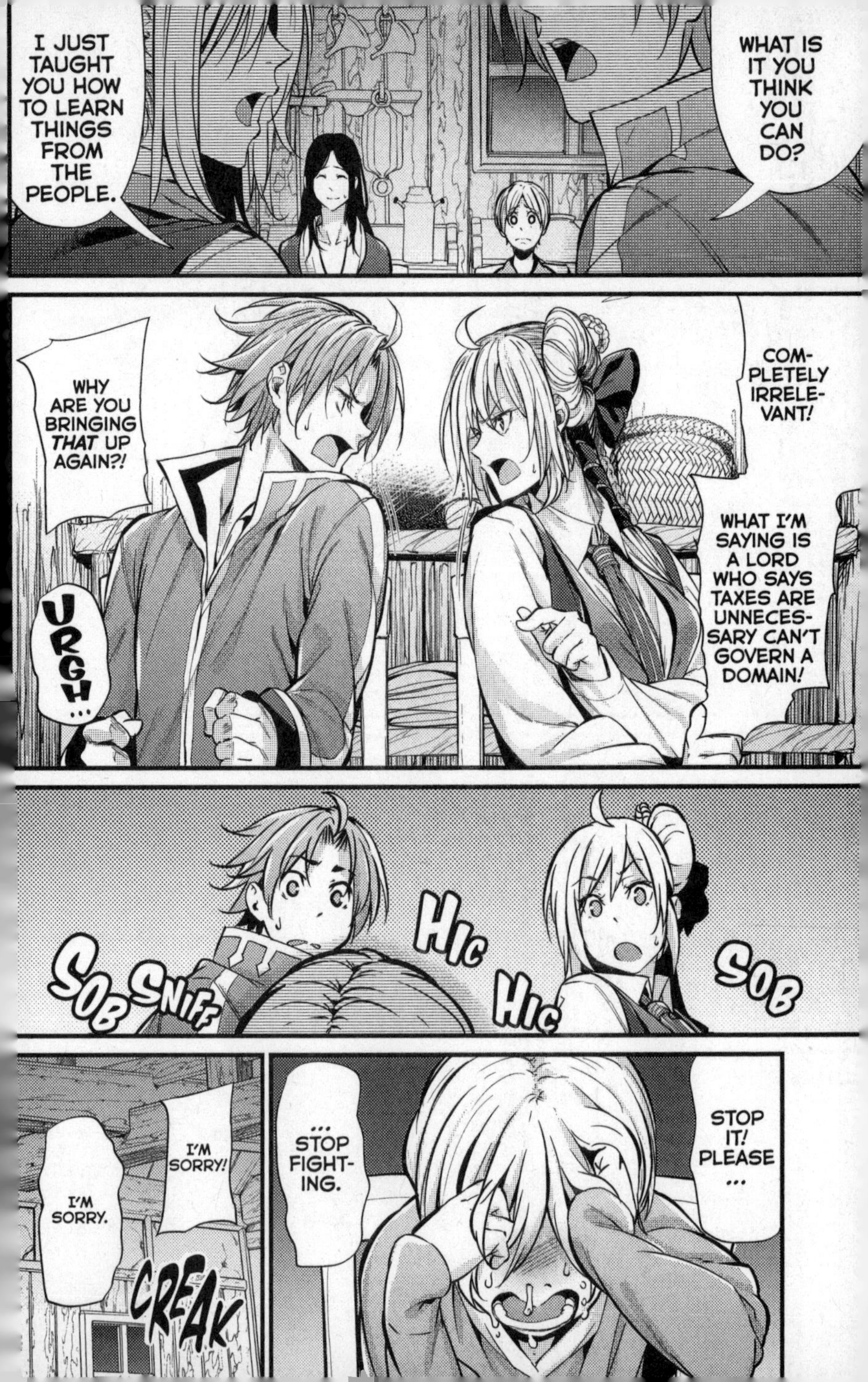
WHAT IS IT YOU THINK YOU CAN DO?
I JUST TAUGHT YOU HOW TO LEARN THINGS FROM THE PEOPLE.
COMPLETELY IRRELEVANT!
WHAT I'M SAYING IS A LORD WHO SAYS TAXES ARE UNNECESSARY CAN'T GOVERN A DOMAIN!
WHY ARE YOU BRINGING *THAT* UP AGAIN?!
URGH...
SOB
HIC
HIC
SNIFF
SOB
STOP IT! PLEASE...
...STOP FIGHTING.
I'M SORRY!
I'M SORRY.
CREAK

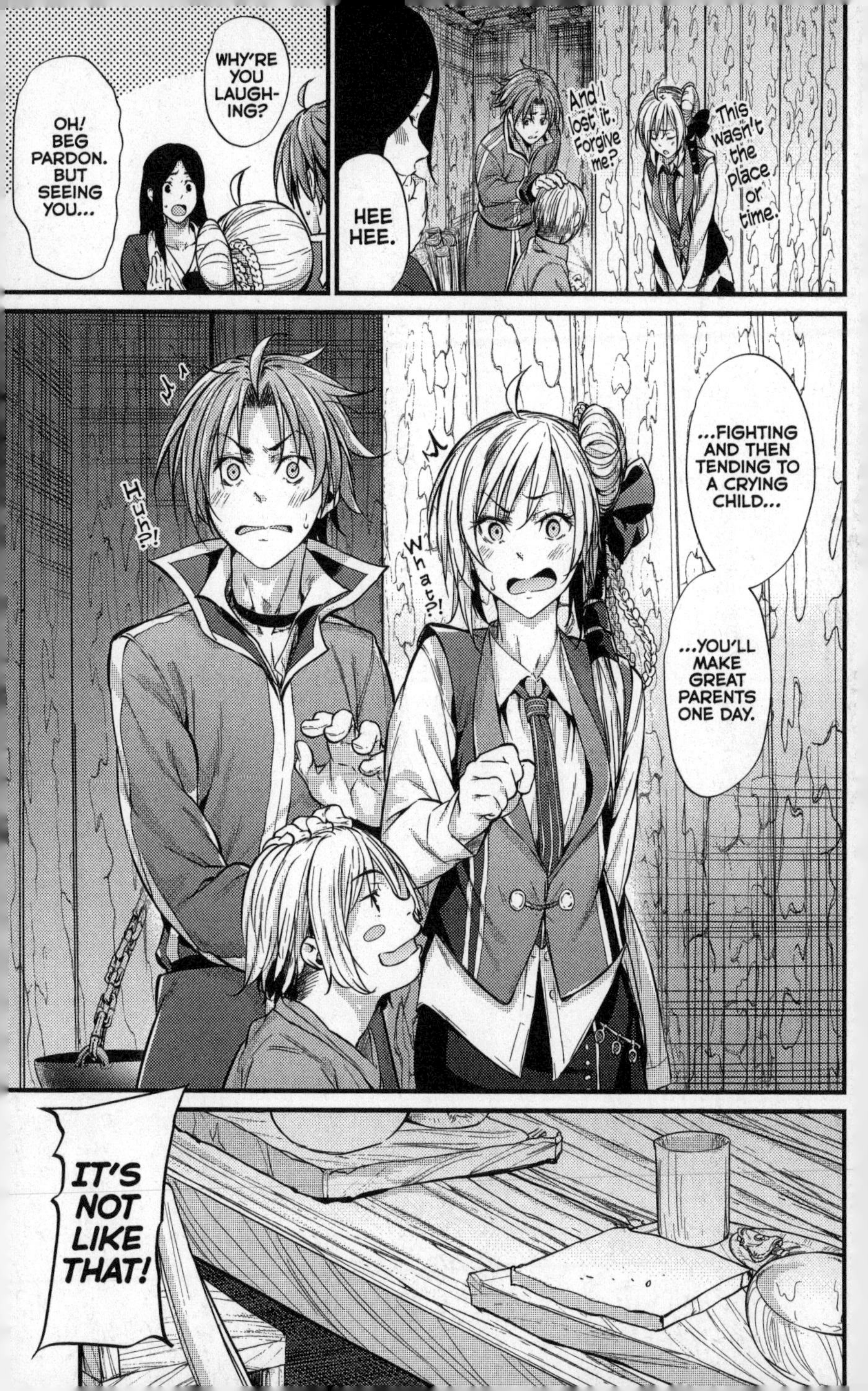
This wasn't the place or time.
And I lost it. Forgive me?
HEE HEE.
WHY'RE YOU LAUGHING?
OH! BEG PARDON. BUT SEEING YOU...
...FIGHTING AND THEN TENDING TO A CRYING CHILD...
...YOU'LL MAKE GREAT PARENTS ONE DAY.
What?!
Huh?!
IT'S NOT LIKE THAT!

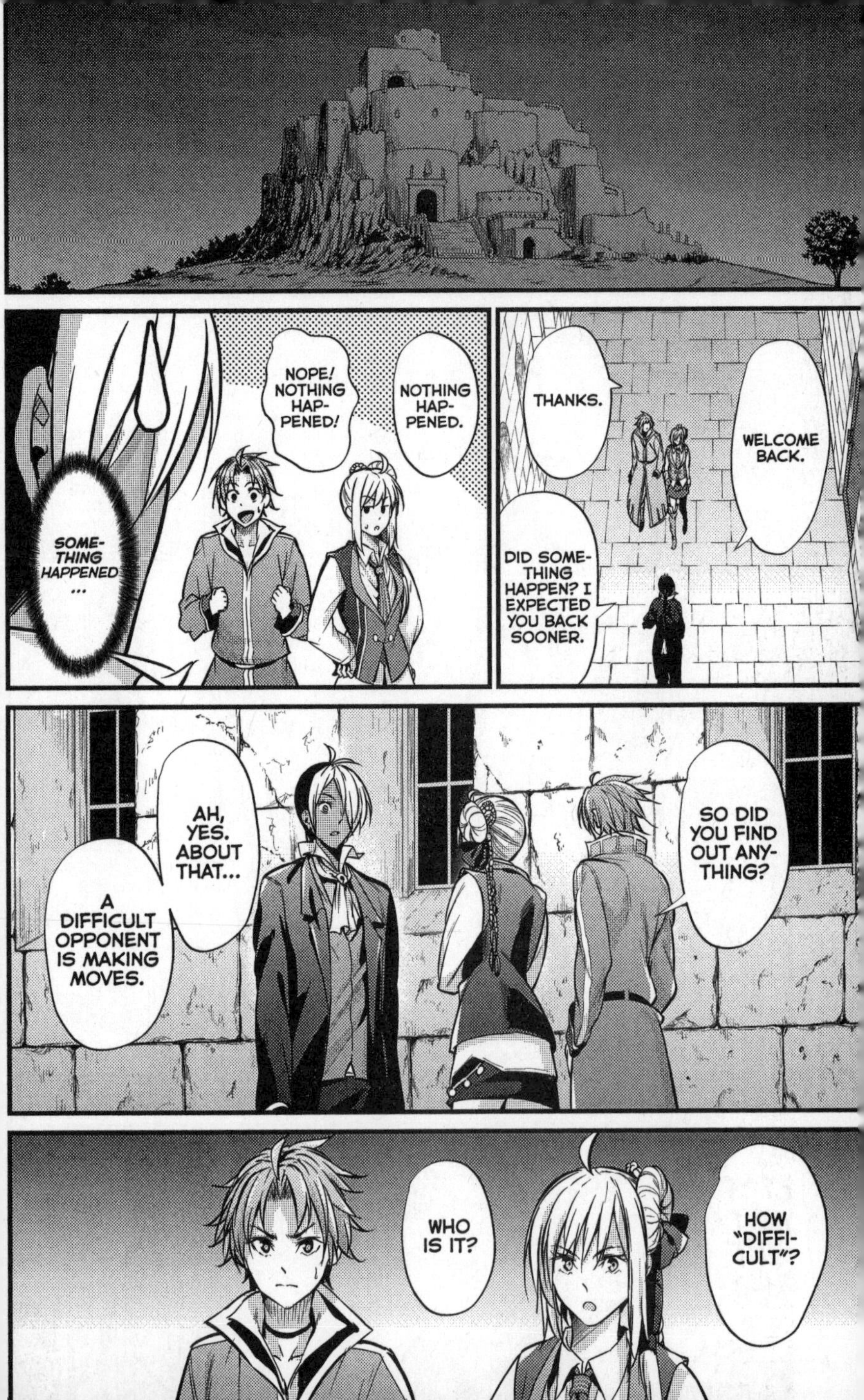
WELCOME BACK.
THANKS.
DID SOMETHING HAPPEN? I EXPECTED YOU BACK SOONER.
NOTHING HAPPENED.
NOPE! NOTHING HAPPENED!
SOMETHING HAPPENED...
SO DID YOU FIND OUT ANYTHING?
AH, YES. ABOUT THAT...
A DIFFICULT OPPONENT IS MAKING MOVES.
HOW "DIFFICULT"?
WHO IS IT?

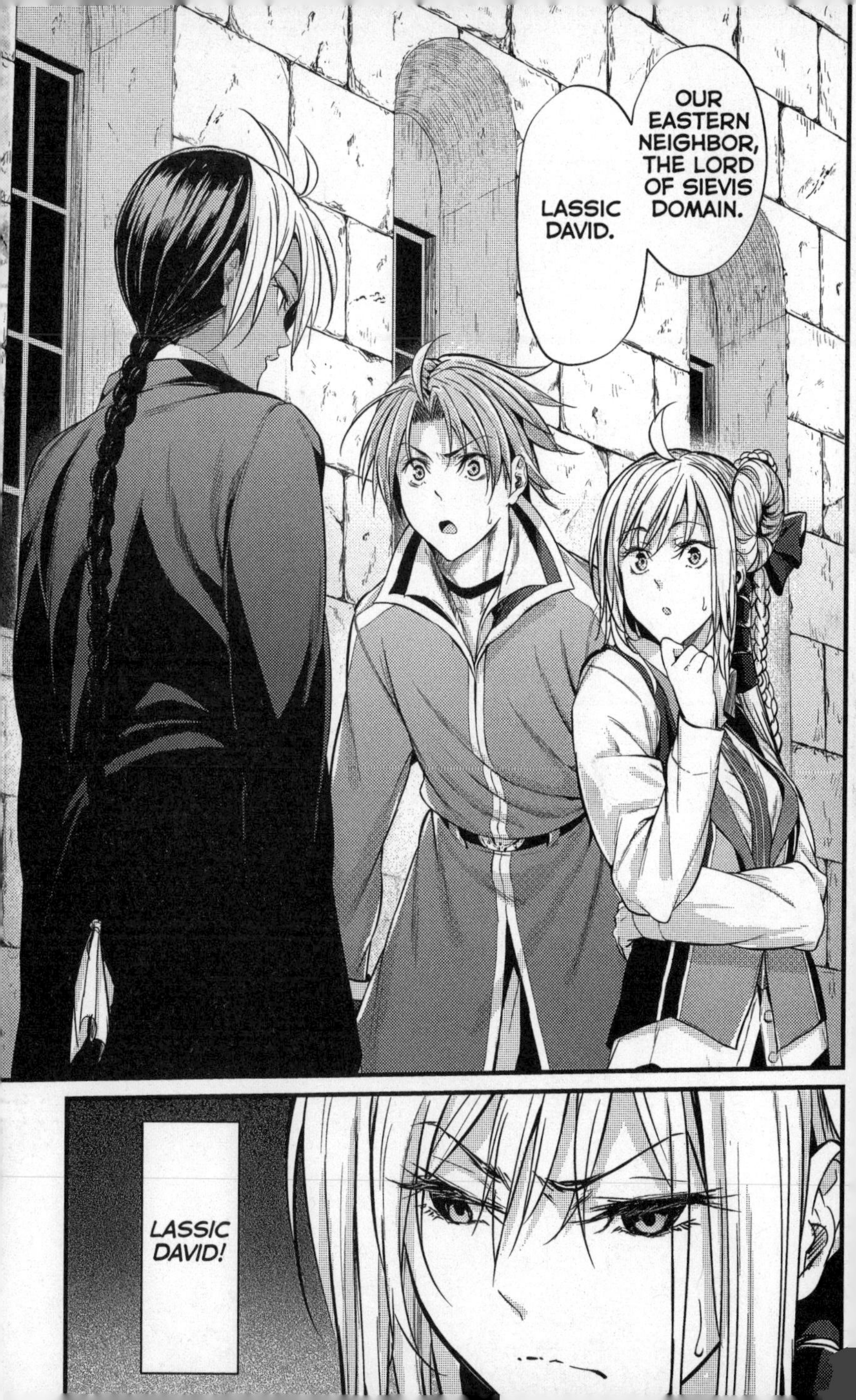
OUR EASTERN NEIGHBOR, THE LORD OF SIEVIS DOMAIN.
LASSIC DAVID.
LASSIC DAVID!

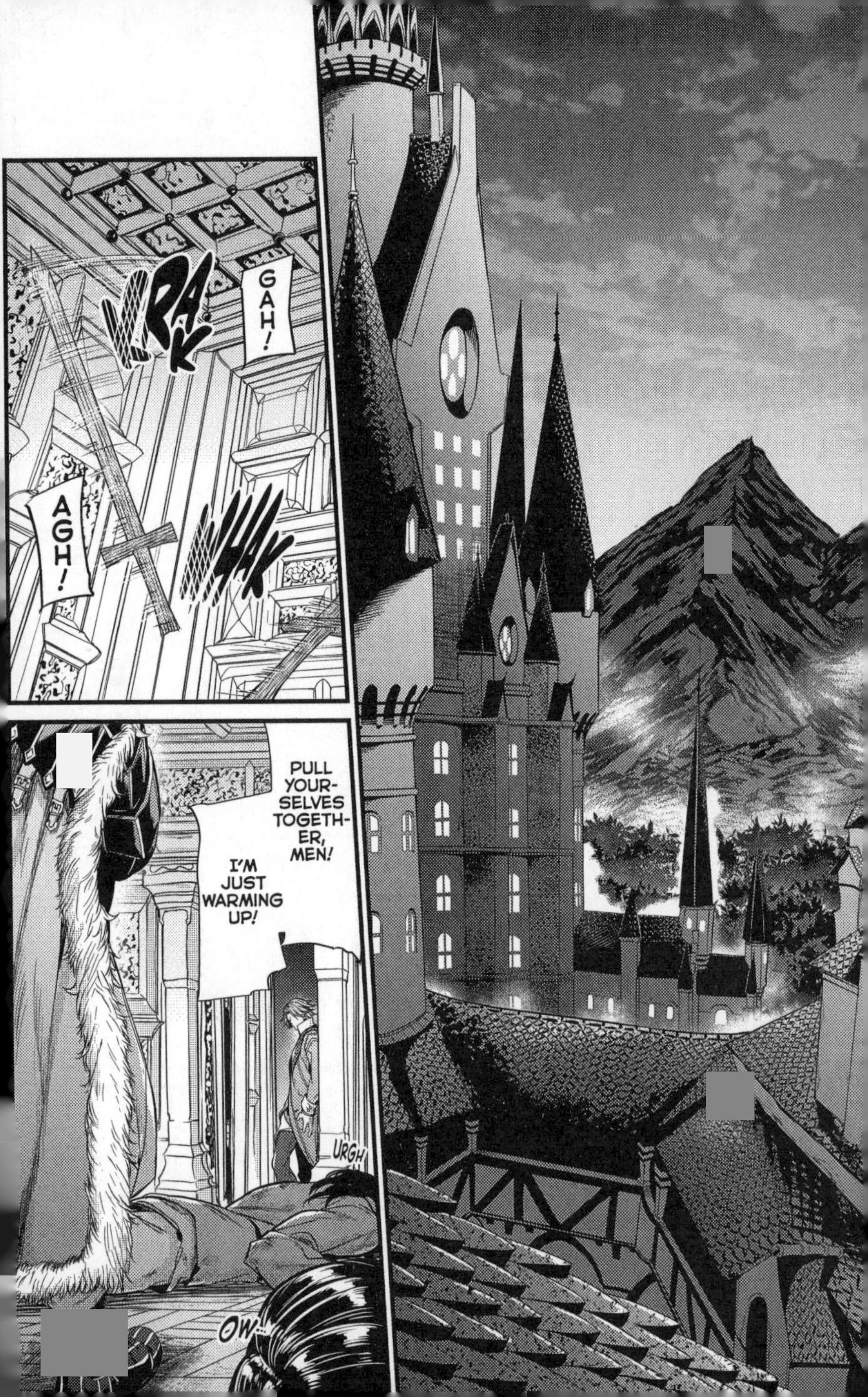
GAH!
VRAK
WHAK
AGH!
PULL YOURSELVES TOGETHER, MEN!
I'M JUST WARMING UP!
URGH
OW...

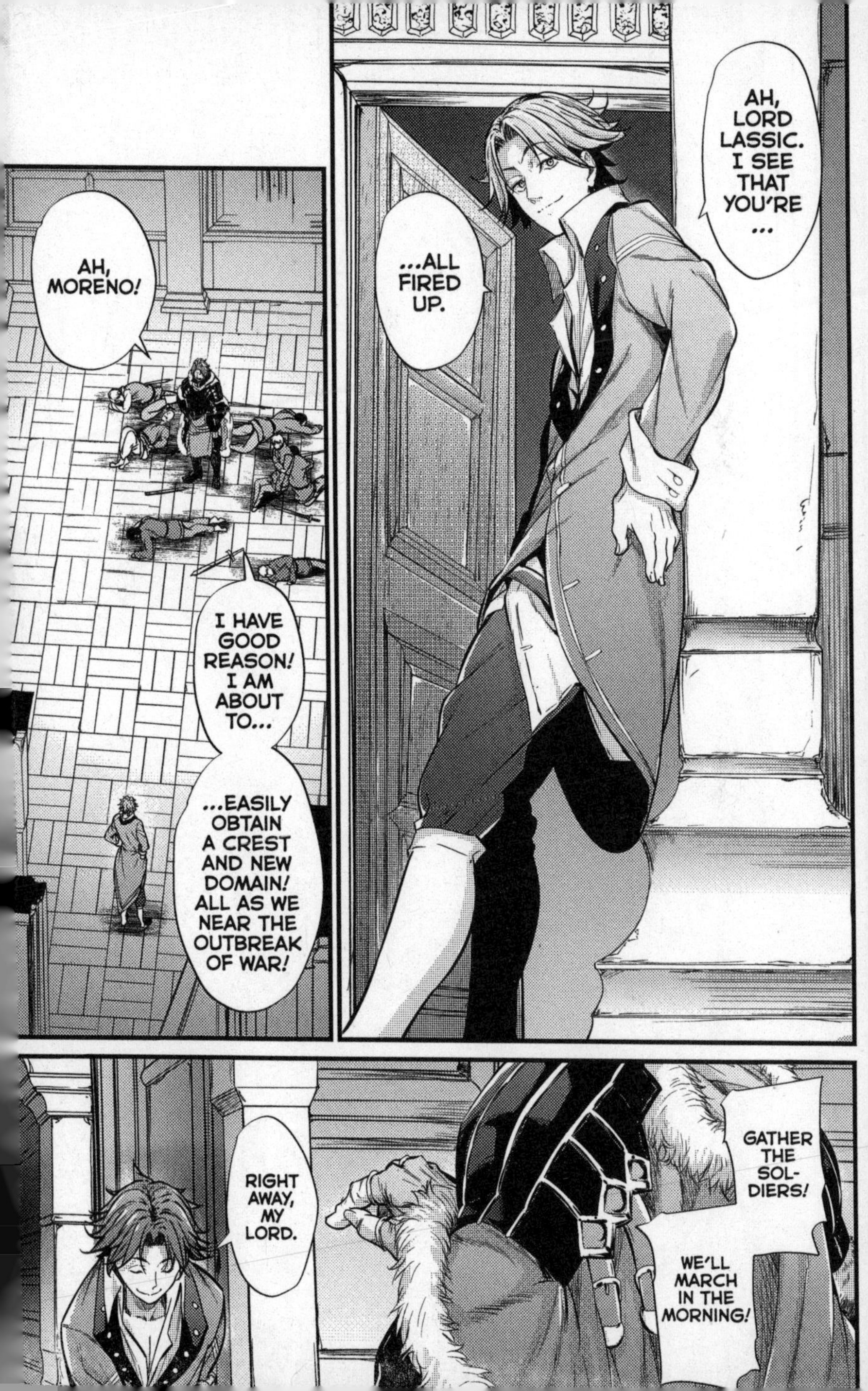
AH, LORD LASSIC. I SEE THAT YOU'RE ...
...ALL FIRED UP.
AH, MORENO!
I HAVE GOOD REASON! I AM ABOUT TO...
...EASILY OBTAIN A CREST AND NEW DOMAIN! ALL AS WE NEAR THE OUTBREAK OF WAR!
GATHER THE SOL-DIERS!
WE'LL MARCH IN THE MORNING!
RIGHT AWAY, MY LORD.

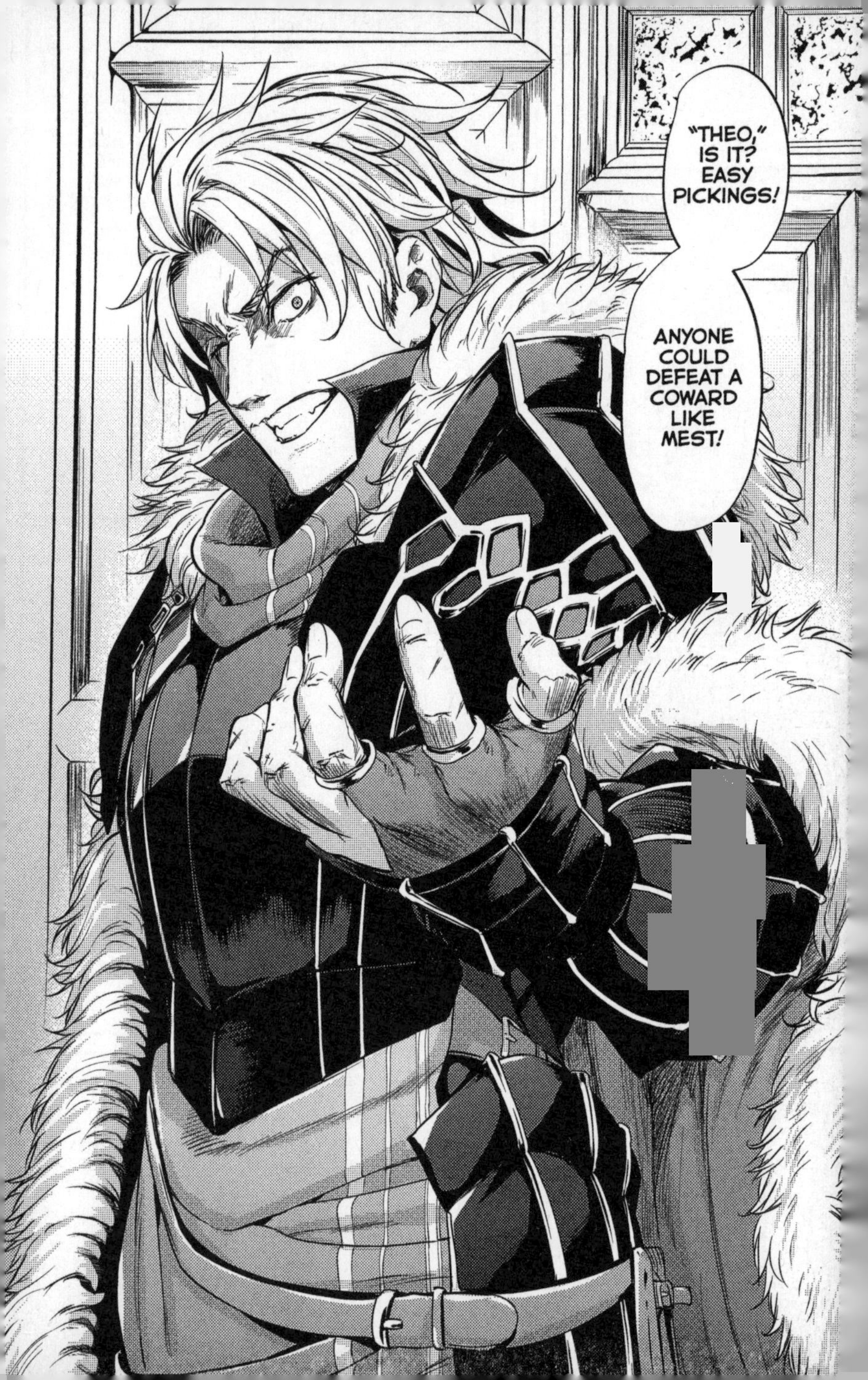
"THEO," IS IT? EASY PICKINGS!
ANYONE COULD DEFEAT A COWARD LIKE MEST!

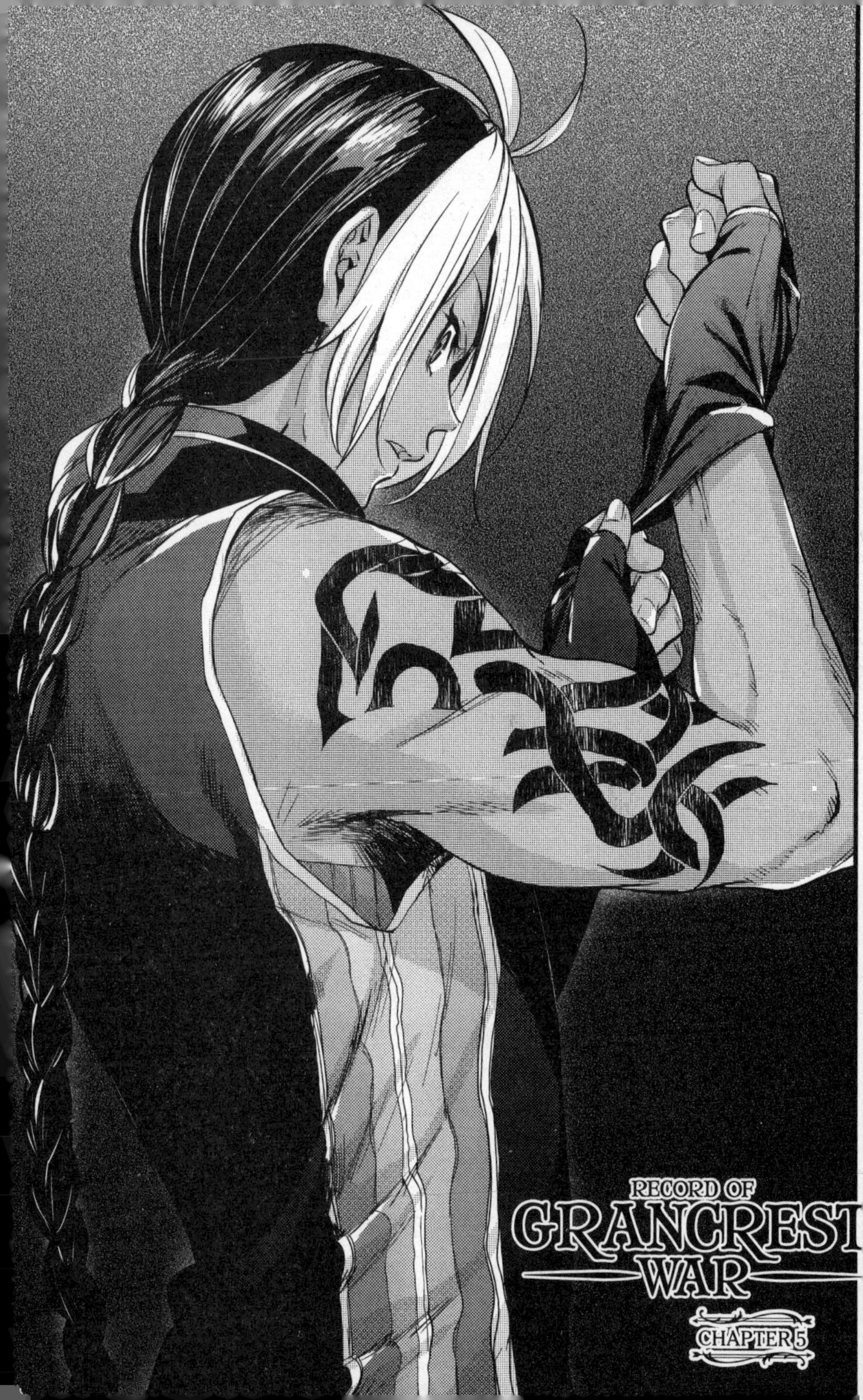
RECORD OF
GRANCREST
WAR
CHAPTER 5

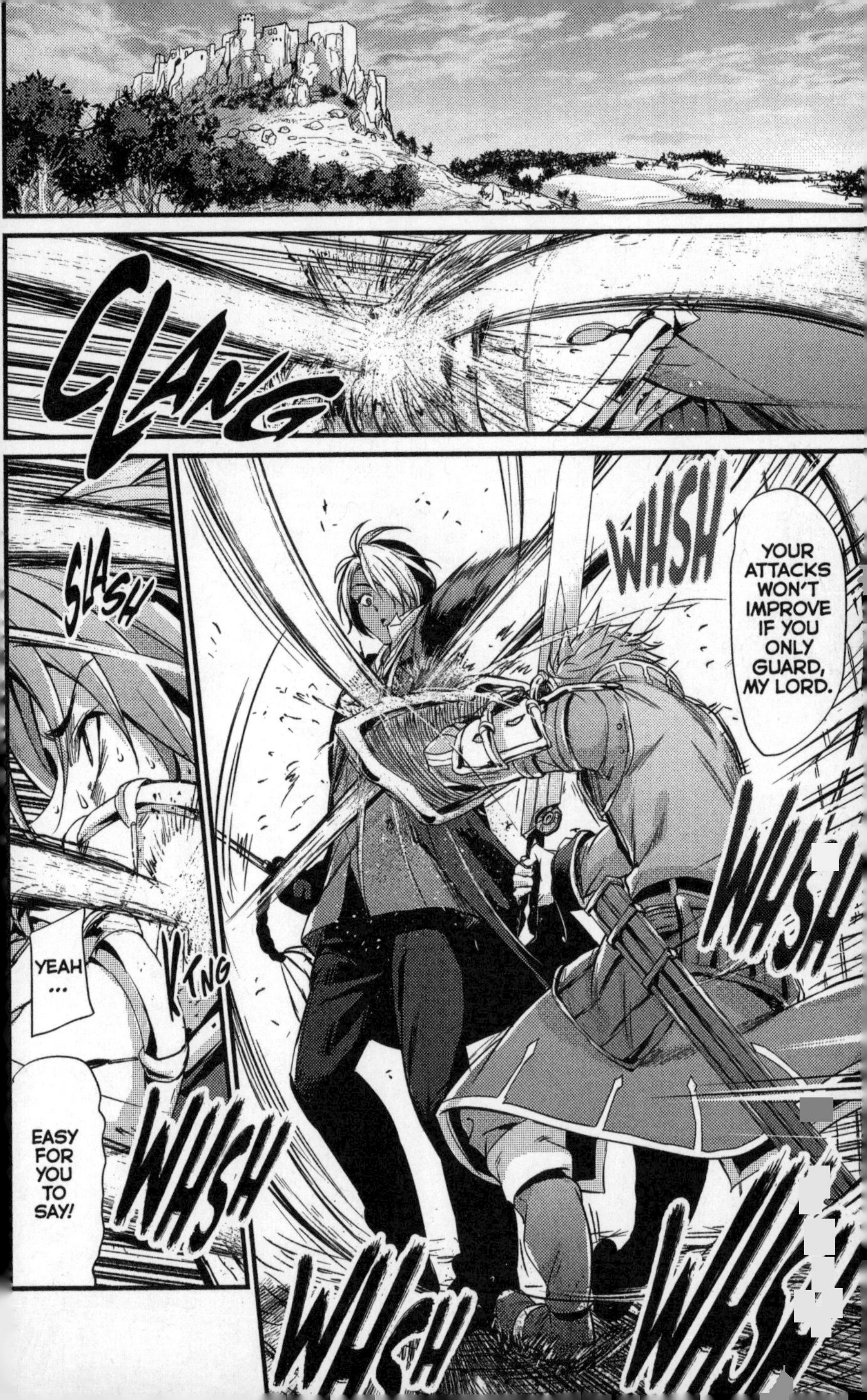
CLANG
WHSH
YOUR ATTACKS WON'T IMPROVE IF YOU ONLY GUARD, MY LORD.
WHSH
SLASH
YEAH...
KTNG
EASY FOR YOU TO SAY!
WHSH
WHSH
WHSH

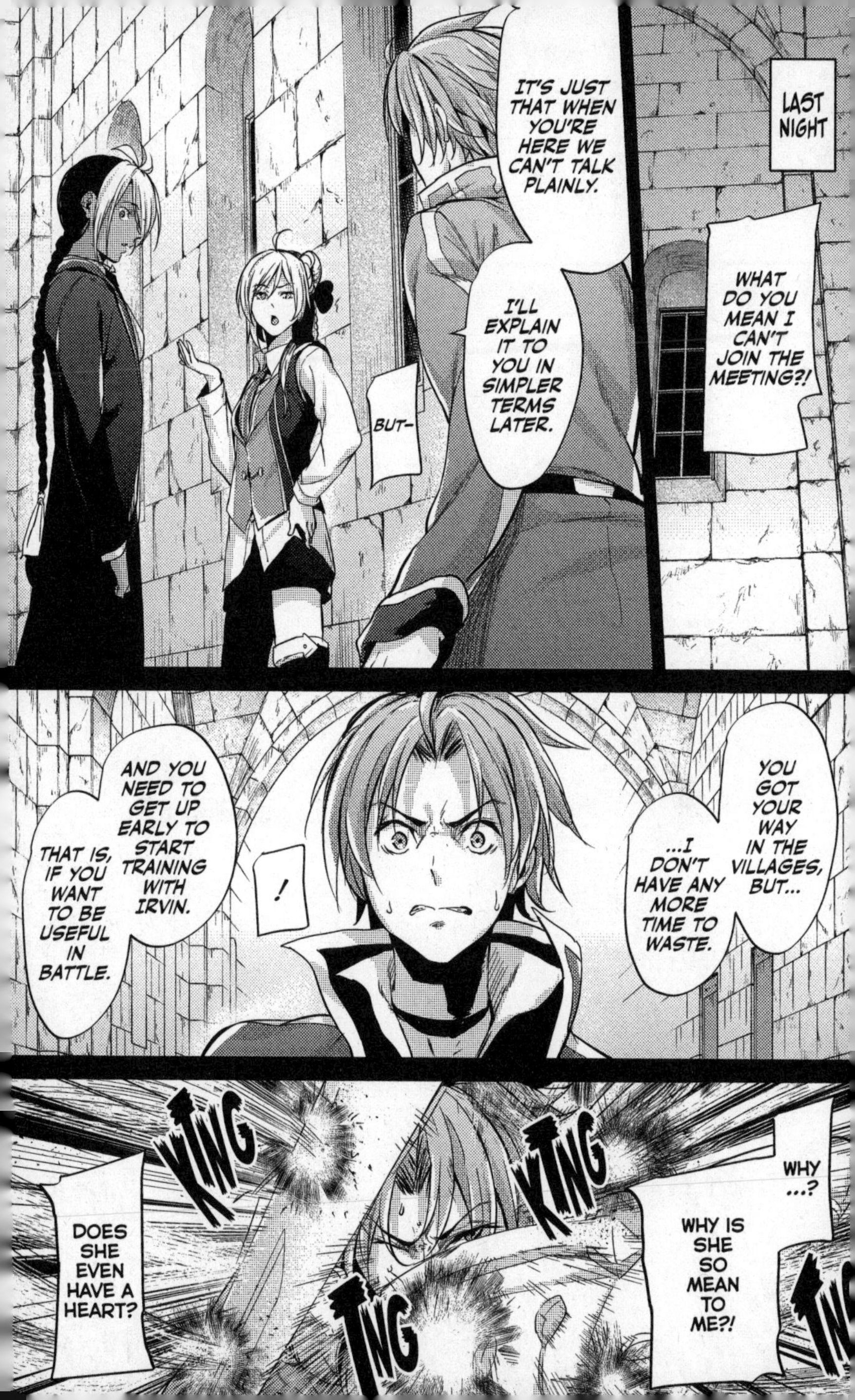
LAST NIGHT
WHAT DO YOU MEAN I CAN'T JOIN THE MEETING?!
IT'S JUST THAT WHEN YOU'RE HERE WE CAN'T TALK PLAINLY.
I'LL EXPLAIN IT TO YOU IN SIMPLER TERMS LATER.
BUT–
YOU GOT YOUR WAY IN THE VILLAGES, BUT...
...I DON'T HAVE ANY MORE TIME TO WASTE.
!
AND YOU NEED TO GET UP EARLY TO START TRAINING WITH IRVIN.
THAT IS, IF YOU WANT TO BE USEFUL IN BATTLE.
WHY ...?
WHY IS SHE SO MEAN TO ME?!
TING
KING
KING
TING
DOES SHE EVEN HAVE A HEART?

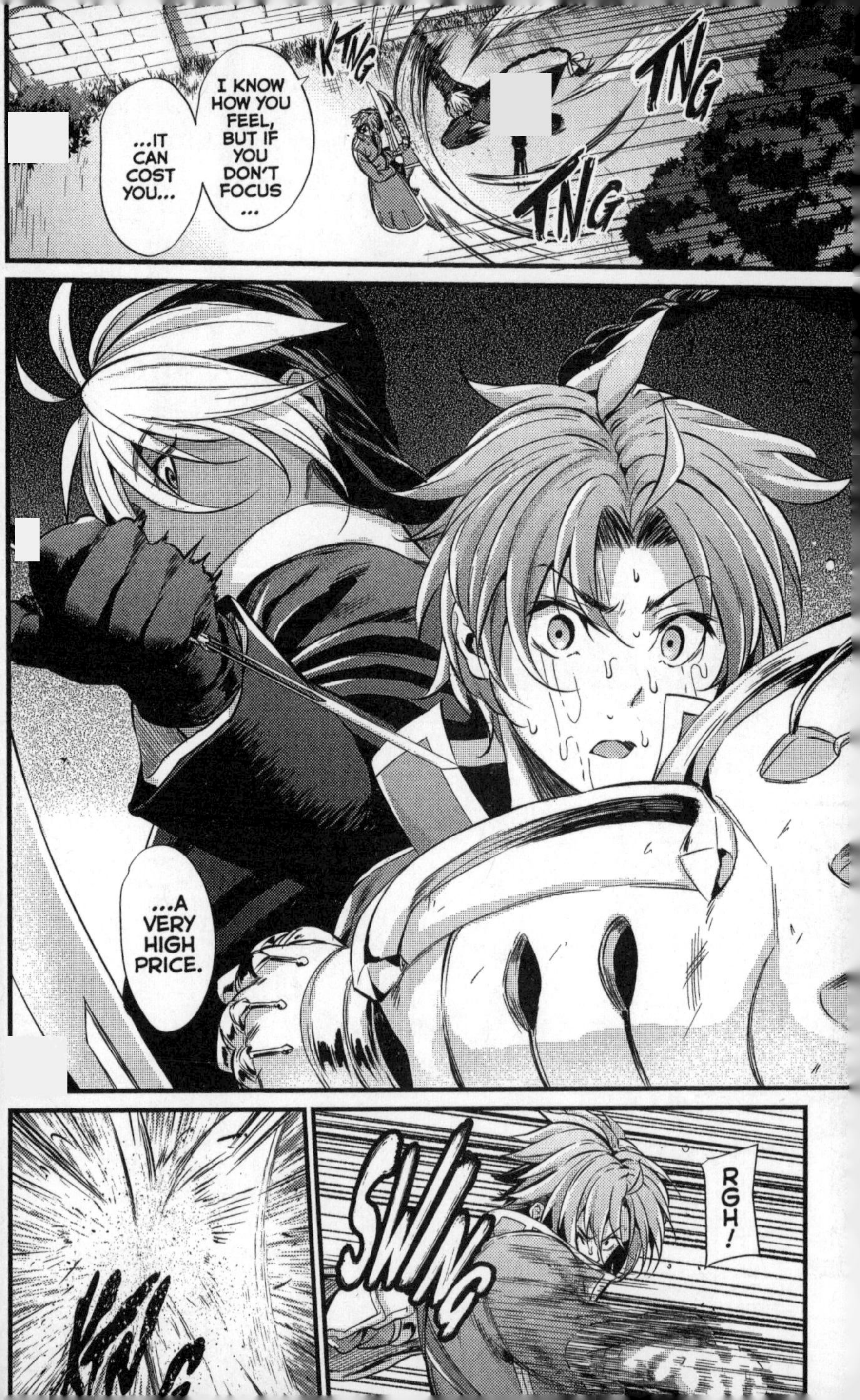
TNG
TNG
KTNG
TNG
I KNOW HOW YOU FEEL, BUT IF YOU DON'T FOCUS...
...IT CAN COST YOU...
...A VERY HIGH PRICE.
RGH!
SWING

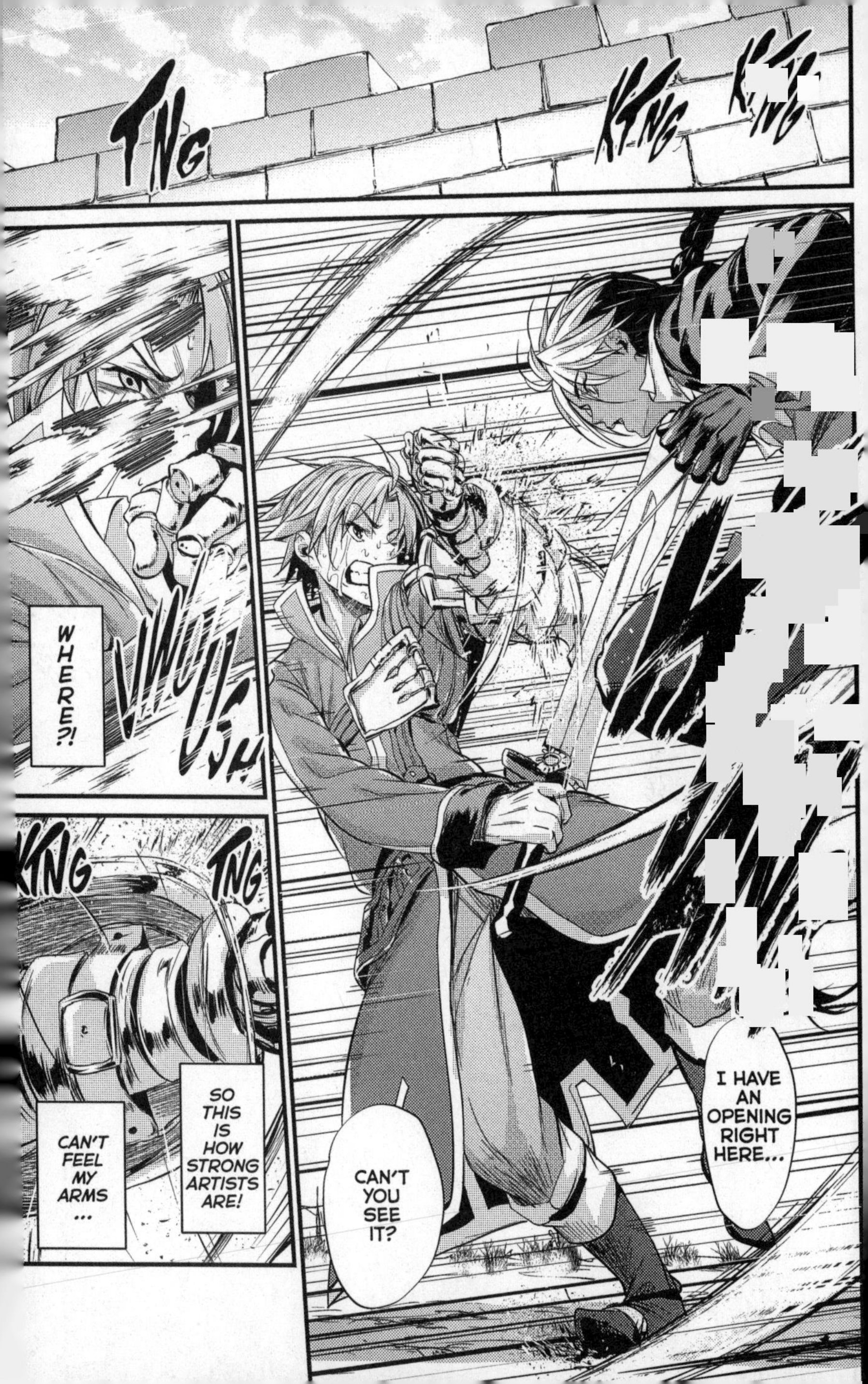
KING
KING
TNG
I HAVE AN OPENING RIGHT HERE...
CAN'T YOU SEE IT?
WHERE?!
VWUSH
TNG
KING
SO THIS IS HOW STRONG ARTISTS ARE!
CAN'T FEEL MY ARMS...

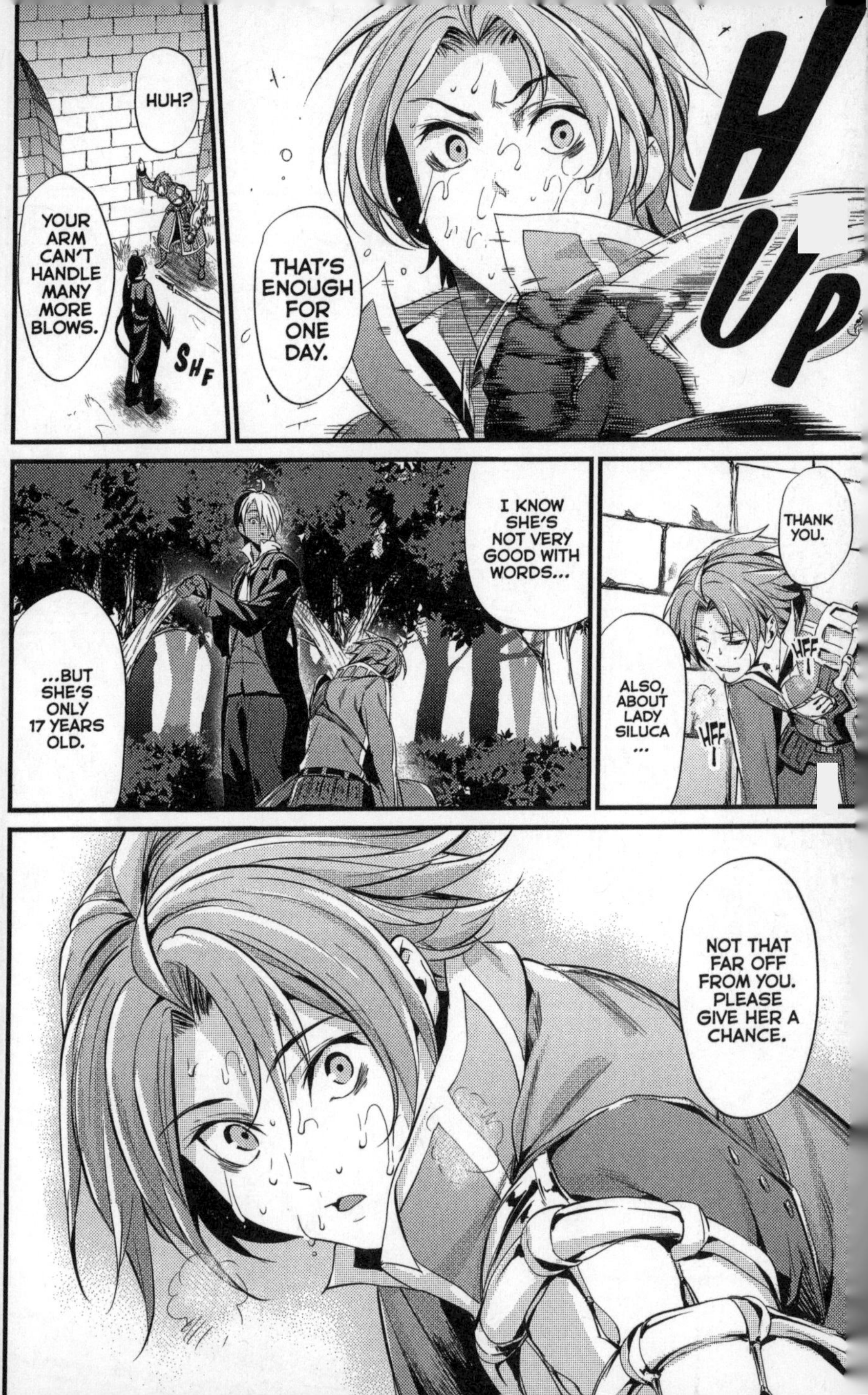
HUP
THAT'S ENOUGH FOR ONE DAY.
HUH?
YOUR ARM CAN'T HANDLE MANY MORE BLOWS.
SHF
THANK YOU.
HFF
ALSO, ABOUT LADY SILUCA...
HFF
I KNOW SHE'S NOT VERY GOOD WITH WORDS...
...BUT SHE'S ONLY 17 YEARS OLD.
NOT THAT FAR OFF FROM YOU. PLEASE GIVE HER A CHANCE.

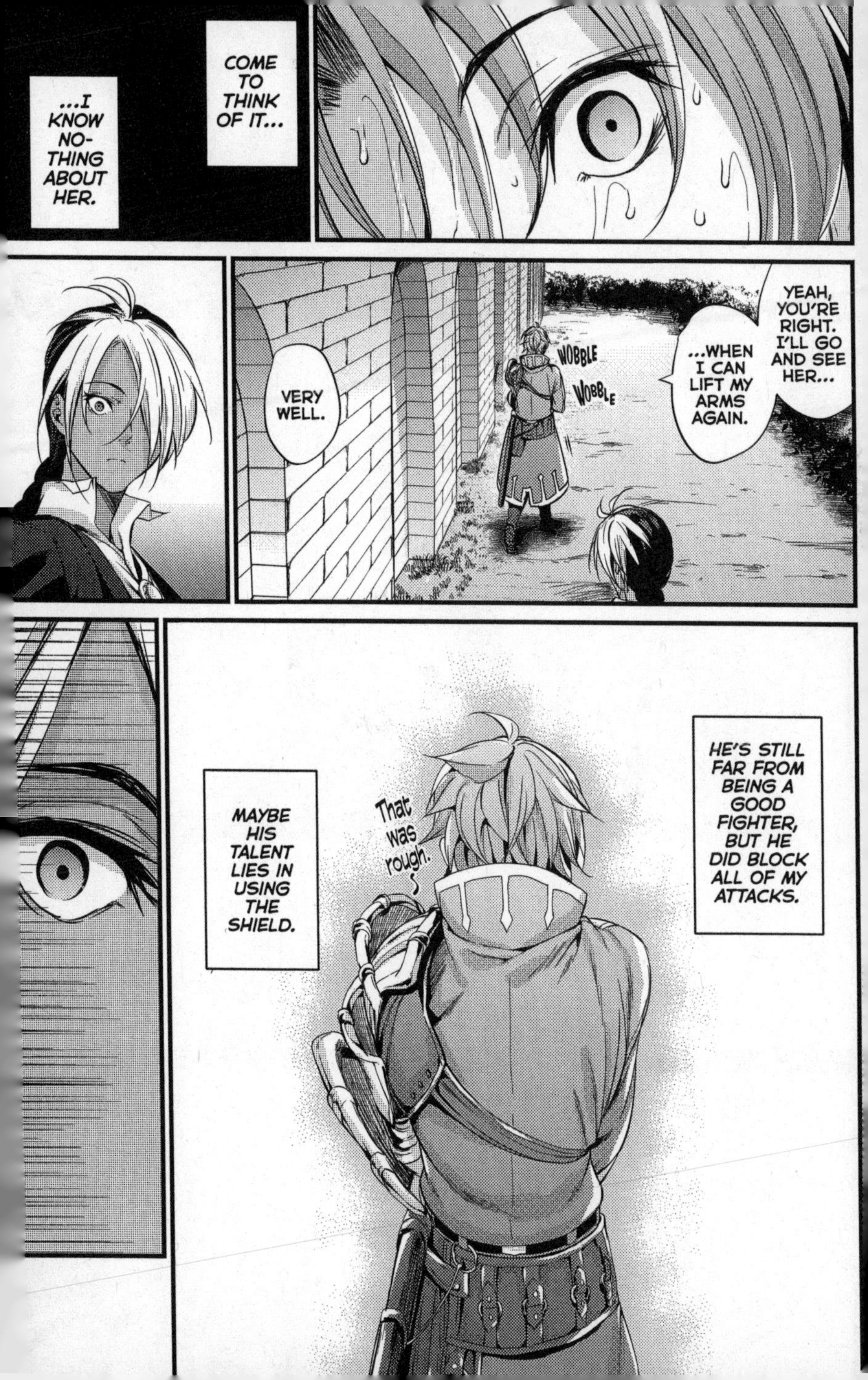
COME TO THINK OF IT...
...I KNOW NO-THING ABOUT HER.
YEAH, YOU'RE RIGHT. I'LL GO AND SEE HER...
...WHEN I CAN LIFT MY ARMS AGAIN.
WOBBLE
WOBBLE
VERY WELL.
HE'S STILL FAR FROM BEING A GOOD FIGHTER, BUT HE DID BLOCK ALL OF MY ATTACKS.
That was rough.
MAYBE HIS TALENT LIES IN USING THE SHIELD.

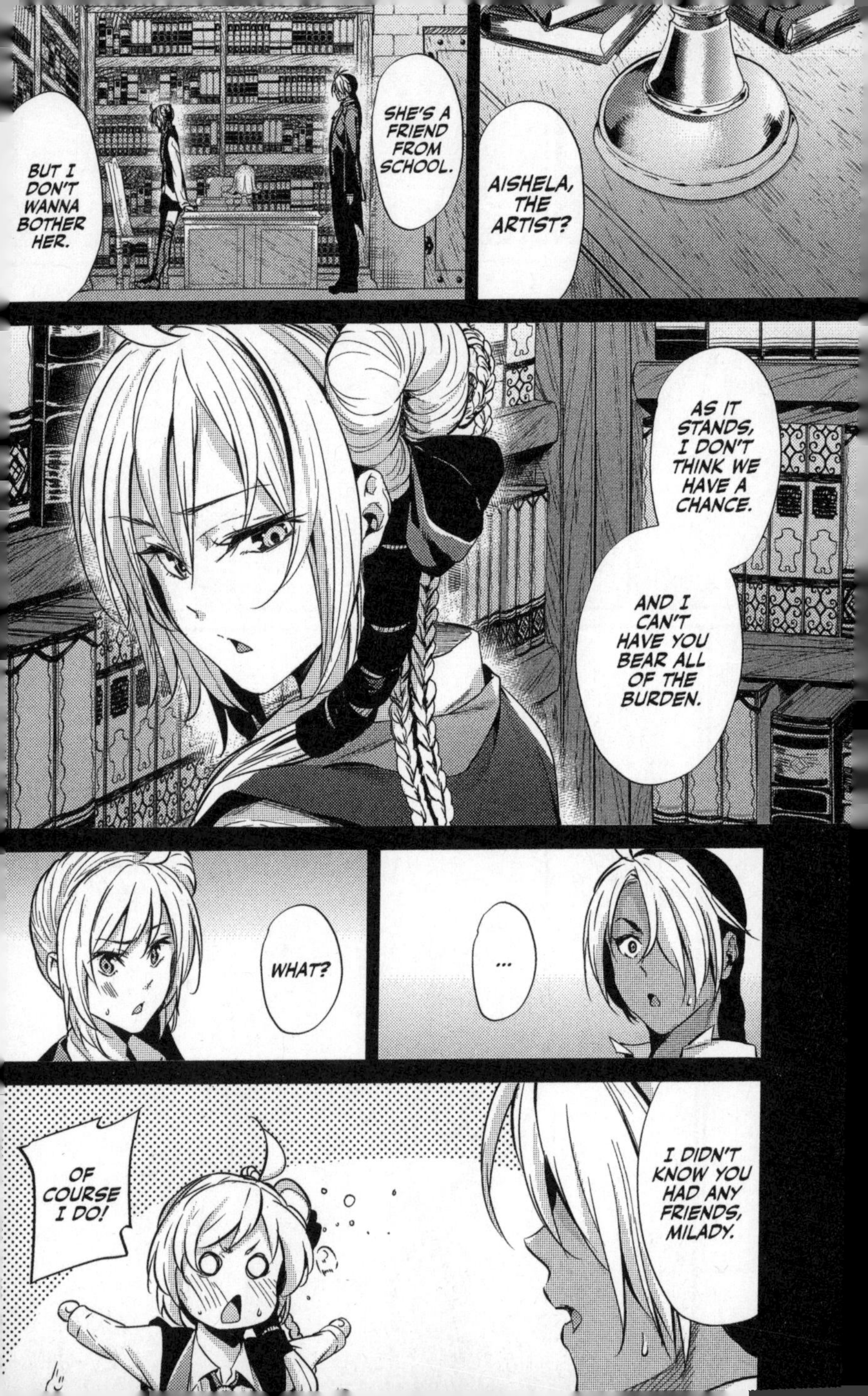
AISHELA, THE ARTIST?
SHE'S A FRIEND FROM SCHOOL.
BUT I DON'T WANNA BOTHER HER.
AS IT STANDS, I DON'T THINK WE HAVE A CHANCE.
AND I CAN'T HAVE YOU BEAR ALL OF THE BURDEN.
...
WHAT?
I DIDN'T KNOW YOU HAD ANY FRIENDS, MILADY.
OF COURSE I DO!

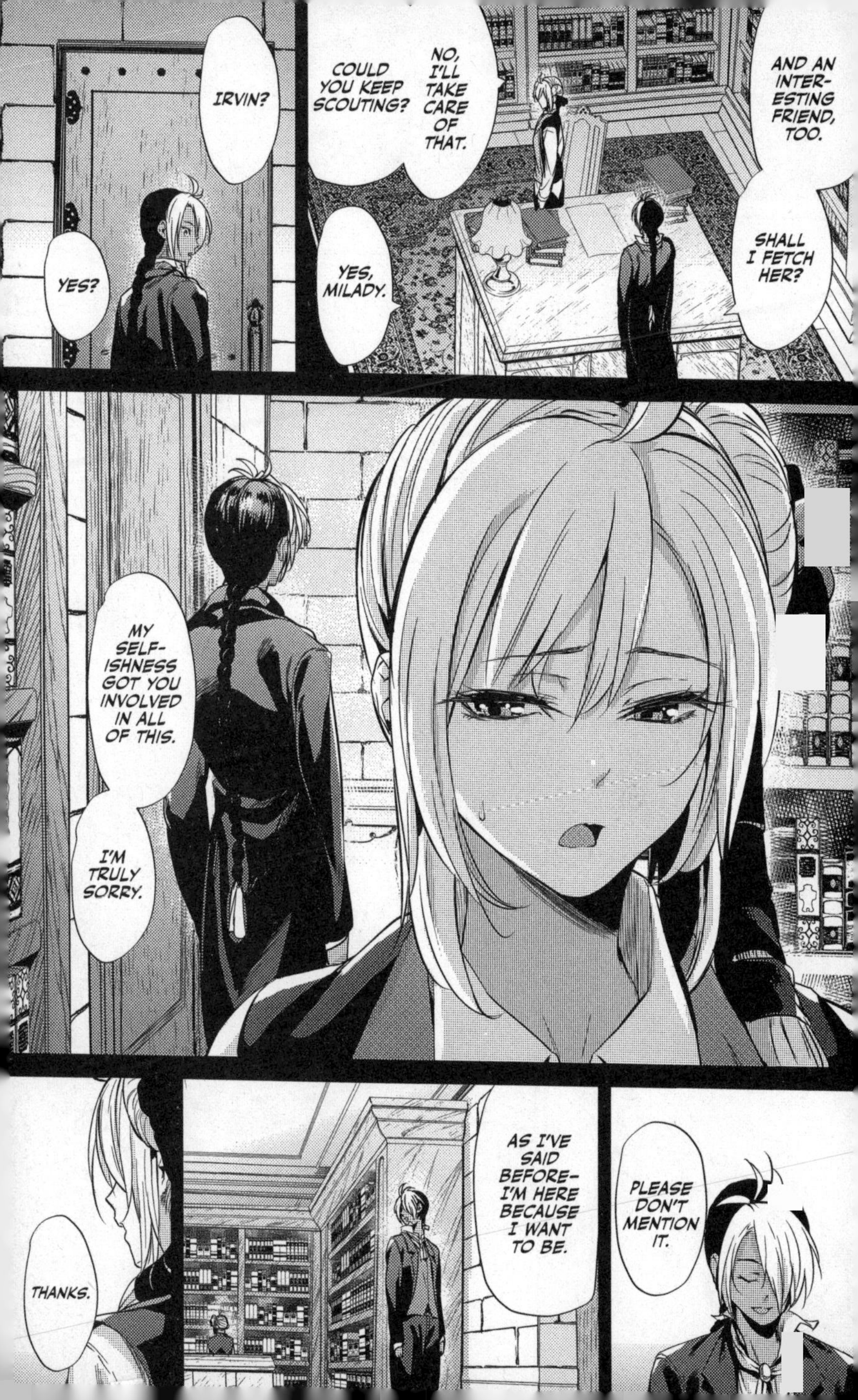
AND AN INTERESTING FRIEND, TOO.
SHALL I FETCH HER?
NO, I'LL TAKE CARE OF THAT.
COULD YOU KEEP SCOUTING?
YES, MILADY.
IRVIN?
YES?
MY SELFISHNESS GOT YOU INVOLVED IN ALL OF THIS.
I'M TRULY SORRY.
PLEASE DON'T MENTION IT.
AS I'VE SAID BEFORE— I'M HERE BECAUSE I WANT TO BE.
THANKS.

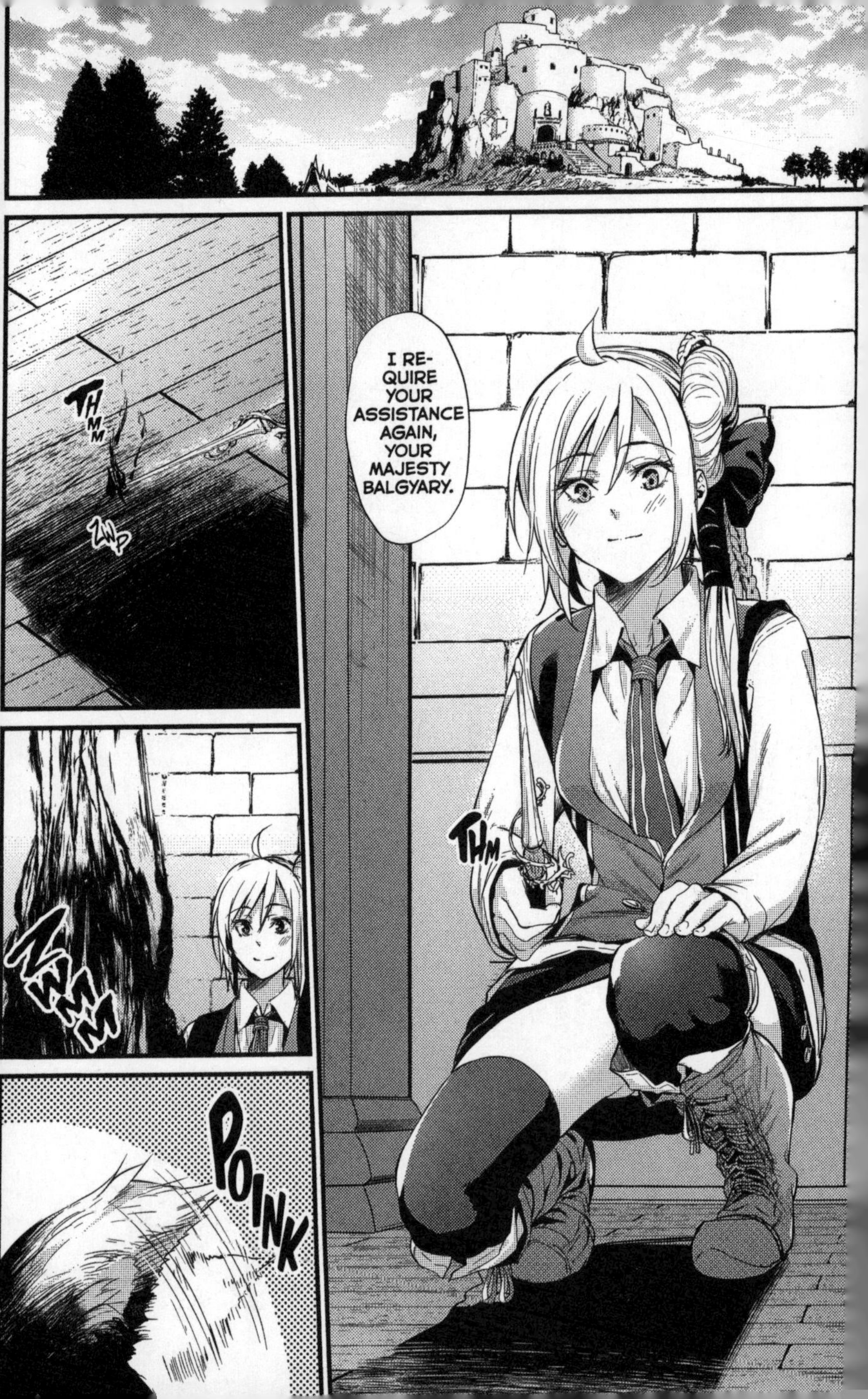
I RE-QUIRE YOUR ASSISTANCE AGAIN, YOUR MAJESTY BALGYARY.
THM
THMM
POINK

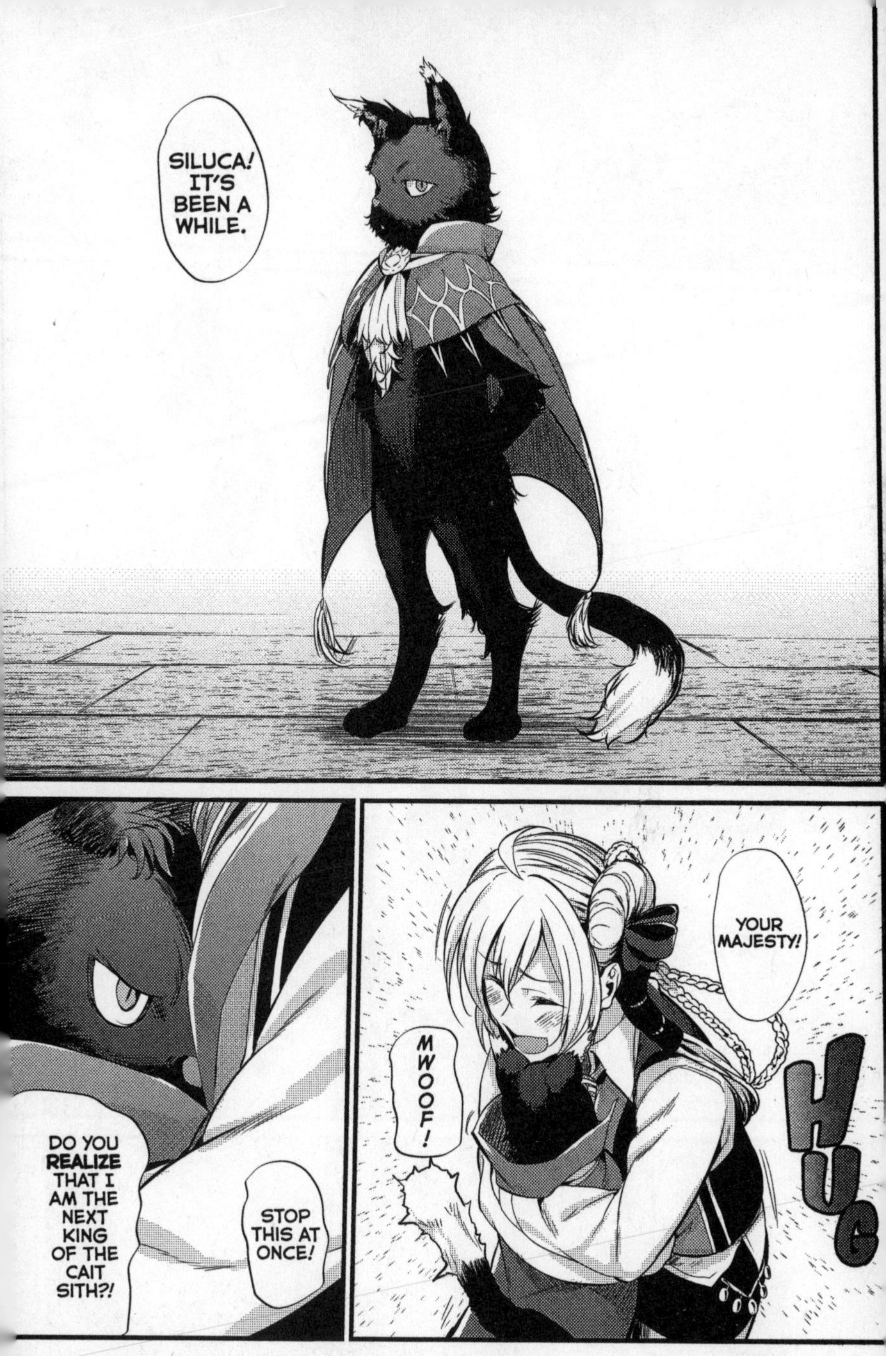
SILUCA! IT'S BEEN A WHILE.
YOUR MAJESTY!
HUG
MWOOF!
STOP THIS AT ONCE!
DO YOU **REALIZE** THAT I AM THE NEXT KING OF THE CAIT SITH?!

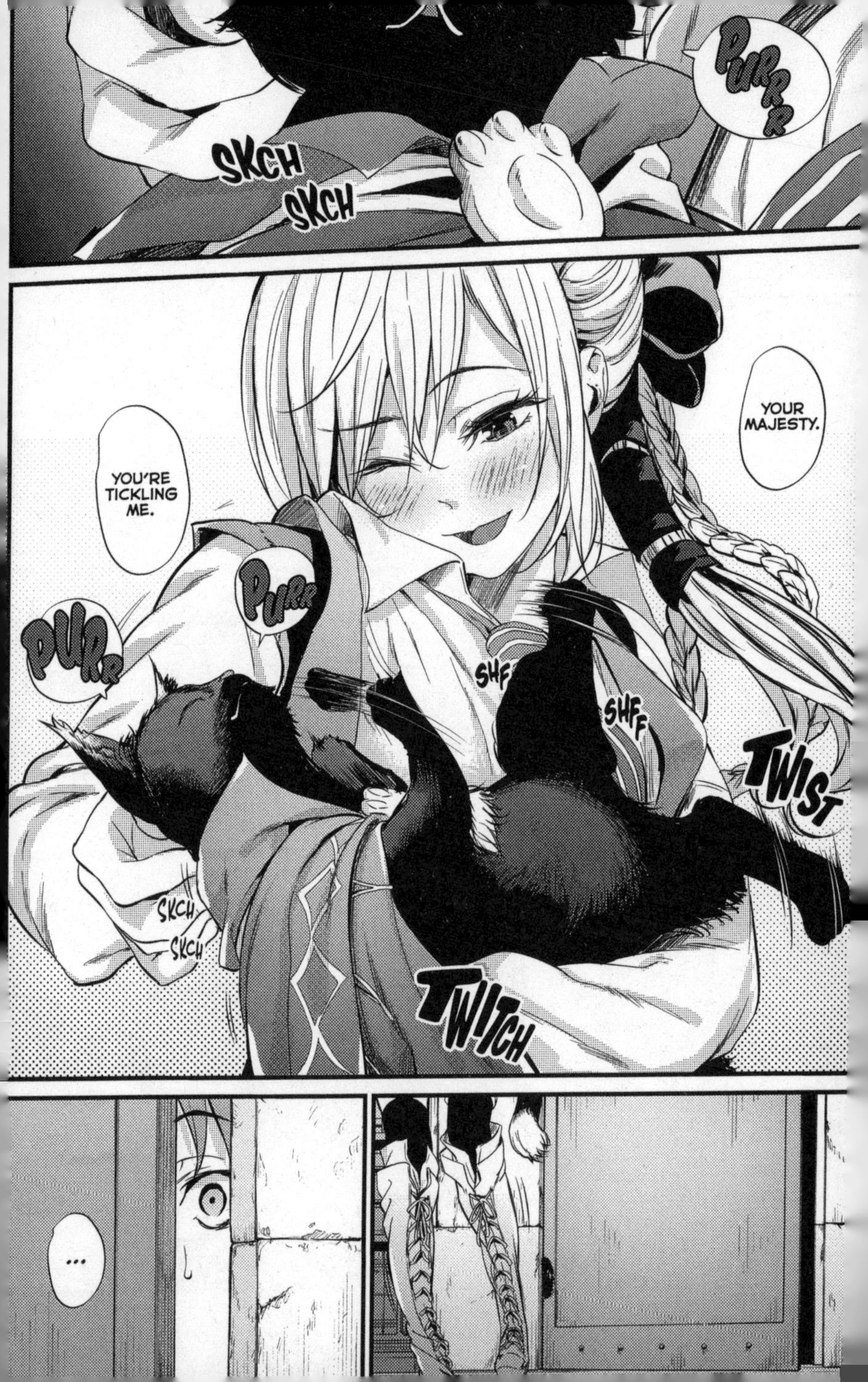
PURRR
SKCH
SKCH
YOUR MAJESTY.
YOU'RE TICKLING ME.
PURR
PURR
SHF
SHFF
TWIST
SKCH
SKCH
TWITCH
...

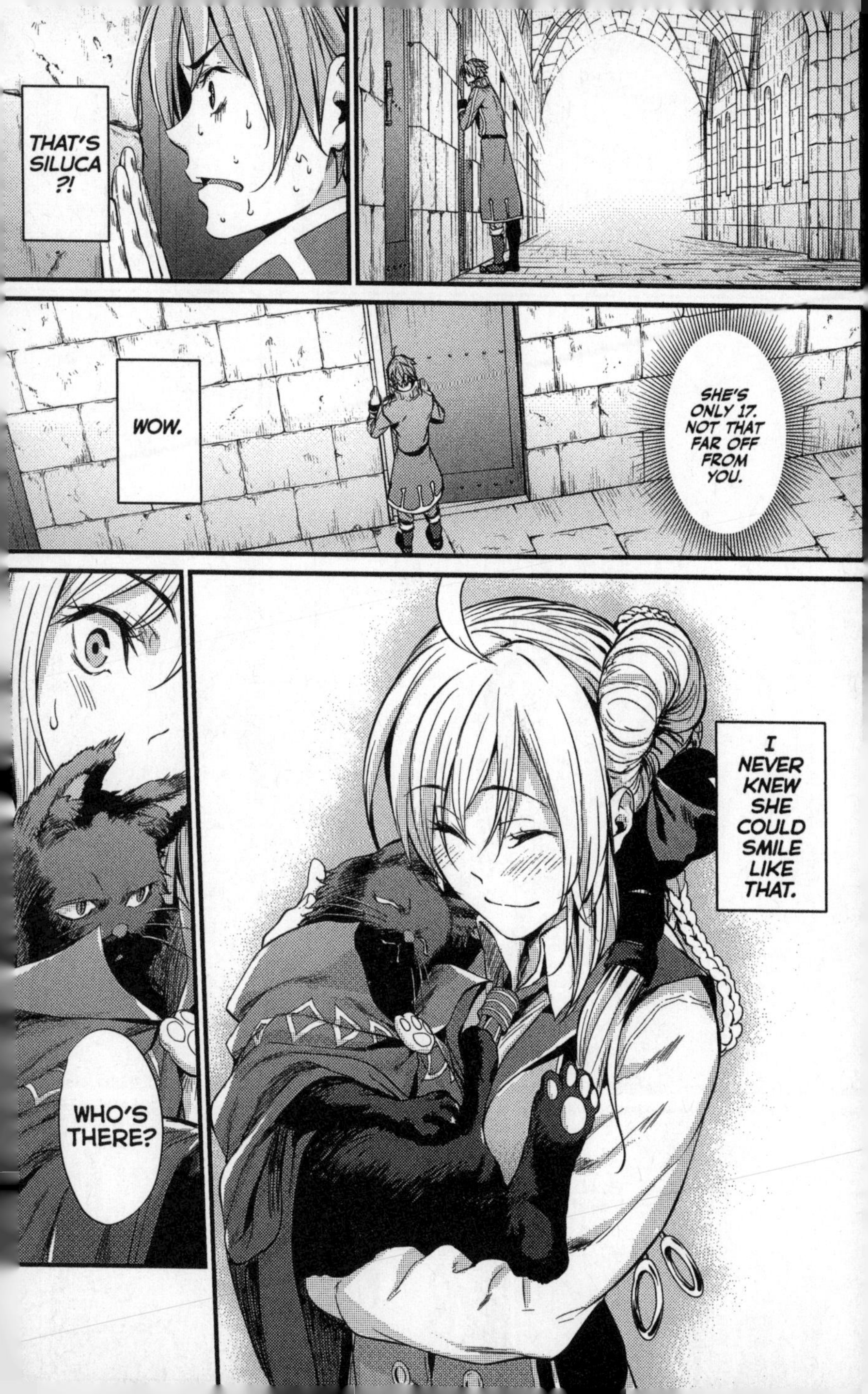
THAT'S SILUCA ?!
SHE'S ONLY 17. NOT THAT FAR OFF FROM YOU.
WOW.
I NEVER KNEW SHE COULD SMILE LIKE THAT.
WHO'S THERE?

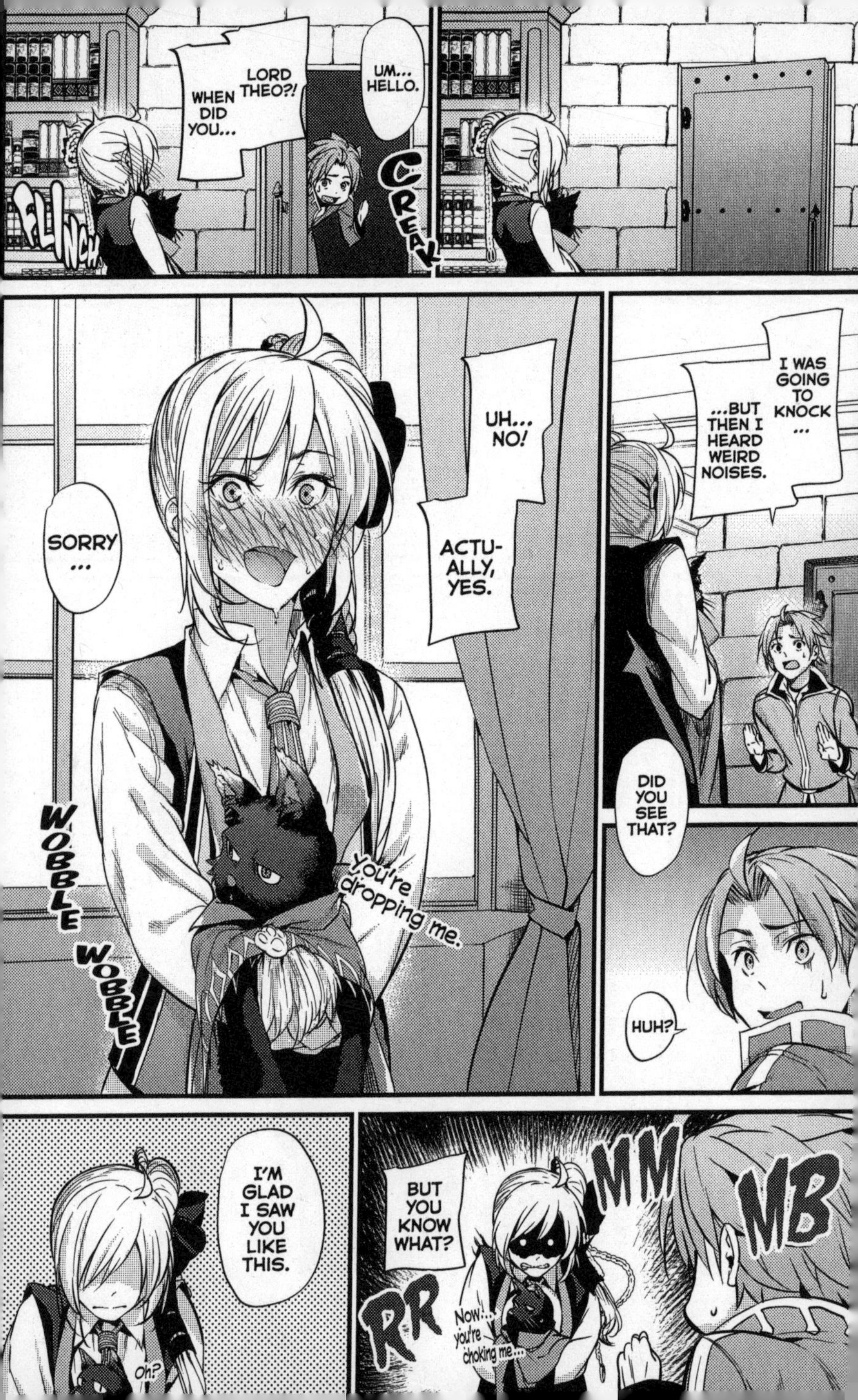
UM... HELLO.
CREAK
LORD THEO?! WHEN DID YOU...
FLINCH
I WAS GOING TO KNOCK...
...BUT THEN I HEARD WEIRD NOISES.
DID YOU SEE THAT?
HUH?
UH... NO!
ACTU-ALLY, YES.
SORRY...
You're dropping me.
WOBBLE
WOBBLE
BUT YOU KNOW WHAT?
MMMMB
RR
Now... you're choking me...
I'M GLAD I SAW YOU LIKE THIS.
Oh?

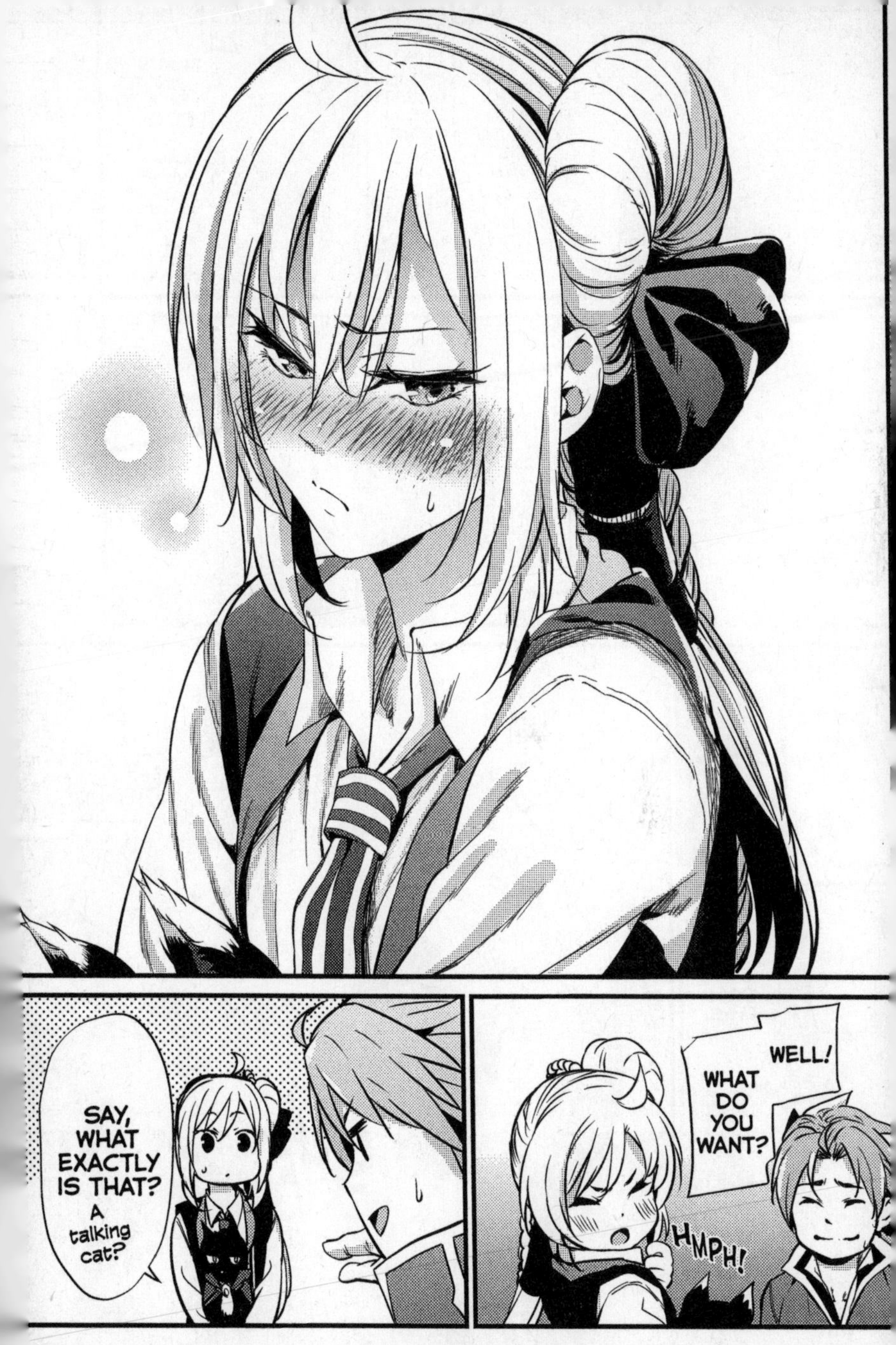
WELL! WHAT DO YOU WANT?
HMPH!
SAY, WHAT EXACTLY IS THAT? A talking cat?

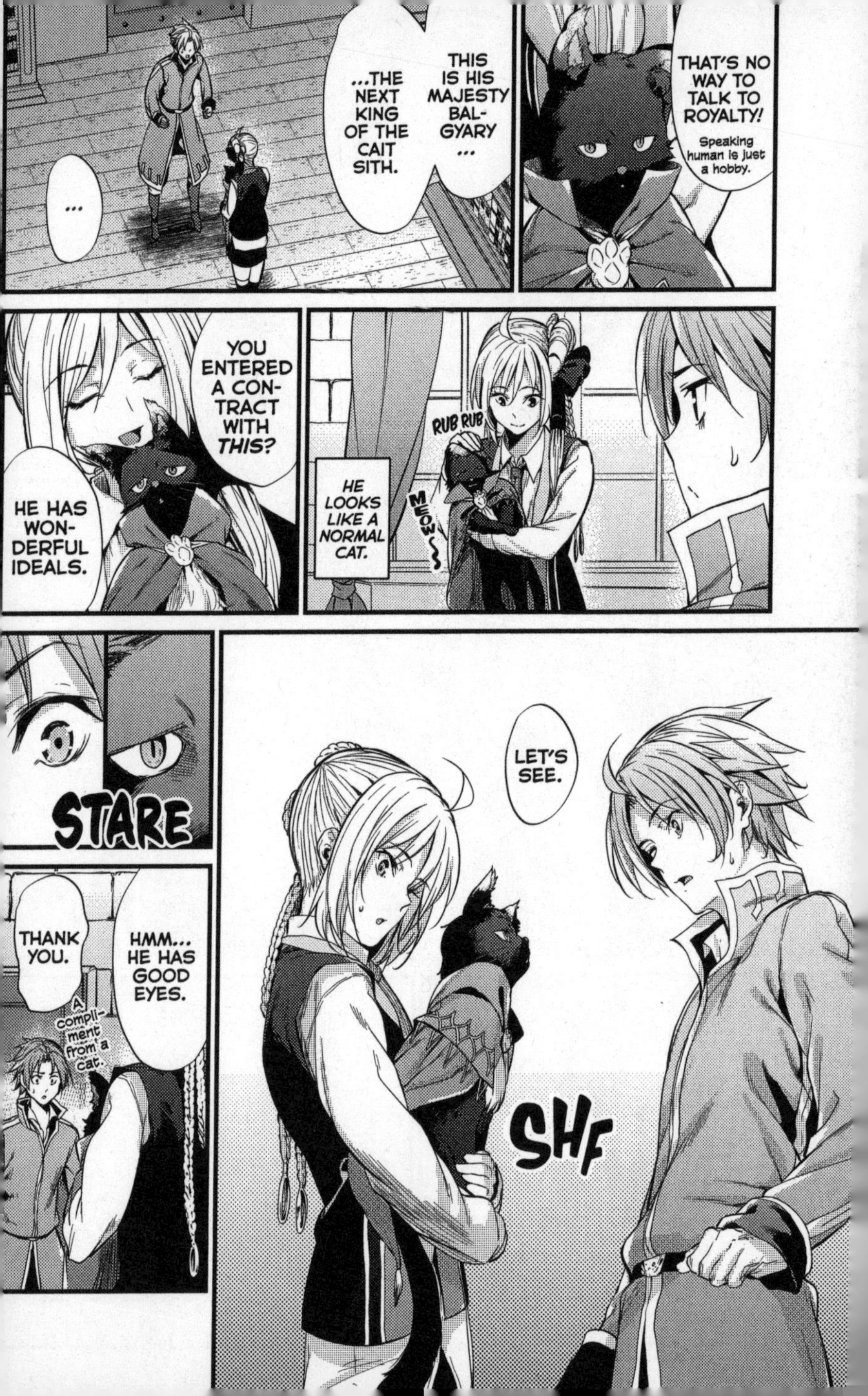
THAT'S NO WAY TO TALK TO ROYALTY!
Speaking human is just a hobby.
THIS IS HIS MAJESTY BAL-GYARY...
...THE NEXT KING OF THE CAIT SITH.
...
RUB RUB
MEOW~
HE LOOKS LIKE A NORMAL CAT.
YOU ENTERED A CONTRACT WITH *THIS?*
HE HAS WONDERFUL IDEALS.
LET'S SEE.
SHF
STARE
HMM... HE HAS GOOD EYES.
THANK YOU.
A compliment from a cat.

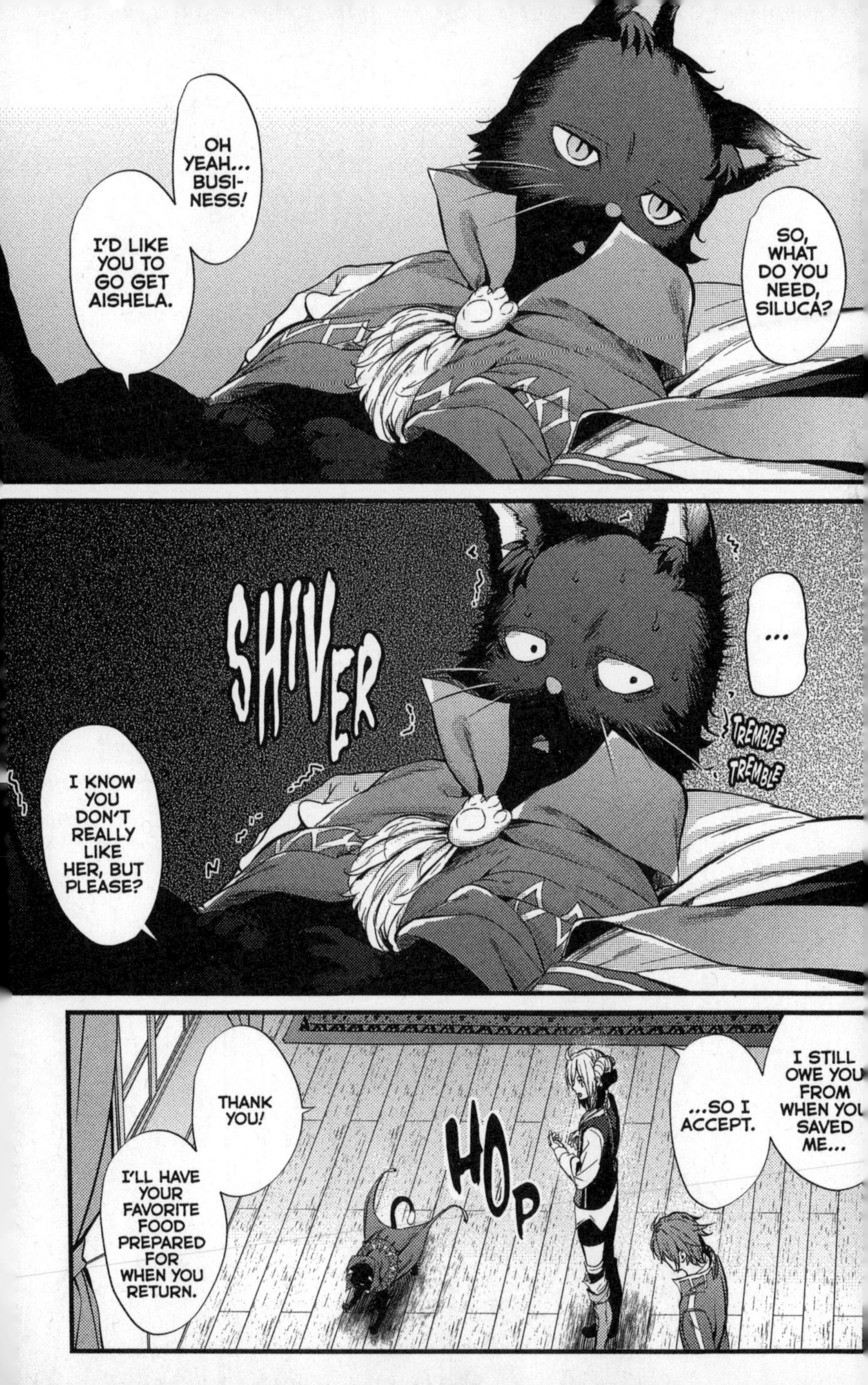
SO, WHAT DO YOU NEED, SILUCA?
OH YEAH... BUSINESS!
I'D LIKE YOU TO GO GET AISHELA.
...
TREMBLE TREMBLE
SHIVER
I KNOW YOU DON'T REALLY LIKE HER, BUT PLEASE?
I STILL OWE YOU FROM WHEN YOU SAVED ME...
...SO I ACCEPT.
HOP
THANK YOU!
I'LL HAVE YOUR FAVORITE FOOD PREPARED FOR WHEN YOU RETURN.

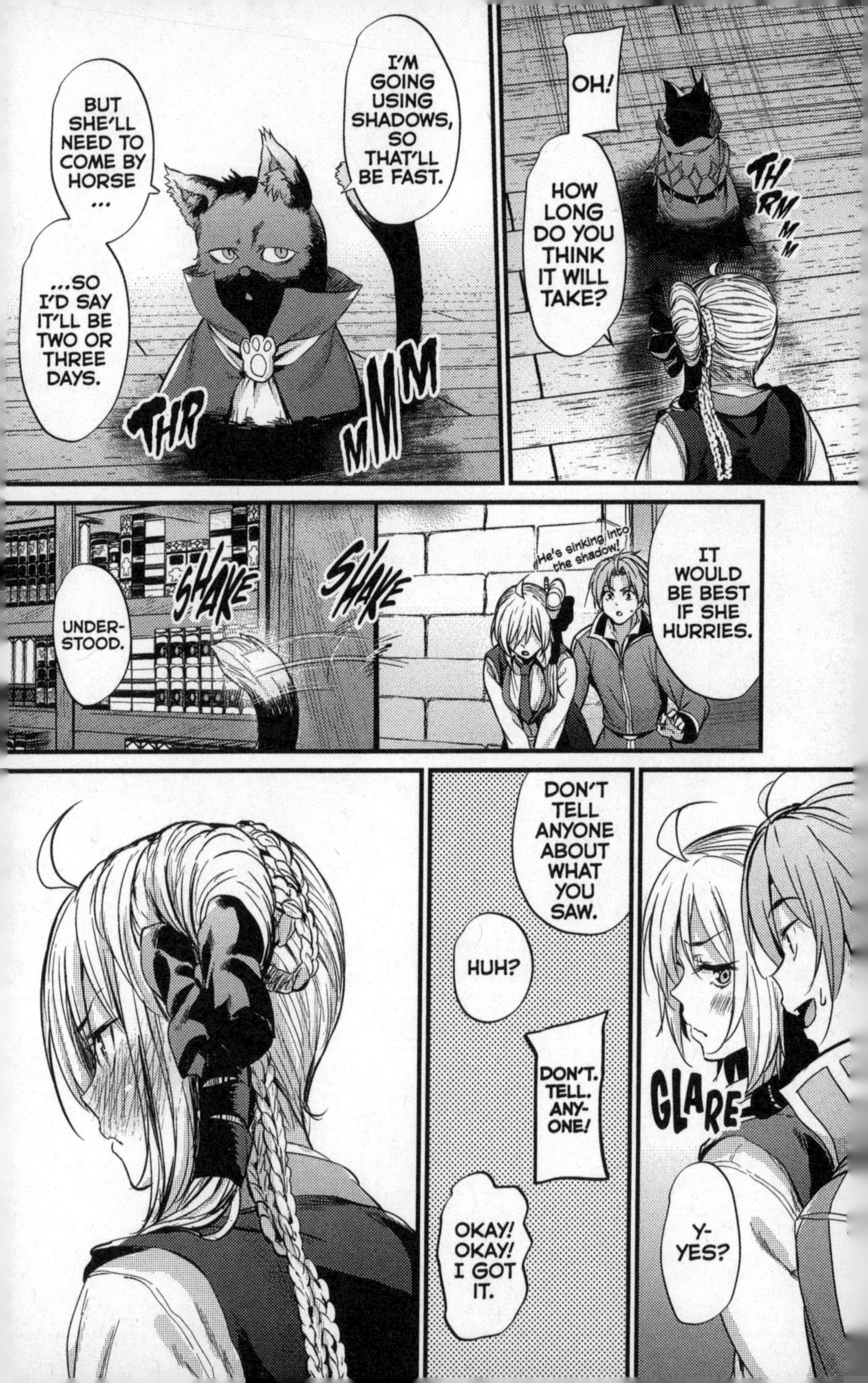
OH!
HOW LONG DO YOU THINK IT WILL TAKE?
THRMMM
I'M GOING USING SHADOWS, SO THAT'LL BE FAST.
BUT SHE'LL NEED TO COME BY HORSE ...
...SO I'D SAY IT'LL BE TWO OR THREE DAYS.
THRMMM
IT WOULD BE BEST IF SHE HURRIES.
He's sinking into the shadow!
SHAKE
SHAKE
UNDER-STOOD.
DON'T TELL ANYONE ABOUT WHAT YOU SAW.
HUH?
DON'T. TELL. ANY-ONE!
GLARE
Y-YES?
OKAY! OKAY! I GOT IT.

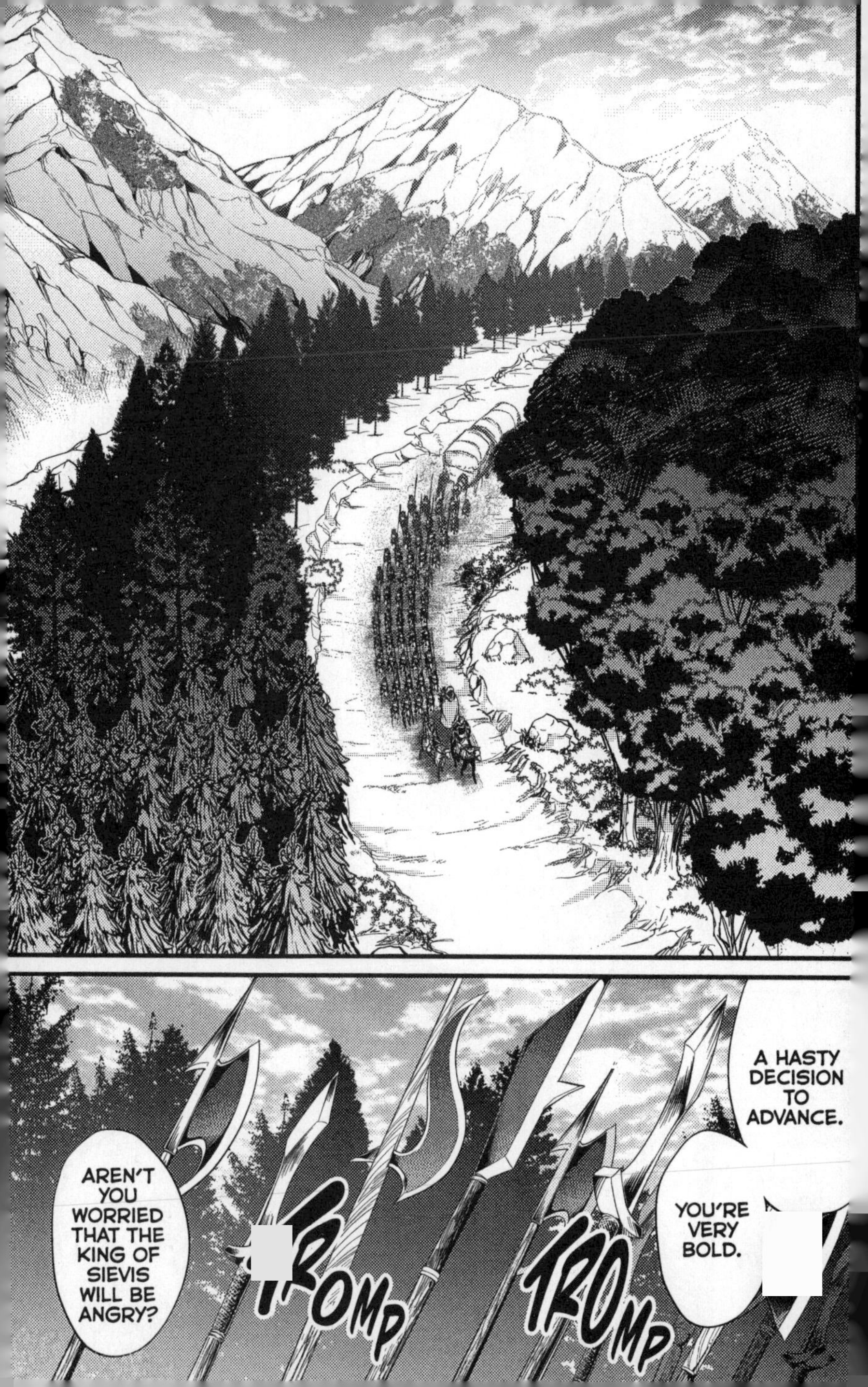
A HASTY DECISION TO ADVANCE.
YOU'RE VERY BOLD.
TROMP
AREN'T YOU WORRIED THAT THE KING OF SIEVIS WILL BE ANGRY?
TROMP

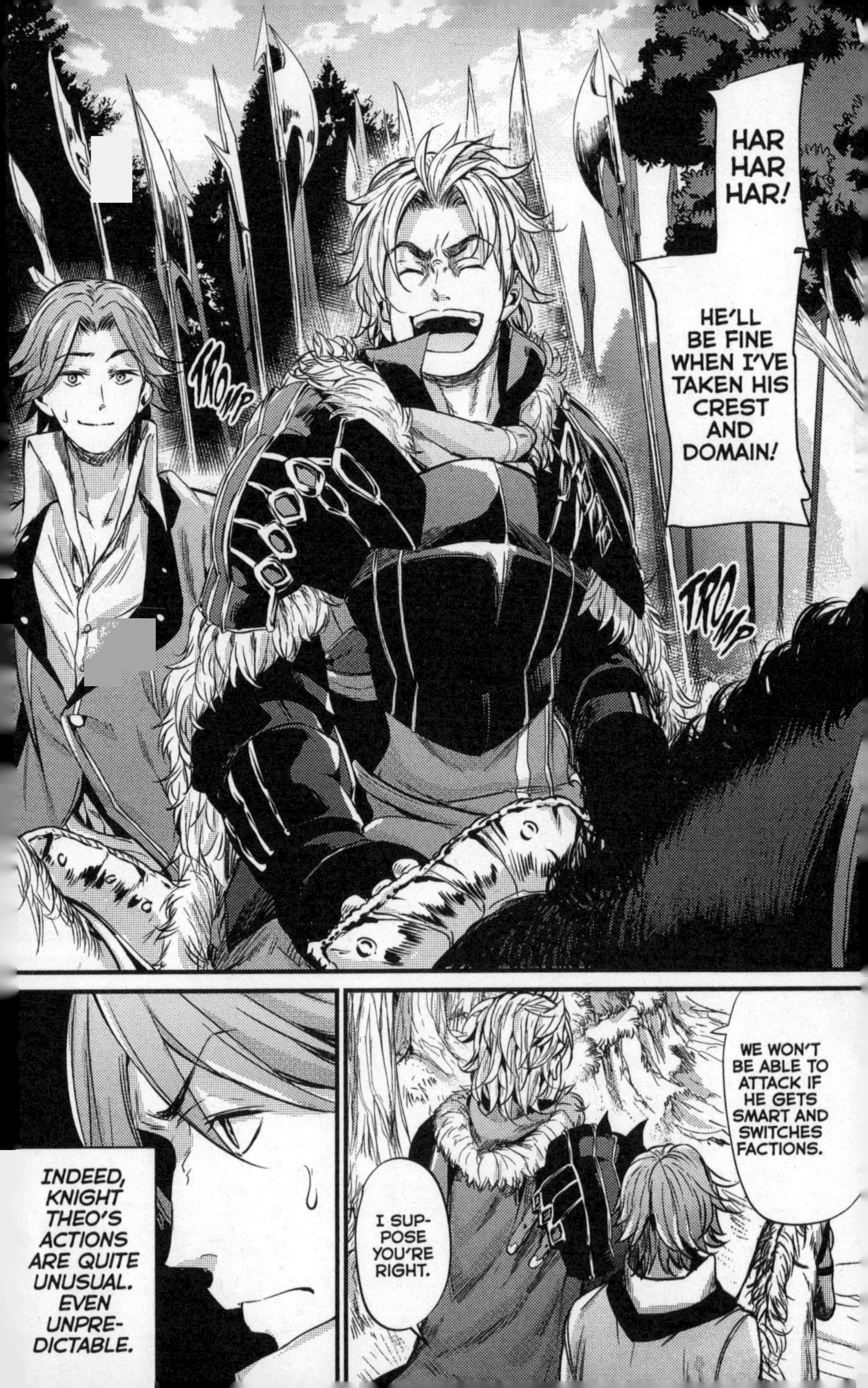
HAR HAR HAR!
HE'LL BE FINE WHEN I'VE TAKEN HIS CREST AND DOMAIN!
TROMP
TROMP
WE WON'T BE ABLE TO ATTACK IF HE GETS SMART AND SWITCHES FACTIONS.
I SUPPOSE YOU'RE RIGHT.
INDEED, KNIGHT THEO'S ACTIONS ARE QUITE UNUSUAL. EVEN UNPREDICTABLE.

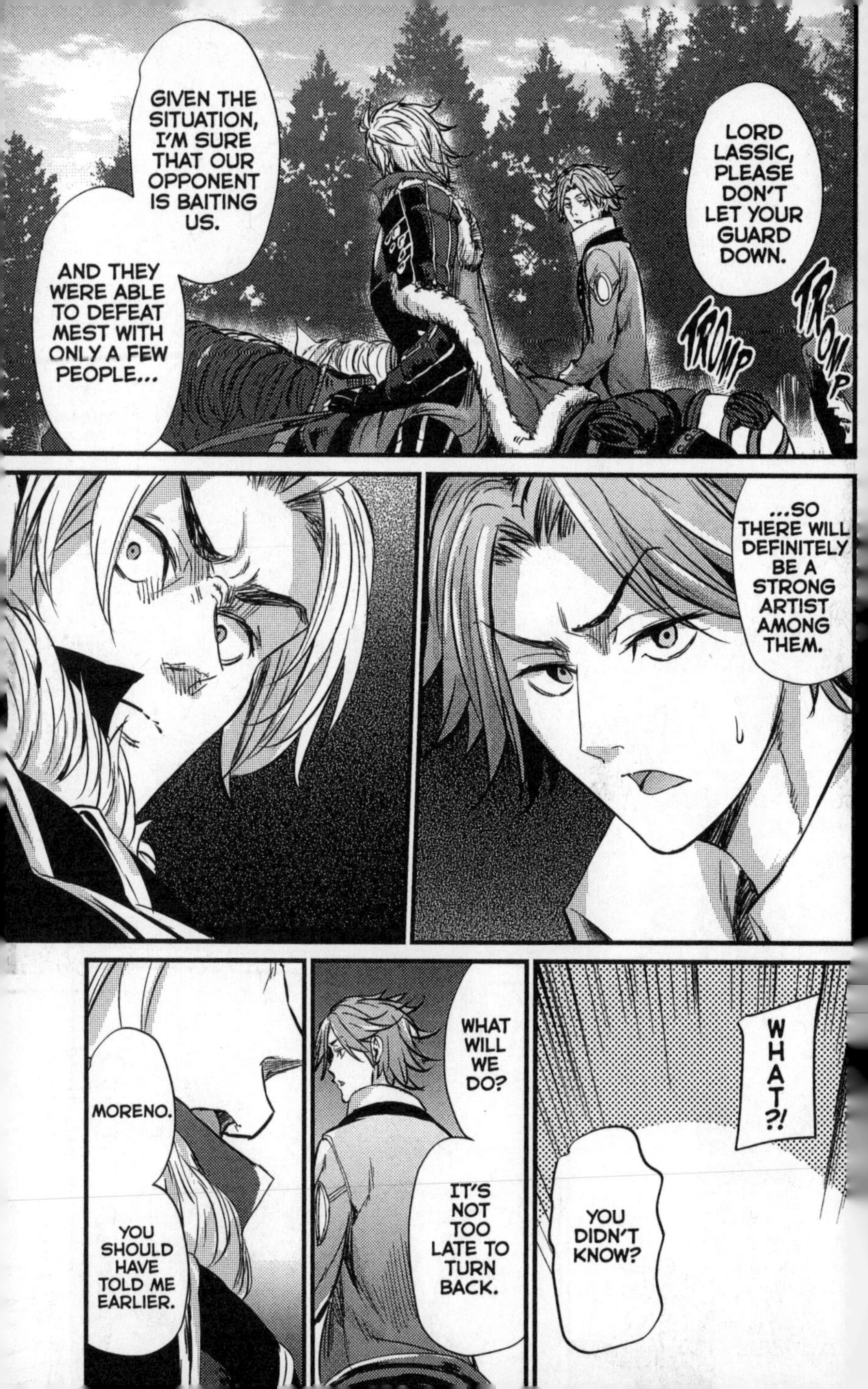
LORD LASSIC, PLEASE DON'T LET YOUR GUARD DOWN.
TROMP
TROMP
GIVEN THE SITUATION, I'M SURE THAT OUR OPPONENT IS BAITING US.
AND THEY WERE ABLE TO DEFEAT MEST WITH ONLY A FEW PEOPLE...
...SO THERE WILL DEFINITELY BE A STRONG ARTIST AMONG THEM.
WHAT?!
YOU DIDN'T KNOW?
WHAT WILL WE DO?
IT'S NOT TOO LATE TO TURN BACK.
MORENO.
YOU SHOULD HAVE TOLD ME EARLIER.

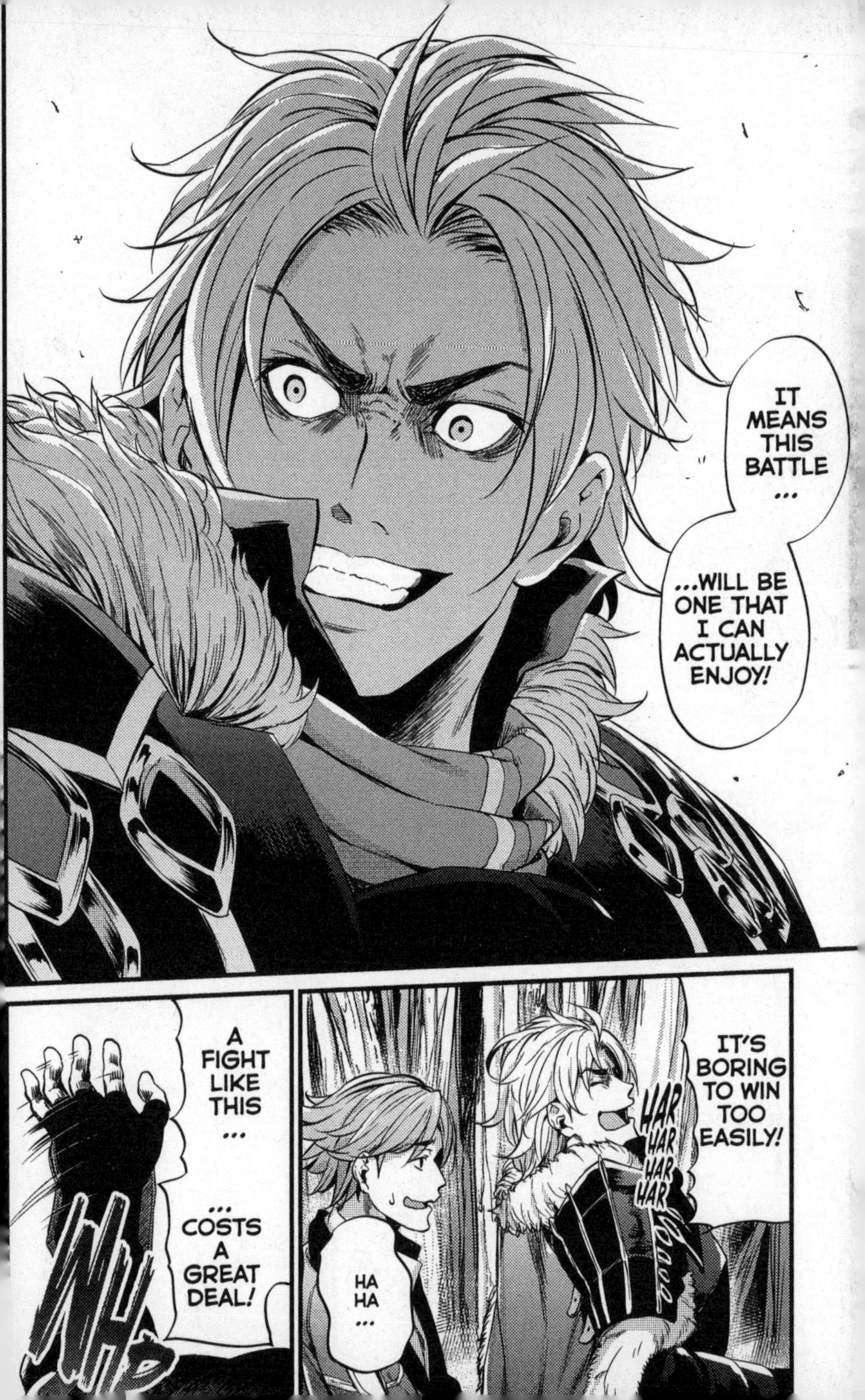
IT MEANS THIS BATTLE...
...WILL BE ONE THAT I CAN ACTUALLY ENJOY!
IT'S BORING TO WIN TOO EASILY!
HAR HAR HAR HAR
HA HA...
A FIGHT LIKE THIS...
...COSTS A GREAT DEAL!

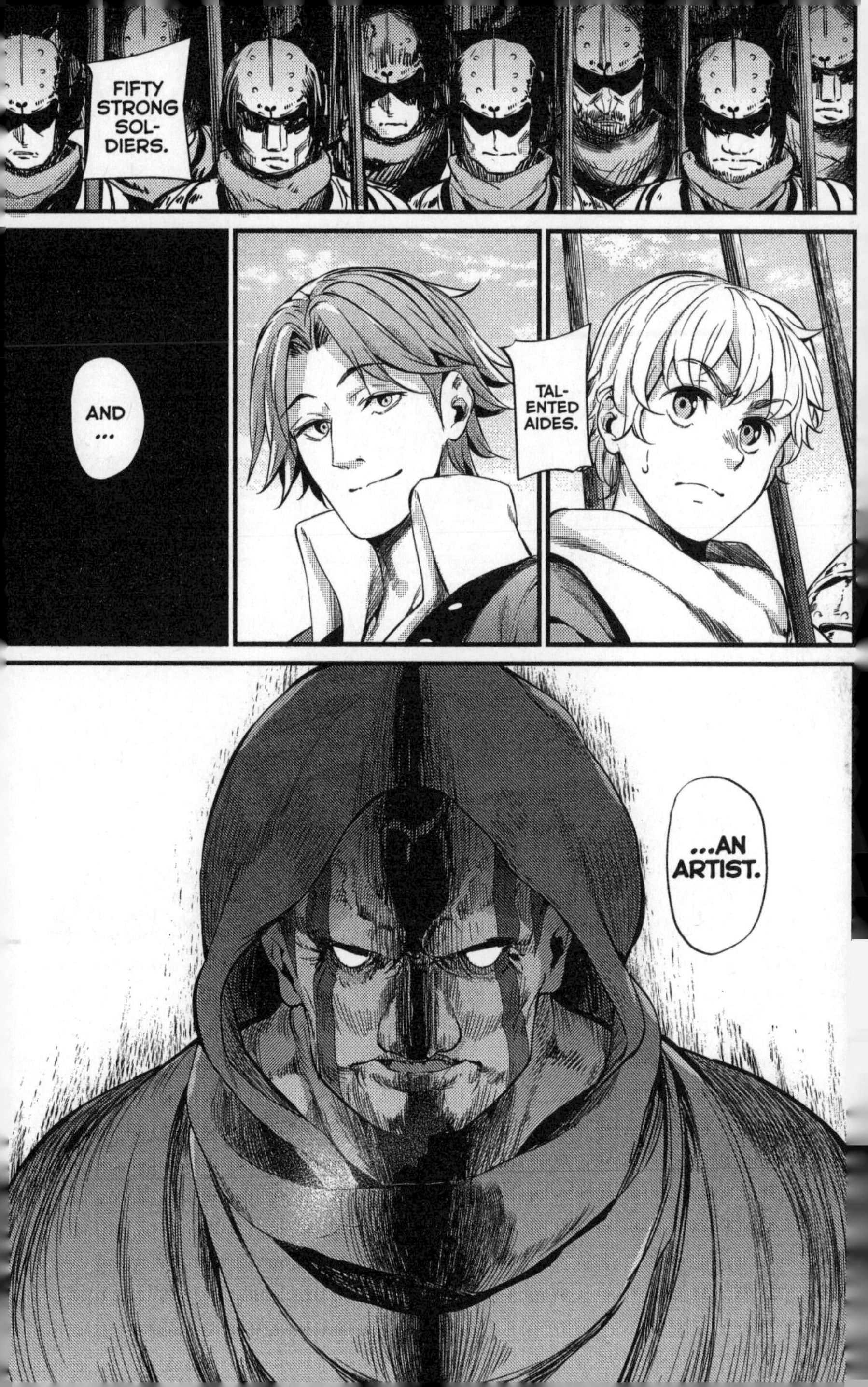
FIFTY STRONG SOL-DIERS.
TAL-ENTED AIDES.
AND ...
...AN ARTIST.

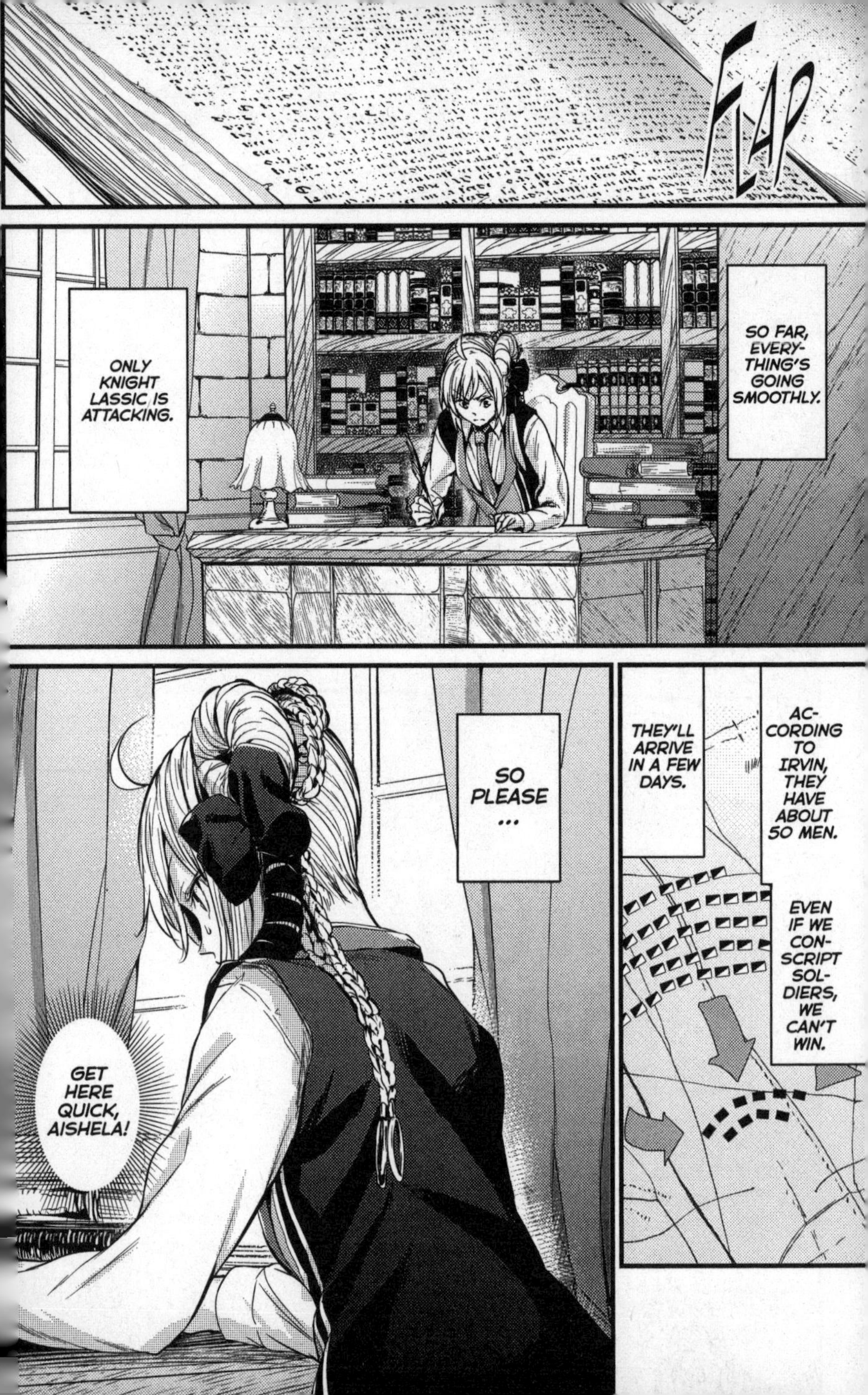
FLAP
SO FAR, EVERYTHING'S GOING SMOOTHLY.
ONLY KNIGHT LASSIC IS ATTACKING.
ACCORDING TO IRVIN, THEY HAVE ABOUT 50 MEN.
THEY'LL ARRIVE IN A FEW DAYS.
EVEN IF WE CONSCRIPT SOLDIERS, WE CAN'T WIN.
SO PLEASE...
GET HERE QUICK, AISHELA!

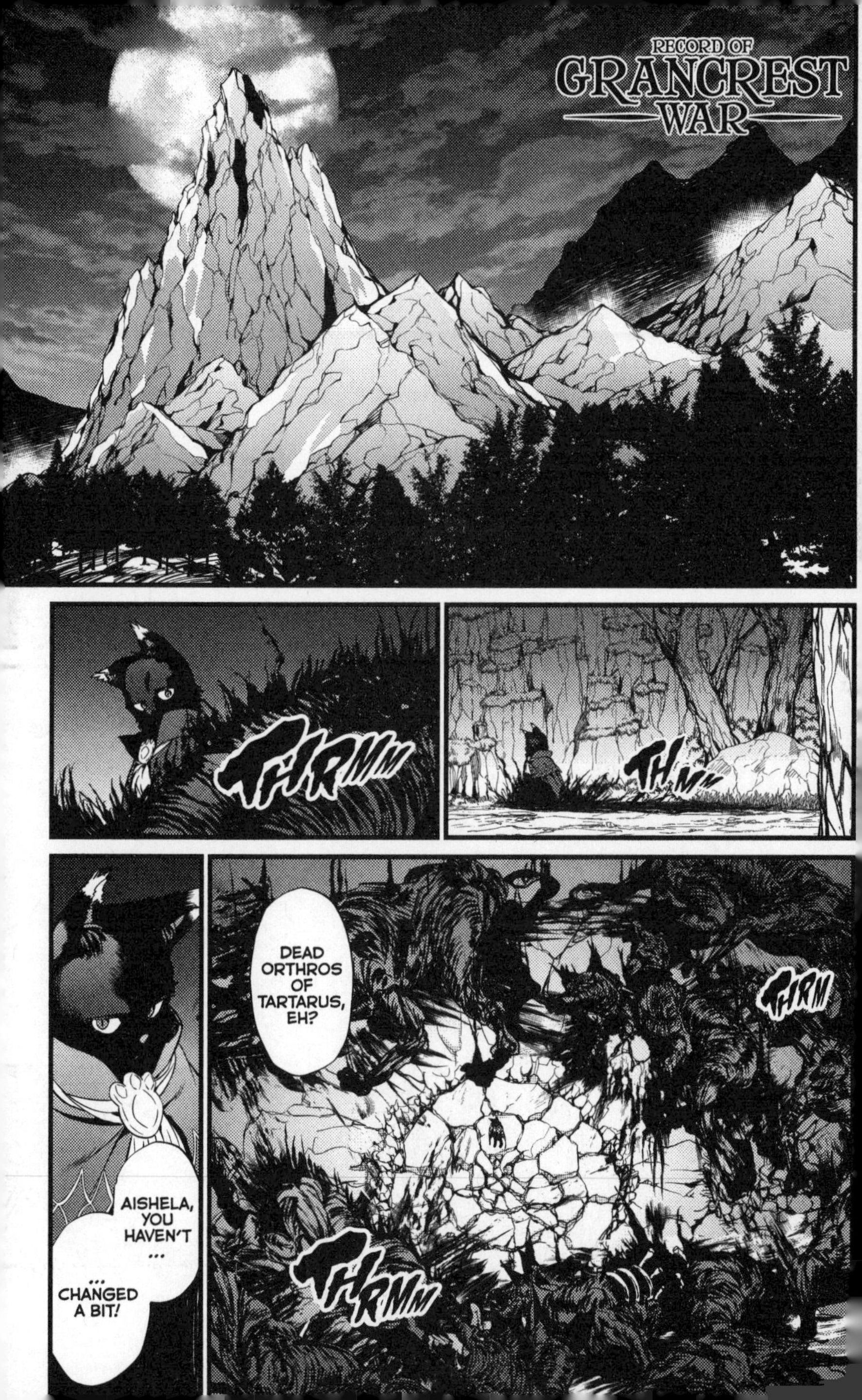
RECORD OF
GRANCREST
WAR
THMM
THRMMM
DEAD ORTHROS OF TARTARUS, EH?
THRM
THRMM
AISHELA, YOU HAVEN'T ...
... CHANGED A BIT!

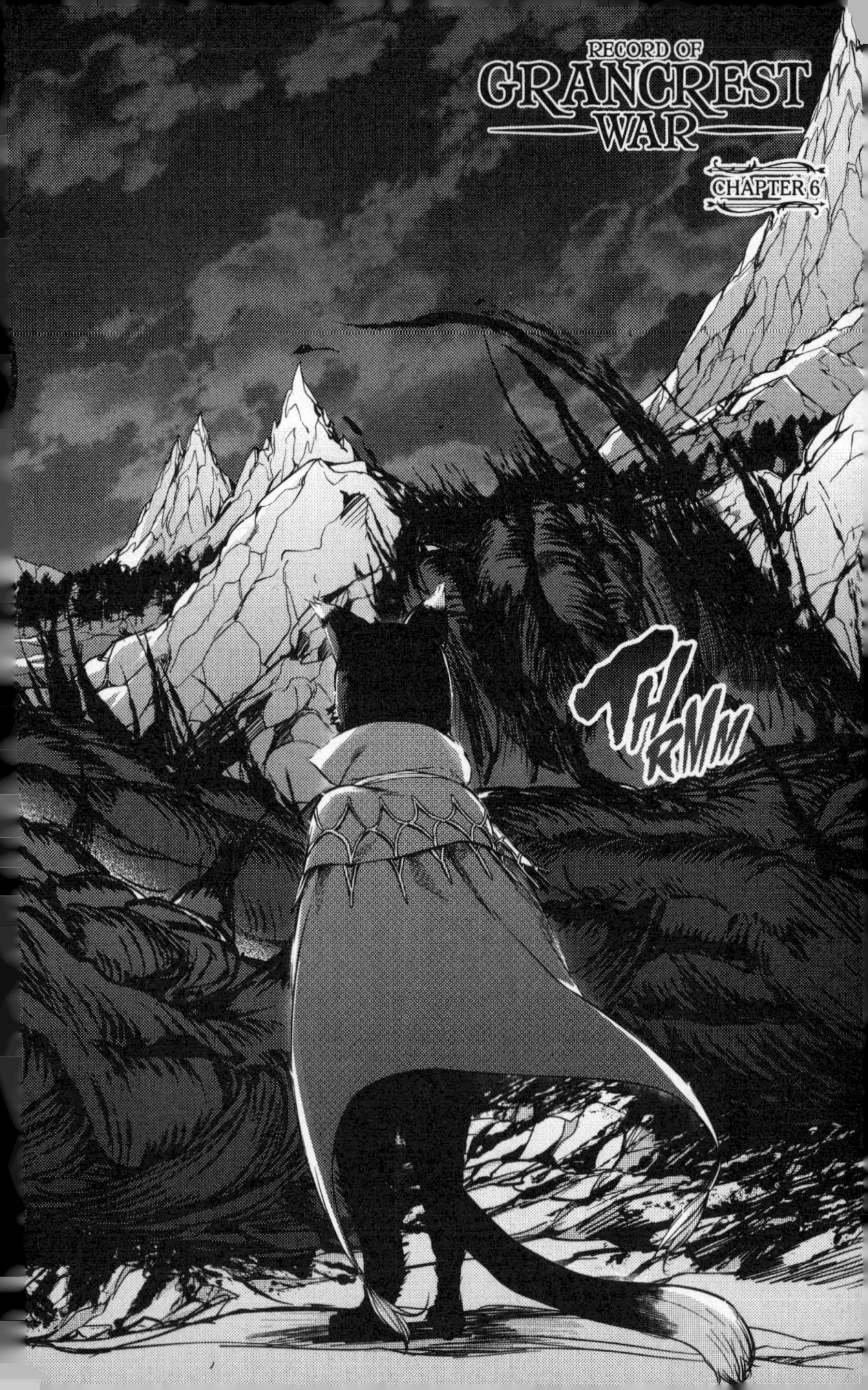
RECORD OF GRANCREST WAR
CHAPTER 6
THRMM

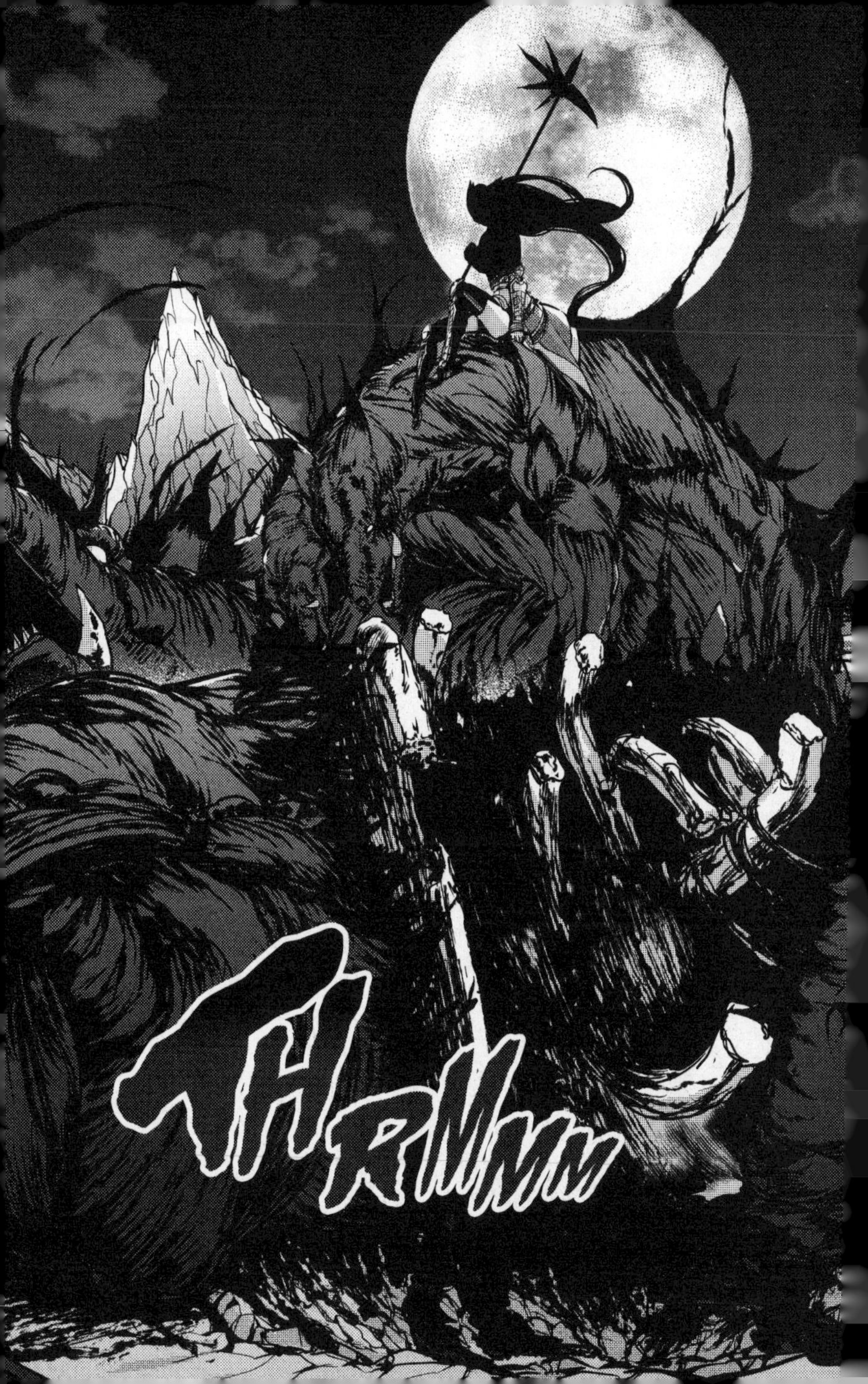
THRMMM

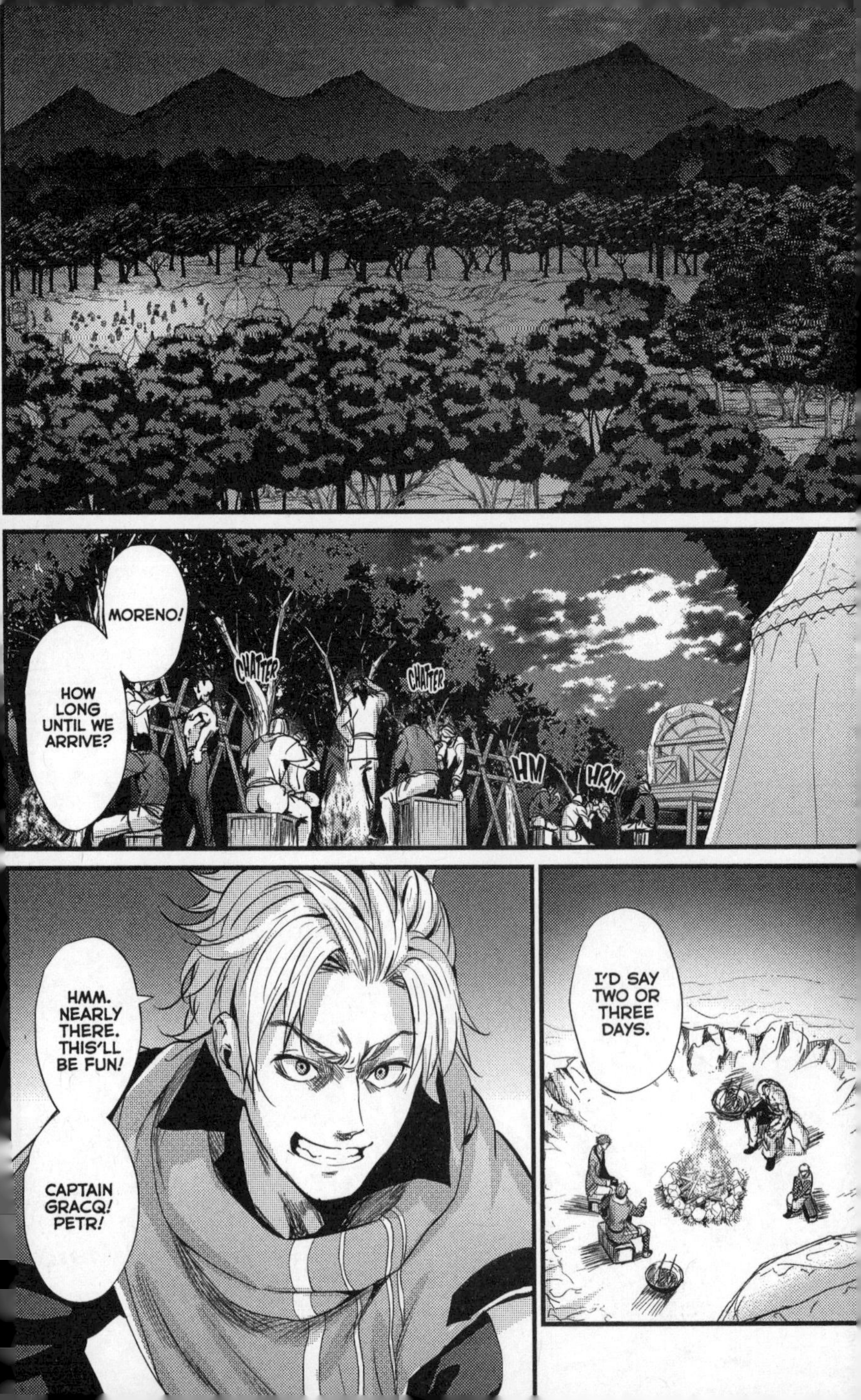
CHATTER
HRM
HM
CHATTER
MORENO!
HOW LONG UNTIL WE ARRIVE?
I'D SAY TWO OR THREE DAYS.
HMM. NEARLY THERE. THIS'LL BE FUN!
CAPTAIN GRACQ! PETR!

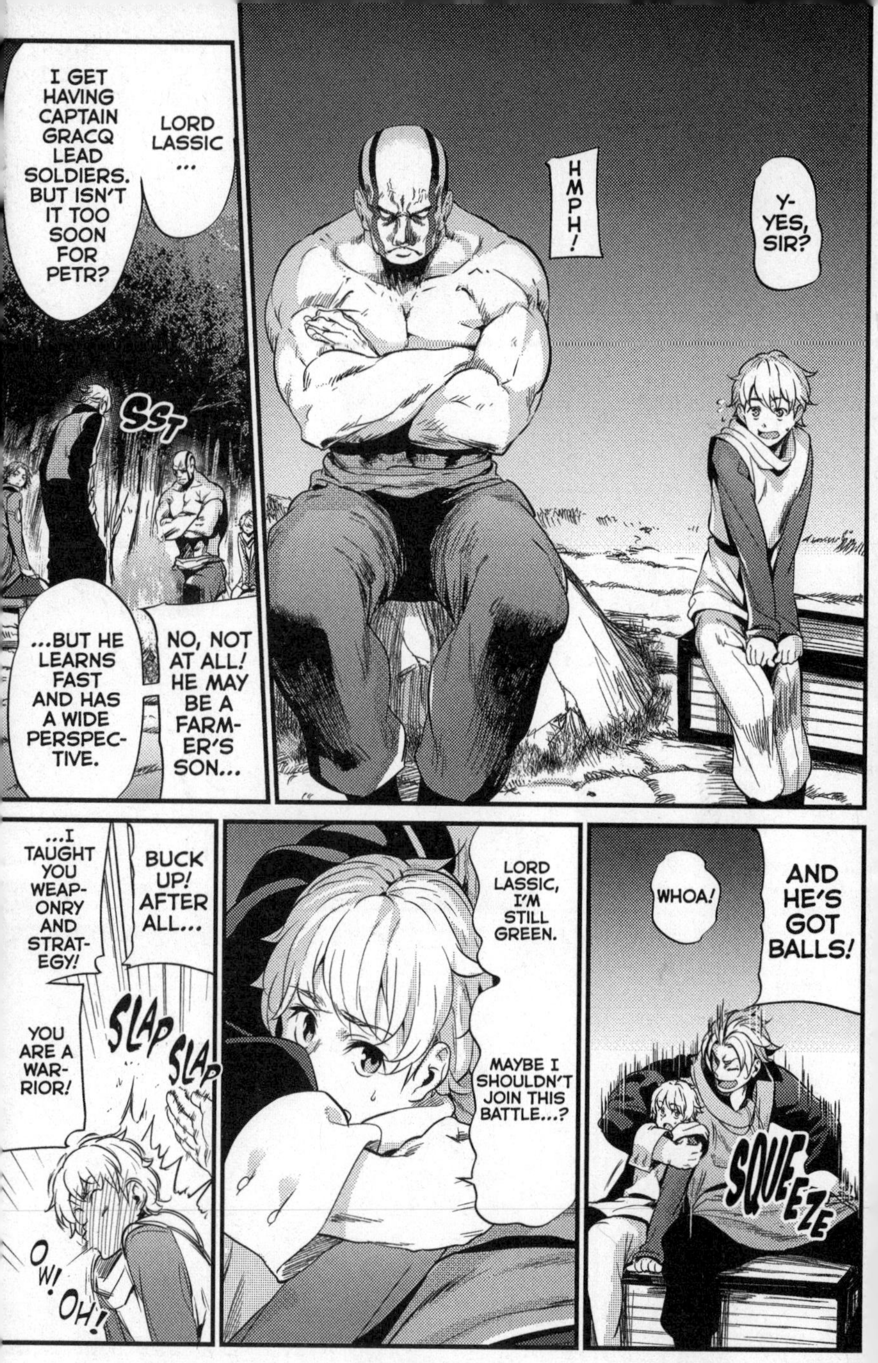
Y-YES, SIR?
HMPH!
LORD LASSIC...
I GET HAVING CAPTAIN GRACQ LEAD SOLDIERS. BUT ISN'T IT TOO SOON FOR PETR?
SST
NO, NOT AT ALL! HE MAY BE A FARMER'S SON...
...BUT HE LEARNS FAST AND HAS A WIDE PERSPECTIVE.
AND HE'S GOT BALLS!
WHOA!
SQUEEZE
LORD LASSIC, I'M STILL GREEN.
MAYBE I SHOULDN'T JOIN THIS BATTLE...?
BUCK UP! AFTER ALL...
...I TAUGHT YOU WEAPONRY AND STRATEGY!
SLAP SLAP
YOU ARE A WARRIOR!
OW! OH!

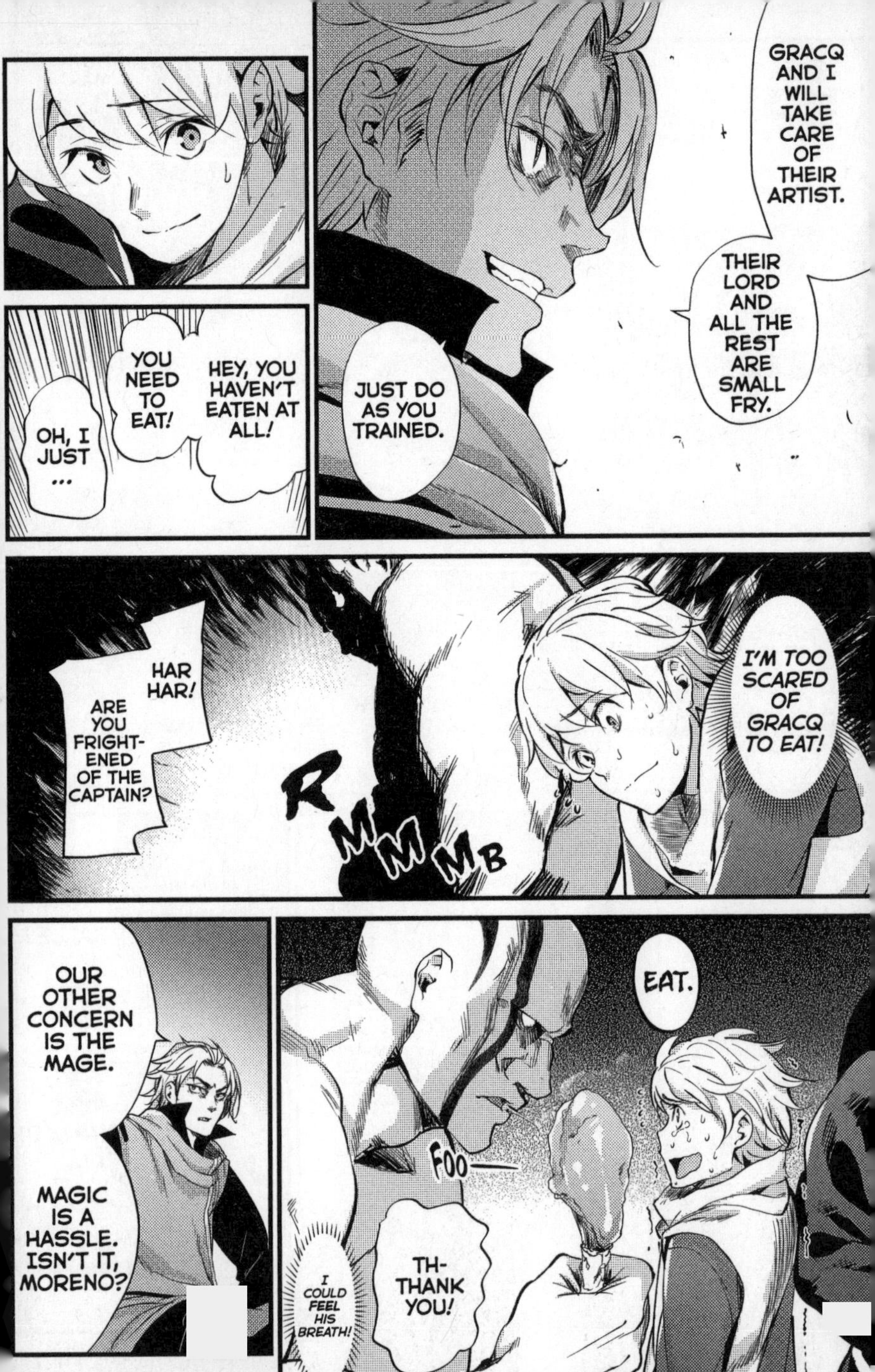
GRACQ AND I WILL TAKE CARE OF THEIR ARTIST.
THEIR LORD AND ALL THE REST ARE SMALL FRY.
JUST DO AS YOU TRAINED.
HEY, YOU HAVEN'T EATEN AT ALL!
YOU NEED TO EAT!
OH, I JUST ...
I'M TOO SCARED OF GRACQ TO EAT!
HAR HAR! ARE YOU FRIGHT-ENED OF THE CAPTAIN?
RMMMMB
EAT.
FOO—
TH-THANK YOU!
I COULD FEEL HIS BREATH!
OUR OTHER CONCERN IS THE MAGE.
MAGIC IS A HASSLE. ISN'T IT, MORENO?

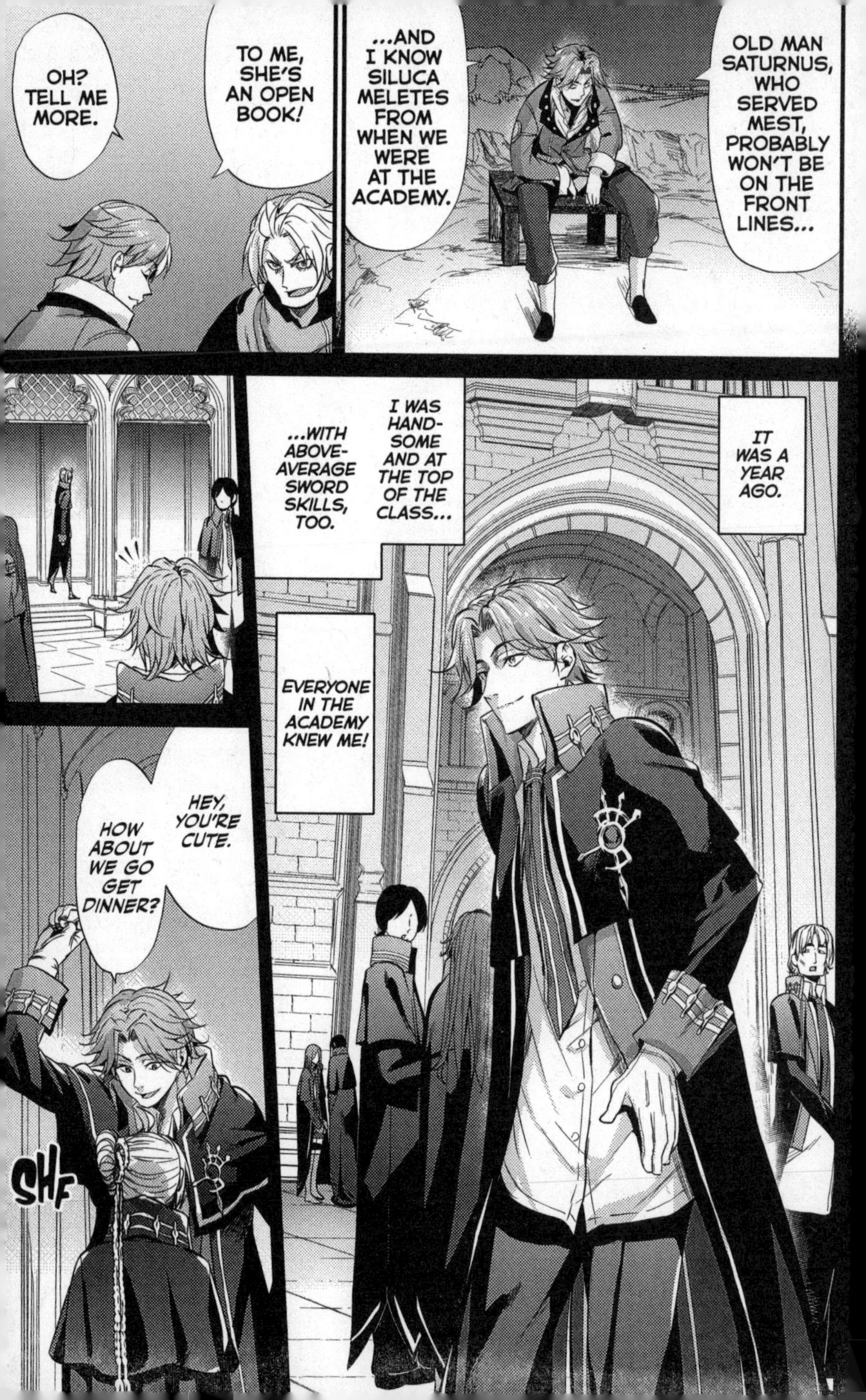
OLD MAN SATURNUS, WHO SERVED MEST, PROBABLY WON'T BE ON THE FRONT LINES...
...AND I KNOW SILUCA MELETES FROM WHEN WE WERE AT THE ACADEMY.
TO ME, SHE'S AN OPEN BOOK!
OH? TELL ME MORE.
IT WAS A YEAR AGO.
I WAS HANDSOME AND AT THE TOP OF THE CLASS...
...WITH ABOVE-AVERAGE SWORD SKILLS, TOO.
EVERYONE IN THE ACADEMY KNEW ME!
HEY, YOU'RE CUTE.
HOW ABOUT WE GO GET DINNER?
SHF

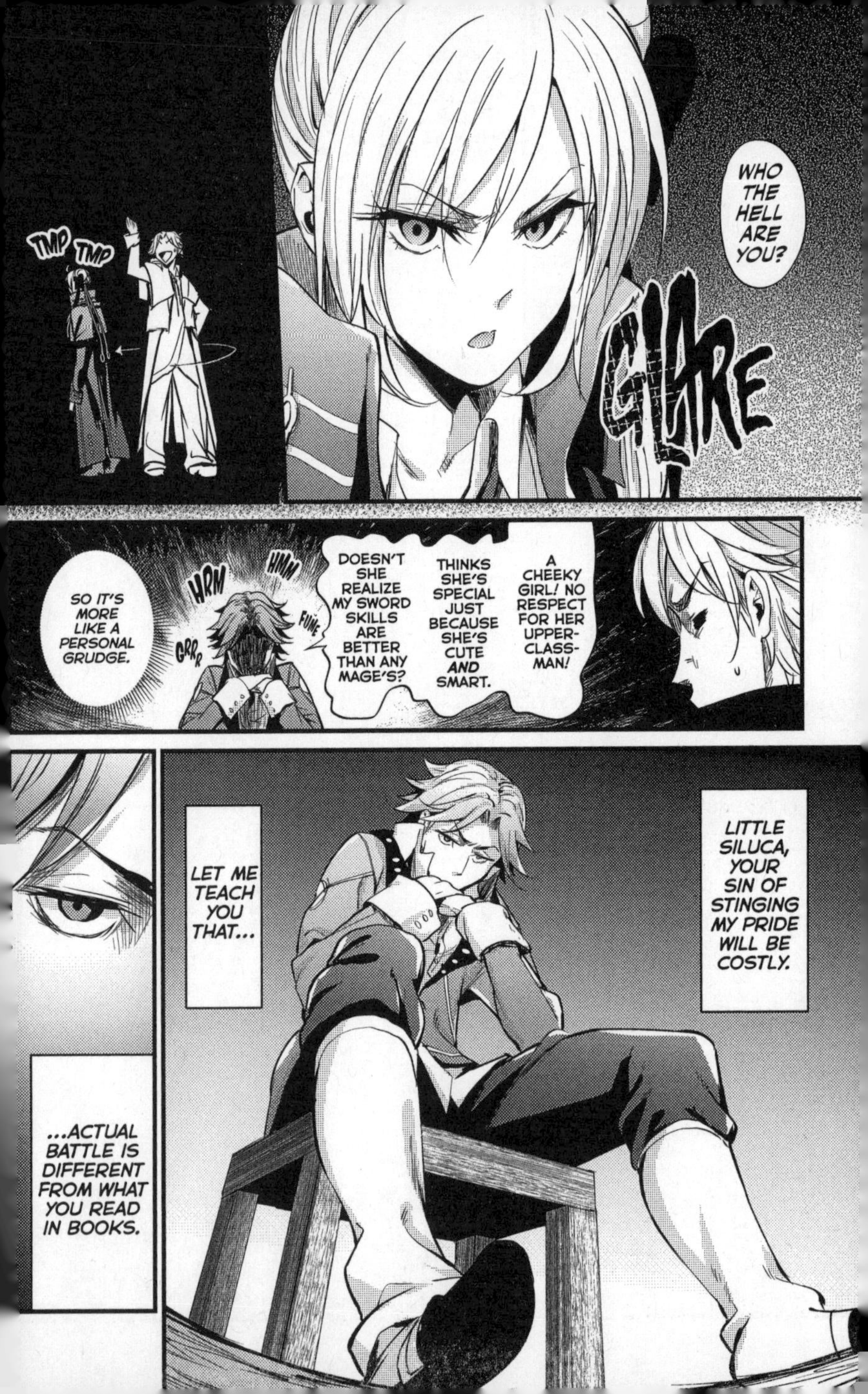
WHO THE HELL ARE YOU?
GLARE
TMP TMP
A CHEEKY GIRL! NO RESPECT FOR HER UPPER-CLASSMAN!
THINKS SHE'S SPECIAL JUST BECAUSE SHE'S CUTE *AND* SMART.
DOESN'T SHE REALIZE MY SWORD SKILLS ARE BETTER THAN ANY MAGE'S?
HMM
FUME
HRM
GRRR
SO IT'S MORE LIKE A PERSONAL GRUDGE.
LITTLE SILUCA, YOUR SIN OF STINGING MY PRIDE WILL BE COSTLY.
LET ME TEACH YOU THAT...
...ACTUAL BATTLE IS DIFFERENT FROM WHAT YOU READ IN BOOKS.

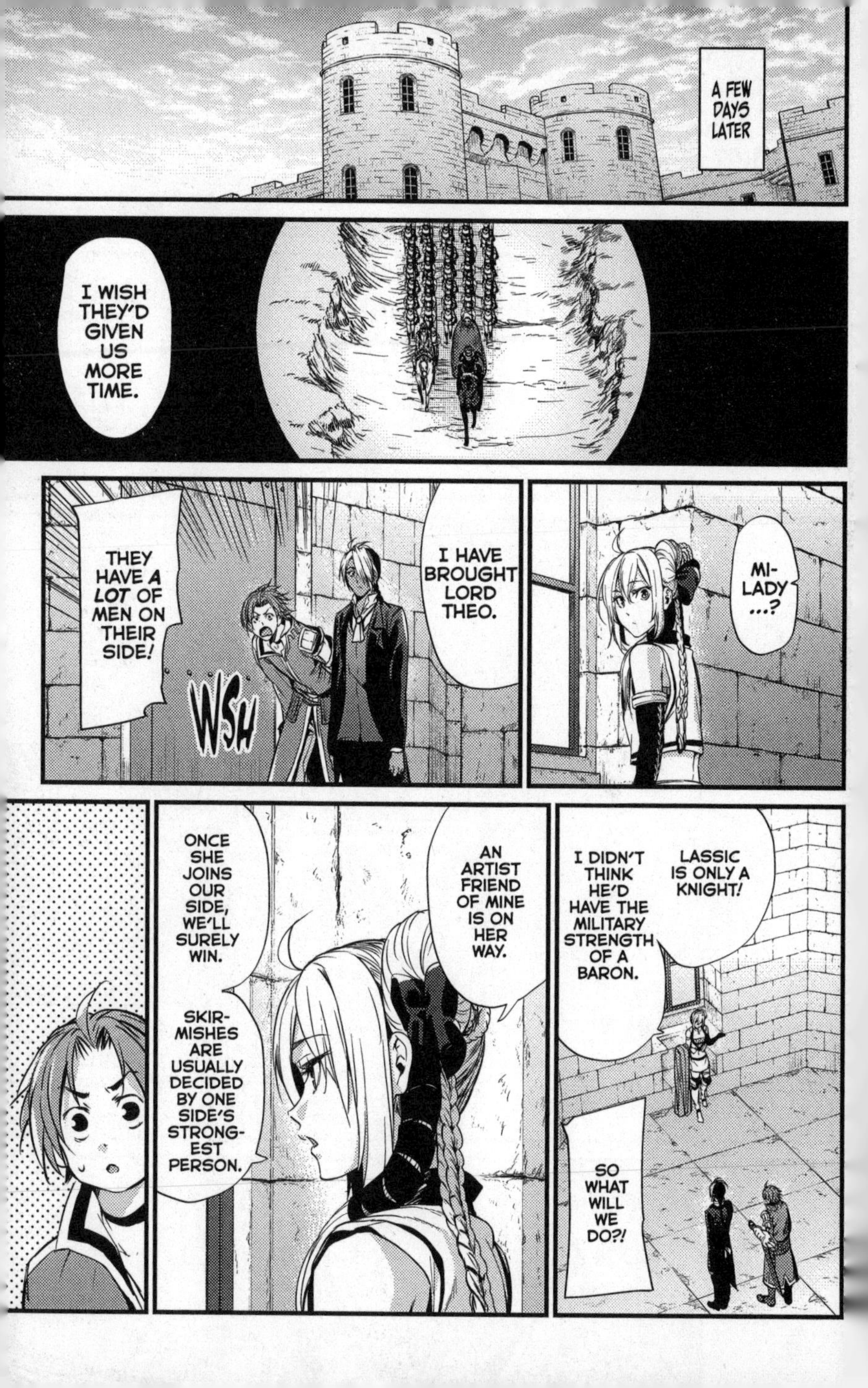
A FEW DAYS LATER
I WISH THEY'D GIVEN US MORE TIME.
MI-LADY ...?
I HAVE BROUGHT LORD THEO.
THEY HAVE A *LOT* OF MEN ON THEIR SIDE!
WSH
LASSIC IS ONLY A KNIGHT!
I DIDN'T THINK HE'D HAVE THE MILITARY STRENGTH OF A BARON.
SO WHAT WILL WE DO?!
AN ARTIST FRIEND OF MINE IS ON HER WAY.
ONCE SHE JOINS OUR SIDE, WE'LL SURELY WIN.
SKIRMISHES ARE USUALLY DECIDED BY ONE SIDE'S STRONGEST PERSON.

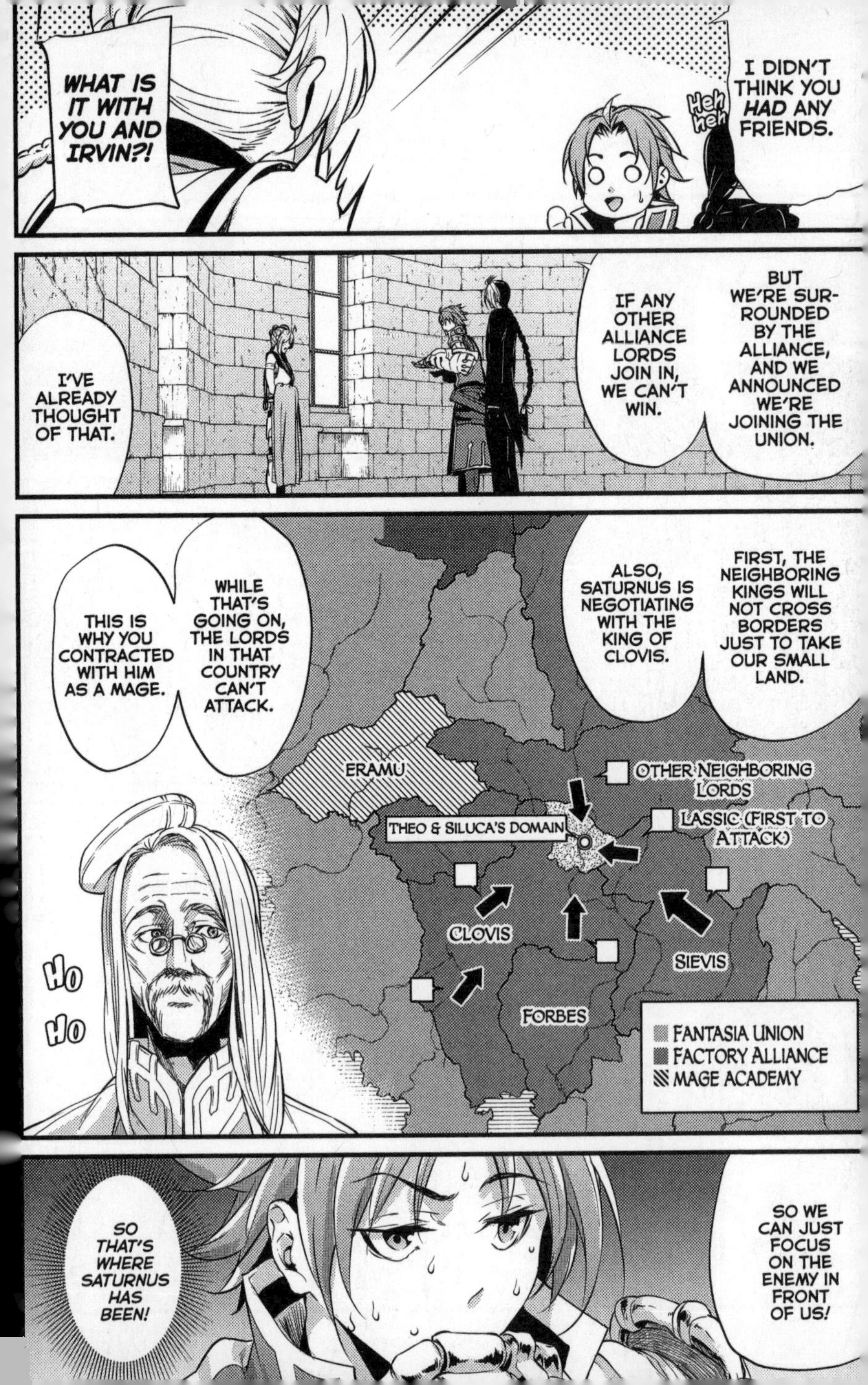
I DIDN'T THINK YOU HAD ANY FRIENDS.
Heh heh
WHAT IS IT WITH YOU AND IRVIN?!
BUT WE'RE SURROUNDED BY THE ALLIANCE, AND WE ANNOUNCED WE'RE JOINING THE UNION.
IF ANY OTHER ALLIANCE LORDS JOIN IN, WE CAN'T WIN.
I'VE ALREADY THOUGHT OF THAT.
FIRST, THE NEIGHBORING KINGS WILL NOT CROSS BORDERS JUST TO TAKE OUR SMALL LAND.
ALSO, SATURNUS IS NEGOTIATING WITH THE KING OF CLOVIS.
WHILE THAT'S GOING ON, THE LORDS IN THAT COUNTRY CAN'T ATTACK.
THIS IS WHY YOU CONTRACTED WITH HIM AS A MAGE.
ERAMU
OTHER NEIGHBORING LORDS
THEO & SILUCA'S DOMAIN
LASSIC (FIRST TO ATTACK)
CLOVIS
SIEVIS
FORBES
FANTASIA UNION
FACTORY ALLIANCE
MAGE ACADEMY
HO HO
SO WE CAN JUST FOCUS ON THE ENEMY IN FRONT OF US!
SO THAT'S WHERE SATURNUS HAS BEEN!

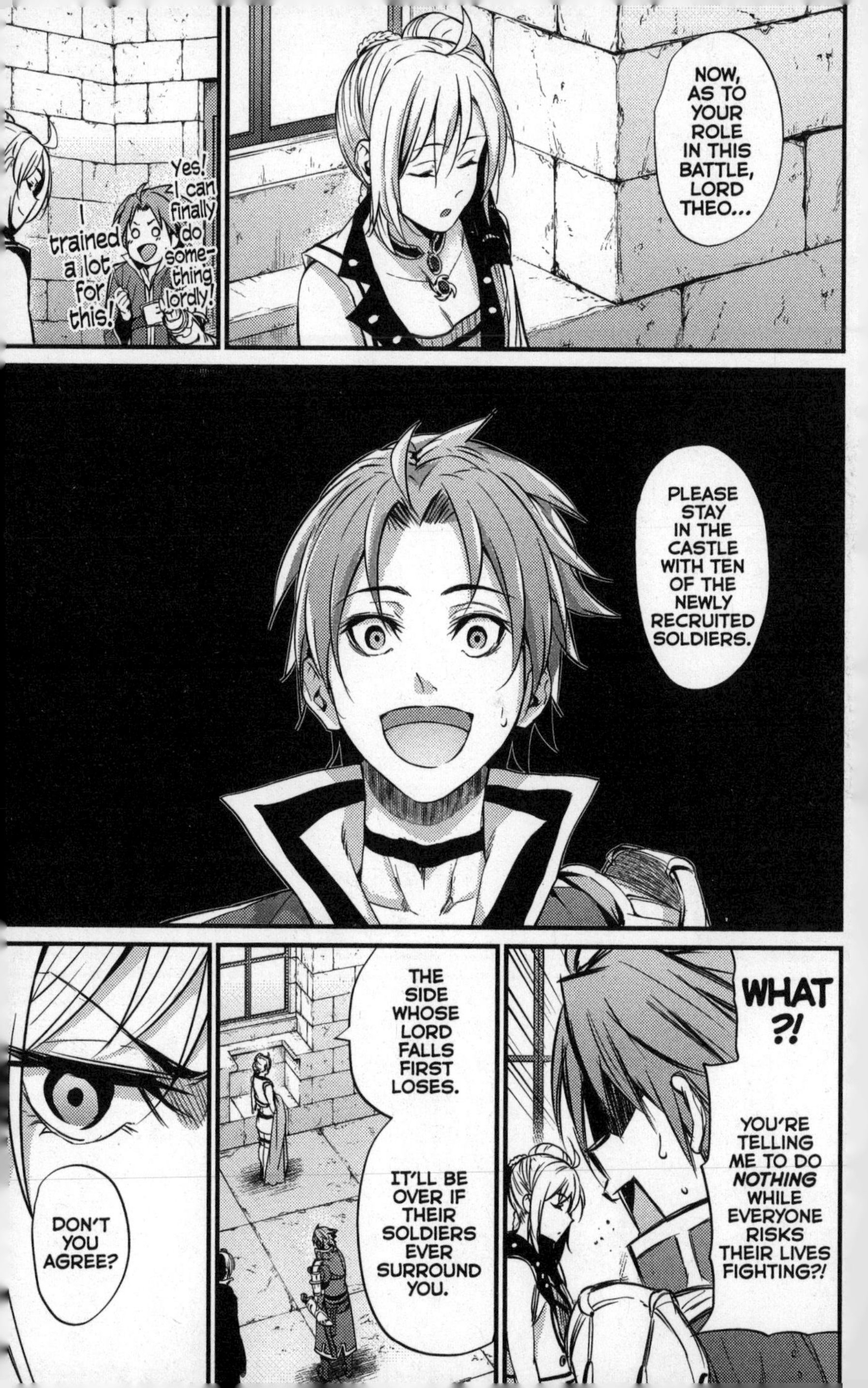
NOW, AS TO YOUR ROLE IN THIS BATTLE, LORD THEO...
Yes! I can finally do something lordly!
I trained a lot for this!
PLEASE STAY IN THE CASTLE WITH TEN OF THE NEWLY RECRUITED SOLDIERS.
WHAT?!
YOU'RE TELLING ME TO DO *NOTHING* WHILE EVERYONE RISKS THEIR LIVES FIGHTING?!
THE SIDE WHOSE LORD FALLS FIRST LOSES.
IT'LL BE OVER IF THEIR SOLDIERS EVER SURROUND YOU.
DON'T YOU AGREE?

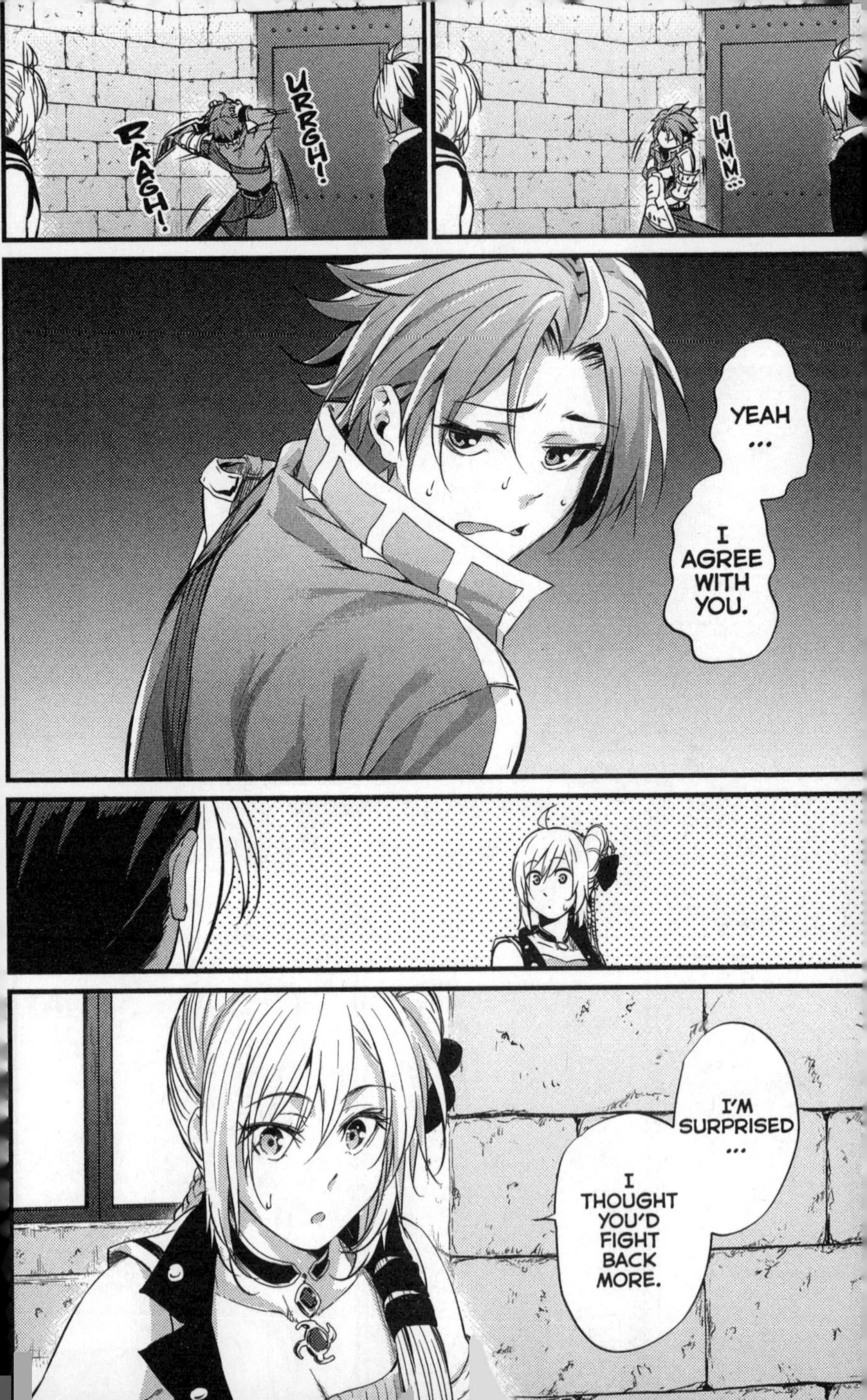
HMM...
URRGH!
RAAGH!
YEAH...
I AGREE WITH YOU.
I'M SURPRISED...
I THOUGHT YOU'D FIGHT BACK MORE.

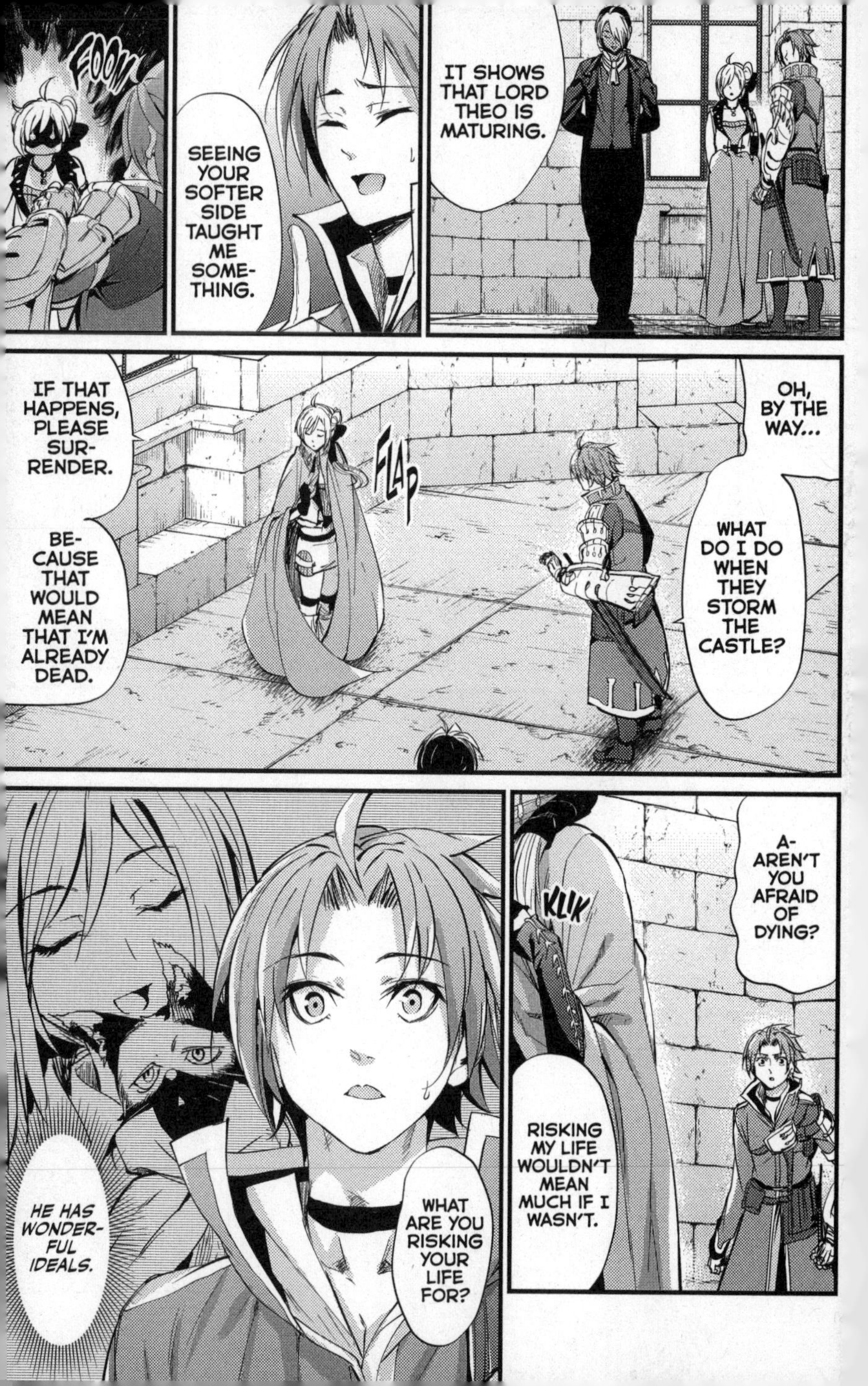
IT SHOWS THAT LORD THEO IS MATURING.
SEEING YOUR SOFTER SIDE TAUGHT ME SOMETHING.
FOOM
OH, BY THE WAY...
WHAT DO I DO WHEN THEY STORM THE CASTLE?
FLAP
IF THAT HAPPENS, PLEASE SURRENDER.
BECAUSE THAT WOULD MEAN THAT I'M ALREADY DEAD.
A- AREN'T YOU AFRAID OF DYING?
KLIK
RISKING MY LIFE WOULDN'T MEAN MUCH IF I WASN'T.
WHAT ARE YOU RISKING YOUR LIFE FOR?
HE HAS WONDERFUL IDEALS.

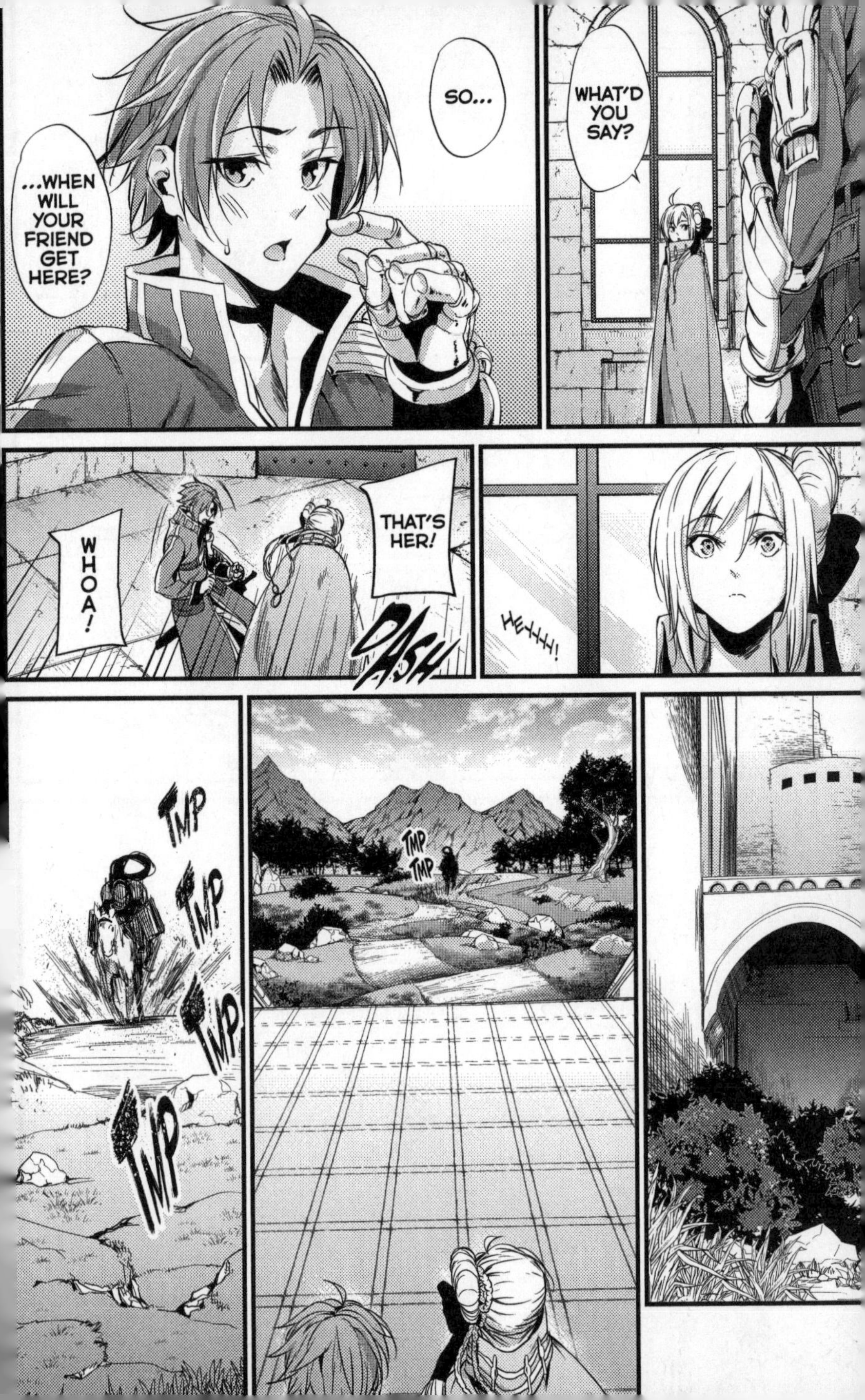
WHAT'D YOU SAY?
SO...
...WHEN WILL YOUR FRIEND GET HERE?
HEYYYY!
THAT'S HER!
DASH
WHOA!
TMP TMP
TMP
TMP
TMP
TMP
TMP

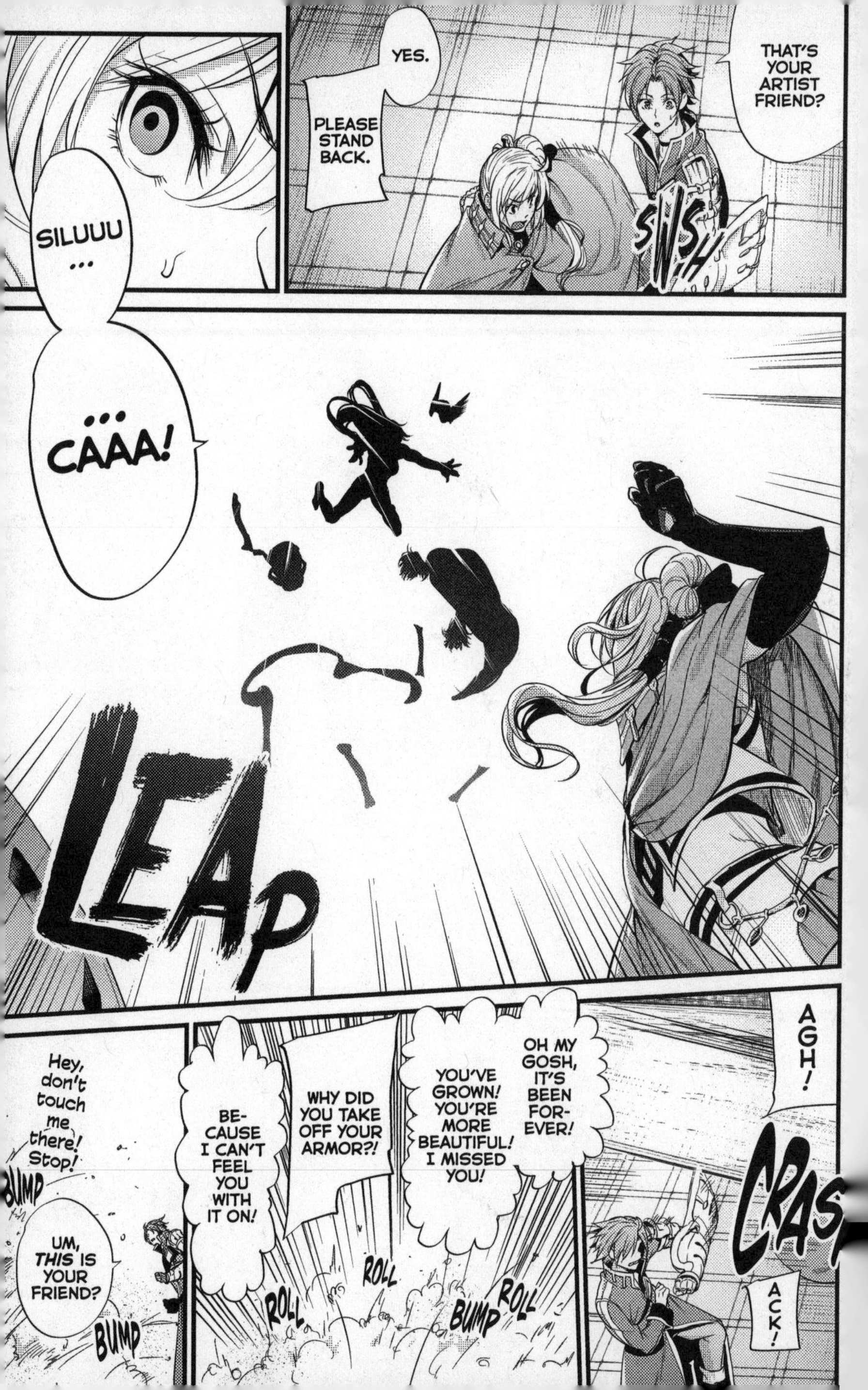
THAT'S YOUR ARTIST FRIEND?
YES.
PLEASE STAND BACK.
SILUUU ...
... CÄAA!
LEAP
AGH!
CRAS
ACK!
OH MY GOSH, IT'S BEEN FOR-EVER!
YOU'VE GROWN! YOU'RE MORE BEAUTIFUL! I MISSED YOU!
WHY DID YOU TAKE OFF YOUR ARMOR?!
BE-CAUSE I CAN'T FEEL YOU WITH IT ON!
ROLL
BUMP
ROLL
ROLL
Hey, don't touch me there! Stop!
BUMP
UM, THIS IS YOUR FRIEND?
BUMP

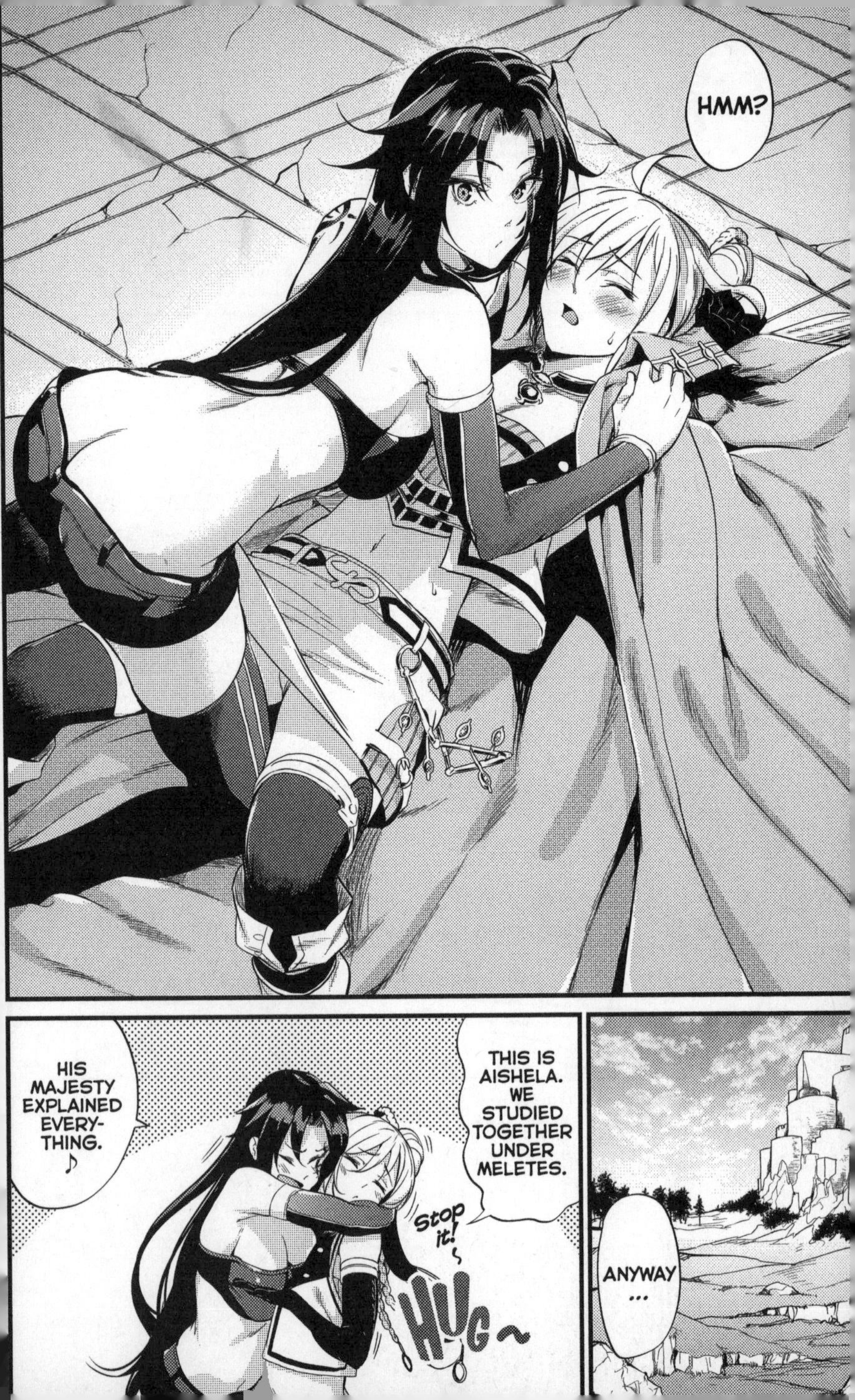
HMM?
ANYWAY ...
THIS IS AISHELA. WE STUDIED TOGETHER UNDER MELETES.
Stop it!~
HUG~
HIS MAJESTY EXPLAINED EVERY-THING. ♪

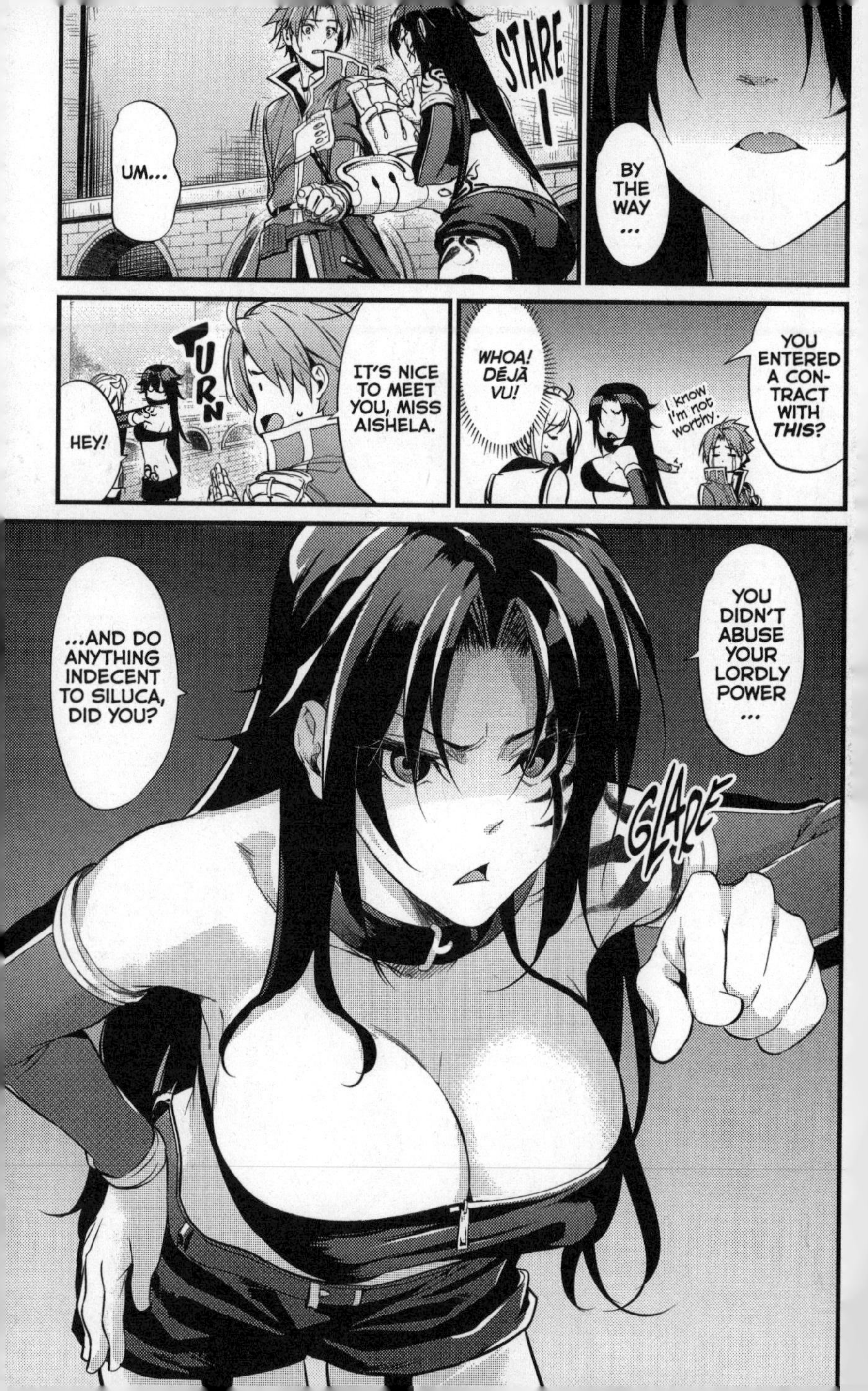
BY THE WAY...
STARE
UM...
YOU ENTERED A CONTRACT WITH *THIS*?
I know I'm not worthy.
WHOA! DÉJÃ VU!
IT'S NICE TO MEET YOU, MISS AISHELA.
TURN
HEY!
YOU DIDN'T ABUSE YOUR LORDLY POWER...
GLARE
...AND DO ANYTHING INDECENT TO SILUCA, DID YOU?

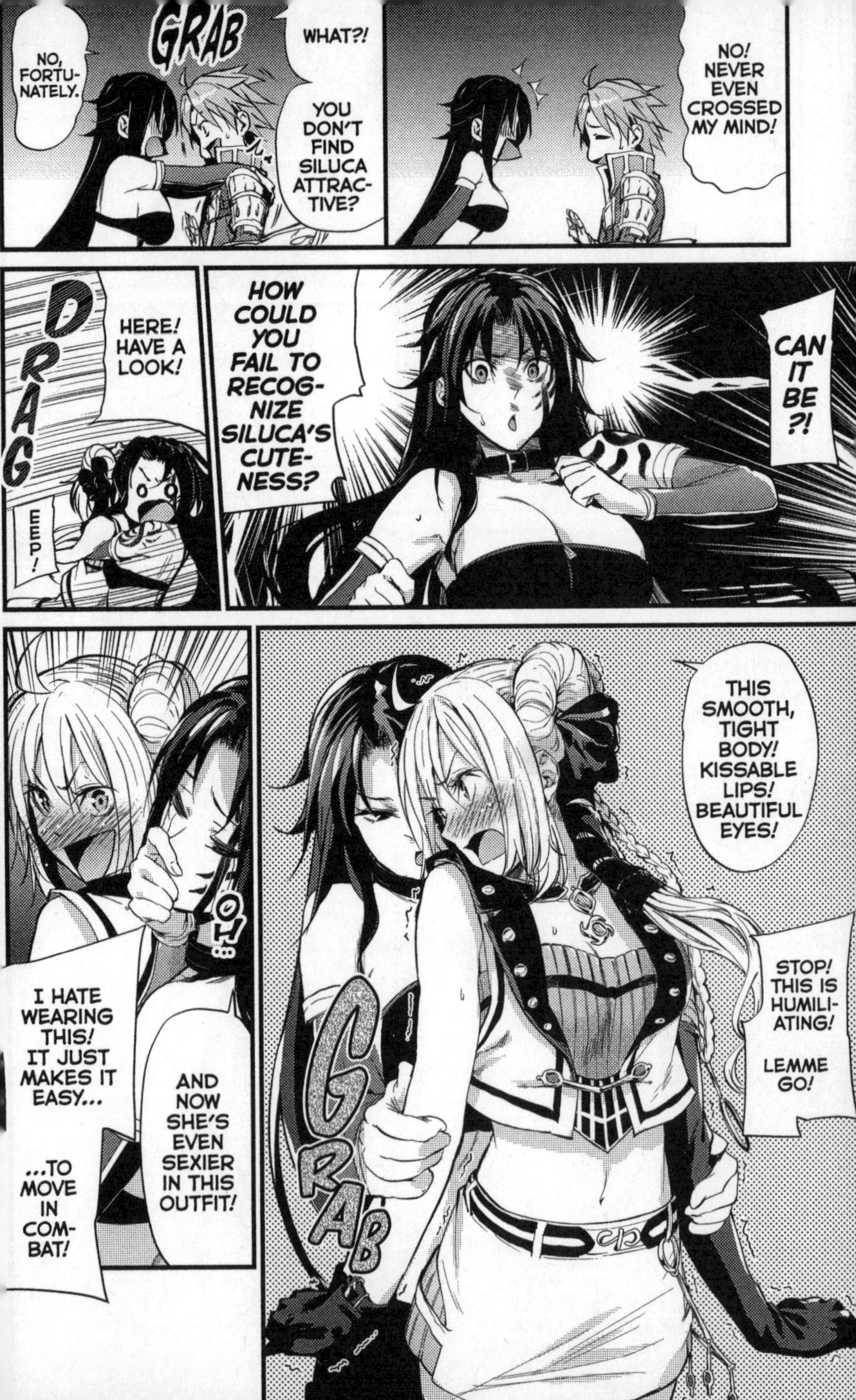
NO! NEVER EVEN CROSSED MY MIND!
WHAT?!
YOU DON'T FIND SILUCA ATTRACTIVE?
GRAB
NO, FORTUNATELY.
CAN IT BE?!
HOW COULD YOU FAIL TO RECOGNIZE SILUCA'S CUTENESS?
HERE! HAVE A LOOK!
DRAG
EEP!
THIS SMOOTH, TIGHT BODY! KISSABLE LIPS! BEAUTIFUL EYES!
STOP! THIS IS HUMILIATING!
LEMME GO!
GRAB
OH!!
I HATE WEARING THIS! IT JUST MAKES IT EASY...
AND NOW SHE'S EVEN SEXIER IN THIS OUTFIT!
...TO MOVE IN COMBAT!

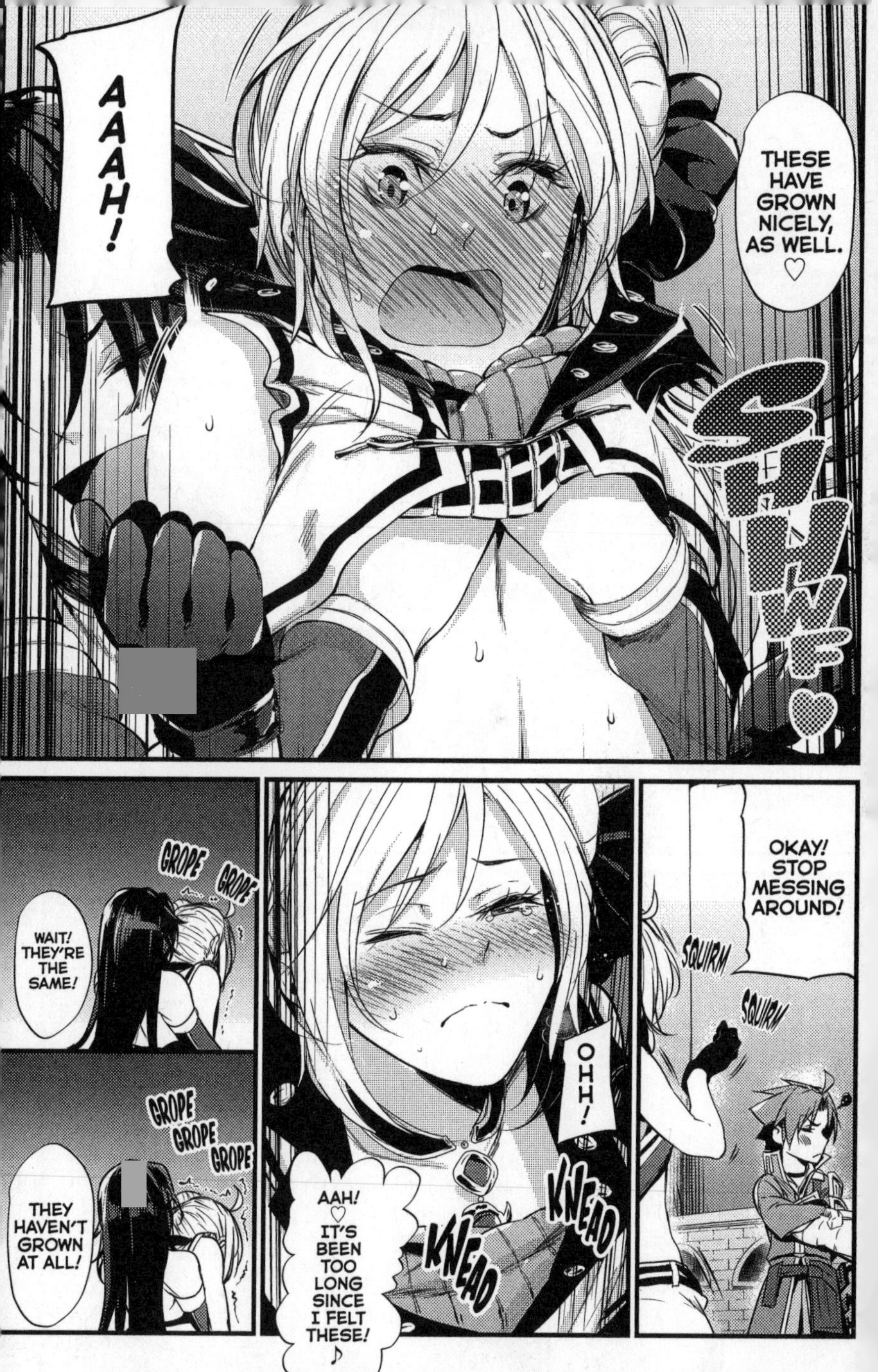
THESE HAVE GROWN NICELY, AS WELL. ♡
SHWF ♡
AAAH!
OKAY! STOP MESSING AROUND!
SQUIRM
SQUIRM
OHH!
KNEAD
KNEAD
AAH! ♡ IT'S BEEN TOO LONG SINCE I FELT THESE! ♪
GROPE
GROPE
WAIT! THEY'RE THE SAME!
GROPE
GROPE
GROPE
THEY HAVEN'T GROWN AT ALL!

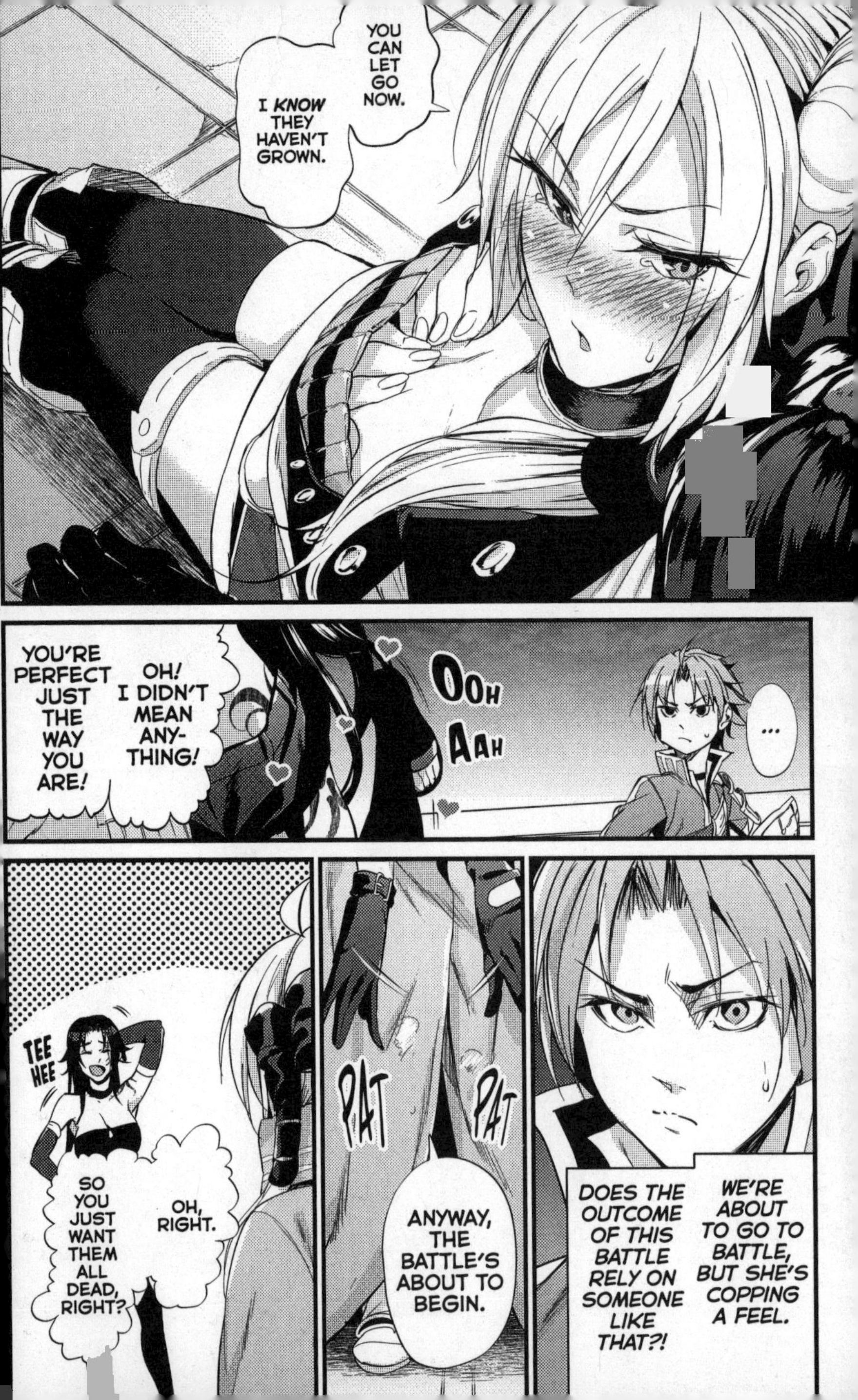
YOU CAN LET GO NOW.
I *KNOW* THEY HAVEN'T GROWN.
...
OOH AAH
OH! I DIDN'T MEAN ANY-THING!
YOU'RE PERFECT JUST THE WAY YOU ARE!
WE'RE ABOUT TO GO TO BATTLE, BUT SHE'S COPPING A FEEL.
DOES THE OUTCOME OF THIS BATTLE RELY ON SOMEONE LIKE THAT?!
PAT PAT
ANYWAY, THE BATTLE'S ABOUT TO BEGIN.
TEE HEE
OH, RIGHT.
SO YOU JUST WANT THEM ALL DEAD, RIGHT?

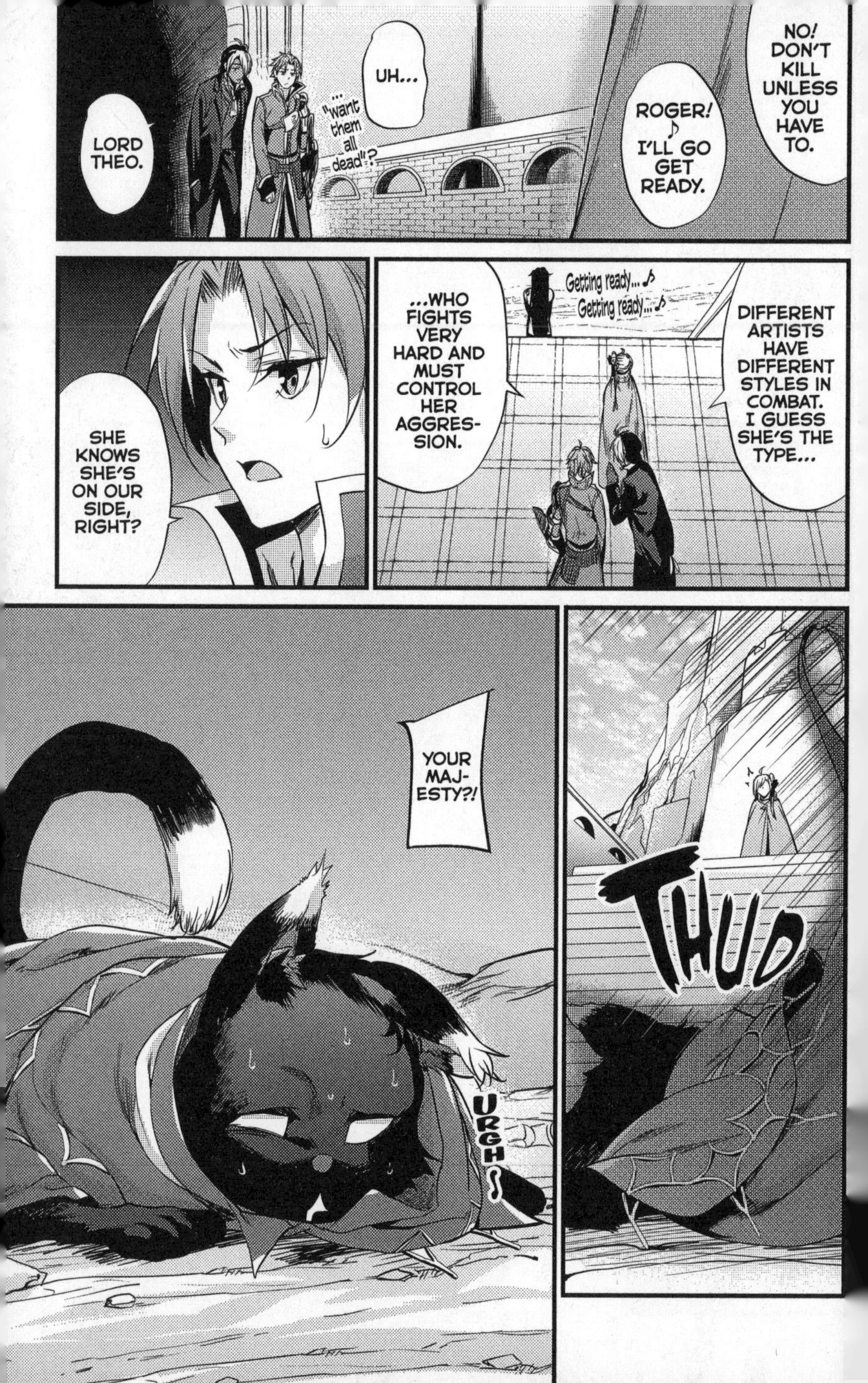
NO! DON'T KILL UNLESS YOU HAVE TO.
ROGER! ♪ I'LL GO GET READY.
UH...
..."want them all dead"!?
LORD THEO.
DIFFERENT ARTISTS HAVE DIFFERENT STYLES IN COMBAT. I GUESS SHE'S THE TYPE...
Getting ready...♪
Getting ready...♪
...WHO FIGHTS VERY HARD AND MUST CONTROL HER AGGRESSION.
SHE KNOWS SHE'S ON OUR SIDE, RIGHT?
THUD
YOUR MAJESTY?!
URGH

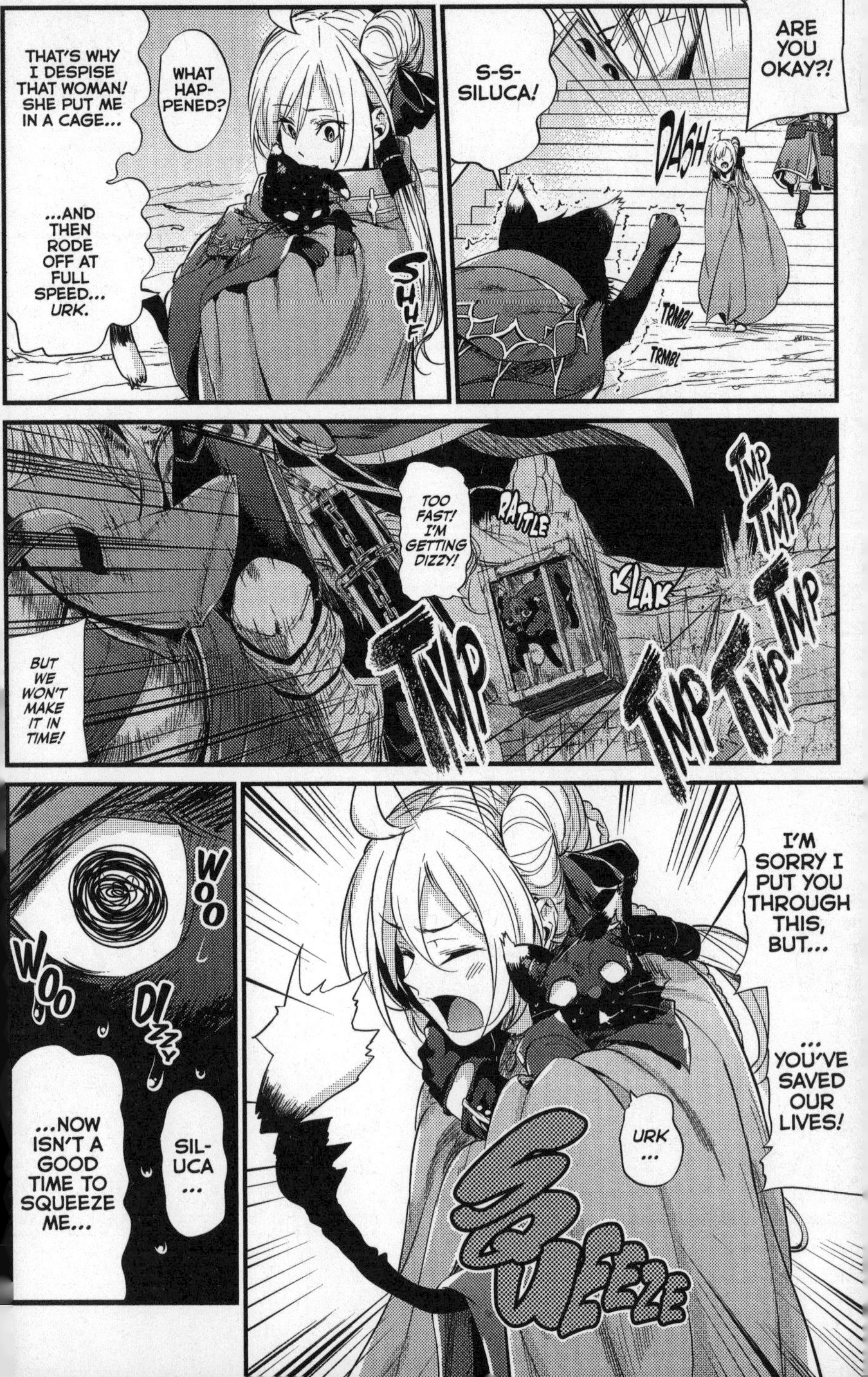
ARE YOU OKAY?!
S-S-SILUCA!
DASH
TRMBL TRMBL
WHAT HAP-PENED?
THAT'S WHY I DESPISE THAT WOMAN! SHE PUT ME IN A CAGE...
...AND THEN RODE OFF AT FULL SPEED... URK.
SHHF
TMP TMP TMP TMP
TOO FAST! I'M GETTING DIZZY!
RATTLE
KLAK
TMP TMP TMP TMP
BUT WE WON'T MAKE IT IN TIME!
I'M SORRY I PUT YOU THROUGH THIS, BUT...
...YOU'VE SAVED OUR LIVES!
URK...
SQUEEZE
WOO WOO
DIZZY
SIL-UCA...
...NOW ISN'T A GOOD TIME TO SQUEEZE ME...

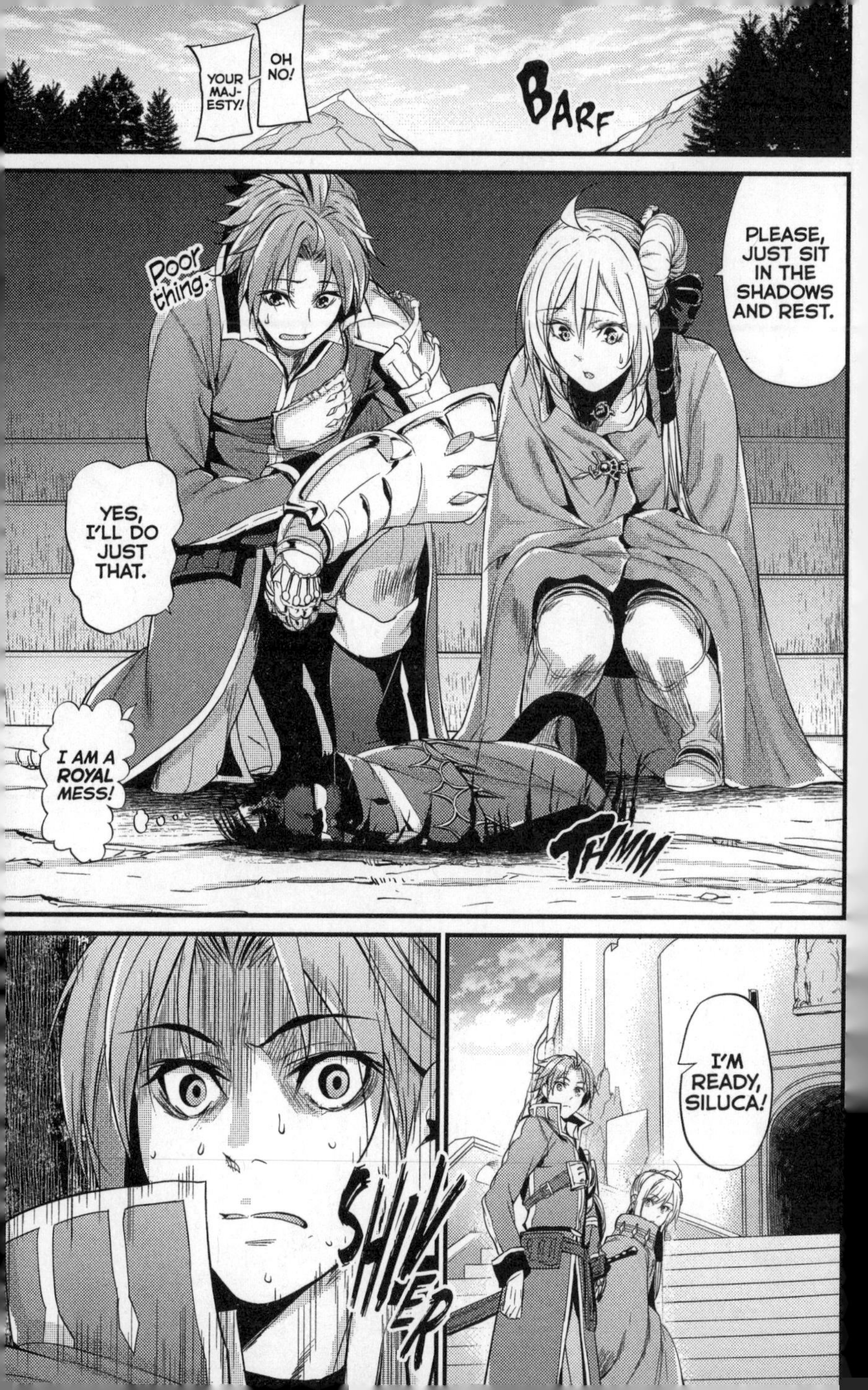
BARF
OH NO!
YOUR MAJ-ESTY!
PLEASE, JUST SIT IN THE SHADOWS AND REST.
Poor thing.
YES, I'LL DO JUST THAT.
I AM A ROYAL MESS!
THMM
I'M READY, SILUCA!
SHIVER

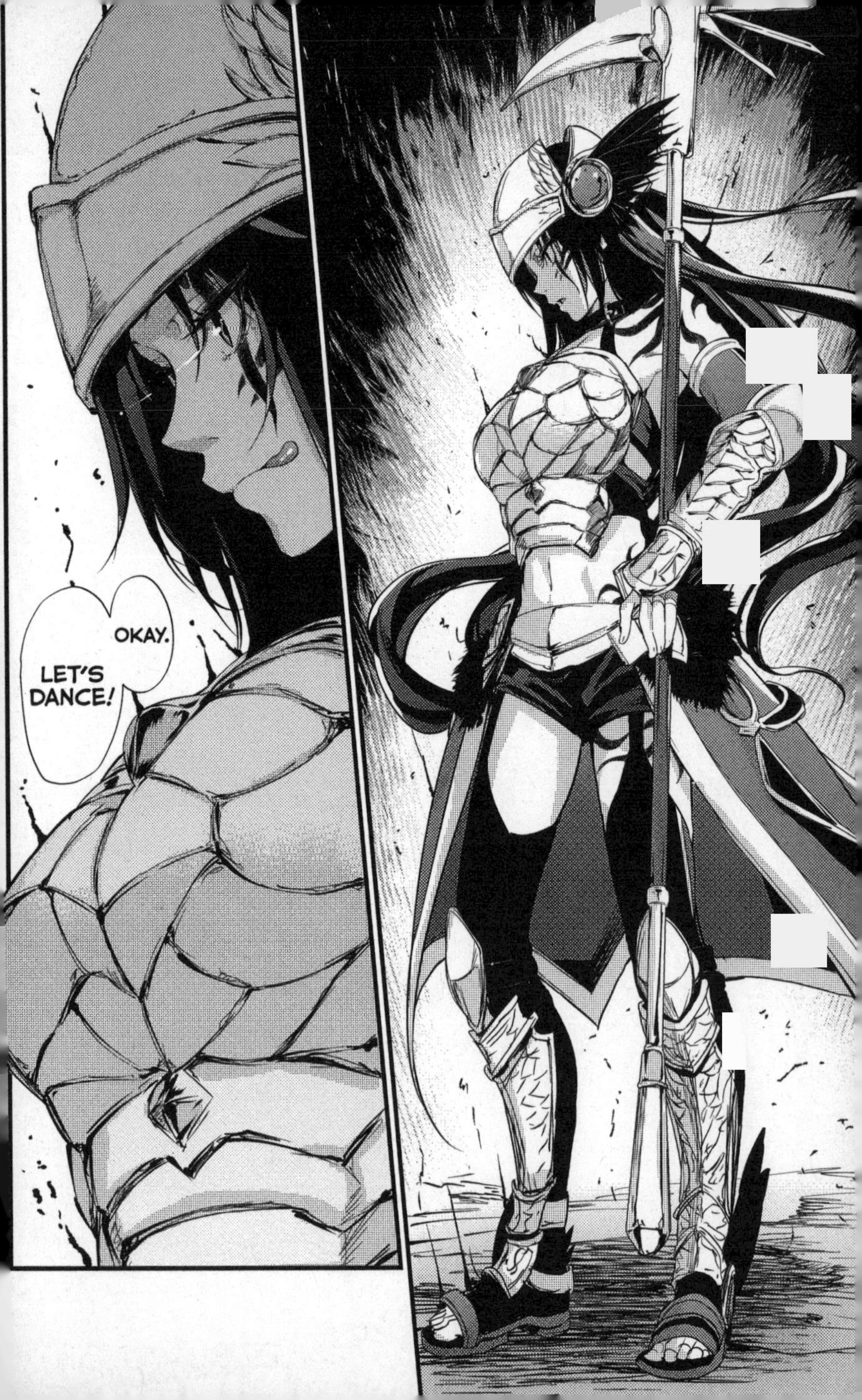
OKAY. LET'S DANCE!

TO THOSE FOR WHOM THIS IS THE FIRST OF MY BOOKS YOU'VE BOUGHT, IT'S NICE TO MEET YOU. TO RETURNING FANS, THANK YOU FOR YOUR CONTINUED SUPPORT. THIS IS MAKOTO YOTSUBA, AND I'M IN CHARGE OF THE MANGA VERSION OF *RECORD OF GRANCREST WAR.*

I HOPE TO MAKE THIS ENJOYABLE BOTH FOR FANS WHO ARE ENTERING THIS WORLD THROUGH THE MANGA, AND ALSO FOR THOSE WHO ALREADY VISITED IT THROUGH THE NOVELS.

SILUCA MAY ACT CRABBY BUT SHE LOVES CATS (AND ALSO WORRIES ABOUT HER BRA SIZE), SO SHE'S NOT ALL BUSINESS.

THEO IS WRAPPED AROUND SILUCA'S LITTLE FINGER, BUT IT WOULD MAKE ME HAPPY IF YOU HELPED KEEP WATCH OVER THEM AS THEY GROW TOGETHER.

I HOPE YOU'LL ALL COME BACK AND VISIT US AGAIN IN VOLUME 2!

MAKOTO YOTSUBA

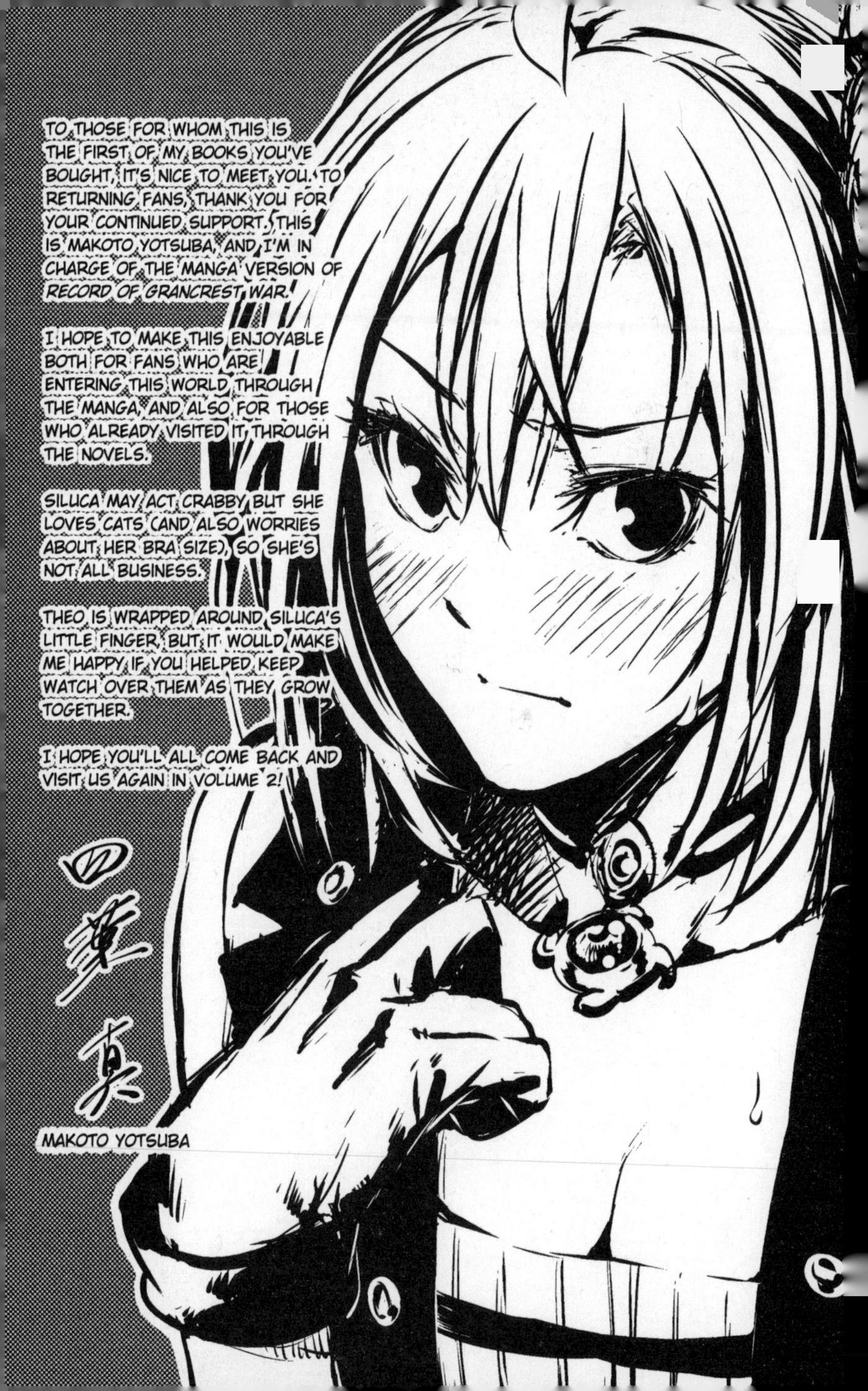

RECORD OF
GRANCREST
—WAR—

VOLUME 1

Original Story by **Ryo Mizuno**
Story & Art by **Makoto Yotsuba**
Character Design by **Miyuu**

Translation: **Satsuki Yamashita**
Touch-Up Art & Lettering: **James Gaubatz**
English Adaptation: **Steven "Stan!" Brown**
Design: **Julian [JR] Robinson**
Editor: **David Brothers**

Printed in U.S.A.

Published by VIZ Media, LLC
P.O. Box 77010
San Francisco, CA 94107

10 9 8 7 6 5 4 3 2 1
First printing, November 2018

viz.com

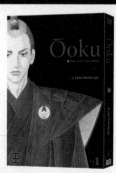

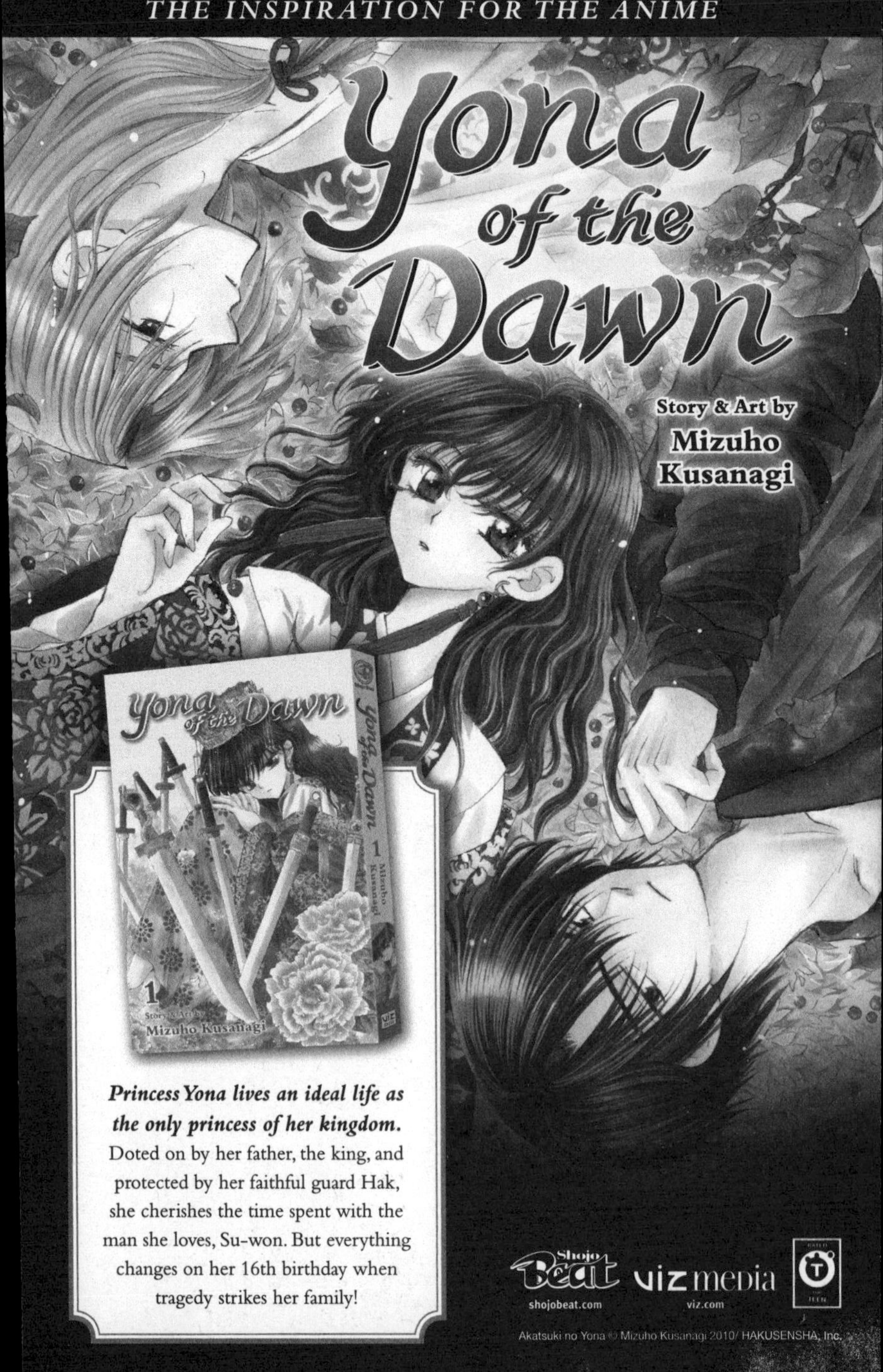
THE INSPIRATION FOR THE ANIME
Yona of the Dawn
Story & Art by
Mizuho
Kusanagi
Yona of the Dawn
1
Story & Art by
Mizuho Kusanagi
Princess Yona lives an ideal life as the only princess of her kingdom.
Doted on by her father, the king, and protected by her faithful guard Hak, she cherishes the time spent with the man she loves, Su-won. But everything changes on her 16th birthday when tragedy strikes her family!
Shojo Beat
shojobeat.com
viz media
viz.com
Akatsuki no Yona © Mizuho Kusanagi 2010/ HAKUSENSHA, Inc.

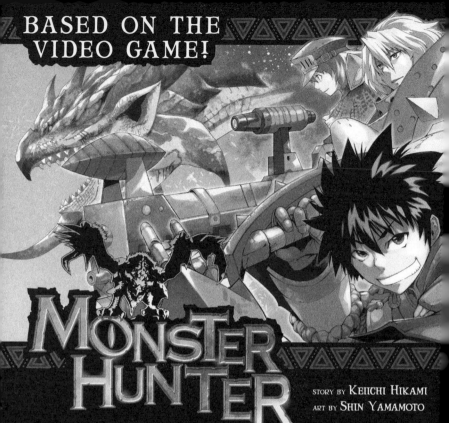

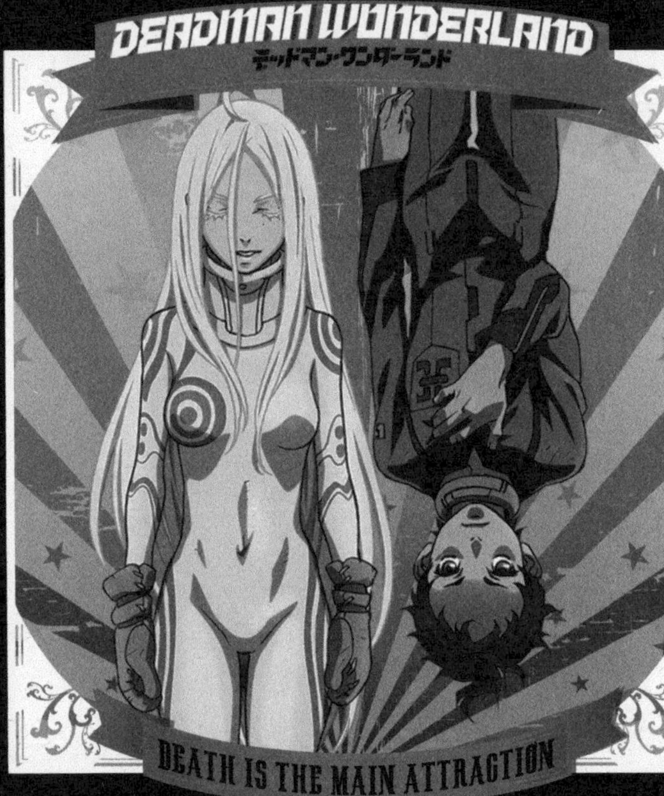
DEADMAN WONDERLAND
デッドマン・ワンダーランド
DEATH IS THE MAIN ATTRACTION

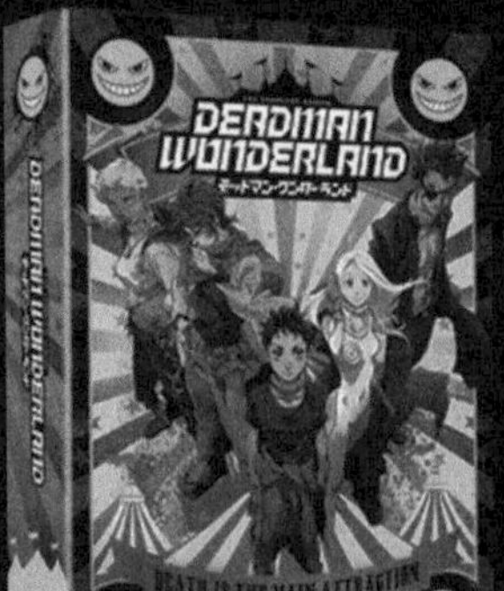
DEADMAN WONDERLAND
デッドマン・ワンダーランド
DEATH IS THE MAIN ATTRACTION

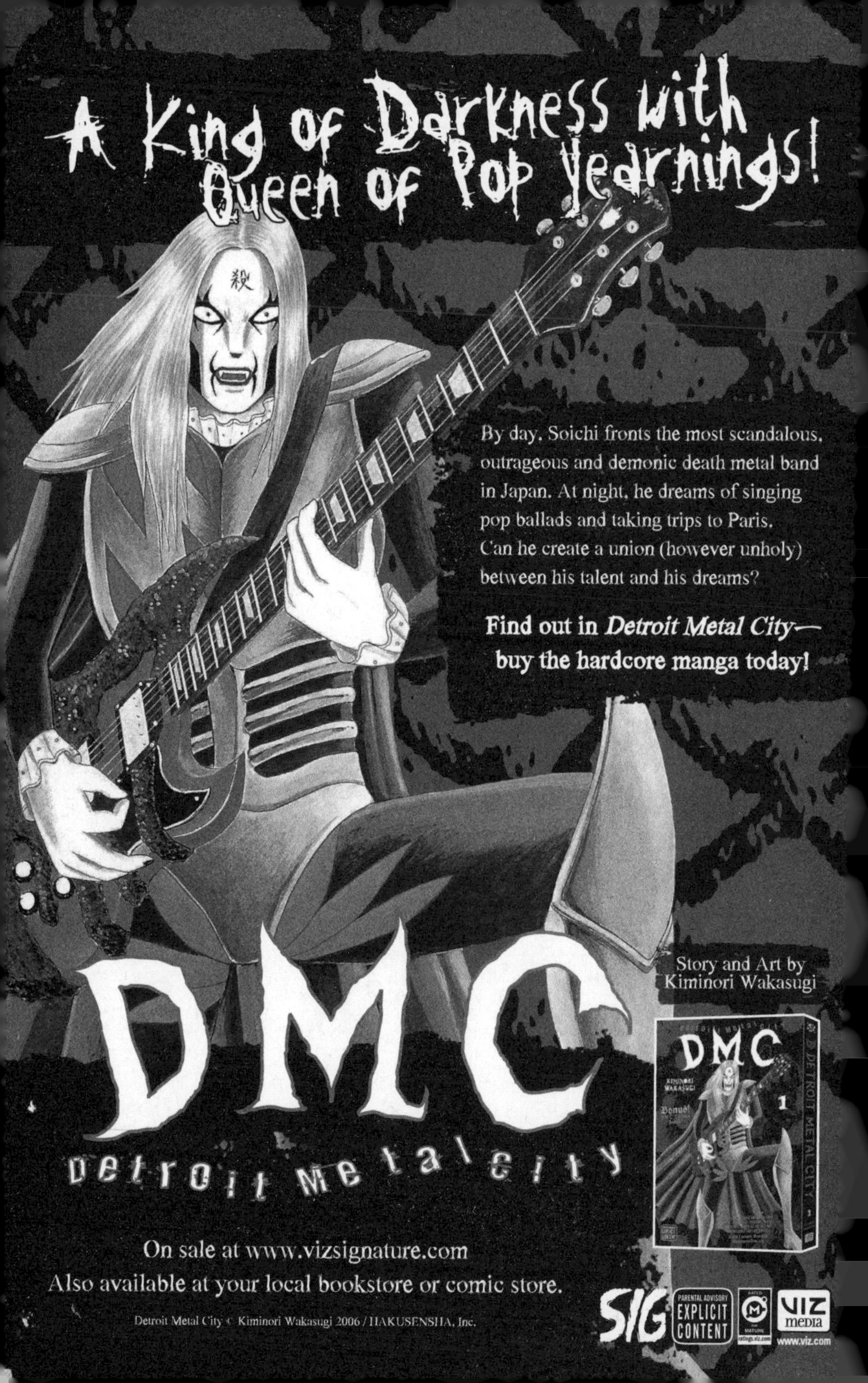

A King of Darkness with Queen of Pop Yearnings!
By day, Soichi fronts the most scandalous, outrageous and demonic death metal band in Japan. At night, he dreams of singing pop ballads and taking trips to Paris. Can he create a union (however unholy) between his talent and his dreams?
Find out in Detroit Metal City—buy the hardcore manga today!
Story and Art by Kiminori Wakasugi
DMC
Detroit Metal City
On sale at www.vizsignature.com
Also available at your local bookstore or comic store.
Detroit Metal City © Kiminori Wakasugi 2006 / HAKUSENSHA, Inc.
SIG
PARENTAL ADVISORY EXPLICIT CONTENT
VIZ media
www.viz.com

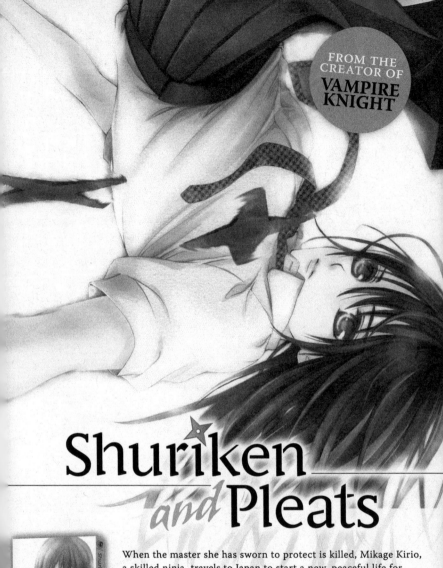

YOU'RE READIN
THE WRONG WA

Record of Grancrest War reads from right t starting in the upper-right corner. Japanese is from right to left, meaning that action, so effects, and word-balloon order are completely reversed from English order.

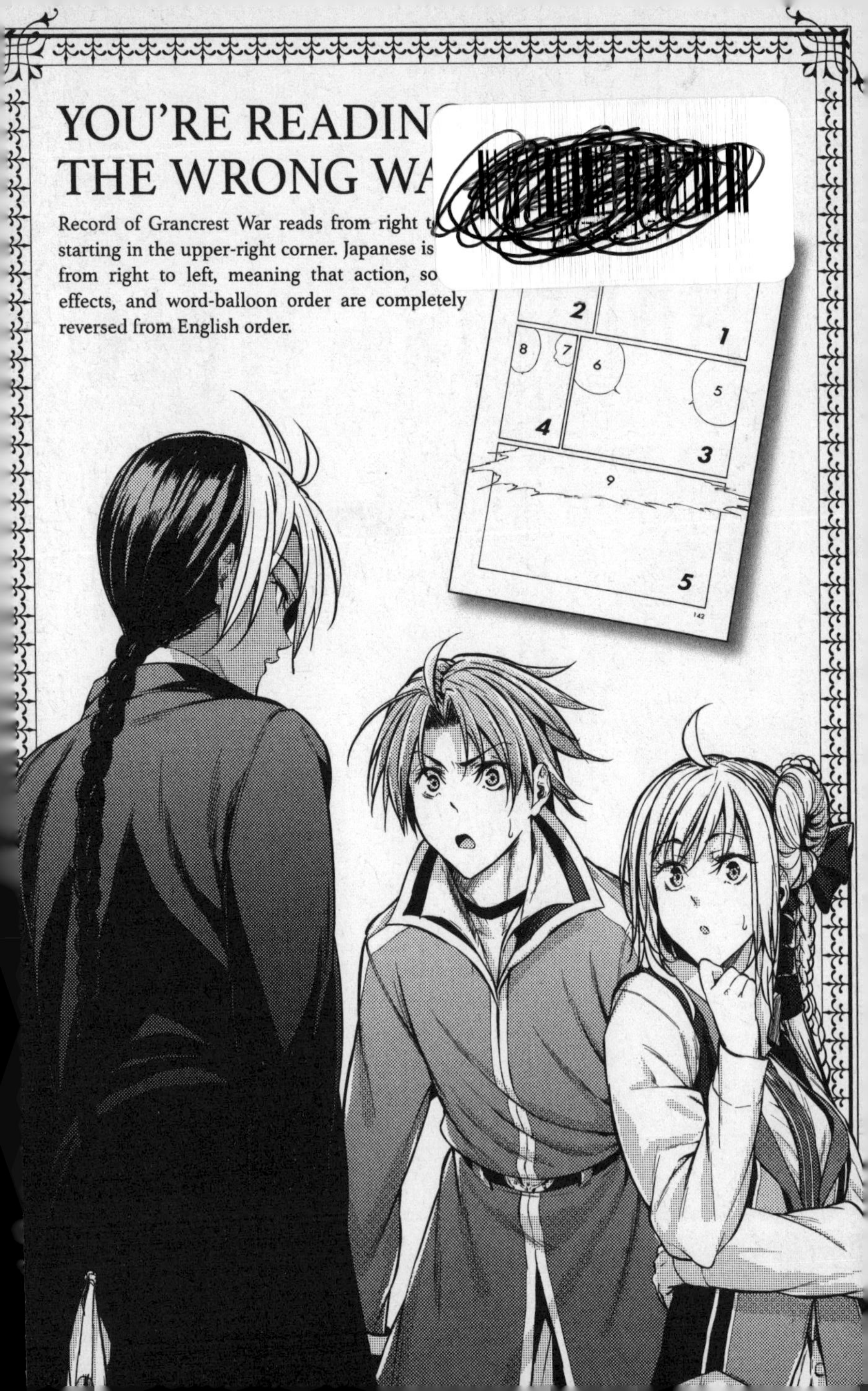

1
2
3
4
5
6
7
8
9
5
142